INTERNATIONAL TRADE AND THE CONSUMER

REPORT ON THE
1984 OECD SYMPOSIUM

ORGANISATION FOR ECONOMIC CO-OPERATION AND DEVELOPMENT

Pursuant to article 1 of the Convention signed in Paris on 14th December, 1960, and which came into force on 30th September, 1961, the Organisation for Economic Co-operation and Development (OECD) shall promote policies designed:

- to achieve the highest sustainable economic growth and employment and a rising standard of living in Member countries, while maintaining financial stability, and thus to contribute to the development of the world economy;
- to contribute to sound economic expansion in Member as well as non-member countries in the process of economic development; and
- to contribute to the expansion of world trade on a multilateral, non-discriminatory basis in accordance with international obligations.

The Signatories of the Convention on the OECD are Austria, Belgium, Canada, Denmark, France, the Federal Republic of Germany, Greece, Iceland, Ireland, Italy, Luxembourg, the Netherlands, Norway, Portugal, Spain, Sweden, Switzerland, Turkey, the United Kingdom and the United States. The following countries acceded subsequently to this Convention (the dates are those on which the instruments of accession were deposited): Japan (28th April, 1964), Finland (28th January, 1969), Australia (7th June, 1971) and New Zealand (29th May, 1973).

The Socialist Federal Republic of Yugoslavia takes part in certain work of the OECD (agreement of 28th October, 1961).

Publié en français sous le titre:

CONSOMMATEURS
ET ÉCHANGES INTERNATIONAUX

TABLE OF CONTENTS

Also available

CONSUMER POLICY IN OECD COUNTRIES – 1983 (October 1985)
(24 85 02 1) ISBN 92-64-12740-2 162 pages   £7.50   US$15.00   F75.00   DM33.00

PRODUCT SAFETY. Measures to Protect Children (July 1984)
(24 84 03 1) ISBN 92-64-12588-4 86 pages   £4.50   US$9.00   F45.00   DM20.00

PRODUCT SAFETY. Risk Management and Cost-Benefit Analysis (December 1983)
(24 83 02 1) ISBN 92-64-12510-8 106 pages   £5.00   US$10.00   F50.00   DM25.00

CONSUMER POLICY DURING THE PAST TEN YEARS. Main Developments and Prospects (November 1983)
(24 83 04 1) ISBN 92-64-12521-3 88 pages   £4.50   US$9.00   F45.00   DM23.00

COMPUTER TECHNOLOGIES AND CONSUMER INFORMATION. Interactive Videotex Systems (February 1983)
(24 82 05 1) ISBN 92-64-12389-X 36 pages   £3.30   US$6.50   F33.00   DM17.00

ADVERTISING DIRECTED AT CHILDREN. Endorsement in Advertising (July 1982)
(24 82 02 1) ISBN 92-64-12276-1 64 pages   £2.70   US$6.00   F27.00   DM14.00

RECALL PROCEDURES FOR UNSAFE PRODUCTS SOLD TO THE PUBLIC (October 1981)
(24 81 05 1) ISBN 92-64-12248-6 64 pages   £3.00   US$6.75   F30.00   DM15.00

SAFETY OF CONSUMER PRODUCTS. Policy and Legislation in OECD Member Countries (June 1981)
(24 80 05 1) ISBN 92-64-12130-7 88 pages   £3.20   US$8.00   F32.00   DM16.00

CONSUMER PROTECTION CONCERNING AIR PACKAGE TOURS (July 1980)
(24 80 02 1) ISBN 92-64-12077-7 44 pages   £2.00   US$4.50   F18.00   DM9.00

BARGAIN PRICE OFFERS AND SIMILAR MARKETING PRACTICES (May 1980)
(24 80 01 1) ISBN 92-64-12033-5 56 pages   £2.70   US$6.00   F23.00   DM12.00

Prices charged at the OECD Bookshop.

THE OECD CATALOGUE OF PUBLICATIONS and supplements will be sent free of charge on request addressed either to OECD Publications Service, Sales and Distribution Division, 2, rue André-Pascal, 75775 PARIS CEDEX 16, or to the OECD Sales Agent in your country.

FOREWORD

by

Jean-Claude Paye
Secretary-General, OECD

From 27th-29th November 1984, more than 150 representatives from governments, international organisations, business and industry, trade unions, universities and consumer organisations gathered in Paris to attend an OECD Symposium on a timely and complex subject: Consumer Policy and International Trade.

It is timely in that the principles for regulating international trade which were laid down in the immediate post-war period are now respected less, or even frankly challenged. Whether open or veiled, protectionism in a variety of different forms is gaining ground and represents one of the most serious threats to world trade and, consequently, to the continuation and spread of economic growth. The OECD is endeavouring to counteract this trend and revive the move towards free trade of all kinds. The Symposium has contributed greatly to these efforts by bringing new ideas into the current debate on international trade.

We have of course all learnt that the true object of economic activity is, ultimately, to improve individual well-being. And we know that free trade provides a powerful stimulus to economic progress through more efficient allocation of resources and abilities. Yet it has to be recognised that protective measures are nowadays being taken with increasing frequency in order to preserve this product or that group of producers. These measures may have advantages -- often overrated or even illusory -- but their costs, on the other hand, are indisputable, particularly for consumers who are deprived of the beneficial effects of competition. The first of this book's three themes examines this issue in detail.

Some of the negative effects on international trade, albeit perhaps unintentional, may stem from impediments introduced by consumer protection policies themselves; this point is taken up in Theme II.

The complexity of the subject lies in finding the best way of ensuring, within bureaucratic structures, that greater recognition is given to consumer interests when trade policy is being debated. Theme III explores the possibilities, together with the essential role that consumer organisations play in this process.

In taking decisions which have implications for trade, governments have to take account of a host of short- and medium-term policy considerations, and also have to contend with structured, well-organised pressure groups. It is difficult in this context for consumers to make their views heard. To enable governments to make rational choices in the balancing of conflicting interests, the OECD Council has approved an indicative checklist for the assessment of trade policy measures. This checklist is designed to help Member governments to undertake as systematic and comprehensive an evaluation as possible of proposed trade and trade-related measures, as well as of existing measures when the latter are subject to review. The list draws attention to the probable economic effects of a given measure and, in particular, its impact on structural adjustment, the functioning of markets and consumer interests. The checklist is an approach which facilitates the decision-making process by establishing the conditions for dialogue between the authorities and the various interested parties.

Following the Symposium, the Consumer Policy Committee adopted a Programme for Action containing suggestions for enhancing the influence of consumer policy considerations on trade policy decisions. These proposals will be followed up in the activities of the Organisation.

The dialogue instituted at the Symposium was an important first step; public discussion on these issues must now continue.

OPENING REMARKS

by

Catherine Lalumière
Secretary of State in Charge of Consumer Affairs, France

The OECD must be congratulated on organising this Symposium on consumer policy and international trade. It is indeed an extremely complex question with a tangle of issues to unravel. The two principal threads -- consumer interests and the facilitating of international trade -- are inextricably interwoven and generally pull in the same direction, but a closer look will show that in certain places there has been a hitch, or the linkages have not been sufficiently tight.

The consumer is a concept which (luckily) is not easy to grasp and codify. It is difficult to distinguish the consumer from the citizen, the worker (wage-earner or professional). There is no typical, average consumer. It was moreover one of the early mistakes of consumerism in the 1960s to have tried to respond primarily to the aspirations of the middle classes who wished to improve their living conditions and to buy more and more, at the cheapest possible price, in an era of apparently limitless growth. The truth is that there is a large number of different types of consumers, many of whom are extremely vulnerable due to their precarious financial position, their age, and their general level of education; there are consumers among the displaced populations and immigrant workers who find themselves in unknown territory, and there are of course the poorest consumers in the world, in certain developing countries, for whom survival is the only and most immediate problem.

Consumer interests cannot therefore be reduced to a standard pattern; needs and aspirations are many and varied, and this only serves to further complicate the task you have undertaken. What is certain is that at this time questions concerning consumption and consumer protection can no longer be dealt with exclusively in the narrow framework of national frontiers. With the many kinds of trade and exchanges that have developed (commercial, human, cultural, scientific), these questions must now take their place in the widest possible framework. This is the responsibility of international organisations such as the OECD, the Food and Agriculture Organisation, the World Health Organisation, the Council of Europe, etc. Here again we must be grateful to the OECD for having been effectively engaged in this field for over fifteen years.

At this opening session I would like simply to put to you a few of the ideas that have come to me after three-and-a-half years of responsibility for consumer affairs in the French Government. In the first place, my conviction is that the development of international trade serves the interests of consumers globally, whether the consumer is seen as a purchaser of goods and services or as a citizen, a member of a community with more general interests. For the purchaser, the development of trade means that he will have access to a more extensive, more varied and more attractive choice of products; it also means that the resulting competition on the market between firms in his own country and those in other countries will bring down price levels. He may also hope that this competition will have beneficial effects on quality. As a citizen it is in his interest to belong to a dynamic, economically efficient community.

While not wishing to pass judgement as concerns their justification, national regulations designed to protect the consumer frequently constitute obstacles to the free movement of goods and to international trade. They lead to the division of markets and increase firms' production costs, complicating their work and thus reducing their dynamism and their competitiveness. They constitute barriers providing artificial protection for the national market with which firms timidly entrench themselves and suffer a slow decline.

At the same time I am afraid that the principle of free trade and the systematic elimination of all constraints may become a dogma, a religion to which one sacrifices, indiscriminately, important aspects of consumer safety, quality of life, and the progress made towards control of the economic environment. Free movement of goods is not an end in itself. The real target of all economic activity is an improvement in living conditions. The measures envisaged to facilitate international trade and business activity must necessarily be accompanied by an active policy in favour of consumers, and if possible the international alignment of such policies.

The development of international trade does not in fact have only advantages for consumers. There are also a certain number of dangers and obstacles.

From the point of view of safety and health, the dangers have been considerably increased by the wide dissemination of products, the impossibility of monitoring their conditions of production, the limitation of controls or the abolition of rules that are considered to be impediments. It is therefore necessary to offset this by developing at the international level strict rules concerning standards of safety and health with which products must comply. Exchanges of information must also be developed between the authorities responsible for controls, with a view to identifying and removing from the market any defective products. (The OECD has played an important role in this respect.) It is, finally, essential to adopt ethical standards to protect consumers in the developing countries.

From the quality aspect, it is to be feared that strong competition resulting from the development of trade could lead to levelling down to the lowest common denominator. Price is an important criterion for the consumer, but it is not the only one; quality, i.e., the capacity of the product to satisfy the consumer, and to be suitable for the purpose intended, is also a very important criterion. To prevent a gradual fall-off in quality, it is necessary to work out a policy for the education and information of consumers, enabling them to make a more rational, better-informed choice. The consumer organisations have a very important role to play in this connection; the development of their activity and influence is therefore indispensable.

As concerns the economic protection of consumers, it has to be acknowledged that the balance of power is not equal, whatever the virtues of the market system. The consumer is in a situation of inferiority vis à vis his other economic partners, and this inferiority is all the more serious if he belongs to a poorer and more vulnerable social category. It is the duty of governments to help to redress the balance both by aid to consumer organisations and by establishing regulations, taking care however that they are not so unnecessarily detailed that they paralyse economic activity.

Among the components of an active policy in favour of consumers, which I consider must go hand in hand with further liberalisation of international trade, I would emphasize the role of the consumer organisations. These associations are more numerous in some countries than in others, and more or less powerful. Their political colouring varies, as is normal given the different interests, both objective and subjective, of consumers. But beyond these differences, it is essential that consumer organisations be recognised as representing the interests, the demands and needs of consumers who are too isolated, too scattered to exert a lasting influence individually. Consumers need organisations to group together, incorporate their different points of view, and exert an influence where decisions are taken affecting their daily lives.

In the case of both agriculture and industry, the economic decision-makers have remained practically deaf to consumer concerns. Their arguments and practices are, I feel, a serious mistake. Economic dynamism demands that consumers should no longer be regarded as lesser beings or as a nuisance, when they are among the protagonists of economic life.

The consumers, for their part, are gradually becoming aware that it is possible to obtain satisfaction without systematic contestation. Manufacturers are discovering that by their demands, users can oblige them to question and rethink their methods of work. From the design of the product to its distribution, acquired habits must be reviewed.

The economic and social dialogue must therefore bring together business organisations, trade unions, consumer associations and the public authorities. I for my part have tried patiently to organise this dialogue from the inside wherever economic decisions are taken and policies relating to agricultural or industrial products defined. I have also experimented with new forms of co-operation, on a non-institutional basis, between consumers, the business community, employees and their trade unions. Current observation of the consumer sector in the present time of crisis and change shows it to be even more necessary than in the past to break down the divisions between the world of producers, that of distributors and that of consumers.

The organisation of this Symposium by the OECD and the discussions to take place are, I am glad to say, a new step in this direction.

Virginia H. Knauer
Director, United States Office of Consumer Affairs;
Special Adviser to the President for Consumer Affairs

We meet today in light of the reality that international trade is a very real concern of nearly every nation on this earth. There is a strong interrelationship between trade policy and consumer policy. Indeed, in the minds of many people, it can be argued that free trade itself may well be the most powerful consumer protection policy of them all.

I believe it a matter of some significance that as we meet, there is another meeting being held concurrently in Geneva of the contracting parties of the GATT. They will be evaluating the results of a two-year programme undertaken at the request of the Ministers of both the OECD and the GATT to review trade problems and opportunities likely to face us in multilateral trade areas during the 1980s. Heads of government at the Williamsburg Economic Summit in June of 1983 and at the London Economic Summit in June of 1984 endorsed this work, pointing to the possibility of new multilateral trade negotiations. And to underscore this point, President Reagan, in his State of the Union message of 25th January 1984, pledged that the United States would "work with our trading partners for a new round of negotiations in support of freer world trade, greater competition and more open markets".

The United States remains committed to the process of liberalising trade and strengthening the international trading system. And, because we do, we welcome this Symposium as an opportunity to exchange views and experiences concerning the relationship between trade policy and consumer policy, and the challenge of articulating consumer interests in the formulation of trade policy. It is in that context that I wish to share with you several of my thoughts concerning the work before us.

I commend those persons within the Secretariat and others who supplied all of us with the excellent and thorough background materials which will be very helpful as we explore together the three themes of our meeting.

Those of us who were privileged to work within the Committee on Consumer Policy will recall our lively discussion in developing this programme. From the beginning, I believe, there was recognition that the problem before us, that of how best to relate a nation's consumer and trade policies, was extremely complex. In fact, if one contemplates for a moment the many implications for consumers in what we propose, the thought is overwhelming.

We started, in the Committee, with a premise that consumers have a right and responsibility to directly influence their nation's trade policy which, in turn, would affect the trade policy -- and consumers -- in other nations. Given the complexities of today's market-place, it can easily be foreseen that, while consumers in one country might often share the same objectives with those in other countries, they often may not share them when an individual's consumer role is in conflict with his producer role. We sensed that the area of international trade might make that fundamental conflict even more evident.

In another area, I am not certain that we have clarified for this meeting what we mean when we talk about that key concept "the consumer interest", and its relation to the "public interest". In a democracy the public interest manifests itself in actions the public, or its representatives, take by way of formulating policies and in making decisions in matters of public concern. The consumer interest, on the other hand, is most readily identified with consumer rights. Basic among these is the right to strive to improve one's station in life, and the freedom to consume according to one's choices and resources. These rights preceded the four rights enunciated by President Kennedy in 1962 and, I might add, endorsed by all subsequent United States Presidents, and which since have been quoted widely around the world: the rights to choose freely, to be informed, to be heard, and to be safe.

But we of the Committee on Consumer Policy were confident, then as now, that these problems are solvable. And so I believe we resolved the best approach for this meeting, choosing our three themes: first, the effect of trade policy on the consumer's interest; second (as a corollary to the first), the impact of consumer protection on trade policy; and third, how the consumer's interest may be better integrated into the process of trade policy development. These themes flowed naturally from the basic objectives we have set forth -- to exchange views, to increase awareness of the issues and to be catalysts for future discussions.

However, as we proceed to explore these issues I hope we do not lose sight of fundamental purposes implied in our work but not elsewhere stated. The essence of why we are here, in my view, is to put theory into practice, and to do so within the limited resources available to us. We are privileged to start a process at the international level to stimulate and assist individual nations to assess the concerns of their consumers regarding international trade, and to devise ways to bring those collective concerns into the process of national and, ultimately, international trade policy development. But the challenge between theory and practice remains before us.

Let me highlight what I mean with the following three points.

First, we agree, in theory, that there is a need for considering the impact on consumers of trade policy development. But we cannot yet convincingly prove that point. Our presence here is not, in itself, enough to convince others. The data we have at hand is not, in itself, enough. Our personal declaration that the consumer is the one who "ultimately pays" is not, in itself, enough. Clearly then, we must take a serious look at the need to gather convincing data which better describes the costs and benefits of trade policies upon consumers and which will enable national leaders to justify the case for greater consumer impact on trade policy development.

Second, we agree, in theory, that there should be mechanisms which provide ways for consumers to influence their nation's trade policy development, and through nations, to influence international trade policies. But we cannot yet offer suggested approaches for national leaders to assure objective sampling of a wide number of consumers on specific subjects. Clearly, then, we need to work on practical suggestions to assist national leaders in obtaining consumer comment.

And third, we assume, in theory, that consumers are in some way thoroughly conversant with international trade issues and all of the ramifications.

For example, among ourselves we all know the numerous benefits to consumers of free trade. We speak of lowered costs, reduced inflation, greater efficiency and productivity, structural flexibility/job creation and higher living standards. We know too that often protectionist measures may appear to offer easy solutions to problems of unemployment or protection of domestic industries but that, in the long term, such measures only distort markets, impede adjustment and often even provoke foreign retaliation. Do consumers generally know that the task of assuring free and open trade would be substantially easier if all trading nations were to engage in a process of negotiations designed to improve the structure of the multilateral trading system and liberalise international trade relations? Do consumers generally know enough of the interrelationship of these factors to offer the quality of comment which gives weight to their counsel on complex issues such as international trade?

Let me digress a moment here. There are a number of issues for discussion and further work in the context of consumer policy and international trade. One which particularly concerns the United States is the counterfeiting of consumer products. Last year over $18 billion worth of counterfeit goods were illegally sold in the United States alone, most coming from the Far East and South America. The world-wide figure is vastly higher, and the problem is intensifying! In speaking of these bogus goods, I am referring not only to luxury items such as counterfeit handbags, watches, designer jeans and credit cards, but also to products affecting the health and safety of consumers, such as unsafe counterfeit automobile replacement parts, artificial heart valves and cosmetic and pharmaceutical products, not to mention helicopter and airplane parts. The 1982 GATT Ministerial established a work programme on counterfeiting. This is an important first step toward an eventual -- and much needed -- GATT code on counterfeiting. I also see a major role for the OECD in stamping out counterfeit consumer products that threaten our lives and damage our pocket-books. President Reagan recently signed into law a Trademark Counterfeiting Act that levies tough criminal sanctions against those that make and traffic in counterfeit products, with fines of up to a million dollars and fifteen years in jail. With stiff enforcement, we hope to take the profit out of counterfeiting. But to achieve this result, we need the support of all of you here, your organisations and governments.

Clearly, we know that most consumers do not understand these complexities. Therefore, we must deal with the necessary consumer education and information needs implied in any recommendations we develop. Unless consumers clearly understand trade policy issues, or their authorised institutions can articulate their viewpoints, the consideration of consumer interests in the making and execution of trade policy may become a mere formality or, perhaps worse, policy-makers will mistake their own judgement or that of the opportunists for the real concerns of the consumer constituency.

As we go forward into this meeting and the topics before us, let us do so in the spirit of producing practical, workable steps we can take or recommend in the context of the realities of our time and limitations. There is a popular quotation I favour and use frequently to encourage my staff: "Make no small plans for they have not the power to stir the soul". But I quickly add that exciting plans need achieveable goals and practical results.

I would hope that in making our plans stirring we would make our initial steps firm yet limited. Our alternatives are several. First, we can appear to take action on these proposals, but in reality leave only a list of dreams. We must not do this because our personal integrity and commitment to consumers will not permit us to do so. Second, in our enthusiasm, we could too hastily suggest the need for sweeping new programmes and structures, while ignoring the limitations we have and the mechanisms already in place. But we must not do this because we all recognise that any steps we support will have to compete with other programme choices which government officials must reconcile with very stressed national budgets and programmes. Any measures we suggest which call for substantially increased budgets are likely to be ignored. And third, as I suspect you know, we can recognise that we are privileged today to open a new area, to open a dialogue at the international level on a very critical but long-term consumer need: that of ensuring that consumer concerns will influence all nations' trade policy development. We will be judged by the practicality of our recommendations, and so I suggest that we take firm, measured, limited steps now that will bring recognisable gains to consumers. We must assure that what we do here helps, and does not hinder, the long-term interest of consumers. Net gains in the consumer interest are made only when balanced with the legitimate interests of all citizens and national interests as a whole.

Our challenge is to build a firm foundation for present programmes, and for the future programmes which time and experience will refine. Our challenge is to see that what we start here today works and endures.

Torsten Löwbeer
Competition Ombudsman, Sweden;
Chairman, OECD Committee of Experts on Restrictive Business Practices

A great many points of common interest exist between competition policy and consumer policy. In a real sense, consumers are the ultimate beneficiaries of actions taken under competition laws to create and maintain open, dynamic and efficient markets for products and services. These efforts, in turn, lead to a greater choice of goods and services at different levels of quality and price, and have contributed to the rise in living standards. Thus, there is a very real link between the work done by the OECD Committee of Experts on Restrictive Business Practices (RBP Committee) and that of the Consumer Committee.

I would like to discuss two main topics. First, I will relate some of the analysis and conclusions developed in the recently published OECD report on the interface of competition and trade policy, particularly concerning consumer interests. Second, I will explore the role that competition policy can play in ensuring that consumer interests are adequately considered in national trade policy decisions.

Let me now turn to the recent work done by the RBP Committee on trade and competition policy. In 1982, the OECD launched an examination of trade issues by asking different committees of the organisation to explore these issues from their particular discipline. This move was undoubtedly prompted by the sluggishness in the world economy and by the rise of protectionism, or as some call it, "managed trade". The RBP Committee was particularly called upon to examine approaches for developing a framework to improve co-operation and for dealing with problems arising at the frontier of trade and competition policy. In response to this mandate, the Committee decided to prepare a report looking into both sides of this issue, that is, the effect of competition laws and policy on trade flows and, conversely, the effect of trade policy on competition in markets. To better understand the linkage of these two issues, a bit of history is in order.

Consumer protection is largely a feature of the period following the Second World War. The post-war economic boom and the growing affluence of consumers provoked new concerns as to the appropriate rules to govern commerce. These developments led to the enactment, in many OECD countries, of laws and regulations to protect the consumer in the purchase of goods and services. Similarly, this has been a very active period for the development of competition laws. In the 1950s and 1960s, most OECD countries enacted competition laws or strengthened existing ones, and devoted increased efforts to applying them. Generally, these laws address three major areas of conduct by corporations: 1) collusion among firms to control output and prices, the so-called cartel; 2) abuses by firms of dominant positions in markets; and 3) acquisitions leading to excessive market power through mergers. In 1953, for example, Sweden adopted an Act to counteract restraint of competition in business, which was amended in 1956, 1966 and 1970. In 1982, the Swedish Parliament passed a new law involving merger control provisions.

The development and application of competition policy was one of the principal building blocks of the post-war recovery. Until the 1950s, large international cartels had controlled a significant percentage of world trade through agreements to divide markets. In that decade, a series of enforcement actions by competition authorities broke up these cartels, opening markets and leading to new opportunities for trade. More recently, competition authorities have sought to ensure that competition remains vigorous in national markets, and that private firms do not act illegally to exclude foreign competitors.

In Part I of our report, we looked at the way in which competition policy is applied to business conduct and the effects on trade. We examined export and import cartels, licensing of technology, trading companies, countertrade agreements and intra-group arrangements by multinational enterprises. To simplify things somewhat, we generally concluded that the effective implementation of competition laws and policy serves to facilitate entry into markets and to foster increased trade. We did note several problems, however, particularly regarding the role of governments in commercial activity.

Another example involves voluntary export restraints (VERs). These measures involve decisions taken by export firms or their governments to limit their exports to certain markets, usually at the request of their trading partners. Many VERs bear a close resemblance to cartels and produce many of the same effects, i.e., reduced competition, higher prices, etc.

In Part II of our report, we examined the effect of different trade-restrictive measures on competition. The recent period has been marked by a sharp reduction in tariffs through the various GATT Agreements, but a rise in the so-called non-tariff barriers. These include VERs, orderly marketing agreements (OMAs), quotas and administrative barriers.

In general, trade exercises a healthy effect on competition in domestic markets. The presence or possible entry of foreign firms stimulates productivity, technological development, adjustment and more efficient use of resources. This, in turn, leads to increases in the goods available to consumers and in the range of price and quality of products.

By removing or limiting some or all of foreign competition, restrictive trade measures curtail the pro-competitive aspects of foreign trade. But the effects of these measures can vary greatly. For example, while tariffs place a price disadvantage on foreign goods, they do not set an absolute limit on the quantity that can be imported. Thus, domestic firms will lose their advantage if they set their prices above the tariff-created level. Similar restraints do not exist when VERs, OMAs or other quota-like measures are adopted. Here, if the domestic firms form an oligopoly or possess market power, the domestic producers can charge excessive prices once the import quota is reached.

As our report indicates, studies in this area suggest that non-tariff barriers not only are anti-competitive, but also sharply affect consumer welfare. At present, a significant percentage of trade in such consumer products as automobiles, electronics, clothing and shoes is covered by VERs or OMAs. According to studies cited in both the competition policy report and the consumer report, these trade restrictions add on billions of dollars to the prices of products and services each year.

Since trade-restrictive measures and barriers reduce competition and harm consumer welfare, the question arises as to why governments adopt such measures. Since this is one of the key subjects of this Symposium, let me share with you some ideas developed by the RBP Committee on ways to expand trade policy decisions.

Among the OECD countries, there is a wide variety of government and institutional structures to implement trade and competition policies. In most countries, informal procedures exist for competition authorities to offer their views on pending trade matters, and in a few countries there are formal arrangements. But experience shows that existing procedures are not adequate to ensure that decisions on trade policy properly consider the impact on competition. To improve this situation, the report of the RBP Committee sets forth an indicative checklist of factors to be considered by trade policy-makers. The checklist not only focusses on competition concerns, but also sets out a broad list of economic and social criteria. Among the effects to be considered are those on the sector seeking protection, on consumers, on government revenues, on competition and the structure of markets, and on trading relations. This checklist approach is designed to ensure that policy-makers undertake a systematic and comprehensive evaluation of the likely effects of a trade measure. Competition authorities are prepared to co-operate in the use of such a checklist to offer their views and analysis of the likely effects of a trade measure on markets, on competition and on consumer welfare, as well as other relevant concerns. Of course, we realise that each government will need to decide what weight to attach to each item in a checklist when taking decisions.

Another area in which competition authorities can contribute to trade policy involves laws attempting to establish rules for fair competition in import trade through regulation of dumping, subsidies and countervailing duties. While they share the objective of removing artificial distortions in the market, laws dealing with unfair trade practices seek to protect domestic industry, whereas competition laws are designed to preserve competitive domestic market structures and the efficient allocation of resources. As a result, different standards are applied to import pricing practices under two sets of laws. Thus, actions brought under trade laws can reduce competition in domestic markets through the foreclosure of foreign firms.

In some countries, proceedings under trade laws do provide for the consideration of consumer interests or for limited participation by competition authorities. In the United States, for example, the competition authorities at the Federal Trade Commission have intervened in several proceedings to comment on such issues as whether imports are a substantial harm to domestic industry and what remedies would be most effective in particular cases. In Sweden, my office has commented against planned import restrictions in the cement industry, and we have offered our views on ways to measure whether import prices constitute dumping.

Despite these efforts, it seems that significant differences remain between the approaches taken under competition laws and trade laws concerning import practices. For that reason, our Committee recommended that consensus be sought on the extent to which consideration can be given to the impact of trade law proceedings on competition in domestic markets. We have also recommended that all interested parties be given an opportunity to express their views in the course of such proceedings.

Finally, I want to share with you a more personal idea I have been thinking about for some time. If it could be realised, I am sure it would strengthen the possibilities for consumer interests to be considered properly. We have within the OECD a Business and Industry Advisory Committee (BIAC) and a Trade Union Advisory Committee (TUAC). But so far, we have no COAC (Consumers' Advisory Committee), a permanent organisation that has as its main task to analyse and put forward the consumer interests. In today's world, politicians are exposed to strong and well-organised interest groups. A strengthening of the consumer voice in this choir is needed for a harmonious balance. So, why not a COAC side by side with BIAC and TUAC?

The RBP Committee has always taken an active interest in the work of the Consumer Committee, and it will continue to do so in the future. The goals that competition authorities seek to attain in monitoring different markets are designed to improve the standard of living of consumers. In the coming years, competition and consumer policy have important roles to play in strengthening the resistance against protectionism. We look forward to working with the Consumer Committee in that effort.

CONSUMER POLICY AND INTERNATIONAL TRADE

INTRODUCTION

by

Joop Koopman
Head of the Consumer Policy Directorate, Ministry of Economic Affairs,
Netherlands
Chairman of the OECD Committee on Consumer Policy

Since its establishment exactly fifteen years ago, the OECD Committee on Consumer Policy has witnessed a momentous period for consumer issues. With the development of the post-war economy, consumer interests have gained new prominence, and many OECD countries have responded by enacting laws to protect consumers. The Committee has actively followed these developments and has issued reports on topics such as product safety, advertising, product information and labelling, consumer credit and marketing practices. Many of these reports have led to recommendations by the OECD Council.

The Committee has always recognised the importance to consumers of an open trading system. Its terms of reference include a provision that it should examine and comment on policies which could contribute to the fostering of international trade. Given the limited resources available to the Committee, we have focussed our attention on product safety aspects of trade. Recently, the growth of protection and measures to limit trade has led to an increased awareness of the harm that trade barriers can cause consumers, making this issue an important concern in consumer policy.

As a consequence, the Committee acted in 1982 on an internal memorandum from the then Secretary-General of the OECD seeking comments from various OECD Committees on trade issues in the 1980s.

The Chairman of the Consumer Policy Committee replied on behalf of the Committee after consultation with its members. In that reply the Committee expressed its support for the adoption of liberalised trade policies, made a number of concrete suggestions and pledged to take up a number of issues in this field in its future programme of work.

The OECD Council discussed the Secretary-General's note and the various contributions from within the Organisation in May 1982, and requested the

Consumer Policy Committee to examine the practical possibilities for giving greater weight to consumer policy considerations in the work of the OECD on trade and trade-related issues. With the organisation of this Symposium and its report entitled "Consumer Policy and International Trade", the Committee on Consumer Policy gives a first response to that request.

The report essentially deals with the three major themes of the Symposium: first, the identification of the consumer interest in foreign trade and measurement of all relevant effects, direct and indirect, of trade policies for society as a whole, and especially the consumer; second, the effects of consumer protection measures on international trade; and third, the ways and means to give greater weight to consumer policy considerations in trade matters.

As to the first theme, consumer interests and trade liberalisation share a common objective. Free international trade enlarges the choice of goods and lowers prices through enhanced competition. Though restrictive trade policy measures may temporarily protect other societal interests, they will generally result in net welfare losses in the long term. Even in the short run the intended positive effects may not be brought about, or may be very small compared to the collective loss to consumers. Therefore efforts should be encouraged to develop methods for a comprehensive ex ante evaluation of costs and benefits of contemplated trade policy measures. A consumer impact statement should be an essential part of such an evaluation. The report draws attention to a checklist of questions which will facilitate the identification and assessment of all relevant effects of proposed trade policy measures.

The report cites a number of studies and presents data on costs to consumers of particular trade-restricting measures. Needless to say, I hope these evaluations are not purely academic exercises, because crucial policy decisions have to be made shortly regarding many products. I want to mention just one example. That is the new trade regime for textiles and clothing that will come into force after the current highly protectionist Multifibre Arrangement expires in 1986. Clearly the products of this sector are of basic concern for consumers, and we are aware of the strong sectoral resistance against liberalisation.

As I indicated before, the second theme, "Impact of Consumer Protection on International Trade", and especially those originating from product safety objectives, has always been a major concern of the Committee. Aiming at the protection of consumers against hazardous products, the Committee has considered measures to minimise negative effects on international trade. I recall the OECD Council Recommendation of 1979 in which, inter alia, governments of Member countries were urged to ensure that those goods banned or withdrawn from sale within their territories because they are inherently so hazardous that they present a severe and direct danger to the life, health or safety of any consumer, are not exported to other countries. In the same Recommendation, mention is made of notification procedures.

Product safety is, however, a complicated matter. On the one hand, we have consumers who expect the products they purchase or acquire to be safe. On the other hand, there is the problem of defining operationally the concept "safe", which results in a multitude of different safety standards in various countries and no safety standards at all in other countries. In the absence of effective international measures, national actions result in trade distortions without any guarantee that the intended protection of the consumer will be achieved. To a certain extent, these problems also arise with other quality aspects of goods. All of this calls for the need for joint approaches toward product safety regulations and international harmonization of product standards.

Having defined and assessed the consumer interest in foreign trade and established the desired level of consumer protection, the question arises as to how the consumer interest will be considered in the trade decision-making process. This is the subject of the third theme.

At the national level, a number of countries have formal procedures in which consumer organisations can air their views on trade policies. At the level of the EEC, the European Union of Consumer Organisations (BEUC) plays an important role. And what about the OECD itself?

Under the new mandate of the Committee on Consumer Policy adopted in October 1982, the Committee will obtain the views of international consumer organisations on an informal basis. However, there is no international consumer organisation at the level of the OECD. BEUC is too small; IOCU is too large. But rather than organising our own counterpart international consumer organisation, we have informally met with IOCU and BEUC. They have provided us with their views for the organisation of the Symposium, and I am happy they are in our midst to contribute to the success of our endeavour.

The background report of the Committee also lists a variety of procedural arrangements which exist in Member countries to ensure that consideration is given to consumer interests in the trade decision-making process. The Committee recognises that policy-making structures vary from country to country. Its recommendations therefore are of a general nature. Consensus exists that decision-makers often experience difficulty in concretely identifying consumer interests. As in many areas of consumer policy, these interests are usually widespread among a large population of consumers. The loss to the individual consumer resulting from protectionist measures is naturally small in comparison to the expected or real sectoral gain which is the objective of the measure, though the collective consumer welfare loss may be massive. Finally, there is often insufficient agreement on the methodology for evaluating gains and losses of a prospective trade measure.

All these factors necessitate action to increase the transparency of trade-restricting measures, raise problem awareness, and further a common approach toward assessment and evaluation of proposed trade measures. There is also a need for the introduction of mechanisms to integrate these results in the decision-making process.

We hope that this Symposium will yield concrete results and will help the Committee to develop recommendations which will give the consumer interest its proper place in the formulation and execution of trade policies at the national and international levels. "Its proper place" means in balance with other interests, which, for the consumer as citizen, include employment and business activities. I am pleased to note that BIAC and TUAC, the two official advisory bodies to OECD, not only made constructive contributions to the organisation of the Symposium but are also here to present their views.

I sincerely hope that we shall have a dialogue, that in the true tradition of our Committee we will be able to listen to one another and see the viewpoint of the other interests, and that we shall be flexible enough to build bridges where the different societal interests seem to clash.

As a basis for discussion, the Committee's report has suggested a number of proposals for action at the national and at the OECD levels. Following the Symposium the Committee will, after consultation with the OECD's Trade Committee, present proposals to the OECD Council to strengthen the weight given to consumer policy considerations in trade matters. I am convinced that the progress we can achieve during this Symposium and through our future activities will be to our common benefit. We are all consumers.

BACKGROUND REPORT BY THE COMMITTEE ON CONSUMER POLICY

I. INTRODUCTION

The OECD Council, at its meeting at Ministerial level on 10th and 11th May 1982, requested the Committee on Consumer Policy "to examine the practical possibilities for giving greater weight to consumer policy considerations in the work of the Organisation on trade and trade-related issues" (1).

The present report by the Committee on Consumer Policy has been prepared as a first response to this request. It was submitted to the 1984 meeting of the Council at Ministerial level as a background document and has subsequently been derestricted by the Council in June 1984. The report highlights the consumer interest in international trade and trade-related policies, determines the effects of various types of trade measures on these interests, discusses the impact of consumer policy measures on trade and reviews existing arrangements in Member countries to take into account consumer interests in the decision-making on trade policy matters. The report served as a basis for discussion at the Symposium and is presented here in a condensed and re-edited version.

II. SUMMARY AND CONCLUSIONS

A. Defining consumer interests in international trade

Consumers collectively have a wide and direct interest in economic policy. Their specific interest includes the enjoyment of rising living standards, efficient use of economic resources and stability in the general level of prices. Enhanced competition, improved information to consumers, and better quality and safety of products and services are among the basic aims of consumer policies and, at the same time, relevant for international trading relations. In the area of international trade, consumer policy has a specific interest in the growth of trade flows as a guarantee that consumers will have the widest possible choice at competitive prices as regards the goods and services offered on the market.

The development of national consumer legislation, in particular the introduction of product-related safety, packaging and labelling requirements, while not designed to restrict imports, may have an impact on international trade. Concern has been raised that some of these requirements may deliberately or inadvertently be used as barriers to trade. Moreover, the export of hazardous products has caused a number of difficulties in international trade relations.

International trade was a very buoyant factor in the world economy during the 1970s. In the beginning of the 1980s, however, the situation of the world economy deteriorated, resulting in economic stagnation and recession on a world-wide scale and a decline in the volume of world trade. This trend was reinforced by rising protectionism in order to redress unfavourable trade balances and to support domestic industries by limiting or excluding imports from domestic markets.

In order to facilitate the recovery now under way in several OECD countries, the 1983 Ministerial Council called upon governments to reverse protectionist trends and to progressively relax and dismantle trade restrictions and trade-distorting domestic measures, particularly those introduced in the recent period of poor economic growth (2). A closer integration of consumer policy considerations into the decision-making process on trade and trade-related measures can make a useful contribution to this process. The recognition of consumer interests in trade policy is all the more important as protectionist pressures are likely to persist since, despite economic recovery, unemployment is forecast to remain in the medium term at a relatively high level.

Trade liberalisation is generally of direct benefit to consumers. For example, one study conducted in the United States compared the prices consumers paid for imported goods and goods of comparable quality that were domestically produced (3). The sample included 168 products representative of consumption patterns and imports, and excluded automobiles, food products and pharmaceuticals. The study found that imports of apparel were approximately 5 per cent cheaper than domestic equivalents, imports of footwear were 12 per cent cheaper, and hard-goods imports were 12 per cent cheaper. Overall, imported goods were 10.8 per cent cheaper than comparable domestic products. The study estimated that consumers in the United States saved $2.2 billion annually by buying imported goods at prices lower than domestic goods.

Consumer interests and trade liberalisation share a common objective. Free international trade undoubtedly creates benefits for consumers: they can buy products not produced domestically, they can buy at the cheapest source of supply internationally and their choice of goods of varying quality at competitive prices is enlarged. These interests are usually served by competition policies designed to promote the effective functioning and the competitiveness of markets, and such policies are often based on the grounds of enhancing consumer welfare and economic efficiency. Nevertheless, restrictive trade policy measures and attempts to shelter domestic industries against foreign competitors may have a significant impact on the effective implementation of competition policy (4).

Trade policies, especially those designed to limit or ban imports, have a significant impact on consumer interests. In particular, trade barriers can affect the price, quantity and quality of goods, patterns of consumption and the distribution of incomes. Consumers may also be affected indirectly by the overall impact of these trade measures on the growth and dynamism of national economies. Restrictive trade policies have often been justified on the grounds that they bolster domestic industries, preserve employment in these industries and help to overcome balance-of-payment problems. Such policies shift economic losses to consumers and the costs for the economy as a whole may be high. Yet, international trade issues tend to be discussed without sufficient attention to their impact on consumer interests.

Obviously, in a complex network of societal concerns and group interests, consumer policy considerations are competing and sometimes conflicting with other aims of economic policy. Thus, trade policy decision-makers have to deal with a wide range of interests. It is the purpose of the present report to highlight specific consumer interests which are often neglected in the decision-making process, and to contrast them with more sectoral concerns which are generally represented by well-organised groups and tend to play a relatively important role in trade decisions. The report suggests an approach for balancing these interests in a way which would give greater weight to consumer policy considerations.

B. Taking into account consumer policy considerations in the decision-making process in international trade

The present report examines various procedures and institutional arrangements in Member countries to take into account consumer policy considerations in the decision-making process on trade and trade-related matters. Several countries have reported a complete absence of any institutional requirements to obtain the views of consumer policy authorities or consumer representatives preceding the adoption of trade policy measures. In these countries, consumer policy considerations seem to have little or no impact on decisions in the trade area. In other countries, procedures such as inter-departmental committees involving consumer policy representatives exist but their importance and actual impact on trade policy decisions seem to be declining. Several other countries frequently have recourse to informal inter-departmental contacts and exchanges of views with non-governmental organisations including consumer representatives. Most of these countries consider such an approach broadly satisfactory, although they do not exclude the possibility of making certain improvements. In a few countries, there exist statutory requirements for trade authorities to proceed through formal enquiries or public hearings in which all interested parties, including consumer bodies, can make their views known, but available evidence suggests that representations by these bodies did not carry much weight in the final decisions adopted.

There are several reasons why consumer interests thus far have had a rather limited impact on the formulation and implementation of trade policies. First, as this report shows, decision-makers may sometimes experience difficulties in clearly identifying consumer interests and distinguishing them from other societal concerns. Second, while aggregate losses caused by specific trade restrictions will in many cases exceed the aggregate gains, the gains are typically shared by a limited number of producers and employees in a particular industry, while the losses are distributed among an enormous number of taxpayers, consumers and firms in other industries and, therefore, are less visible. Third, there is still a lack of generally accepted analytical approaches for evaluating consumer (as opposed to other) interests. Therefore, the report develops a general analytical framework which the Committee proposes for the use of decision-makers to provide a sounder basis for evaluating the effect of proposed trade measures, including their impact on consumers.

Consumers and consumer representatives are frequently at a disadvantage in terms of influencing trade policy decisions. Consumer interests are generally more diffuse geographically and in terms of product coverage than those of domestic producers of a particular commodity. Further, having focussed their efforts on the implementation of consumer protection laws, for lack of resources or other reasons, consumer organisations may not always have been aware of the consumer impact of trade policy measures; in any case they have not taken full advantage of existing possibilities to exert influence on trade policy decisions. An important obstacle in this respect is the inherent lack of transparency and the complexity of many restrictive trade measures, in particular those most frequently associated with the rise of new protectionism (i.e., voluntary export restraints, administrative and technical barriers). There is a need to address these problems in a pragmatic manner so as to establish the necessary conditions for consumer policy considerations to be given greater weight in trade policy decisions.

III. THE EFFECT OF TRADE POLICY ON CONSUMER INTERESTS

A. General assessment of trade barriers from a consumer perspective

Restrictive trade policies impact directly on consumer interests, as the availability of goods and services is reduced. In particular, trade barriers can affect the price, quantity and quality of goods, patterns of consumption and the distribution of incomes. Consumers may also be affected indirectly by the overall impact of these trade measures on the growth and dynamism of national economies. In the short run, these restrictive trade policies may bolster domestic industries and preserve employment. Their long-term effects, however, can be to shift economic loss to consumers in the form of higher prices, poorer quality of products, reductions in real income and a diminished standard of living.

Decisions to impose or not to impose barriers to imports or to take other trade-distorting measures tend to be a trade-off of domestic producer and consumer interests. For every export subsidy, tariff, quota or other protectionist policy a country considers, there are domestic losers as well as gainers. In many cases, the aggregate losses caused by a particular protectionist trade policy will exceed the gains. But the gains are typically shared by the producers and the workers in a particular industry, while the losses are distributed among an enormous number of taxpayers or consumers. Thus, even when the aggregate losses from a protectionist trade policy exceed the aggregate gains, the losses experienced by any individual will be much smaller than the gains of a subset of the population favoured by these measures. A bias in favour of protectionist trade policies therefore develops because the losses caused by these policies are less visible than the gains and may be underestimated as a result.

The consumer loss caused by a policy directed against imports of a product is most easily seen in the form of higher prices. Economic theory suggests a division into three components; the costs to consumers are: i) the higher cost of imports of the product; ii) the differential between the price of the additional domestic production which the barrier to imports induces consumers to purchase, and the price at which imports of the product would be available in the absence of the trade barrier; and iii) the additional gain to consumers that would result when consumers altered their overall consumption pattern in response to lower price of the product (in the absence of the trade barrier).

Loss component ii) above represents an implicit subsidy of domestic production. In other words, protectionism leads to greater domestic production of the protected goods by diverting factors of production from activities when their output is more highly valued (at world market prices). The loss to the economy is the production foregone in these other sectors which are internationally competitive.

Closely connected with the allocational losses due to the protection are the dynamic losses. The dynamic effects of protection are mainly the result of decreasing intensity of competition. Since competition forces firms to minimise production costs (in order to stay competitive) and, at the same time, to search for new ways of production, new markets and new products, protection from foreign competition reduces dynamic forces. Conversely, the competitive pressures to provide quality products are reduced by protectionist measures. The losses may occur in the form of substitution of inferior goods, non-availability of high technology products, or malfunctioning and more frequent product failure.

Macro-economic analysis of trade policies usually centres on the quantitative aspects of international trade. From a consumer point of view, however, it would be desirable to include some of the often neglected aspects of international trade and consumer behaviour, e.g. the development of quality preferences, the changing consumption patterns and the impact of advertising and objective consumer information on them, which have contributed to the wide and hitherto unknown acceptance of foreign goods and cannot always be explained by a mere monetary comparative advantage arising from international trade.

Seen in this light, the relationship between trade policy and consumption patterns becomes more apparent. The success of imports in recent years is attributable not only to lower prices, but also to quality, reliability and/or attractiveness of foreign goods or the ability of importers to supply innovative, new or previously unavailable products. Each or all of these factors may diminish the effects of some types of trade policy to induce consumers to purchase domestic goods. Efforts to persuade consumers to prefer domestic products, such as "buy domestic" campaigns or labelling and other requirements to show the origin of imported goods have been made in various countries, but as a whole, and although it is obviously very difficult to evaluate the actual effect of such measures, it seems fair to assume that they have rarely had a significant impact on consumer behaviour.

C. Selective trade restrictions and the consumer

For illustrative purposes, it may be useful to mention two examples where trade policies have been considered to have a significant impact on consumers: restrictions on textiles and clothing imports under the Multifibre Arrangement (MFA) and trade-restrictive agricultural policies.

The contents of the MFA will not be summarised here. Nor will its effects on certain developing countries be discussed. Rather, its impact on specific consumer interests in industrialised countries will be briefly mentioned. The latter have been studied in more detail in two consecutive studies by consumer organisations (5). Both reports recognise that a policy decision to restrict imports is necessarily the result of a trade-off between a number of competing policy considerations (employment, inflation, structural adaptation, consumer interests, etc.). However, as regards the MFA, the studies did not find any evidence that the advantages claimed have in fact emerged. According to these reports, the direct effects of the restriction in quantitative terms and the indirect side-effects have been increased prices, restricted choice of products and, at the time the reports were issued, no significant change in the structure of domestic industry had occurred.

The quota system implemented under the MFA was designed not only to restrict the quantities available but also to encourage shifts in production of the exporting country. Since the MFA quotas only monitor quantity, the natural reaction of exporters in developing countries was to move out of the most basic and cheapest product range and to produce higher quality with higher profit margins. Thus, the report notes that even designer-label high-cost clothing can be manufactured in certain developing countries, which means that competition with EEC countries is in fact intensified in areas which the MFA was intended to protect. Another phenomenon noted by these reports is the fact that in certain exporting countries, the MFA imposes a "scarcity premium". Quotas are bought and sold between manufacturers in the exporting countries, and the premiums for such transactions are considered as a component in the sellers' price. On the importing side, the quota restriction creates similar "scarcity" value for these goods, which, as the report suggests, could incite importers and retailers to apply higher margins than they would obtain on a free market.

One of the main conclusions to emerge from these reports is that the MFA has resulted in considerable price increases and that the availability of low-cost clothing, in particular children's clothing, which is of special importance to low-income consumers, has been reduced.

Agricultural protection is another example to illustrate the long-term and cumulative effects of insulating sectors from world markets. Many OECD countries operate restrictive agricultural policies which result in domestic prices that differ from world market prices. For instance, the domestic dairy sector tends to be protected in most OECD countries, which results in price increases for dairy products. The economic costs of the border protection combined with internal support measures for agriculture are large and real income losses by consumers and the burden to taxpayers appear to be much higher than the income gains of farmers (6).

Available survey evidence provides some indications of the magnitude of consumer welfare loss due to trade-restrictive barriers. While these studies largely focus on the cost to consumers, in light of the significant impact on consumer welfare, they further suggest the need for a careful consideration of the potential benefits of a trade measure prior to its adoption.

In Canada, one study estimated the cost (net of government tariff revenue) to Canadian consumers of the 25 per cent customs set on furniture imports at between $57-$125 million annually. The estimate of the cost of the tariff to consumers was based upon comparison of factory prices in Canada and the U.S. for comparable items. Of this estimated loss to consumers, $55 million is the higher cost of domestically produced furniture, $2-3 million is additional consumer surplus from increased consumption, and $0-67 million is the value of the wider range of choice that would result from the removal of the customs tariff (7). Another study estimated the cost to Canadian consumers of tariffs and quotas on imports of footwear and clothing to be as high as $150 million per year on footwear and $1 billion annually for clothing (8). The basis for the study was analysis of the Census of Manufacturers cost-of-production data, utilising the "effective rate of protection" concept.

In the United States, several studies have been conducted on the effects of trade-restrictive measures on consumers. A series of sectoral studies done for the U.S. Federal Trade Commission showed that the net welfare gain of the removal of import restraints on apparel was estimated to be $1.319 billion in the first four years, due to a $1.532 billion reduction in deadweight losses and $213 million costs for adjustment. The study found the cost of the tariff on sugar to amount to $155 million over four years, and, in the non-rubber footwear industry, the study estimated that removal of the existing tariff and Orderly Marketing Agreement would result in benefits to U.S. consumers of $288 million per year (9).

The findings of the above FTC report were incorporated in a subsequent study, which attempted to measure the overall effect of trade restraints on U.S. consumers. This study, conducted at the Center for the Study of American Business, estimated the direct costs that U.S. protectionist policies placed on American consumers in 1980 to be $58.4 billion (10). That figure was considered to be an underestimate, since not all trade-restrictive practices are identifiable. Thus, the study concentrated on the cost to consumers of tariffs and other quantitative restrictions. The study concluded that trade restraints impose a "hidden tax" on consumers.

D. Comparative analysis of specific trade restrictions

As it appears from the preceding discussion, trade restrictions affect consumer interests because it is the consumer who finally in one way or the other bears the economic cost of trade restrictions. However, the actual cost of such measures and the way they are perceived by the public vary considerably according to the types of measures taken. The reasons are manifold: first, the freedom of consumers to choose as well as the freedom of (foreign) producers to produce is reduced differently by different types of interventions; second, since uncertainty arising from ignorance has costs of its own, some trade barriers can be regarded as less harmful than others due to their relative transparency; third, government revenues and, fourth, government's expenditures for administration of trade barriers differ according to the trade policy pursued (also, there may well be differing dynamic implications such as long-term effects on the competitiveness of the economies considered); fifth, protection-induced quality changes must be considered.

For the purpose of this analysis, the various restrictive trade measures can be organised in three categories:

-- Tariffs and tariff-like provisions;

-- Quantitative restrictions, e.g. import quotas determined by volume or value, voluntary export restraints (VERs) and Orderly Marketing Agreements (OMAs);

-- Administrative and other non-tariff barriers.

In addition, consideration is given to laws relating to unfair trade practices (anti-dumping, countervailing) which, if improperly used, can constitute restraints to trade and competition and affect consumer interests.

The main problem with evaluating these measures is that most of them are hard to quantify (e.g. non-tariff protection), and that a number of such measures lack transparency. The latter is particularly true for the new forms of protectionism, e.g. VERs, OMAs and administrative barriers which have increased in importance during the past decade. A comparison of the relative importance of the different types of trade measures clearly indicates a trend towards these more subtle and unquantifiable forms of trade restrictions. As a result of the subsequent rounds of international trade negotiations, tariffs in most member countries are no longer used as the main instruments of protection, although in certain sectors, relatively high tariff protection has been maintained.

The last decade has brought a wave of non-tariff protectionism. Empirical evidence of a systematic and comprehensive nature, however, is difficult to obtain as many of these measures, notably "voluntary" export restraints, are not notified within GATT. Available sources of information, nevertheless, show a growing trend towards managed international trade through non-tariff barriers and protective arrangements between Member countries on a bilateral or regional level. A considerable number of these measures do not only concern labour-intensive traditional industries facing structural adjustment problems, but also the established manufacturing sectors and newly emerged industrial sectors involving high technologies.

The changing pattern of trade-restrictive measures is of considerable importance from a consumer perspective. In this respect, relative disadvantages and advantages of the different types of measures can be summarised as follows.

Unless they are definitely prohibitive, tariffs may prove less harmful to consumers than other types of restrictions to the extent they still allow consumers to buy foreign goods. In addition, they have a relatively high degree of transparency as regards price and cost effects. A further argument to be taken into consideration in this context is the fact that, under certain circumstances, exporting manufacturers faced with tariff walls or tariff-like protection may endeavour to partly compensate their competitive disadvantage by an agressive price policy. A comparative study in car prices in the EEC member countries undertaken by the Bureau Européen des Unions de Consommateurs

(BEUC), for example, shows considerable differences in the net prices of passenger cars which attempt to partly compensate the differences in sales and other taxes imposed on cars (11). A comparison of net prices expressed as a percentage rate of the highest net price in member countries, for instance, shows that the net price in the country with the highest sales tax is about half the maximum net price. Although not directly referring to tariffs, this example clearly demonstrates that exporters can in certain circumstances more easily adjust to tariff protection or tariff-like measures than to other forms of trade restrictions.

A tariff on imports of a commodity raises its prices to consumers (above the price at which it is traded internationally) by as much as the amount of the tariff. The price of imports is, of course, above the "world price" by the amount of the tariff, and this margin [which corresponds to the consumer loss component i) mentioned above] accrues as revenue to the government of the importing country. Of course, the cost to consumers is also manifested in the prices of domestic production [consumer loss component ii) mentioned above]; as a result of the tariff, the price of domestic production may exceed the price at which the commodity is traded internationally by as much as the tariff. However, if the price differential between domestically produced goods and the world market price is small, even a modest tariff can raise the price of imports significantly above the price of domestic production.

A quantitative restriction on the volume of imports of a product is effected by i) allocating limited entitlements to imports, and ii) permitting only imports corresponding to these authorised entitlements. By the very nature of an import restriction, entitlements to import are scarce and these entitlements are therefore valuable rights. The price of imports to the consumer increases by the amount of the associated scarcity premium. Thus, some of the effects of quantitative restrictions on consumers are identical to those of tariff-like provisions. There is a basic difference, however, in that the margin between the resulting price of imports to consumers and the (lower) "world price" accrues to holders of the rights to import unless it is taxed away by governments through fees for entitlements to import. The size of the margin gained by importers will depend, inter alia, on the demand for imports, price flexibility and the structure of the market affected. In highly concentrated markets, for instance, where one or few domestic producers have market power, a quantitative restriction will normally result in a higher domestic price than would a tariff which allows the same level of imports (12).

An additional possible impact of quantitative restrictions is that they affect the product quality chosen by importers. If the restriction applies to the number of physical units imported, and if import profits are approximately proportional to the value of sales, then importers have incentives to substitute higher-quality units for what they would otherwise choose to sell. The rationale is that higher-quality units would command higher prices, so that the value of sales and profits would be greater while the quantity imported would still meet the restriction.

Of particular concern from the consumer standpoint is the often distributional effects of quantitative restrictions such as quotas, OMAs and VERs. Where trade restrictions induce exporters to increase the unit value of their traded goods, the costs can be particularly severe for low-income consumers, particularly where a product that is a "necessity" is involved. For example, footwear imports to the U.S. were subject to an OMA for the 1970s until 1981. A study of this arrangement showed that the quota increased the price of imported shoes, resulting in larger percentage increases for the low-priced footwear that is generally purchased by low-income groups. Second, the OMA induced an increase in the relative supply of higher-quality (and higher-price) footwear, thereby resulting in lower price increases for those shoes that are generally purchased by higher-income groups. As a result, the restraint on footwear imports tended to act as a regressive "tax" on lower-income consumers (13).

Administrative barriers, from the perspective of exporters and consumers, can constitute a serious impediment to trade flows, because of the inherent lack of transparency and their largely discretionary nature which introduces an element of unpredictability in trading relations, not only with regard to the circulation of goods, but also with regard to the marketing and sales efforts of countries and individual enterprises. An example of administrative barriers is more intensive inspection of imports, which may involve significant delays at Customs if there is an inadequate number of government officials available to perform the examinations. Another area of concern arises from the fact that product safety regulations, or other product-related measures, can in some instances be inadvertently applied or even deliberately misused as a protectionist device. These concerns are discussed in Section IV below.

Another example in this context are "buy national" campaigns, whereby governments seek to encourage the sale of domestic products but do not exercise any direct influence on the quantity and the price of imported products. These campaigns may be on a formal or informal level, with varying degrees of government involvement. The effect on trade is not presently quantifiable. However, national consumer groups have, on several occasions, opposed campaigns to encourage consumers to purchase domestic products, since they run contrary to the general notion that consumers should base their selection of products on objective factors such as price and quality and because it can often be difficult to define precisely what is or is not a domestically produced product. In the EEC, the European Court has held that one such campaign violated the Treaty and Community Directives relating to the free circulation of goods within the Common Market, since it found direct government involvement in that the country was providing financial assistance to the campaign to promote consumer purchase of domestic goods (14). Of course, national campaigns to promote domestic products abroad or in other member states would not violate EEC laws.

While laws relating to unfair trade practices are designed to adjust competitive disequilibria brought about by injurious trade practices (dumping, subsidisation), the enforcement of such laws can, under certain circumstances, restrict competition in domestic markets and have harmful effects on consumer interests. In this respect there are several fundamental concerns which are discussed in detail in the Report of the Committee on Restrictive Business Practices dealing with issues arising at the frontier between competition and trade policies (15). One is whether private firms abuse trade laws by bringing unfounded actions with a view to either controlling or excluding the presence of foreign competitors in domestic markets. Another question is whether the effects on competition and consumer interests are adequately considered in proceedings under laws relating to unfair trade practices. In its conclusions, the Report of the Committee of Experts on Restrictive Business

Practices recommends that policy-makers and enforcement authorities give consideration to the impact of enforcement of these laws on competition in domestic markets. It is recommended, _inter alia_, that injury to domestic industry and its causal relationship to unfair trade practices which, under GATT and the 1979 implementing agreements, is a prerequisite for the imposition of anti-dumping or countervailing duties, should continue to be assessed on the basis of objective criteria and following procedures where all interested parties are given an opportunity to express their views (16). These conclusions are also valid from a consumer policy perspective and merit support.

IV. THE EFFECT OF CONSUMER PROTECTION MEASURES ON INTERNATIONAL TRADE

An important issue in the context of this report is the impact of consumer laws and policies on international trade. In the past decade, many OECD countries have enacted laws to establish consumer rights and curb abuses in the market-place and have increased their enforcement activities. These laws address such problems as product standards, warranties, deceptive advertising, packaging and labelling, and product safety. While enhancing the ability of consumers to make purchase decisions, these requirements inherently limit consumer choice and so involve real costs. For the most part, such laws apply with equal force to all products and do not discriminate against imports. While not designed to restrict imports, such consumer laws may, however, impose a particular burden on exporters as compared to domestic producers if exporters have to meet a variety of product-related requirements and regulations in each market in which they desire to sell their products regarding the different conditions under which products may be used. For example, different product standard requirements may compel importers to modify and redesign their product for each national market. In this regard, care should be exercised so that consumer policies do not inadvertently create barriers to trade.

An important issue in this context, which clearly shows the growing international dimension of consumer policy and its links with international trade, concerns national product safety measures and their application in connection with internationally traded goods. The Committee on Consumer Policy has been dealing with these issues since its creation in 1969 and has constantly stressed the need for international co-operation in this field. The informal notification procedure concerning product safety measures (regulations, product bans and recalls, safety research) set up by the Committee was a first step in this direction; the improvement of this procedure and further work on problems related to the export of hazardous products will continue to be given high priority. The Committee is co-operating with the Trade Committee on these issues. Moreover, the Committee seeks to promote the adoption by Member countries of a systematic approach towards product-related safety problems which includes the use of reliable sources of accident data and the application of risk management and cost-benefit methods in the decision-making process preceding the introduction of new product safety measures (17). A comprehensive study on methods used in Member countries for the elaboration and implementation of product safety measures is under way.

International harmonization of product standards merits support not only from a consumer policy but also from a trade perspective and the exchanges of views and experience within the Committee on problems encountered in specific product areas are useful in this respect. Progress in this direction has also been achieved by international standardization bodies, in particular the International Organisation for Standardization (ISO) and the International Electrotechnical Commission (IEC). It nevertheless has to be recognised that harmonization is a long-term objective which, in many areas, may be difficult to achieve. Co-operative efforts are therefore necessary to prevent different national standards from being used as significant barriers to trade.

Product-related standards affecting international trade are subject to international discipline under the 1979 GATT Code on Technical Barriers to Trade. This Code contains specific provisions designed to avoid the creation of unnecessary obstacles to trade, to accord national and non-discriminatory treatment to imports and to ensure through notification that signatories are kept informed about standards or technical regulations under preparation when these have a significant effect on trade. A Committee on Technical Barriers to Trade has been established to deal in particular with the settlement of disputes and to elaborate necessary procedures.

Trade problems arising from the application of different product standards are highlighted by a number of decisions of the Court of Justice of the European Communities in application of Art. 36 of the EEC Treaty concerning the free circulation of goods within the Common Market. The relevant principles developed by the Court in its "Cassis de Dijon" decision can be summarised as follows:

-- As a general rule, products lawfully produced and marketed in a member state have to be admitted for sale in other member states;

-- National product standards and technical rules can only be used to restrict or exclude imports of foreign products for imperative reasons, such as the protection of health and safety, fair competition and consumer protection, provided that such rules are not disproportionate and that no alternatives less harmful to trade are available;

-- Where product standards differ between member countries, it is important to determine whether the standards of the exporting country, while different, provide an equivalent degree of protection to meet the basic concerns of the regulations in the importing country (18).

Although applying within the rather specific context of efforts seeking to integrate markets and harmonize national laws within the EEC, the "Cassis de Dijon" doctrine exemplifies many of the issues involved in balancing trade interests against the need to regulate imports to protect consumers. With respect to product purchasing and content regulations, the Court has recognised that labelling requirements can provide sufficient safeguards without resorting to import bans. At the same time, the Court has indicated that considerations of public health can be used to justify import bans, even with respect to products that are lawfully sold in other countries. For instance, in a recent decision, the European Court of Justice declined to set aside a Dutch law that requires permission by national health authorities for the sale of beverages and foods to which vitamins have been added. The Court recognised that due to the uncertainty as to the health risks of food additives, member states must enjoy a broad margin of discretion in the implementation and enforcement of laws designed to protect human health. Of course, the health justification underlying an import ban must be genuine to be upheld, and not a pretext for blocking imports.

Another significant issue concerns the supply and prices of spare parts and after-sales service, which form an integral part of the cost, quality and durability of a specific product. Problems in this area can arise where restrictions on distribution (selective distribution) exist. Problems may also arise concerning the dependence on foreign supply of spare parts, especially in countries with no domestic production of the products or parts concerned.

V. APPROACHES TO ASSESS THE DIFFERENT SOCIETAL INTERESTS

As already mentioned, consumer policy considerations in the decision-making process will have to be balanced with other, sometimes conflicting policy objectives. Three of these objectives will be briefly discussed here: the fight against unemployment, the promotion of specific -- high-technology -- industries, and national security interests.

Much of the public appeal of protectionist measures is due to the belief that jobs endangered by foreign supplies can be saved by import barriers. It is, therefore, no surprise that protectionist pressures and measures have been and are most numerous in sectors where the degree of market penetration by foreign imports is high. The negative effects of protection have been discussed in earlier chapters: a decrease in consumer surplus, inefficient allocation of resources and an increase of the barriers to the competitive process. Moreover, income losses of the exporting country resulting from trade-restrictive measures may reduce its import capacity and this can have repercussions on exports and production in the protectionist country itself. From an international point of view, the situation can become even worse whenever labour intensities of production are different among countries; for instance, protection in industrialised countries may, in many cases, destroy a multiplicity of jobs in less-developed countries. Finally, the possibility of retaliation by the countries affected by restrictive trade measures must be taken into account. Retaliation will usually be directed against those sectors of the country which provide most of the income and employment generation in an economy and which are internationally most competitive.

Responding to concerns arising from unemployment, governments have in a number of cases found it necessary to take measures designed to gain time in order to carry out adjustments and thus reduce their social costs. Such measures can entail short-term employment benefits, or rather, avoidance of the dislocating costs of industrial adjustments. The size of this decrease in social costs depends on such factors as: the degree of skill of the labour force concerned, the level of wages of this labour force, the unemployment compensation and the average length of the unemployment period. As stated in the General Orientations for Positive Adjustment Policies adopted by Ministers in 1978 and confirmed in 1982, a constructive approach to these problems is to further adjustment to new conditions, relying as much as possible on market forces to encourage mobility of labour and capital to their most productive uses. Where governments are pursuing social and political objectives to assure a fair sharing of the burden of adjustment, it is essential that these goals be sought through policies which minimise any resulting costs in terms of reduced economic efficiency (19).

Another argument for restrictive trade measures or for subsidisation policies is the desire to stimulate or protect domestic production, e.g. in high-technology sectors. Governments, for instance, may seek to promote the competitiveness of their national industries in key sectors with the long-term purpose of creating the industrial base required for the expansion of the entire economy. In fact, subsidies for research and development constitute an important element in most countries' industrial and technological policies, and in some instances such policies are flanked by restrictive trade measures.

Thus the "infant industry" argument is often advanced to justify trade restrictions. Measures of that kind, which in the short run clearly affect consumer interests, may, in certain circumstances, produce longer-term economic benefits in cases where two basic conditions are fulfilled. First, the measures concerned should be temporary. Second, they should be part of an overall policy designed to facilitate an increasing participation of the industries concerned in international competitive markets, and government intervention should be kept to a minimum.

For illustrative purposes, it is worth mentioning the voluntary export restraint concerning Japanese exports of videotape recorders to the Common Market. An ostensible reason for the arrangement was to enable the European producers to establish a viable position in this newly emerging industry. In early 1983, Japan for the first time decided to exercise export moderation of particular products to the entire EEC, this arrangement taking the form of a series of official forecasts of Japanese exports to the EEC countries. The number of video tape recorders (VTRs) it sells in the EEC, establishment of a floor price for VTR sales, and a market for 1.2 million units produced by European manufacturers are provided for in the arrangement.

These types of arrangements, however, may impact negatively on consumer interests. They distort competition in home and world markets with the subsequent losses being borne by consumers, at least in the short run. In contrast to the short-term losses, possible economic benefits are uncertain and if they arise, may only do so after a considerable lapse of time (20).

Finally, trade restrictions have often been justified by the need to avoid undue dependencies of a country's economy on sources of foreign supplies (e.g. in the agricultural and energy sectors). This implies higher prices imposed on consumers as a premium for foreign policy or strategic reasons. Where such measures are considered unavoidable, an effort should be made to minimise their negative effects by limiting trade barriers to those necessary to protect the minimum-scale domestic production required for national security, by restricting the sectors involved and by considering alternative policy instruments to trade barriers such as stockpiling of supplies or regional diversification of imports. Considerations of self-sufficiency should not be misused to justify measures of excessive protection or support for domestic industry.

Consumer interests in trade policy measures must compete with other economic policy objectives which decision-makers have to take into account. In view of the far-reaching effects of trade-restrictive measures on the national and international economy and the many interests involved, a systematic and comprehensive evaluation of such measures is to be recommended. The purpose of such an evaluation is to make visible to the maximum extent possible the effects and costs of trade-restrictive measures so as to enable decision-makers to make a rational choice, having given proper consideration to consumer interests and the impact of trade policies on the economy as a whole.

While a variety of methodologies exist that are relevant to the analysis of trade restrictions, a commonly accepted and comprehensive approach has not yet emerged. One useful methodology available seems to be the cost-benefit approach which has been used increasingly in other policy areas.

As reports by Member countries show, cost-benefit methods are not widely used in the trade field. Only Australia, Canada, New Zealand and the United States have occasionally used such methods in this area. The majority of Member countries do not apply them, and several Member countries question their reliability in this specific context.

In Australia, cost-benefit methods are used by the Industries Assistance Commission to assist it in its deliberations during inquiries into both specific industries' and broad industries' assistance measures. The IAC takes into account such factors as the level of competitiveness of locally produced as opposed to imported goods, employment, profitability, long-term viability, production levels, cost of input, effects on user industries, etc.

In New Zealand, cost-benefit criteria are applied by the Industry Development Commission when they investigate an industry group, e.g. i) to what extent should other sections of the economy be required to pay higher prices following from additional protection given to one sector, and ii) to what extent is a disproportionately high protection accorded to one sector likely to reduce demand and, through it, employment opportunities in the rest of the economy?

In Canada, the positive and negative implications of trade measures are integral components of the decision-making process of such measures. In this context, the implications for consumers of action against imports are taken into account. In some cases, quantitative estimates of the consequent cost to consumers are provided. Further, a number of non-official studies have attempted to measure the impact of import restrictions (21).

Another example of the use of a cost-benefit estimate in trade proceedings arose in the 1982 investigation by the U.S. Department of Commerce with respect to the imposition of countervailing duties on important steel products. In an Annex to its comments in the proceeding, the FTC provided an estimate of the losses to the U.S. economy and to consumers, as well as the gains to domestic producers of steel and the increase in tariff revenue that could arise. The analysis concluded that imposition of a 15 percent tariff on imported steel products could provide annual gains to domestic steel producers of approximately $223 million, additional tariff revenues to the government of $0-19.6 million (depending on the market share of non-restrained foreign suppliers) and losses to consumers totalling $480.9 million. This could produce annual dead-weight losses to the economy (i.e., costs imposed on consumers which are not redistributed to other sectors of the economy) ranging from $237-257 million. The study also estimated the costs of increasing domestic jobs and concluded that each job would cost the economy, in efficiency losses, $28 795 to $31 082 annually.

It is necessary to recognise at the outset the limitations of cost-benefit methods. There are obvious difficulties in quantifying all effects of a policy and to take proper considerations of non-economic factors. Despite these problems, cost-benefit analysis is the best method currently available, provided that it is complemented with an assessment of qualitative factors and is applied with great caution. Further, a variety of methodologies exist that are relevant to the analysis of trade restrictions, and cost-benefit analysis need not be interpreted as a particularly narrowly defined analytical technique. Rather, the objective is to enhance the quality of policy decisions through consideration of effects of trade-restrictive measures on the basis of a set of objective criteria.

Specifically, a comprehensive checklist is proposed, indicating the factors that should enter into a quantitative and qualitative appraisal of alternative trade policy measures that are being considered. Such a checklist would serve as a guide to decision-makers, it being understood that government policy considerations would determine the weight to be given to the various factors. Before undertaking such an analysis, Member countries should, of course, be guided by their international obligations, in particular under GATT, which will circumscribe the available policy options.

From the perspective of consumer policy, the consideration of factors like price effects of trade policy measures, their costs to consumers, their impact on specific groups of consumers and their effects on availability and quality of products and the structure and competitive process in domestic markets are of particular importance. In addition to considering the effects on the national economy of alternative trade measures, governments should take into account the interest of their trading partners and the common objective of maintaining an open multilateral trading system. The proposed rationalisation of national trade policies would heighten awareness of the domestic costs of protection and, therefore, tend to narrow the range of issues to be resolved at the international level.

The following checklist is largely drawn from the report of the Committee of Experts on Restrictive Business Practices dealing with questions arising at the frontier between competition and trade policies (22). While it includes all factors mentioned in that report, a few more specific consumer policy considerations have been added:

a) What is the expected effect of the measure on the domestic price of the commodity concerned and on the general price level?

b) What are the expected direct economic gains to the domestic sector, industry or firms in question (technically the increase in producer's surplus)?

c) What number of jobs are expected to be created or protected by the measure? In the absence of the trade protection measure, what are the expected costs in relation to unemployment compensation, taking into account the average-length period of unemployment?

d) What are the expected gains to government revenues (e.g. from tariffs, import licences, tax receipts) and/or increased government costs (e.g. export promotion, government subsidies, lost tax revenues)?

e) What are the direct costs to consumers due to the resulting higher prices they must pay for the product and the reduction in the level of consumption of the product (technically the reduction in consumer's surplus)?

f) Are there specific groups of consumers which are particularly hit by the measure?

g) What is the likely impact of the measure on the availability, choice, quality and safety of goods and services?

h) What is the likely impact of the measure on the structure of domestic markets and the competitive process within those markets?

i) Will the measure encourage or permit structural adaptation of domestic industry? What will be the expected effect on investment by domestic firms and by foreign investors?

j) What would be the expected economic effects of the measure on other sectors of the economy, in particular, on firms purchasing products from and selling products to the industry in question?

k) How are other governments and foreign firms likely to react to the measures and what would be the expected effect on the economy of such actions? Is the measure a response to unfair practices in other countries?

l) What are the likely effects of the measure on other countries? How can prejudice to trading partners be minimised?

VI. THE REPRESENTATION OF CONSUMER POLICY CONCERNS IN THE DECISION-MAKING PROCESS ON TRADE AND TRADE-RELATED ISSUES

This section of the report, which is based on information submitted by Member countries, shows to what extent consumer policy considerations and other policy concerns actually interrelate in the decision-making process on trade and trade-related matters. First, the role of national and international consumer organisations in this area is discussed. Second, this section provides a survey of existing procedures for participation of consumer policy authorities in the formulation and implementation of trade policies. Third, existing possibilities for consumer organisations to make their views known either through formal or informal channels are examined.

A. The contribution of consumer organisations to trade policy discussions

As the previous chapters have shown, consumers should have a strong and active interest in matters concerning international trade. However, international trade policy matters have not always been a subject of primary concern for consumer organisations. Historically, consumer organisations have mainly grown on the basis of their direct assistance in the improvement of the relationship between individual consumers and suppliers of goods and services and of the legal framework governing these relations. The pursuance of this objective, which guided the activities of the consumer movement in its early years, coincided with a period of strong economic growth and of a considerable growth of international trade. Moreover, the relatively scarce financial and manpower resources of the majority of consumer organisations imposed a concentration of their activities on those services which would be directly beneficial to consumers, namely consumer information in the widest sense, co-operation with governmental bodies on matters of consumer legislation and questions of product safety. Nevertheless, trade problems and their implications for consumers have been increasingly recognised by consumer organisations. The following paragraphs summarise to what extent consumer organisations at national and international levels have shown an active interest in trade matters.

The need to maintain and strengthen an open international trading system is generally endorsed by consumer organisations, both at national and international levels. The ways and means of defending this position range from general statements, position papers and press releases which reflect trade policy aspects, to consumer information activities which give a neutral view on the performance of products, regardless of their origin. The latter aspect, though part of the traditional information activities of consumer organisations, should not be underestimated in this context. Comparative product tests undertaken in Member countries have certainly contributed to a wider acceptance of imported goods, and a comparison of product tests in the same product area undertaken at intervals of, say, ten years would clearly show how the interpenetration of markets has been beneficial to consumers from a price and quality point of view and with regard to the wider choice of products available.

Moreover, consumer organisations have quickly become aware of the imperfections in international trade. Several Member countries refer to studies comparing prices of the same or similar goods in different countries which show price differences that go far beyond the effects of different levels of turnover or sales taxes, transportation costs and other relevant factors. In Austria, for example, the prices for cameras and electrical appliances were compared with those of other countries, and in Norway comparative studies of the same kind showed considerable differences between domestic prices and the prices applied abroad. The conclusion which is put forward by both countries is that large -- often multinational -- firms tend to charge higher prices in small countries with no significant domestic production.

Quite apart from this direct interest in international trade matters, national and international consumer organisations have become increasingly involved in the policy discussion concerning international trade during the late seventies. In its final Resolution, the 1978 Congress of the International Organisation of Consumers Unions (IOCU) stated that the "General Assembly of IOCU expresses concern at the resurgence of protectionism in world trade caused by current economic recession; recognises the extent to which further import controls would threaten the already depressed living standards of developing countries while restricting choice and raising prices in industrial countries; and calls on governments to combat recession, reduce unemployment and protect the consumer interest by pursuing through GATT and in other ways an orderly growth of world trade, coupled with policies of domestic expansion" (23).

At about the same time, the Bureau Européen des Unions de Consommateurs (BEUC) became more actively interested in the subject. The main product areas, which gave rise to criticism on the part of BEUC, were food products (covered by the Common Agricultural Policy), textiles and clothing (regulated by the Multifibre Arrangement) and cars. These three product areas were also mentioned, in the same order of priority, by several Member countries.

Agricultural products are definitely at the top of the list of products arousing trade-related consumer concern (24). This is not limited to members of the European Community, where the Common Agricultural Policy constitutes, in the eyes of consumer organisations, an institutionalised system of trade restrictions. Similar concern is felt by consumer organisations in non-EEC Member countries, for example Norway and Switzerland with regard to their agricultural policies.

The second issue which has attracted the attention of consumer organisations, both at national and international levels, is the Multifibre Arrangement. In 1979, the Consumers' Association in the United Kingdom published its study on the impact of the MFA on consumers (25), which was soon afterwards followed by a study undertaken by BEUC (26). The Netherlands mentions, in addition to the above issues, the area of pharmaceuticals, the sector of automobiles and the operations of oil companies as the main targets of growing consumer interest.

In addition to tackling specific sectors, consumer organisations in various Member countries have expressed their concern about the rising wave of protectionism. In Germany, for instance, the consumer organisation "Arbeitsgemeinschaft der Verbraucher", at its November 1982 General Assembly, adopted the following resolution:

"The consumer associations regard the danger of growing protectionism both within and outside the European Communities with great concern. Increasing trade protectionism is unequivocally contrary to the interests of consumers. It impedes competition amongst suppliers with regard to both prices and the quality of products and thereby curtails consumers' freedom of choice. All protectionist measures, no matter what form they take nor which objective they serve, have a negative effect on consumers' purchasing power. The Arbeitsgemeinschaft der Verbraucher appeals to the Federal Government to undertake every effort to counter protectionist tendencies both within and outside the European Communities. At the same time, it should increase its endeavours to raise public awareness of the negative consequences of protectionist measures. Enterprises and sectors which demand such measures should simultaneously disclose the extent to which these measures burden both the overall economy and consumers" (27).

Similar examples can be found in other countries, e.g. in the United Kingdom, in Canada and in Norway. The Consumers' Association in the United Kingdom is by far the most active consumer organisation in this field. It has published numerous studies, position papers and briefings dealing with questions of international trade and consumer interests (28). The United Kingdom National Consumer Council, a semi-public consumer body, is also strongly involved in the discussion of trade matters. The Consumer Council has recently submitted a statement by its Chairman to the Minister for Trade which underlines the fact that consumer interest can easily be overlooked in the debate about protection for sectoral interests: "This is a particular problem in Parliament, where Members very understandably will be extremely concerned about developments in their constituency and, it is unlikely that an interest which spans all constituencies will be so powerfully represented" (29). The Consumer Council therefore requested that the industry given protection should have clear objectives for using its advantage, that the reasons for giving protection should be publicly stated, that the effects of protection should be monitored and that the protection should not be renewed without examination.

The Consumers' Association of Canada (CAC) has also been very active in the trade policy field. CAC has initiated representations to and been consulted by ministers on specific issues. CAC has, for example, made submissions to official inquiries by the Tariff Board, the Textiles and Clothing Board, and the Anti-Dumping Tribunal (30).

In Norway, the Consumer Council, a semi-official consumer body, has discussed the import restrictions in textiles and clothing in 1981 and adopted the following resolution:

"The Consumer Council wishes to raise the question of whether the present protection of Norwegian products does not result in an unsatisfactory distribution of costs. In our opinion, it is unreasonable that the main burden of costs should fall on consumers. When import restrictions are applied, costs are to an excessive degree borne by families with children and by those who can only afford the cheapest clothing, because the restrictions particularly affect low-price imports. The various forms of trade restrictions tend to preserve the existing distribution chain, with the possibility that certain firms can dominate the market as a result of quota allocations. Although the Consumer Council is not in favour of an indiscriminate dismantling of trade restrictions, it is of the opinion that, in the somewhat longer term, various types of support for the textile and clothing industry should be considered. One possibility would be to apply more direct subsidies to industrial concerns. The manner in which this is to be done must be studied more closely. A dismantling of trade restrictions would result in a direct reduction in prices to consumers. If the quota system were suspended, competition could increase, resulting in more efficient and cheaper distribution of textiles and articles of clothing" (31).

As a whole, the information made available by Member countries shows that today, the consumer movement at national and international levels is fully aware of the detrimental impact that restrictive trade policies can have on consumers. While recognising that consumer interests have to be assessed within a wide and complex network of societal concerns, consumer organisations feel that such interests often do not receive thorough consideration by decision-makers in the area of trade policy.

B. Procedures for taking into account consumer policy considerations in the decision-making process concerning trade matters

The survey conducted by the Committee has revealed the following -- not mutually exclusive -- procedural arrangements applied in a number of Member countries to ensure that consideration is given to consumer interests in the area of trade policies:

-- Cabinet-level representation of consumer policy authorities;

-- Concentration of tasks relating to policy areas of interest to consumers in one government department;

-- Participation of consumer policy authorities in interdepartmental committees or task forces dealing with trade matters;

-- Informal interdepartmental co-ordination on trade policies;

-- Statutory requirements to take into account consumer interests in legislative proposals or other measures including those related to trade policy;

-- Existence of independent bodies dealing with the implementation of trade policies and/or the assessment of government interventions.

The following paragraphs provide illustrative examples for each of these arrangements.

Consumer policy structures vary from country to country and institutionalised representation of consumer policy authorities at cabinet level is not widespread. In Canada, the inclusion of the Department of Consumer and Corporate Affairs in the membership of the cabinet basically enhances the potential for consideration of consumer interests. Consumer and Corporate Affairs also participates in a number of interdepartmental committees. Although it is recognised that such committees have played a declining role in trade matters, this structure provides at least a strong formal basis for the Department to keep involved in trade matters. A study on this subject commissioned by Consumer and Corporate Affairs Canada (32) concludes that the Department's role in this respect has not yet been sufficiently recognised and could be substantially improved. In most of the other countries where responsibility for consumer interests is concentrated in a separate unit, these units are generally part of a ministry with broader consumer policy responsibilities like Economic Affairs or Trade and Industry.

Member countries have tackled the problems of interdepartmental co-ordination in various ways. In Japan, for instance, a number of interdepartmental bodies have been set up in the trade policy area which include members who can represent consumer interests; these bodies include:

a) The Customs Tariff Council which deliberates on any amendments to the tariff annexed to the Customs Tariff Law and any other important matters concerning tariff rates;

42

b) The Export-Import Trade Council which deliberates on any important matters concerning the export-import trade, purchase and distribution of goods;

c) The Export Inspection and Design Council, which considers matters relating to export inspection, including those relating to improvement of design of products.

All these Councils can submit their findings to the competent Minister in the form of a recommendation. Furthermore, in Japan, ministries and agencies in charge of trade policy have sections in charge of consumer policy. Another example which has already been referred to is Canada, where several inter-departmental committees, such as the Committee on Low-Cost Imports, have been set up which involve the participation of Consumer and Corporate Affairs. The Canadian Combines Investigation Act is also worth mentioning in this context. It provides that the Director of Investigation and Research, who is responsible for the administration of competition policy, may make representations or submit evidence to government agencies "in respect of the maintenance of competition". This authority has been utilised on occasion to make submissions on behalf of consumers in the context of inquiries into matters relating to Canada's import policies.

An alternative solution chosen by some other Member countries consists in concentrating several tasks of interest to consumer and trade policies in the same government department. Thus in Germany, the Netherlands and Switzerland, for instance, the Ministry for Economic Affairs is responsible for both consumer and foreign trade policies. In the United Kingdom the Department of Trade and Industry deals with issues of foreign trade, industrial policy and consumer policy, and the Office of Fair Trading is competent for the implementation of both competition and consumer policy. The latter policy areas are also regrouped within the same department or government agency in several other countries, e.g. Canada (Consumer and Corporate Affairs), U.S. (Federal Trade Commission).

In the United States, limited procedures exist for consideration of the impact of trade measures on competition and consumer welfare. In enforcement proceedings under certain trade legislation before the U.S. International Trade Commission, e.g. anti-dumping and countervailing actions, procedures exist for the competition authorities, the Department of Justice and the Federal Trade Commission, to comment on such public interest concerns as the potential effects of these proceedings on domestic competition and consumer interests. In several instances, the Federal Trade Commission has commented specifically on the estimated quantitative impact of pending trade measures and proceedings on consumer welfare. For example, prior to the implementation of the voluntary export restraint by Japan on passenger car exports to the U.S., the Federal Trade Commission estimated that among its effects, the proposed VER would cost American consumers between $3 billion and $5 billion annually.

In most Member countries, interdepartmental co-ordination on trade policy matters is handled on an informal, ad hoc basis. While some countries see considerable advantage in the flexibility of these procedures, others believe that where co-ordination does not take place in a more systematic or formal way, consumer policy authorities have little or no impact on trade policy decisions.

Some countries do have formal requirements to take into account consumer interests when adopting laws, regulations and policy decisions in the area of trade and other related areas. For instance, in the UK, the government is required by legislation to consult interested parties when proposing changes in that legislation in various fields, including certain trade-related areas. Consumer organisations are often included in such consultations, particularly where there is a direct consumer interest. In New Zealand, consumer interests are formally recognised in the Commerce Act. As stated in the Preamble, the Act promotes "... the interests of consumers and the effective and efficient development of industry and commerce through the encouragement of competition ...". Germany refers to a 1973 decision of the federal government according to which all consumer-related proposals submitted to the cabinet for consideration should include a "consumer clause", i.e., a description of the impact which the proposed measures are likely to have on consumers. In principle, that also applies to proposals in the trade field.

In several Member countries, independent official bodies have been set up for the implementation of specific trade policies or for the assessment of the economic impact of trade or trade-related measures. The role of the U.S. International Trade Commission in the enforcement of injurious or unfair trade laws has already been mentioned (33). In Canada, there exist several independent bodies dealing with trade matters, in particular the Tariff Board, the Textile and Clothing Board and the Anti-Dumping Tribunal.

In Australia, the Industry Assistance Commission Act of 1973 has created a statutory body, the Industry Assistance Commission (IAC), with the task to advise the government on the nature and extent of assistance, including trade protection granted to industry. In the exercise of its functions, the Commission is required to have regard to the Australian Government's desire, inter alia, "to recognise the interests of consumers and consuming industries likely to be affected by measures proposed by the Commission". The enabling legislation further requires the IAC to hold public inquiries to enable interested parties, including consumers, to present submissions. Its conclusions appear in draft reports which are open to public scrutiny and comment before final recommendations are presented to the government.

C. Possibilities for consumer organisations to make representations to government bodies on trade issues

Several countries mention a somewhat institutionalised form of consumer representation in trade discussions. In the other countries, various types of informal representation seem to prevail, which are either based on the presumption that trade policy is in any case bound to take into account the "general public interest" or rely on informal contacts between consumer organisations and the political representatives.

The Australian Federation of Consumer Organisations (AFCO), which comprises 54 member organisations with a total membership of 2 million consumers, has consistently made submissions to those IAC inquiries with a substantial consumer interest. The IAC takes all views presented to it into account in formulating its recommendations. However, these recommendations are not binding on the government although they form part of the decision-making process.

44

AFCO is represented on the Australian Manufacturing Council (AMC) and the Economic Planning Advisory Council (EPAC). The former provides advice to the government on matters of relevance to the manufacturing sector to facilitate the development of efficient and internationally competitive manufacturing industries. The AMC comprises representatives from the trade union movements, industry bodies, State and Commonwealth representatives, the consumer movement and the chairpersons of ten individual industry councils which deal with specific manufacturing industries. EPAC's functions are to:

-- Draw together the views of community representatives on prospective economic conditions and appropriate policies;

-- Identify feasible and desirable goals and targets for the economy as a whole;

-- Provide perspectives on the medium- and longer-term economic outlook;

-- Develop policies to help realise the maximum growth potentialities of the economy and assist in the achievement of sustained economic growth.

EPAC is made up of seventeen members, with representatives drawn from Commonwealth, State and local governments, the business sector, the rural sector, the trade union movement, welfare organisations, consumer and community groups. Clearly, these two Councils consider and provide advice to the government on issues which affect trade policy.

Since 1974, the Australian Attorney-General's Department has arranged and hosted an annual international trade law seminar designed to involve businessmen, legal practitioners, academics and representatives of State and Commonwealth Governments in considering and exchanging views on developments in the field of international trade law. An official report of the seminar containing the papers and speeches is printed and tabled in Parliament by the Attorney-General. This forum provides an opportunity for consumer views with respect to trade policy measures and trade-related issues to be raised.

As has already been mentioned, consumer organisations in Canada may express their view in formal public enquiries conducted by independent bodies such as the Tariff Board, the Textile and Clothing Board and the Anti-Dumping Tribunal. The same situation exists in the U.S. for public hearings organised by the International Trade Commission.

In Germany, consumer organisations similar to other interest groups are free to express their views on trade policies. This can be done informally or in a more formal manner, e.g. in hearings which can be held in conjunction with the preparation of new legislation. In addition, the Consumer Advisory Board to the Federal Ministry of Economics, an independent body advising the federal government on consumer policy issues, can also comment on aspects of trade policy which are relevant to consumers. In fact, the Consumer Advisory Board has urged the federal government to resist protectionist pressure.

In Switzerland, the "Commission consultative de politique économique extérieure" (Consultative Committee on Foreign Trade Policy) comprises 36 members representing the various interested parties. Consumer organisations and trade unions have two seats each. The distribution sector, which frequently defends similar viewpoints, also participates in this Committee. Moreover, the "Commission d'experts pour le tarif douanier et la limitation des importations" (Expert Commission on Tariffs and Import Restrictions), as well as several more specialised working groups, in particular in the field of agricultural products, also include consumer representatives.

In Denmark, although there are in general no formal ways in which consumer's views are presented in trade policy discussions, the Consumer Council is a member of the special committees under the Ministries of Agriculture and of Fisheries, under which the Danish position on EEC questions is prepared.

In other countries, the representation of consumer interests is largely determined by the general institutional background in the economic policy field. In the United Kingdom, for example, whilst there are no formal arrangements for consumer organisations to express their views on trade issues, informal contacts are well established and are extensively used between consumer organisations and government officials, between one government department and another and between separate divisions of the same department. It is considered that the informality and flexibility of such arrangements has worked to the benefit of all concerned. In the Netherlands, the consumer organisations hold periodical meetings with the Minister concerned with consumer policy, where matters concerning trade policy can be informally dealt with. Similar possibilities of informally influencing decision-making actually exist in other Member countries as well.

One of the important features of the increase in consumer protection legislation during the past decade has been the creation of specific legal rights enabling consumers individually, and in some cases collectively, to initiate litigation to correct illegal practices in the sale of goods and services. Through such procedures as class actions and recoupment of attorney's fees and court costs, consumers were put in a position to be able to monitor the market-place and to correct practices that harmed or threatened their welfare. For the most part, consumers and consumer groups do not enjoy similar rights to protect themselves against trade practices or policies that affect their interests but are not subject to consumer protection legislation. In a few countries, consumer groups possess limited rights to file a complaint or offer their views in proceedings under unfair trade statutes. For the most part, however, consumers and consumer groups lack legislative authority to bring legal action against trade measures or policies, e.g. VERs, quotas, that affect consumer welfare. This is generally due to the fact that government decisions are broadly exempted from the requirements of consumer (or competition) laws and that consumers are not directly empowered under laws to prosecute private practices that restrain trade. One of the few cases involving this issue arose in the United States, where in 1972 the Consumers Union filed a lawsuit to enjoin operation of the arrangements provided for in a voluntary export restraint concerning steel exports to the U.S. from Japanese and European producers. The consumer group alleged that the VER exceeded the commerce powers of the executive. The case was ultimately dismissed and the agreement upheld, but the standing of the consumer group to challenge the trade agreement was not contested (34).

At the international level, consumer organisations have limited access to policy-makers in international trade matters. GATT proceedings do not provide for observer status for non-governmental organisations. At the UN level, IOCU is represented among the non-governmental organisations accredited with the Economic and Social Council of the United Nations (ECOSOC). Within the OECD, the new mandate of the Committee on Consumer Policy requests the Committee to obtain as appropriate the advice of international consumer organisations.

An attempt to include consumers in a somewhat institutionalised form of the decision-making process has recently been undertaken by the European Communities where Council Regulation No. 288/82 of 5th January 1982 provides for public hearings to receive evidence from "interested national and legal persons" in the case of selective import controls from non-EC countries. Although not yet widely used, this procedure could open up the possibility for consumer organisations to voice their views on trade issues. Another EC mechanism, the Consumer Consultative Committee, provides a platform for consultations on technical issues, e.g. the product safety and quality standard aspects of internationally traded goods.

NOTES AND REFERENCES

1.   C(82)58(Final), Point 15(a).

2.   Communiqué, Press/A(83)25, paragraph 14.

3.   William R. Cline, "Imports and Consumer Prices: A Survey Analysis", Journal of Retailing 55 (1979) at 3-24.

4.   The Committee of Experts on Restrictive Business Practices has carried out a study on the issues arising at the frontier between competition and trade policy and reported to the OECD Council at Ministerial level in May 1984; see Competition and Trade Policies: Their Interaction, OECD, 1984.

5.   "The Price of Protection", A Which? Campaign Report, Consumers' Association, London, 1979. The European Community, the Consumer and the Multi-Fibre Arrangement, Bureau Européen des Unions de Consommateurs, Brussels, November 1981.

6.   There are estimates according to which the total economic burden of measures taken within the framework of the Consumer Agricultural Policy for a given period have been one-and-a-half to two times higher than the income gain to agriculture. See H. Dicke and H. Rodemer, Gesamtwirtschaftliche und Finanzwirtschaftliche Auswirkungen des Agrarschutzes in der EG, Kieler Arbeitspapiere No. 146.

7.   David E. Bond and Ronald J. Wonnacott (1968) "Trade Liberalization and the Canadian Furniture Industry", The Impact of Trade Liberalization, Private Planning Association of Canada, University of Toronto Press.

8.   Craig J. Campbell, The Impact of Barriers to Footwear Imports on Canadian Consumers and the Canadian Economy and The Impact of Barriers to

<u>Clothing Imports on Canadian Consumers and the Canadian Economy</u>, Consumer and Corporate Affairs, Canada (unpublished).

9.   Morris E. Morkre and David G. Tarr, <u>Effects of Restrictions on U.S. Imports: Five Case Studies and Theory</u>. Staff report of the Bureau of Economics to the Federal Trade Commission. Washington: U.S. Government Printing Office, 1980. The study used a partial equilibrium model to study the effects of various methods of protection on the industries selected.

10.   Michael C. Munger, "The Costs of Protectionism: Estimates of the Hidden Tax of Trade Restraints" (Working Paper No. 80), and Murray Weidenbaum, "Toward A More Open Trade Policy", Publication 53, Center for the Study of American Business, Washington University (1983).

11.   Report on car prices and on the private import of cars in the EEC countries, Bureau Européen des Unions de Consommateurs (BEUC), Brussels, 1981.

12.   For a further discussion of the distributional consequences of various quantitative restrictions on imports, see the Report of the Committee of Experts on Restrictive Business Practices, <u>supra</u> no. 4, at Chapter II (Section B/3)(b).

13.   See Jooh N. Suh, "Voluntary Export Restraints and Their Effects on Exporters and Consumers: the Case of Footwear Quotas", Working Paper No. 71, Center for the Study of American Business, Washington University (October 1981), cited in Murray Weidenbaum, "Towards a More Open Trade Policy", at 9.

14.   The decision is reported in Judgement of 24th November 1982, Case 249/8 and the relative laws were Article 2 of the Directive 10/50.

15.   See Report by the Committee of Experts on Restrictive Business Practices, <u>supra</u> no. 4.

16.   Id., at Chapter II, Section C(5).

17.   See e.g. <u>Data Collection Systems Related to Injuries Involving Consumer Products</u>, OECD, 1978; <u>Product Safety -- Risk Management and Cost-Benefit Analysis</u>, OECD, 1983.

18.   For a detailed discussion of the "Cassis de Dijon" doctrine and related case law, see A. Mattera, "Les nouvelles formes du protectionnisme économique et les articles 30 et suivants du Traité CEE", Revue du Marché Commun 1983, pp. 252 et seq.

19.   Council Communiqués of 15th June 1978 [C(78)96(Final) Annex II] and of 11th May [C(82)57(Final) Annex].

20.   As to the economic and legal analysis of voluntary export restraints, see the above-mentioned report by the Committee of Experts on Restrictive Business Practices, op. cit., Chapters I and II.

21. See e.g. <u>Trade Liberalisation and the Canadian Furniture Industry</u>, Private Planning Association of Canada, University of Toronto Press, 1968; Craig J. Campbell, <u>supra</u> no. 8; Glenn P. Jenkins, <u>Cost and Consequences of the War of Protectionism</u>, Harvard University, 1980.

22. See Report by the Committee of Experts on Restrictive Business, <u>supra</u> no. 4, at Chapter II, Section B(I)(b).

23. Proceedings of the 9th IOCU World Congress, London, July 1978, IOCU, The Hague, page 5.

24. In Germany, for example, about 50 per cent of the issues of a weekly consumer news release published by the consumer organisation "Arbeitsgemeinschaft der Verbraucher", <u>Verbraucherpolitische Korrespondenz</u>, Bonn, carry articles dealing with agricultural policy and its cost to consumers.

25. See Consumers' Association, <u>supra</u> no. 5.

26. <u>The European Community -- The Consumer and the Multifibre Arrangement</u>, BEUC, Brussels, 1981.

27. <u>Verbraucherpolitische Korrespondenz</u> -- "Arbeitsgemeinschaft der Verbraucher", Bonn, No. 47 of 23rd November 1982.

28. See position papers, e.g "EEC Trade Policy", May 1979, consumer briefing to candidates for the European Parliament; press interviews, e.g. on the GATT Ministerial Meeting in "Consumers for World Trade", Newsletter, Washington, D.C., Jan. 1983; annual briefings to the UK Government, European Parliament, EC Commission and the Press on the "EEC Farm Price Proposals", 1982/83, 1981/82, 1980/81, 1979/80; election candidate briefings, e.g. to candidates for the European Parliament, May 1979; briefing to the UK and European Parliaments, the UK Government, EC Commission and the press on "The EEC's Negotiating Stance on the Next Multi-Fibre Arrangement", June 1981.

29. Quoted from a submission by the UK Consumer Council.

30. September 1975: Submission to the Clothing and Textile Board on Imposition of Restraints on Imported Men's and Boys' Shirts
    November 1975: Submission to the Textile and Clothing Board re: Outerwear;
    November 1976: Submission to the Textile and Clothing Board re: Clothing Imports;
    March 1979: Submission to the Standing Senate Committee on Agriculture on Bill s13 re: An Act to Control the Importation of Beef into Canada;
    February 1980: Submission to the Textile and Clothing Board;
    September 1980: Submission to the Anti-Dumping Tribunal on Footwear;
    October 1981: Submission on Meat Import Legislation for Canada.

31. Resolution adopted by the Norwegian Consumer Council on 25th November 1981.

32. Frank Stone, Consumer Interest in Canadian Trade Policy -- A study prepared by the Department of Consumer and Corporate Affairs, Carleton University, Ottawa, 1982.

33. For a further discussion, see Report of the Committee of Experts on Restrictive Business Practices, supra no. 4, at Chapter II, Section C(3).

34. Consumers Union of US, Inc. v. Kissinger, 506 F. 2D 136 (D.C. 1974); cert. denied, 421 US 1004 (1975). The power of the executive to enter into OMAs has subsequently been clarified by new legislation in the U.S. but this authority does not, at present, extend to VERs.

Theme I

THE EFFECT OF TRADE POLICY ON CONSUMER INTERESTS

SUMMARY

by

T. Russell Robinson
Assistant Deputy Minister, Bureau of Policy Co-ordination,
Consumer and Corporate Affairs, Canada

In our session for Theme I we were invited to consider the following:

a) How the consumer interest can be defined and distinguished from other societal objectives, with the trade policy regime as our frame of reference;

b) How restrictive trade measures impact on consumers -- not just generally, but differentially, depending on the type, nature and degree of such measures;

c) How these effects can best be researched and evaluated -- benefit-cost types of analysis, for example -- and by whom.

Much of the discussion quite properly addressed the issue of what the so-called "consumer interest" is and who should be expected to speak for "it". Does the "consumer interest" constitute an independent perspective that can legitimately join other interests in contributing to policy discussions and decisions? With a couple of small qualifications, I believe the papers and speakers confirmed the hypothesis in the OECD background document: there is certainly a legitimate consumer interest or consumer perspective that should be explored, articulated and presented in many areas of policy-making, including trade policy.

It was pointed out many times that individuals can and do play several roles, and therefore can "wear" different interest "hats", whether as voters, taxpayers, employees, employers, investors and so on. But the consumer hat is a legitimate one, reflecting the role of individuals and families as users of funds, as spenders, as purchasers of final goods and services. The economist's distinction between sources and uses of funds is instructive. As workers or employees, we seek funds by selling services; as investors we try to improve our sources of income in one form or another. But as consumers we use or dispose of funds: we buy goods and services, and with good market information, good access and informed choice, we translate that spending/buying activity into our ultimate standard of living.

So we can and do differentiate our interests as consumers from our interests as producers, employers, taxpayers, etc. And these interests can be in conflict as they involve different needs, weights and characteristics. This does not mean that consumer interests are always at odds with the other roles or interests. It simply means that they are not the same, and therefore can have something separate and additional to say about public policy issues. If this distinction is accepted, it then follows that groups representing other perspectives such as business associations, trade unions, taxpayer interest groups, etc. will not automatically ensure that consumer interests are respected on all issues at all times. They may indeed broaden their reach and address consumer concerns from time to time, and many of their interests from their own perspective will be consistent with consumer interests, but this is not guaranteed, nor should it be asserted or accepted as an act of faith. Other groups must be free to disagree as well as to find common cause.

When we apply these considerations to the field of trade policy, we find both "good news and bad news". The good news is that there is considerable scope for agreement and "common cause" between consumers and other "stakeholders" in trade policy matters. Restrictive trade measures not only "tax" consumers; they can also adversely affect importers and retailers. Other businesses as well are users or "consumers" of imported supplies, equipment, services, and other forms of "intermediate goods". Access to imports at competitive prices are important for business productivity as well as for consumer welfare. Domestic exporters can suffer from import restrictions, either directly as a result of retaliation of one form or other, or more generally as production and marketing patterns are distorted, or as reduced exchange earnings abroad inhibit access to those markets. ("We cannot sell if we do not buy!") Obviously consumers are not alone in reaping the benefits from an open and expanding trading system, so they should not stand alone in opposing distortions or restrictions to that system. They can and should join forces with many other interested participants, whose voices in turn are also not always well developed.

The bad news, of course, is that in a period where unemployment is high due to a continuation of recession and rapid structural change, conflicts between different interests can become particularly sharp. The unemployed (or those threatened) and the industries most likely to face major change (including disappearance!) are more numerous in these times, and public policy, in the name of the more comprehensive public interest, must seek judicious compromises among the competing, conflicting demands -- a much more difficult task than that faced in more buoyant, dynamically stable periods.

But perhaps there is another element of good news to be found in the "structural change" component of our current economic situation. Adjustment, adaptation and structural change are formidable challenges, but there can be no doubt that "consumer interests" are generally served if these changes are achieved. So again we find common cause with business groups concerned with building future competitiveness, with governments trying to accommodate change and to encourage and assist adjustment, and with all those hoping for least costly methods of accomplishing these public purposes.

When some analysis is done of the modalities of trade policies -- particularly forms of trade restrictions -- some messages emerge that our authors and speakers agree upon as useful criteria for evaluating "better versus worse" forms. It was widely recognised that trade restrictions ultimately have to do with redistribution (e.g. from consumers/taxpayers /exporters/etc. to the particular industry protected). Furthermore, questions relating to the degree of distribution and who will benefit are social/political questions, not analytical/economic ones. Nevertheless, the analysis (of ways and means, alternatives, pros and cons, etc.) can make the underlying distributional matters more transparent, and more clearly and widely understood, thereby reducing the risk of miscalculation (or even gross error), or at least help to clarify the choices and the priorities so as to minimise the resultant burdens or costs. It was pointed out that in some cases, restrictive trade policies have inadvertently exacerbated the problem by causing increased pressure on the "protected" producer, while rewarding the foreign exporter, at the expense of the domestic taxpayer/consumer!

In any case, there can be no doubt that better analytical work needs to be done, supported by relevant background research, if we are to minimise losses or costs, maximise efficiencies, and encourage the needed adjustments when trade restrictions are deemed necessary as a compromise among competing interests. As regards the consumer perspective, a series of criteria emerged from the papers and commentary. To the fullest possible extent, restrictive trade measures should be:

--- Transparent rather than disguised;

--- Direct rather than indirect;

--- General rather than specific;

-- Temporary rather than permanent (and scheduled firmly, rather than continuously renegotiated which causes additional problems due to uncertainty).

Further, any property rights (or benefits or windfalls) resulting from restrictive measures should if possible be captured domestically, and used to finance or encourage the adjustments that are needed to complement the measure, so as to ensure that the measures will be temporary, and that the consumer/taxpayer/business and foreign "contributors" will in fact see an end to their "burden" and a positive result from their "involuntary investment". The reference to "foreign contributors" is of course a reminder that not only domestic or national interests are at stake, and it is not only domestic stakeholders who pay for protective measures. By definition trade is an international issue, and the "public interest" is global, not just national.

While there can be no doubt that improved analysis and better understanding of policy choices can help reduce costs and improve the effectiveness of trade policies, some of the analysis already reminds us that restrictive trade policies can only explain a part of the relative slow-down in the growth of trade recently, and only part of the dynamics of trade pattern adjustments. The great driving forces of global trade development and structural change are inexorable: there may be some opportunity to "manage" the process in ways that may be effective in certain cases, but the "grand lines" are not to be denied or reversed. Restrictive trade policies may indeed be costly, but they will not stem the tide of history, and those who would rely on them to "insulate" their country or their industry are probably short-sighted and naïve. The other side of this coin, of course, is the fact that total elimination of all trade barriers would not guarantee an end to recession, or the disappearance of the necessity and pain of major structural changes in our economies. Macro-economic policies and international policy co-operation are the "grand lines" affecting trade development, and there must be some truth to the claim that at least some of the growth of protectionist measures have been an understandable response to conditions which we must ultimately improve by these other means. Thus we need to keep the specific trade measure questions in broader perspective, even as we try nevertheless to improve our performance in the trade policy realm itself.

These questions of perspective came up time and again in our papers and discussions, even when we dipped into the esoteric world of analysis and methodology. It was acknowledged that our supportive research and policy analysis should be, for example:

-- As broadly based as possible (i.e., more general equilibrium analyses are preferred over a partial equilibrium focus or work even more specific or narrow in scope);

-- Dynamic rather than static (we must acknowledge incentives, indirect factors, and adjustments over time, with evaluation embracing a longer rather than shorter time horizon);

-- International rather than strictly national (if we are to respect the true nature of the issues, and the need for international as well as national consensus and co-operation).

Of course these are desirable characteristics of research and analysis of any field of policy, but they are particularly important for those of us worrying about trade policy from a consumer point of view. The issues are complex enough to require sophisticated attention in any case. But our interests as consumers can be well served only if we do have that more comprehensive analysis on the table. And if we can find ways and means to make that happen, we will earn that seat at the table, and be welcomed as a thoughtful, useful contributor.

If I had to attempt a more distilled summary for Theme I of the Symposium, it might be this:

a) The issue is not whether there is a differentiable thing called "the consumer interest in trade policy", but whether and how that interest is or can be a useful contributor to policy-making processes; whether it can bring its perspective "to the table" in an effective way, so that when the inevitable compromises are made, they are judicious compromises -- ideally enlightened compromises -- based on a fuller understanding of all the relevant costs and benefits of policies being considered;

b) In the trade realm, consumers have common cause with many others. Exporters, business (as users of imported "inputs"), taxpayers and others all suffer along with consumers when trade barriers are present in inefficient forms, when productivity and economic

54

adjustments are inhibited unduly, and when efficiency costs far outweigh the redistributional effects which are usually at the heart of
protectionist inclinations. Ideally, restrictive trade measures
would be accepted only temporarily, and only where they contribute
to minimise difficulties while at the same time aiding and encouraging effective, efficient and speedy structural adjustment;

c) Consultation, co-operation and concertation at both national and
international levels are important and needed, and consumers' interests should be part of such processes. More effective participation, however, will depend greatly on the quality of the contributions brought "to the table". Better research and relevant policy
analysis is essential, both for the credibility of the participants
and for the success of the policies chosen.

THE ECONOMIC EFFECTS OF TRADE POLICY MEASURES

by

Hartmut Scheele
Counsellor, Federal Ministry of Economics, Bonn, Germany

World-wide protectionism is one of the main threats to global economic
recovery.

Elimination or at least regulation of the classic instruments of protectionism -- tariffs, quantitative restrictions and traditional safeguard
measures -- is provided for in the GATT, the governing framework for the
multilateral system of free world trade. The GATT laid the cornerstone for
the unexampled expansion of world trade in the first twenty years after GATT's
establishment in 1947. But since the end of the sixties, the open multilateral trading system has had to cope with mounting difficulties. In the
face of world-wide economic problems, there has been an increasing tendency to
protect domestic producers by sealing off markets from foreign competitors;
the GATT was more successful in reducing tariffs than in progressively eliminating quantitative import restrictions. Trade barriers in the form of quotas
have been increasing. The Multi-Fibre Arrangement (MFA) has contributed extensively to this development.

Besides the traditional protectionist measures, new forms of protectionism threaten to undermine the liberalisation successes of the GATT (including those of the latest major round of negotiations, the Tokyo Round from
1973 to 1979) and to lead to an erosion of the open multilateral trading
system. Some examples of these are: administrative and other non-tariff
barriers; orderly marketing agreements (OMAs); voluntary export restraints
(VERs); excessive subsidisation; "buy national" campaigns; harassment by
improper use of regulations relating to unfair trade practices; proposed
tariff increases for the protection of so-called infant industries; and
industrial targeting: excessive industrial concentration tolerated or even
promoted by governments.

The protectionist fortress mentality tends to look at trade relations more and more from a bilateral and sectoral angle than from a multilateral point of view. This reduces the exchange of goods to the level of the lowest bilateral common denominator. The increasing number of orderly marketing agreements and voluntary export restraints, which take place in a grey area outside GATT, is an example of this dangerous shift. Furthermore, governments must refrain from relieving business of its responsibility to adjust, in that they distract them from undertaking the necessary steps toward restructuring by an increasing process of subsidisation. There can be no argument to support socialising business losses and burdening healthy companies and private taxpayers -- not to mention consumers -- in order to sustain the existence of companies otherwise not competitive any more. Above all, it is not acceptable for a certain sector in one country to receive government support, thus ruining the companies in another country which have to live without such support.

Nobody will gain from an erosion of the open multilateral trading system. Loss of confidence in investment, of competitiveness, of markets for exports and of jobs are the consequences.

Consumers are also affected by protectionist trade measures, suffering from the slow-down of growth and dynamism of an economy and the consequences thereof: price increases, less quality and limited choice due to the absence or weakening of healthy competition. In the field of agriculture, the EEC countries for some time now have been living with a dangerous combination of import protection, price guarantees, surplus production and export restitutions. In the steel area, the U.S. has introduced additional tariffs and quotas on certain specialty steel products. Japan has undertaken several voluntary export restraints or so-called forecasts for a number of products, including video tape recorders. While it is difficult to assess how much these measures cost the consumer, there can be no doubt that the sacrifice is high.

Unfortunately, while the dangers of protectionism have been recognised world-wide, there has been very little concrete progress in removing protectionist measures. Yet the fact remains that trade liberalisation is clearly in the interests of consumers. And certainly the initiative of the Secretary-General of the OECD for the rollback of protectionist measures and efforts to strengthen the open multilateral trading system by implementing the GATT Work Programme and preparing a new round of trade negotiations within GATT (dealing with, inter alia, new forms of protectionism) are also in the interests of consumers.

TRADE ISSUES AND CONSUMER INTERESTS:
THE JAPANESE EXPERIENCE

by

Koichi Hamada
Professor of Economics, University of Tokyo

Yoshiro Nakajo
Deputy Director, First Consumer Affairs Division,
Economic Planning Agency, Japan

I. INTRODUCTION

The welfare of consumers is naturally the ultimate goal of an economic system. Particularly in a market economy, economic activities are guided by price signals in such a way as to serve the needs and desires of consumers. Thus, consumer sovereignty is the basic principle of a market economy. Quite often, however, consumer sovereignty may be only a myth because of various imperfections in the market and unnecessary interventions by states.

It has been recognised that international trade is an effective way of increasing the welfare of nations. Naturally, free trade benefits consumers. The question is whether present-day consumers in various countries enjoy the full benefit of free trade. We shall address this question, referring to the experience of the Japanese economy (1).

In the argument against free trade, reference is often made to "the national interest". For example, one hears about how the Japanese Government should protect "the national interest" in the face of foreign pressures to open its agricultural and service markets. In general, however, no single abstract "national interest" exists in any country.

In the process of progress in free trade, there are people who gain from liberalisation of trade and those who lose in participating countries. For example, if Japan exports automobiles of high quality to the U.S., American consumers will gain while the management as well as workers of the American automobile industry may be harmed in the form of reduced profits and unemployment. Similarly, if low-priced agricultural products are imported to Japan, the Japanese consumers will gain while Japanese farmers will be threatened by the competition.

Thus, trade friction is by no means a simple conflict between national interests in the two countries. Instead, conflicting interests within both the U.S. and Japan are interwoven in a structure of multiple layers. The interest of the Japanese automobile industry coincides with the interest of American automobile users; the interest of American farmers has much in common with that of Japanese food consumers. In this way, consumer and producer interests meet across the ocean.

In light of these observations, one can see that, for instance, the role of Japan's trade missions is more than just a survey of opinions of

Japan's trading partners, though these missions are usually not given any authority to conduct formal negotiations representing the government. When Japan's mass media report that pressure from foreign countries is so strong, they may help to resolve some of the conflicts between various national groups in Japan.

The development of trade friction will explicitly reveal the conflicting relations among various groups in each country, which already existed but were understood only implicitly. Trade frictions will force people to make decisions concerning such questions as how much sacrifice consumers should make to protect the domestic industries, agriculture or service industries that face competition from imports.

Consumer interests are widely scattered over a large number of consumer products, so that consumer voices are hard to organise as a political pressure. Although consumers use a great number of products, the quantity of each product consumed is small. In contrast, liberalisation of imports will directly affect the living conditions of people who are engaged in import-competing industries. Consequently, the interest of those people who directly suffer is more concentrated and political pressure is more easily formed. In many cases, the collected gains that consumers receive are larger than the losses that competing domestic industries suffer in the free trade. Thus an imbalance exists between the representation of producer interests and that of consumer interests. One of the roles of consumer groups should be to study their own interests objectively, to represent them faithfully and to counteract protectionist pressure from producers.

II. GAINS FROM TRADE AND CONSUMER INTERESTS

In this section we shall survey the degree of openness in various sectors of the Japanese economy and examine to what extent Japanese consumers benefit from trade, and to what extent they are prevented from enjoying the benefits of free trade.

A. Manufacturing sector

In its efforts to open the markets for industrial products, Japan can certainly be proud of its record, compared to that of most advanced countries. Japan has lowered its import duties several times since the Tokyo Round Agreement went into effect in April 1980. Furthermore, in 1984, Japan lowered tariff rates on 47 individual items and decided to accelerate by two years the implementation of tariff reductions on industrial products agreed by the Tokyo Round. As a result, the average tariff rate is now around 3 per cent, compared with slightly more than 4 per cent in the U.S. and slightly less than 5 per cent in the EC countries (estimated by the GATT). The number of products under import restriction in mining and manufactured sectors in Japan is only five (compared with six for the U.S., 27 for France and one for Germany).

With respect to some Japanese exports of industrial products, we have encountered many instances of trade friction. In order to ease political tensions caused by the sharp increase in export volume and shares of specific products in the market, Japan has often been asked to impose voluntary export restraints (VERs) for several products into American and European markets, or obliged to announce forecasts for its exports to the EC. For example, in May 1981, Japan decided to introduce a voluntary restriction on autombile exports to the U.S. for a period of three years in the hopes that the American automobile industry would make efforts at restructuring. Although such a VER is certainly harmful to the interests of consumers in the partner country, it was introduced as a temporary measure to prevent the importing country from imposing a direct import restriction.

Table 1

EXAMPLE OF VER AND EXPORT FORECAST

Automobiles		Video Tape Recorders	
VER intended to U.S. (thousand units)		Export forecast intended to EC (thousand units)	
1981	1 680	Knock-down Kits	Finished
1982	1 680		
1983	1 680	4 550	
1984	1 850	600	3 950

In 1984, because of the slump in the U.S. steel industry, the steelmakers' and steelworkers' unions (USW) appealed to the U.S. Administration for relief measures. Acting on the President's decision in September 1984, the U.S. has decided to negotiate with countries where exports to the U.S. are sharply increasing, and to conclude an arrangement with them to confine their exports. According to this measure, the import share of steel products in the U.S. (from Brazil, Spain, South Korea and Japan) is expected to drop to about 18.5 per cent -- compared with 25.2 per cent for the period from January to July 1984.

It is instructive to cite the statement by Kindleberger and Lindert, which clearly indicates that a VER is by no means voluntary.

"First in textiles, and later in steel and other products, the U.S. Government found itself wanting a quota or its equivalent in order to ease protectionist lobbying pressures. Yet the U.S. Government wanted to avoid the embarrassment of imposing import quota itself while still professing to be leading the world march toward free trade. It thus intimidated foreign suppliers into allocating a limited quota of exports to the U.S. market among themselves. The result was a quota on U.S. imports -- but the foreign suppliers, who had previously competed among themselves, were forced to collude like a group monopoly and apparently responded by charging their few U.S. buyers the full U.S. price instead of delivering at a competitive world price. The result: the same U.S. losses as with an equivalent tariff plus the failure to keep the price mark-up within the United States." (2)

59

If the government of an importing country resorts to import quotas, the country will receive the goods at a world price and can collect the gains due to the price difference between the higher domestic price and the cheaper world price (3). However, if the quota is enforced by the foreign government or by an organisation of foreign exporters, this gain will be completely lost from the importing country. The exporters in the exporting country, the intermediating business organisation, or the government agency that allocates licences for exports, can instead collect the rent due to the price difference between the export price and the domestic price in the exporting country.

Under the competitive assumption, consumers in an exporting country such as Japan would seem to have no reason to complain of VER procedures. For example, if the amount of automobile export is limited, not only could automobile producers gain from a type of monopoly rent as was just mentioned, but consumers of the exporting country could also benefit from the reduced price of automobiles due to the VER, or at least from the lack of pressure to increase the domestic price of automobiles due to export demand. Selfish consumers in Japan thus would welcome VER arrangements. However, the existence of VERs may facilitate cartel-type activities among Japanese producers and unnecessary interventions of the government. These effects could work against the consumers' interest.

Moreover, the Japanese consumers should be concerned about the possible dangers resulting from protective customs, such as the VER, which may substantially erode the system of international free trade. The system of free trade itself is a kind of international public good. The maintenance of this public good is in the common interest of all consumers in all countries. There is a need for international co-operation between consumers and consumer groups. Thus Japanese consumers would be better off to encourage foreign, particularly U.S., consumers to fight against such non-transparent practices which solicit other countries to put VERs on their imports.

B. Agricultural Sector

Table 2 shows the comparison in food prices between major cities in the world and Tokyo, reported by Tatsuya Kugo (4). These figures must be viewed with caution because they vary considerably depending on the exchange rates used and because the percentage of increase in commodity prices in the subsequent period differs from city to city. However, even with such a caveat, it is clear from this table that foodstuffs in Japan have been costly compared with those of other countries in the world and that this has been most conspicuous in beef. These figures seem to indicate that agricultural and livestock industries are protected at the expense of consumer interest. Of course, Japan is not the only country that protects agricultural production.

The costs of price support are borne by consumers who must buy farm products at prices higher than the international price levels, and are also financed by government expenditure. These two represent incomes transferred to farmers from consumers and from the general public as taxpayers. (The transfer incomes include the amount transferred from farmers as taxpayers to farmers, but the amount is negligible in Japan.) Hayami and Honma (5) measured the ratio of these transfers in the total agricultural income, a measure called the nominal rate of protection.

Table 2

FOOD PRICES IN THE WORLD'S MAJOR CITIES IN 1981

(Unit: Yen)

Commodity	Tokyo	New York	London	Paris	Düsseldorf
Beef (fillet, 1 kg.)	7 000	1 290	3 030	2 820	1 900
Chicken (1 kg.)	1 200	490	2 560	610	540
Milk (1 litre)	220	141	158	117	135
Eggs (1 dozen)	280	202	349	322	404
Flour (1 kg.)	170	96	107	113	240
Lemon (1 kg.)	500	740	558	282	481
Refined Sugar (1 kg.)	268	150	163	141	221

Exchange rates: $1 = Y 224.20   DM 1 = Y 96.14   FF1 = Y 40.25   £1 = Y 464.88

Source: Tatsuya Kugo, "On the Liberalisation of Imports of Agricultural Products", MC News-letter (Mitsubishi Corporation, August, 1981).

Thus, they defined the ratio of producer support (PSR) as:

$$PSR = \frac{(domestic\ price -- international\ price) \times domestic\ production}{domestic\ price \times domestic\ production}$$

The loss to consumers is the amount obtained by multiplying the volume
of consumption (instead of production) by the difference between domestic and
international prices. Accordingly, they defined the ratio of consumer loss
(CLR) as:

$$CLR = \frac{(domestic\ price -- international\ price) \times domestic\ consumption}{domestic\ price \times domestic\ consumption}$$

They included six items of grain (wheat, rye, barley, oats, corn and
rice), five items of livestock (beef, pork, chicken, egg and milk) and sugar
beets and potatoes. They added these items and calculated the (weighted)
average PSR and CLR for various countries.

They made no attempt to calculate loss of efficiency due to trade restriction, i.e., the dead-weight loss. The authors consider that because the price elasticity of supply and demand in farm products is small in most cases, the dead-weight loss is much smaller than the transfers represented in the table. However, the dead-weight loss for rice is quite substantial (6).

From Table 3, in which we cite their results for the U.S., EC countries and Japan, we can see that the rate of protection of the agricultural sector in Japan in terms of the PSR and the CLR has been rapidly increasing. The PSR grew from about 15 per cent in 1955 to 45 per cent by 1980. The more detailed comparison between grains and livestock provided in their paper shows that the rates of protection in both groups increased but that the rate of protection for grains was higher. Incidentally, they report that PSR for livestock in Japan (28.7 per cent) is not higher than in EC countries (29.3 per cent) in 1980.

C. Service sector and public utilities

In service industries and public utilities, there are also cases where consumer interests seem to be sacrificed in order to protect business interests. Nippon Telegraph and Telephone Corporation (NTT) is reportedly planning to introduce a price system in which long-distance telephone rates will be lowered to about one-third of the present rates, while the current charge of ten yen for local calls will be doubled -- an early indication of the efficiency effect of the expected future deregulation (and resulting competitive pressures). Thanks to foreign pressure for internationalisation of standards and liberalisation, service rates that consumers pay will be adjusted to adequately reflect cost and benefit structures.

More problematical are the telephone rates charged by KDD (Kokusai Denshin Denwa Co. -- International Telegraph and Telephone Co.). Before the rates were revised in April 1984, there was a large difference between the tariff charged for a call to the U.S. from Japan and that for a call to Japan from the U.S. during the economy hours. This difference has been considerably narrowed by the KDD's revision in rates and the introduction in April 1984 of special reductions by 10 to 20 per cent for Sunday and night calls. Nevertheless, the percentage of discount on the rates remains lower in Japan.

Another example is air fare. The advanced purchase excursion tickets (APEX) system is not applicable to flight services from Japan to Europe, so that even if the same flight is used, those individual travellers who are qualified for the APEX from London to Tokyo pay about three times less than those travelling from Tokyo to London. The agreement of the IATA (International Air Transport Association) functions as a kind of international cartel agreement among airline companies. And Japanese travellers are hardly in a position to fight such a "cartel", particularly as it is supported by protective government policies.

Banking services provide a third example. When we remit membership fees to academic associations abroad, or subscriptions to international scientific journals, we have to send a small amount of money. If we draw a dollar cheque, say 30 dollars, at a Japanese bank, we are charged 3,000 yen as a service fee. In other words, we must pay the bank a service fee amounting to more than one-third of the actual remittance. The interest of Japanese consumers is harmed by the fact that banks in Japan take advantage of their

Table 3

ESTIMATES OF AVERAGE PSR AND CLR FOR THIRTEEN GOODS (%)

	Production Support Ratio (PSR)						Consumer Loss Ratio (CLR)					
	1955	1960	1965	1970	1975	1980	1955	1960	1965	1970	1975	1980
U.S.	2.3	0.9	7.6	9.8	3.8	△0.1	3.8	3.1	9.5	11.2	9.6	3.4
EC (a)	23.3	24.3	28.1	31.5	20.8	26.0	22.7	25.0	29.0	31.8	20.7	26.8
FRANCE	23.8	18.5	21.9	30.6	21.9	22.8	21.8	18.1	22.4	30.2	23.0	23.9
GERMANY	21.9	28.9	31.9	30.7	26.4	29.6	22.4	28.9	32.0	29.4	25.0	27.8
ITALY	29.5	29.9	34.7	37.1	23.3	32.9	29.2	30.8	34.1	38.0	25.6	33.8
NETHERLANDS	10.7	18.1	23.5	25.7	22.4	20.2	9.1	17.9	24.2	28.1	22.4	23.5
UK	25.9	25.4	15.9	19.9	5.3	24.3	25.3	24.8	15.0	18.3	2.7	23.8
DENMARK	4.3	3.1	4.3	13.6	15.5	19.6	3.4	2.4	5.4	20.0	18.3	23.8
SWEDEN	23.8	28.7	31.7	38.0	29.0	35.6	23.2	28.9	32.3	38.8	30.4	36.4
SWITZERLAND	34.7	35.5	39.4	45.7	46.5	53.1	35.7	37.6	39.7	46.3	45.5	53.3
JAPAN	15.0	29.3	40.3	42.1	42.7	45.5	15.2	28.2	38.7	42.3	39.0	48.3

a. For 1955-1970, the figure given is the weighted average for four countries (France, Germany, Italy, Netherlands); for 1975-1980, the figure is the weighted average for six countries (adding the UK and Denmark).

Source: Hayami and Honma.

63

protection from international competition to work out an agreement on the service fees among themselves. The same argument applies to the brokerage fees that securities companies charge to Japanese traders; such fees are, by international standards, quite high.

Over the years, depositors of small amounts in Japan have had to be content with a low interest rate uniformly established across the country. In the period of Japan's rapid economic growth, people had to settle for an interest rate much lower than the market interest rate. At the expense of these depositors, Japan's industrial circles were able to obtain funds at a low rate, and banks themselves were able to recruit highly educated employees, offer them high salaries and build large office buildings on the main streets. Only recently have people been provided with the means for more profitable investments, thanks to the introduction of new savings instruments, including trust funds nicknamed "big", "wide" or "jumbo". Interest rates on bank deposits are now more flexible.

What then will be the major effect of liberalisation, internationalisation and deregulation? Needless to say, deregulation will make the service industry more competitive, resulting in more efficient use of resources. Individual economic incentives will be promoted positively. Since prices reflect benefit and cost structures, some prices may be raised. For example, the local telephone rates may be doubled. If banks can no longer enjoy the full advantage of deposit rate ceilings, they may discontinue visiting depositors' homes to solicit and collect deposits. However, consumer interest will be increased on the whole. The number of vacant seats on air lines will be reduced, and bank employees will spend less time competing with each other to collect deposits.

III. QUALIFICATIONS TO THE CLASSIC FREE TRADE ARGUMENT

So far we have reviewed the gains from trade to be reaped by consumers from the standpoint of the traditional theory of trade, and argued that Japanese consumer interests are hampered in several forms. Needless to say, the conclusions from the traditional trade theory are often qualified in several ways.

A. Security for food supply

Farming land in Japan is extremely scarce (only 0.046 ha. per capita) compared with that in the U.S. and European countries. Japan's self-sufficiency in calorie production was only 53 per cent in 1982 and has been decreasing, while in Germany and the UK, the figures in 1978 were, respectively, 75 and 60 per cent, and have been increasing. Japan's average net import of farm products was about 17 billion U.S. dollars between 1980 and 1982. Japan is the largest importer of farm products, exceeding Germany. Meanwhile, the world supply-and-demand condition of farm products may tighten in the long run because demand for food imports is expected to grow in developing countries as well as in the Soviet Union. Thus, there is a danger that Japan will suffer from a sharp fluctuation of food prices if it further increases its dependence on food imports. In order to maintain security for food supply, a case can be made for applying a certain brake to the liberalisation of agricultural imports. In particular, the Japanese people should have enough rice fields to at least provide the minimum calories for subsistence in case of emergency.

B. The problem of industrial adjustment

According to the traditional argument on gain from trade, free trade increases the welfare of each country, assuming that resources are smoothly transferred across different industries. However, in practice, neither capital, nor equipment nor workers are easily moved from sector to sector. When the costs of these industrial adjustments are taken into account, it sometimes may be wise to moderate the speed of trade liberalisation.

First, let us begin with the problem of industrial adjustments in agriculture. In its adjustment process, labour productivity increases while the number of persons engaged in agriculture decreases, maintaining a certain level of production and a certain amount of arable land. Any drastic adjustment in agricultural production in local communities would force farmers in rural villages to move and to take an unstable side job, such as temporary daywork. This would extensively affect local communities which depend heavily on agriculture. Thus, at least in the short run, a slower adjustment, which mainly relies on occupational change accompanying generational changes, would reduce the cost of adjustment. On the other hand, no adjustment implies the reproduction of inefficiency. Some compromise must be made in order to choose an appropriate speed, given these short-run and long-run trade-offs.

Next, let us turn to the problem of industrial adjustment in the manufacturing sectors (7). The number of industries that experienced a sharp decline in production since the 1970s comes to 16, including textile, chemical, pulp, metal, machine and so forth. They range widely from raw materials to processing, from capital-intensive to labour-intensive industries. Major determinants of the changes in industrial structure are a) decrease in the domestic demand, and b) reduced competitiveness of Japanese industries in the international market.

In the textile industry, two packages of structural improvement measures were formulated; one covering 1967-74, the other from 1974-79. Under the former, the government outlayed a total amount of about 378 billion yen for the textile industry, including 220 billion yen in loans and 51 billion yen in subsidies. The effect of such spending during the planned period was as follows: a) the number of enterprises did not decrease; on the contrary, in the knitwear industry the number increased by 27.7 per cent; b) the number of plants decreased as a whole except for plants used for automatic dyeing; c) the looms for knit and for cotton staple fibre decreased by 42.2 per cent and 8.4 per cent, respectively, while other equipment increased slightly; and d) the number of employees dropped by 19.1 per cent. Regarding modernisation of facilities, 70 to 80 per cent of the programme was attained in some subsectors (spinning and fabrics). But in others, the degree of success in accomplishing the target for concentration of enterprises varied.

To cope with further changes in the supply-demand situation, new structural improvement measures (1974-1979) were put into effect under the "Law on Extraordinary Measures for the Structural Improvement of the Textile Industry" in 1974. This was designed to increase research and development efforts, to promote vertical integration of enterprises, and to facilitate resource adjustments to other industries. In the adjustment of equipment (disposal of surplus facilities), among 17 industries involved, eight industries attained this programme by more than 90 per cent, and two other industries by more than 80 per cent. Thus, these programmes were rather smoothly implemented. From 1975 to 1979, the number of approvals of vertical integration of enterprises across different industries was only 56 in knowledge-intensive areas, and the number of approvals for joint use of facilities across firms was 19. The number of approvals of vertical integration subsequently dropped year after year.

In principle, measures for industrial adjustment should be formulated as temporary and emergency relief measures carried out to facilitate modernisation and to promote the smooth movement of resources to industries that have better comparative advantage. If these conditions are met, it is more desirable for the government, hence for the taxpayers, to pay subsidies for industrial adjustments than to let protectionist appeals replace the principle of free trade.

C. Safety of products and safeguard against health hazards and dangers to life

In general, free trade would supply the population with a variety of products at lower costs. At the same time, people desire to lead a safe, healthy daily life as consumers. It is thus necessary to make a thorough check on imported goods, as is done on domestic products, to ensure that they satisfy proper safety standards.

To secure the safety of consumers, the Japanese Government has provided various measures. These measures are mainly legal restrictions under such laws as the Food Sanitation Law, Pharmaceutical Affairs Law and Consumer Product Safety Law. As the volume of imports increases, uncertainty about safety can increase. Regardless of whether products are domestic or foreign, the strict application of safety provisions is necessary for consumers. Because Japan is a food importer, it is particularly important to ensure the safety standards of imported food.

For example, the use of food additives synthesised from chemical products is forbidden -- and prohibited from import -- except for those designated by the Minister of Health and Welfare under the Pharmaceutical Affairs Law.

The necessity of additives used in food varies from country to country, depending on the climate and eating habits of each nation. Therefore, the ultimate right to decide on additives should be left to the national governments. The U.S. and European countries often maintain that Japan's restriction on the use of food additives could work as a kind of non-tariff barrier. The government thus decided to undertake a review of specifications and standards on food additives.

Food additives are evaluated by the Food Sanitation Investigation Council. The Council takes fully into account the changing food environment in recent years, and carefully re-examines the adequacy of each individual additive that has already passed international safety evaluation at FAO/WHO. The number of designated food additives (chemical compounds) changed from 333 in 1976 to 347 in 1983.

Let us turn to the case of pharmaceutical products. Usefulness of drugs must be evaluated by taking their side-effects into consideration. In the past the Japanese position of scrutinising the data obtained in foreign countries again generated criticism that this worked as a possible form of non-tariff barrier. In recent years, to secure reliability of data on experiments with animals, many countries have established the standard for experiments (GLP or Good Laboratory Practice). In Japan, GLP standards were established in March 1982. This paved the way for a mutual acceptance of test data between Japan and foreign countries.

In this manner, the administration pursued, with good reason, rather careful and strict rules regarding the safety of both domestic and imported products.

There is often, however, a short-circuit sentiment in Japan, particularly in consumer groups, that "food products in the U.S. and European countries contain a lot of additives", "additives are harmful", hence "liberalisation of trade is dangerous". The safety of products should be assessed on the basis of scientific analysis. One should refrain from opposing liberalisation of imports for the sake of import competitors, using the safety issues as a pretext.

On the other hand, international exchange of information on product safety is indispensable. In addition to GLP for drugs as described above, Japan was the first country to introduce restrictions on chemical substances such as PCB by establishing laws in 1973 concerning the use and test procedure of chemical substances. Following this initiative, various other countries introduced similar restrictive measures. The agreement reached on the principle of mutual acceptance of test data, i.e., the general provisions of GLP, will prove very useful among OECD countries.

The case of asbestos suggests that we might learn a great deal from the American consumers. Also, Japanese consumer groups can be instrumental in disseminating safety information to developing countries, and in preventing the export of products possibly harmful to the environment.

IV. GENERAL ATTITUDES OF JAPANESE CONSUMER GROUPS

In the pre-war period, there were only 64 consumer groups in Japan. After the war, however, the number rapidly increased, reflecting the dramatic pace of Japan's economic expansion and the diversified needs of consumers. The number of consumer groups increased to 748 by 1954, to 2 660 by 1974, and by 1983, the number reached 7 537, with a total membership of more than 36 million. Among them, 29 are central organisations. Their main activities include holding educational seminars for consumers, testing of the quality of merchandise, arranging for co-operative purchase of commodities, and mediating disputes between consumers and producers regarding defective products. When it comes to trade liberalisation issues, however, many of these consumer groups have taken positions that do not appear to coincide with the common interest of consumers in general.

The Japan Consumers' Federation, one of these central organisations, announced in April 1982 its objection to liberalisation of agricultural imports "for the sake of consumers". It went on to say that "even though the domestic prices of agricultural products may be sustained much higher than the international prices as a result of the import restriction, the Federation members would be happy to bear the added financial burden". The National Liaison Committee of Consumer Organisations, Japan Livelihood Co-operation, Regional Women's Association, and the Housewives' Federation were all reported to be in accord with the Consumer Federation's opinion to object to liberalisation of agricultural imports.

At the national convention of All Japan Consumer Groups held in November of 1981 as well as in 1983, the representatives from various organisations decided to protest against the liberalisation of agricultural imports. According to their contention, the liberalisation would lower the self-sufficiency rate of the Japanese foodstuff supply, which was already low, and could ultimately jeopardise the food security of the nation (8).

It is understandable that the producers who will suffer strongly protest against liberalisation, but hardly believable that consumers who stand to gain would also protest. General consumers are buyers of so many commodities that the benefits they receive individually from the liberalised import restriction on each commodity appear small or even negligible. It is hard in any country to assemble the scattered individual interests for each item in order to form groups capable of exerting political pressure. In order for the consumer groups to truly reflect and represent the real interests of individual consumers, Japanese consumer groups, as well as general consumers, must first recognise the economic logic that import liberalisation in general is to the consumer's own benefit.

Import liberalisation of beef and citrus fruit may cause unemployment problems to the related sectors in Japan. And of course, due consideration should always be given to the security of food supply. It is not hard to understand why so many people want the protection of rice production in Japan in order for the nation to be guaranteed the minimum level of calories for subsistence in an emergency. However, it does not seem appropriate to extend this argument for food supply security to many other agricultural products.

Taking all these security and adjustment problems into account, we should seek a suitable combination of policies whereby we could attain food security with minimum costs of support and with minimum friction. Individual consumers, as well as consumer groups, need to exchange frank opinions with the agricultural producer groups on the merits and demerits of the import liberalisation of agricultural products. It may be inevitable for the consumers themselves to bear some of the costs involved, as a kind of insurance premium payment, but the current situation implies substantial overpayment.

The consumer movements in Japan seem to have worked effectively on such ethic issues as protection against unfair trade practices, sales of dishonestly advertised products and defective products. However, on the prices, qualities and varieties of goods, and on underlying economic logic, consumer groups have paid very little attention. An exceptional concern over prices was shown in their protest against the Large-Scale Retail Store Law in 1978. These large stores could offer better prices on goods than the old small-size retailers, benefitting the general consumer. Unfortunately, their protest seems to have attracted little attention and had only little impact.

Do the consumer groups then really reflect the interest of consumers themselves? Addressing this question, Mitsuo Hosen (9) made interesting observations in his "Basic Study on Consumer Groups" published in 1977. He compared the consumer groups' main concerns with the general consumers' opinions expressed in "The Study of the National Life Situation", conducted by the Japan Consumer Information Centre.

Among the concerns expressed by the national consumer groups, the health problem ranked first, followed by safety and then by prices of merchandise. The 29 larger central consumer organisations throughout Japan said that their members' primary concern was safety, then price and quality standards, in that order. In both surveys, safety was considered more important than price issues. Yet, according to the research conducted by the Japan Consumer Information Centre on the general consumer consciousness, the complaint and anxiety over high prices of merchandise was rated as the prime concern of individual consumers. As of 1981, nearly 70 per cent of housewives expressed their dissatisfaction with the high prices of daily necessities (10). The number of housewives who said that "food additives" (or "food pollution") was their primary concern was less than half the number of those who indicated "high prices" as their biggest headache. This has been the general tendency of consumer opinions in this annual survey for the last ten years since 1974 (11).

Furthermore, according to a public opinion poll taken jointly by Sankei Shimbun and Fuji Television Company in May 1982, 52 per cent of the consumers in the samples expressed their support for beef import liberalisation, and only 23 per cent were against it. In an occupational classification of the responses, only the agricultural and fishery groups of the population contained more "objectors" to than "supporters" of import liberalisation, and even in this category of occupations only 42 per cent indicated opinions strictly against relaxation of import controls. In regard to the import of citrus fruit, 50 per cent of the polls expressed approval of importing liberalisation, and only 26 per cent were against it (12).

According to Hosen there are two ways of interpreting these results. One assessment is that the consumer groups' disapproval of the market-opening policy is soundly based on their long-range view of retaining a high degree of foodstuff self-sufficiency. In short, consumers are not well educated and are short-sighted. The other interpretation, which we consider more appropriate, is that consumer groups do not grasp the real preferences expressed by individual consumers. Consumer groups' objections to import liberalisation seem to have stemmed from their lack of knowledge of the economic advantage that the free-trade system can provide to a great number of consumers, and of the economic mechanism that generates benefits to individual consumers.

One can conceive of several reasons why consumer movements do not correctly reflect consumer interests in Japan. First, a great majority of the consumers actually engage in, or are housewives who engage in, some form of manufacturing or retail business. The number of "pure" consumers, such as teachers or civil servants, is relatively small. Secondly, many individual consumers living in big cities have their own "roots" in farming villages. Twice a year, i.e., at midsummer (Bon) and year-end, there is an exodus of city residents to their native provinces in order to conduct the folk ritual of worshipping their ancestors and celebrating the new year. This characteristic of the Japanese consumer underlies the Japan Consumer Federation's philosophy as regards the market liberalisation issue. It is also understandable that groups like consumer co-operatives, whose chief role is to intermediate the flow of goods between producers and consumers more directly, cannot express the interest of consumers exclusively. Generally speaking, Japanese consumers are more sympathetic with small-size enterprises than with big ones, and with farmers or workers as opposed to employers. This tendency may have contributed somewhat to the mysterious attitudes of many consumer groups in Japan.

Meanwhile, Japan's resistance to market liberalisation might in fact hinder its own export activities in such forms as tariffs, quotas on the part of foreign countries or imposed VERs on the part of Japan. Moreover, if consumers are forced to buy higher-priced domestic goods because of trade restrictions, this will push up wage levels and ultimately the production cost of Japanese exports. In other words, some of the burdens that consumers bear as a consequence of the closed-market policy are shifted to Japan's industrial sectors. Thus, in this issue of agricultural import liberalisation, industrial group interests are in accord with the consumer interests. A possible way out would be for the industrial circles to put strong pressure on the government to lighten the burden of consumers.

There is, however, no guarantee that the same would hold true in other trade issues. If, in the future, imports of industrial products from newly industrial countries (NICs) to Japan show a drastic increase, Japan's industrial circles may wish to restrict them. If they do so, the consumer interests to seek goods of quality at low prices would be impeded by the industrial circles. The consumer groups, therefore, should clearly announce their own interests at that time.

The seemingly closed Japanese market is not merely a creation of the Japanese society. The lack of enthusiasm on the part of foreign businesses to adapt to local business practices, to learn our language, to obtain information on the nature of the Japanese retail market and so forth is partly responsible for their slow penetration into Japanese markets.

V.   THE ROLE OF GOVERNMENT POLICY IN JAPAN

Japan's consumer protection measures have progressed steadily over the last twenty years, and especially after the enactment of the Consumer Protection Fundamental Law in 1968, under which some seventy national legislative acts and many regional regulations have been implemented. About 260 local consumer centres have been established in different locations throughout the country.

These policies have emphasized and successfully protected the rights of consumers regarding product safety, hygienic conditions and truthful description of merchandise. However, the continuing changes and progress of socioeconomic conditions have created new forms of consumer problems (13). Among them, one important issue is the topic of this paper, namely how to protect consumer interests in relation to foreign trade, in the face of the "internationalisation" of our markets.

Japan -- and its consumers -- benefit tremendously from the principle of free trade. In order to pursue this basic policy still further, the Japanese Government has recently implemented various measures to liberalise our markets. With respect to the standards and certification systems for imported merchandise, the government enacted in May 1983 a partial amendment of all the related regulations not to allow any discrimination between nationals and non-nationals in the certification procedure of imports (14). In addition, the administration is improving testing procedures to ensure transparency in the process and to make them conform to international standards by accepting foreign test data. Furthermore, there is close surveillance over the domestic distribution systems from the viewpoint of antitrust laws, in order to facilitate smooth inflows of foreign products.

Each country should make the final decision on its safety standards since the climate, customs and living styles differ from country to country. For example, the incidence of SMON disease allegedly due to the use of chinoform was much greater in Japan than in other countries (perhaps stemming from the fact that the Japanese have a tendency to overuse medicine). However, unnecessary differences in product standards and inspecting systems could be eliminated; traders could thus save extra costs by applying special modifications to their products in order to conform with the standards of the country of destination. Consumer policies should take this kind of problem into account and try to prevent unnecessary friction in international trade. Also, an international exchange of information among governments on the safety standards of the various countries is necessary in order to secure the safety and health of consumers world-wide. For this reason, we call for international co-operation among consumer groups.

Accordingly, the Japanese Government is making an effort to harmonize domestic safety standards with the international standards system. An example of this move was seen already in the application of the principle of Good Laboratory Practice (GLP) for the Safety Test on Pharmaceutical Products (15).

In an effort to promote trade and particularly to make the Japanese market more transparent, the Japanese Government has established a special agency called the Office of Trade and Investments Ombudsman (OTO) in 1982. This office accepts and settles complaints sent to the Japanese authorities with regard to trade issues. The OTO was opened in response to foreign criticism and complaints that the Japanese import testing system is too closed and complicated. Another positive motive for the Japanese Government to establish the OTO was to put a stop to the international rise of protectionism by making our markets more open. Certainly the establishment of the OTO is welcomed by Japanese consumers.

The number of trade-related complaints and proposals received by the OTO since February 1982 is shown in Table 4. As a result of the OTO's effective countermeasures and systematic responses, the number has been declining yearly. The largest number of complaints has come from the U.S. and European countries (see Table 5) (16). Out of a total of 162 complaints received, 157 cases, which are broken down in Table 6, were settled by October 1984. In 38 cases, no change in the situation has been registered (17).

A general review of the nature of the complaints has shown that nearly two-thirds, or 23 cases, were related to human lives and safety. Concrete cases show that most of the proposals that were turned down were closely related to the health and safety of consumers.

In addition to protecting the consumer through the enforcement of legislative controls, the government should make every effort to educate the consumer public at all levels. This will help consumers choose goods (including imported goods) and services independently and with discretion. From this standpoint, both national and local governments are conducting various consumer education programmes.

In school, at the primary and high school level, the subject of consumer protection is taught as a course of study. Also, as a part of the consumer education programme initiated by the government, the Economic Planning Agency and other ministries are actively providing consumers with pertinent information. Furthermore, the government-supported Japan Consumer Information Centre sponsors educational seminars to train consumer leaders and use news media to promote consumer education. The local governments are engaged in educational activity for consumers in general through the local consumer centres. The Japan Consumer Information Centre in Tokyo is now starting to establish an on-line consumer information network throughout Japan, connecting its central computer with the regional consumer centre terminals.

Table 4

NUMBER OF COMPLAINTS RECEIVED

February 1982 -- December 1982	88
January 1983 -- December 1983	50
January 1984 -- March 1984	5
April 1984	3
May 1984	3
June 1984	6
July 1984	1
August 1984	3
September 1984	3
1st-29th October 1984	0
Total	162

Out of 162 complaints, one was refiled (in January 1984).

Table 5

ORIGIN OF COMPLAINTS/PRODUCTS

Origin of Complaints		Origin of Products Involved	
Japan	55	U.S.	67
Overseas	107	EC	47
(U.S.)	(50)	(Germany)	(28)
(EC)	(31)	(UK)	(7)
		Others	31
Total	162	Unspecified	17
		Total	162

Table 6

HOW COMPLAINTS WERE SETTLED

Classification of Processing	Total
Improvements made	42
Misunderstandings cleared	77
(Import promoted)	(50)
(Other)	(27)
Situation unchanged	38
Total	157

Still, the existing educational programmes leave much room for improvement. In particular, the current consumer education conducted in the school curriculum is not quite sufficient for future adults to avoid difficulties concerning defective products, misleading merchandising and sometimes loan sharks, because the consumer public lacks sufficient information.

The subject of international trade issues vis-à-vis consumer interests is dealt with as part of the "Economics" course taught in school. Economics in high schools stresses history, institutions and the explanation of technical terms, but provides little information on the role of the price system in a market economy. In school education, pupils should be taught how to protect themselves from unsafe products and unsound trade practices, how they can take advantage of price mechanisms, and in particular how protective trade practices are harming them. One of the reasons why the Japanese consumer groups do not encourage import liberalisation may lie in their lack of understanding of the basic function of supply and demand.

Concluding remarks

Referring to the Japanese experience, we have discussed in this paper the question of how consumer interests should be promoted in conjunction with the expansion of international trade, or conversely, how consumer interests would be hindered by trade protectionism. We have also examined the attitude of Japanese consumer groups and the basic approach of the Japanese Government concerning this problem.

Japan's consumer groups and government agencies have hitherto conducted their consumer policies by emphasizing the need to retain the safety and health standards of the population as well as the protection of the environment. In their approach to international trade issues, however, they tend to give priority to the issues of safety and security of consumers rather than to the issues of quantity, variety and price of products. The safety and security of a nation must of course be the prime concern and responsibility of any government. It is also an important goal for any consumer group. But, at the same time, we have to watch against the practice of using security problems and health standards as mere excuses to protect import-competing industries. Every effort must be made to prevent the rise of protectionism. In particular, Japan's consumers have ignored the fact that the price mechanism, and accordingly free trade, can be utilised to enhance the welfare of consumers.

What is needed now is for Japanese consumers and their unions to realise their own economic interests without sacrificing other important objectives, such as food security and smooth sectorial adjustments. We hope that this Symposium will contribute greatly to the understanding of economic logic involved in the issues of trade and consumer interests.

NOTES AND REFERENCES

1. The opinions expressed are those of the authors and by no means reflect the views of the Japanese Government. We are grateful to Mr. Hideo Tsuzuki for his helpful assistance in preparing this paper and Mr. Toshiaki Takigawa for his useful comments.

2. Kindleberger, C.P. and Lindert, P.H. (1953) International Economics, Chapter 8, p. 152.

3. The reader may recall the related and well-known argument on the equivalence of tariffs and quotas. In competitive situations, the gain equals the tariff revenues that would be obtained by imposing a tariff to reduce the import by the same amount. Cf. e.g. Bhagwati, J.N. and Srinivasan, T.N. (1983) Lectures on International Trade, Chapter 10.

4. Kugo, Tatsuya (1982) "On the Liberalisation of Imports of Agricultural Product", The Quarterly Study of MITI Policies, Ministry of International Trade and Industry, No. 2 (April).

5. Hayami, Yujiro and Honma, Masayoshi (1983) "The Level of Protection of the Japanese Agriculture from International Comparison", Policy Concept Forum Research Report Series, No. 1.

6. For the importance of the dead-weight loss resulting from rice policy, see Otsuka, Keijiro and Hayami, Yujiro (1984) "Rice Policy in Japan:

Its Costs and Distributional Consequences", <u>Pacific Economic Papers</u>, Australia-Japan Research Centre, Australian National University, Canberra, No. 114 (August).

7.   See Sekiguchi, Sueo (1981) <u>Industrial Adjustment in Japan</u> (June).

8.   Some consumer groups in the western area of Japan, however, realising the economic benefits from imports, expressed their support for the import liberalisation policy. They believe that the free-trade system would provide consumers with more freedom to choose merchandise they like.

9.   Hosen, Mitsuo (1982) "Consumer Groups Against Agricultural Import Liberalisation", <u>Economy Society Policy</u>, E.P.A. (December).

10. Even in the 1983 survey, the ranking of the safety issue remained unchanged. However, in this survey, the price issue was ranked seventh in groups nation-wide and fourth in the larger central groups.

11. In the 1983 survey also, the dissatisfaction and anxiety over the high prices were rated highest and preoccupied 60 per cent of the general consumers.

12. Two of the recent NHK (Japan Broadcasting Corporation) surveys indicated that more than three-fourths of the respondents were for import liberalisation of beef and citrus fruit, but that only one-fourth of them are for the import liberalisation of rice.

13. There has been a mild shift of emphasis from these safety and quality standards to the proper servicing and sales methods of merchandising. The rapid increase in the use of electronic computers is creating new problems.

14. A total of 17 laws, including the Pharmaceutical Affairs Law and Consumer Products Safety Law have been amended to facilitate certification procedures. The purpose is i) to enable foreign suppliers to apply for and obtain certification directly, and ii) to accord foreign products and suppliers treatment substantially equal to that accorded to domestic products and suppliers, with respect to testing method.

15. Refer to Section III (2).

16. Government ministries and agencies concerned with these complaints were, in order of the numbers, the Ministry of Health and Welfare, the main authorities that handle safety standards of commodities imported (62 out of a total of 162), the Ministry of Finance (38), the Ministry of International Trade and Industry (31), and the Ministry of Agriculture, Forestry and Fisheries (15).

17. Among them, twelve complaints are related to the Ministry of Health and Welfare, nine to the Ministry of Finance, seven to the Ministry of Agriculture, Forestry and Fisheries, and five to the Ministry of International Trade and Industry.

BIBLIOGRAPHY

Bhagwati, J.N. and Srinivasan, T.N. (1983) Lectures on International Trade.

Computer Age Corporation (1984) Textile Industry in '70 (July).

Consumer Union of Japan (1982) Consumer Report (July).

Hayami, Y. and Honma, M. (1983) "The Level of Protection of the Japanese
    Agriculture from International Comparison", Policy Innovation Forum
    Research Report Series, No. 1.

Hosen, M. (1982) "Consumer Groups Against Farm Product Import Liberalisation",
    ESP (December).

Japan Consumer Information Centre (1984) The Consumer Review, Vol. 305 (July).

Japan Economic Research Institute (1984) Propositions for International
    Orderly Economics.

Japan Economic Research Institute (1984) Research for Openness of Market in
    Japan (August).

Kindleberger, C.P. and Lindert, P.H. (1953) International Economics.

Kugo, T. (1982) "On the Liberalisation of Imports of Agricultural Product",
    The Quarterly Study of MITI Policies, No. 2 (April).

Kurihara, M. and Ueda, Y. (1984) Hybrid Rice: A Threat of Mystery Rice to
    Japan, NHK Press.

Ministry of International Trade and Industry, Census of Industry (1967, 1972,
    1974, 1979, 1982).

Ministry of International Trade and Industry, Textiles Statistics Annually
    (1967, 1972, 1974, 1979, 1982).

Ministry of International Trade and Industry, White Paper on International
    Trade (1982, 1983, 1984).

Namiki, N. (1978) Textile Industry in Japan (May).

Nihon Keizai Shinbun (1983) Contemporary Economics (Spring).

Nihon Seni Shinbun (1980) Textile Yearbook.

Ogawa, S. and Yamaguchi, M. (1984) "International Comparison of Protection of
    Agriculture", Study of Agricultural Structure, No. 139 (Spring).

Otuka, K. and Hayami, Y. (1984) "Rice Policy in Japan: Its Costs and Distri-
    butional Consequences", Pacific Economic Papers, Australia-Japan
    Research Centre, Australian National University, Canberra, No. 114
    (August).

Sekiguchi, S. (1981) Industrial Adjustment in Japan (June).

THE CONSUMER INTEREST IN TRADE POLICY AND PROTECTIONISM

by

Lars O. Broch
Director, International Organisation of Consumers Unions (IOCU),
The Hague, Netherlands

I. IOCU POSITION AND OUTLINE

During the past decade, the earlier post-war trend towards more open international trade, which accompanied the most vigorous expansion of the global economy ever known, has been put into reverse.

A few key statistics underline the link between trade and growth: in 1913-48 world production rose by 2 per cent, world trade by 0.5 per cent a year; between 1948 and 1973, production rose by 5 per cent and trade by 7 per cent a year. There is widespread agreement that the stampede to protectionism in the 1930s, particularly in the United States, was one of the main factors in prolonging the depression.

Protectionist measures force other nations to import less due to reduced exports followed by a lack of foreign currency. This is particularly so for debt-ridden developing countries. A recent report by Jeffrey J. Schott to the Council on U.S. International Trade Policy notes that 30 to 40 per cent of the exports of non-oil-producing developing countries have been subjected to import restraints. U.S. exports to the two largest debtor countries, Brazil and Mexico, have fallen by almost 50 per cent since 1981, representing 30 per cent of the total decline in U.S. exports during this period. Both countries were forced to restrict imports severely because of a lack of foreign exchange, and the lost exports to Brazil and Mexico alone have cost the United States an estimated 250 000 jobs.

Retaliations between countries and trading blocks have been reported in the press on many occasions, showing the risks of protectionist ripple effects within the international trading systems.

During this decade of re-emerging protectionism, the International Organisation of Consumers Unions, speaking for consumers around the world, has been clear and consistent in its view that free trade between nations best furthers the interest of consumers.

At its seventh World Congress in 1972 in Stockholm, the following resolution was adopted:

"IOCU should work toward the removal of international trade restrictions and of discriminatory practices of all kinds with the twin aims of providing more choice for consumers in developed countries and wider opportunities for people in developing countries to enjoy the basic human right to earn a living".

Three years later in Sydney the Congress resolved:

"That this General Assembly ask the Council of IOCU to urge on Governments the most urgent action to freer world trade in order that economic efficiency may be increased, employment in developing countries may be assisted, inflation may be mitigated and hopefully reduced and consumers everywhere may benefit".

In London in 1978, this resolution was adopted:

"That this General Assembly of IOCU expresses concern at the resurgence of protectionism in world trade caused by the current economic recession; recognises the extent to which further import controls would threaten the already depressed living standards of developing countries, while restricting choice and raising prices in industrialised countries; and calls on governments to combat recession, reduce unemployment and protect the consumer interest by pursuing through the GATT and in other ways an orderly growth of world trade, coupled with policies of domestic expanison".

II. WHY PROTECTIONISM HURTS NATIONAL ECONOMIES AND CONSUMERS

After the war, with memories of the "beggar-my-neighbour" protectionism of the 1930s still strong, governments set up the General Agreement on Tariffs and Trade (GATT) to establish an international framework of rules of trade. These rules specify that trade barriers should be transparent (easily identifiable) and non-discriminatory between countries. And under successive negotiation rounds, tariffs on industrial goods have been cut from an average of 30 to 60 per cent to around 4 to 8 per cent today.

But since 1974 import barriers have increasingly taken the form of quotas, "voluntary" export restraints, "orderly marketing arrangements", administrative delays, restrictive safety or health standards, discriminatory government procurement policies, and export subsidies, not to mention the side-effects of regional aid and industrial investment grants. The GATT has a list some 2 000 pages long of notified non-tariff barriers to trade which go to make up the "new protectionism".

Between 1974 and 1980 the proportion of world trade covered by non-tariff barriers rose by a fifth from 40 to 48 per cent. Virtually all of the increase reflected greater constraints on manufactured trade, and this in turn was alsmost entirely due to new barriers erected by the industrial countries, mostly directed at the exports of the developing world. Since 1980 and the onset of world recession, the new protectionism has spread further, notably in the motor industry and steel.

III. WHY PROTECTIONISM IS HARMFUL BETWEEN NATIONS

Protectionism is harmful for three main reasons. First, it hinders the transmission of economic growth around the world and mutes its strength by dampening positive feedback through trade.

There are particular dangers in the trend towards higher barriers to Third World imports into industrial countries. Less-developed countries (LDCs), which now account for more than 30 per cent of world trade, are as potent an influence on the global economy as the United States, taking a quarter of all OECD exports. If industrial countries refuse to buy their goods, LDCs will have less cash to pay for Western imports and to service the debts owed largely to Western banks. Their economies will suffer. Growth in the industrial world will be held back because export markets are depressed. And if LDCs cannot service their debts, the global financial system is weakened. Its ability to finance growth and investment the world over is impaired.

Secondly, free trade permits countries to specialise in what they are good at -- where they have a "comparative advantage". They can then export these products and services while importing other products and services more cheaply than they could produce them at home. If trade is restricted those signals are blurred. The protected industry has less need to adjust. Resources are kept in the industry when they could be better employed elsewhere. The restrictions encourage the industry to stick with the old uncompetitive products and methods rather than explore new ones which would enable it to compete as and when trade barriers come down.

Import controls may also raise the cost of inputs to other industries (for instance, restricted steel imports may increase the price paid for steel by the car industry) and make them less competitive abroad; they penalise output and jobs in export industries and services such as tourism by maintaining a high exchange rate (because in the short run the trade balance is improved); and they encourage investment in wasteful import substitutes.

The result is likely to be slower economic growth, higher prices, less employment and a less productive and thus lower-paid labour force.

Thirdly, the growth of the new protectionism, largely outside the existing framework of international rules on trade, has produced growing uncertainty in international economic relations. It creates endemic friction between governments, of which the U.S./EC battles over steel and agriculture are symptomatic. Stronger nations are able to bully weaker ones into accepting export restraints for fear of something worse. Industry cannot rely on the international community to uphold the rules and becomes more cautious over trade and investment.

Impact on consumers

Turning to the effects within a domestic market-place, protectionism alters the distribution of income away from consumers towards producers: consumers pay more for less. Lack of competition from abroad relaxes the pressures on domestic companies to lower costs, minimise price increases, improve products or respond to changes in consumer tastes. The results are less choice and higher prices.

The consumer costs of protection are more widely spread and less easy to identify than the highly tangible impact on output and jobs in vulnerable industries of import competition. But what estimates there are suggest the sums involved are extremely large. Many examples are given both in the OECD background paper (1) and in other papers prepared for this Symposium. The attempts which have been made at quantifying the effects of protectionist measures are revealing.

Sometimes -- despite the costs -- the measures do not even achieve what they set out to do; the home industry has in fact not been protected (2). And when the protectionist measures have worked, the costs per job saved have been quite disproportionate.

Recent studies have specifically concentrated upon the non-tariff barriers, especially the "voluntary" export restraints (VERs). All restraints on imports -- whether tariff or non-tariff barriers -- will lead to higher-priced imports, meaning a loss in consumer welfare (partly because they must pay more for the same goods, partly because some are not able to afford the product). But the redistribution of the consumer's money is fundamentally different with tariffs and VERs.

With tariffs being imposed, the added price will be government revenue, and it is not even certain that the consumer will be charged the whole amount. Studies have shown that manufacturers may well pay part of the tariff instead of passing it on to the consumer for fear of otherwise selling less (3). On the other hand, the imposition of VERs will produce a "scarcity premium" or "scarcity rent" -- there are fewer goods available than would be sold at the going price. The reaction of the manufacturer or seller is to increase price rather than have a queue of potential customers and no goods to offer. This price increase represents a free gift not necessitated by any economic change, and may be pocketed by the manufacturer, importer or seller. A recent study (4) on Japanese cars within the U.S. market found that the welfare loss caused by the "scarcity rent" far outweighed the sum of the other forms of welfare losses associated with the VERs (loss due to foregone consumption and welfare loss due to price increase of domestic cars).

The reason for the popularity of VERs or generally Orderly Marketing Agreements (OMAs) in recent years has been summarised as follows:

"Despite the fact that QRs (Quantitative Restrictions) impose the additional costs on the domestic economy of expropriated profits by exporters and the potential for creating domestic monopoly power, they have become increasingly popular in the 1970s. Ironically it is precisely the feature of OMAs that makes them more costly to the domestic economy and makes them politically attractive. In general, the exporting nation can be expected to be a major political obstacle in a protectionist effort. In offering an OMA, however, the exporting nation may be 'bought off' by the possibility of expropriating the scarcity rents; this considerably reduces the possibility of retaliatory trade actions" (5).

Recalling that VERs and other non-tariff barriers to trade have become increasingly popular over the years, it is IOCU's view that the development has been the worst possible: non-tariff barriers decrease international trade and thus competition; they create higher prices on both imports and domestic production, with the bulk of the welfare loss being payment of an unjust scarcity premium. Non-tariff barriers are not transparent; sometimes they are not even known. Whereas tariffs -- being seen as equivalent to taxes -- often are dependent upon parliamentary reports or even decisions, the VERs are often withdrawn from any public or democratic procedure.

The way to turn the present trend around is to insist upon democratic -- open -- treatment of all measures affecting imports and to call for making the effect of these measures transparent, to ensure participation by all economic sectors -- including consumers -- and to focus public attention (through the measures mentioned, case studies, etc.) on how protectionist measures affect every one of us as ordinary consumers.

The other side of the protectionist coin: export subsidies

Protectionist measures try to protect a domestic production which is not competitive in the world market. In some cases the production in question cannot totally be consumed domestically. It is not saleable on the world market at its production price. The answer is often to subsidise exports and ban or restrict imports. A prominent example of this is the Common Agricultural Policy (CAP) of the EEC. Of the £9.7 billion that CAP cost in 1983, more than one-third was used for export subsidies. In 1984 sugar was sold to Eastern Europe at 7 pence per pound, pork at 45 p. per pound, butter at 53 p. per pound and wine at 7 p. per litre (6).

Export subsidies related to specific products should be viewed as one form of protectionism, because the granting of such subsidies is a solid indication of domestic production not being able to compete internationally. Furthermore, if subsidised below normal world market prices (price dumping), export subsidies distort free trade and will easily -- and understandably -- result in a call for protectionist measures by those states which are the object of dumping.

When is protection justified?

Some cases have generally been considered as "appropriate" for protectionist intervention:

- -- Infant industries, including the high-technology sector, that cannot be expected to bear international competition before having become mature;

- -- Old industries, which should be given "breathing space" to restructure;

- -- Preservation of jobs (but as examples show, this may be an extremely costly way of doing it);

- -- Security of supply;

- -- Retaliation against dumping or other misuse of the market.

Arguments for protection are less convincing in practice than in theory. "Infant industries" grow into adulthood still cosseted by controls. "Senile" industries, for which trade restrictions are supposed to provide a breathing space for restructuring, remain propped up indefinitely. "Unfair" or "disruptive" imports may often simply be "cheaper" or "better".

If declining industries are shedding jobs more quickly than can be provided elsewhere, the sources of the problem -- deficient demand, skill mismatch, regional imbalances -- should be addressed, rather than giving the industries protection from the need for change.

Similarly, the desire to avoid undue dependence on foreign suppliers for essential commodities rarely justifies controls on imports. If necessary, direct subsidies to farmers are a more efficient way of encouraging domestic production which bring the costs of maintaining security of supply out into the open.

There can be exceptional cases where protectionist measures may be justified. The Consumers in the European Community (UK) Group have in a report (7) suggested five points which must be met:

"Firstly, criteria to establish when protectionism is absolutely unavoidable should be publicly discussed and decided by Parliament, not by ad hoc arrangements, intimidation of exporting countries, tortuous procedural restrictions and secret agreements by manufacturers' price-fixing cartels.
Secondly, it must be proved that it will positively help the industry.
Thirdly, it should be clearly stated that the proposed protection will be temporary, and time limits set.
Fourthly, it must be shown that the measures will actually protect domestic employment overall in the long term.
Fifthly, the measure should be monitored and the findings published".

IV. PRODUCT SAFETY IN INTERNATIONAL TRADE

Whereas IOCU firmly believes that consumers are best served by the free flow of products over national borders, one aspect of such a free international trade needs to be addressed: how to protect consumers from unsafe products being freely traded internationally.

During the last decade, many OECD countries have introduced or strengthened their legislation relating to general product safety. The purpose of this legislation is to secure that consumers are protected against unreasonably dangerous products, whether domestically produced or imported. But very few of those laws even provide for the possibility of regulating products made for export, and none of them envisage the application of identical safety standards to goods intended for export.

This lack of legal control over exports leads to a series of situations harmful to consumers:

1. Production may wilfully be set up for adherence to a dual standard -- one safety standard for domestic use, and a lower one for some or all exports, partly depending on the legislation in force in the importing country, partly on how that legislation is enforced. Thus, a consumer in Portugal may buy a Norwegian chain-saw, knowing that there are strict safety regulations in Norway for chain-saws but unaware that the chain-saw he buys does not comply with those

regulations, and would be deemed too unsafe to be used within Norway. A pesticide produced in the U.S. does not have to comply with domestic safety standards and does not have to be approved by the authorities if it is made for export;

2. Production standards may be identical but the information given to consumers about the product is systematically geared to meet different domestic safety legislation. It is well known from pharmaceuticals that producers may give wildly varying indications for use and warnings on identical products intended for different national markets. The result is wide misuse of these drugs. Another example is sweetened condensed milk which has been labelled as suitable for infant feeding in some Third World countries while being recognised in industrialised countries as particularly unsuitable for this purpose;

3. A product does not comply with domestic safety standards through an unintentional fault in the production. Though produced for the home market, it is now illegal to sell it domestically. To avoid loss, the producer "dumps" it in another country with no or lower safety standards covering such products. This was the case of the export from the U.S. to Europe in the 1970s of children's pyjamas treated with the cancer-causing fire retardant TRIS, a case that politically brought the dumping issue to the foreground. It has since been repeated on countless occasions, though rarely between developed nations -- much more often from developed to developing countries with larger differences between their product safety legislation and administration;

4. A product is recalled on the domestic market because of a hitherto unknown hazard. It is left on the market in countries where the risk of discovery or the level of product liability is less threatening;

5. A product is imported into a country which refuses its entry on safety grounds. As the country will rarely destroy the product physically, it can thereafter be dumped onto another -- unsuspecting -- country to prevent loss for the producer.

It has been said that imposing one country's safety standards on other countries would be paternalistic and that it is unconditionally a matter for each state to decide upon the level of safety for its citizens. IOCU holds this opinion to be an over-simplification for the following three reasons. First, there are vast differences between countries in available resources for product-safety work and indeed in technical development. Generally, what is dangerous in one country is dangerous in another, but knowledge about what is dangerous will certainly vary. When TRIS was banned in the U.S. but not in Belgium, this did not reflect a difference in opinion over known risks, but a difference in knowledge. Secondly, discovering a faulty product is in itself difficult. After having discovered a faulty stock, it is irresponsible to let it go -- anonymously and unmarked -- to another country, counting on that country's officials to spot it again. Thirdly, consumers often have expectations when buying goods from a specific country. It would indeed surprise most consumers if it were common that Japanese cars, Swiss watches, German beer and U.S. pharmaceutical products -- all of which have earned a reputation for being manufactured with high quality -- were being systematically produced at lower quality for export. It would seem to us that of the different quality aspects, the one decidedly not to vary would be that which determines the level of physical safety, and even more so if it is a mandatory requirement in the country of production.

The OECD has on several occasions proved that product safety is a matter for international action and concern. In 1979 the OECD Council, in Recommendation C(79)202 concerning the safety of consumer products, stated [Operative para. 5(a)]:

"Governments of Member countries should strive to ensure, by means in conformity with their national procedures, that those goods that are banned or withdrawn from sale within their territories because they are inherently so hazardous that they present a severe and direct danger to life, health or safety of any consumer of those goods, are not exported to other countries".

Two years later, in Resolution C(81)7, the Council, in operative para. (ix), recommended:

"Where internationally-traded products are involved in recall procedures, Member countries should, in accordance with paragraphs 4 and 5 of the OECD Council Recommendation C(79)202 (Final) of 18th December 1979, notify other Member countries in the framework of the informal notification procedure and, if available and justified by the product hazard, use their powers to prevent further exports of the products involved".

For several years the Consumer Policy Committee has operated an informal information exchange programme on dangerous products in international trade. Recently, in the field of chemicals, the OECD has instituted a formal information exchange system related to export of banned or severely restricted chemicals [Recommendation C(84)37].

IOCU believes the principles embodied in these various resolutions to be just and sound. We do, however, believe that they now should be expanded to more directly reflect their purpose: that, generally, consumers around the world have the same protection from physical dangers, and that, where there are exceptions, decisions be made by the importing country with full knowledge of the facts.

We therefore hold that national authorities normally should apply mandatory safety standards to all production, and to exports. This view has recently been supported to a very large degree by the United Nations, where the General Assembly in December 1982 passed a resolution on protection against products harmful to health and the environment (Res. 37 137). The first operative paragraph of that resolution reads:

"Agrees that products that have been banned from domestic consumption and/or sale because they have been judged to endanger health and the environment should be sold abroad by companies, corporations or individuals only when a request for such products is received from an importing country or when the consumption of such products is officially permitted in the importing country".

It is IOCU's view that sub-safety-standard exports should be prohibited by the authorities in the country of manufacture unless the importing authority either expressly specifies the goods in question or has taken an express general decision with regard to the specific safety standard in question. However, even in such cases, IOCU holds that if the country of manufacture is made known to consumers, the product should be labelled not in conformity with the safety regulations of that country. To market a product "Made in Utopia" despite the fact that it would be illegal to sell it there is indeed misleading.

V. CONCLUSIONS AND RECOMMENDATIONS

The drift towards greater protection threatens to weaken world economic recovery, impair national growth prospects, put the international financial system at risk, and increase political and economic tensions between nations. Despite resumed growth in the industrial countries, the protectionist ratchet is still on its upward climb.

The result of protectionist measures for consumers is that they receive less and pay more. Competition is reduced and the pressures to lower costs, improve products and respond to changes in consumer choice are relaxed. The forces of the market-place, which are the ground rules for securing maximum economic benefit, are distorted. Because the costs to consumers are widely spread, the magnitude of the loss is all too often ignored. And since consumers generally are unrepresented when questions of international trade are decided, it is all too easy to overlook the impact on them of measures taken.

Especially disturbing has been the growth in non-tariff barriers. They are often non-transparent, they imply a much greater loss of welfare than tariffs, and they often result in unfair shifts in the distribution of income.

Government action to reverse these trends is urgently needed.

IOCU would make the following recommendations:

1. World leaders should impose a moratorium on new protectionist measures and announce a phased programme for the dismantlement of existing barriers, especially those imposed during the recent recession;

2. The GATT should be given power to monitor and supervise trade controls, which should be non-discriminatory and subject to time limits. Non-tariff barriers should be brought within the ambit of GATT rules and progressively removed. Protection should normally take the form of subsidies or tariffs, which are transparent and allow changes in competitiveness to guide investment and trade;

3. The OECD, in collaboration with the GATT, should make available funds for studies on the impact of different trade measures on consumers and issue a yearly "state of world trade" report, to include an assessment of the impact of international trade practices on consumers;

4. Each country should have a body to analyse and publish the costs and benefits of proposed trade controls. Consumers should be represented on that body;

5. Each country should establish criteria for when protectionism is absolutely unavoidable. Such criteria should be publicly discussed and decided upon by the national parliamentary body;

6. Before passing any protectionist measures it should be proved that the measure will positively help the industry and that the measures will actually protect domestic employment overall in the long term;

7. Any protectionist measures should clearly state that they will be temporary, and time limits set. The measures should be monitored and the findings published;

8. Governments should recognise the link between their wish to export and their obligation to see that goods produced in their countries are suitable for export. To this end:

-- The OECD and the Member countries should give legal and technical assistance to developing countries for furthering their work in setting up a legal/administrative machinery on product safety;

-- Governments should normally apply mandatory safety requirements to all production, including exports. Exceptions should only be considered when the importing country specifically has requested a certain product or where such product specifically is permitted in that country;

-- Where the country of origin is marked on a product or otherwise used in its marketing, and the product is not in conformity with that country's mandatory safety requirements, a statement to this effect should be made with the same prominence as the statement of country of origin.

NOTES AND REFERENCES

1. "Consumer Policy and International Trade", Report by the Committee on Consumer Policy, Paris, 1984.

2. See as one example the discussion of the Multifibre Arrangement in the OECD background paper, as well as "The Effect of Trade Restrictions in Selected Sectors -- Consumer Interest in Textile and Clothing Policy" by Teresa Smallbone, also in this publication.

3. See "Report on Car Prices and on the Private Import of Cars in the EEC Countries", Bureau Européen des Unions de Consommateurs (BEUC), Brussels, 1981.

4. "The Welfare Loss of the Voluntary Export Restraint for Japanese Automobiles", Journal of Consumer Affairs, Vol. 18, no. 1 (1984), pages 47 to 63.

5. Ibid, p. 49.

6. "Enough Is Enough", Report on CAP by Consumers in the European Community Group, September 1984.

7. "Why Protectionism is a Mistake", London, April 1983.

THE CONSUMER INTEREST IN TRADE MATTERS:
THE TRADE UNION POINT OF VIEW

by

The Trade Union Advisory Committee to the OECD (TUAC)

At the outset, the complexity of the question "What is a consumer?" must be fully recognised. People have a dual identity, both as producers and consumers. Furthermore, there are different categories of consumers making different choices; for example, in a situation of less than full employment an unemployed consumer would no doubt welcome lower prices but may prefer a job. There is a danger that isolating the position of individuals as consumers without also seeing them as, or dependent upon, producers of goods and services will lead to inappropriate policies. Trade unions have to represent this dual identity; governments continuously have to take decisions to balance these concerns; and international organisations like the OECD have to promote co-operation so that the choices of governments are compatible at the global level. This complexity should moderate the advocacy of simplistic solutions.

There is a presumption in the background documents for this Symposium that by improving the functioning of market forces, the best of all possible worlds will be achieved for consumers. The TUAC wishes to stress that, in the current situation of mass unemployment and unbalanced growth within the OECD area, and austerity programmes in developing countries forcing their production towards exports, the market forces are not giving correct and sustainable price signals. At a time of rapid structural change due to new technologies and trade patterns, it is in the long-term interest of consumers that each country's economy successfully adjust with the minimum of social disruption towards sufficiently diversified and solid economic structures. The adjustment measures which have to be applied necessarily have costs, and at least a part of this cost needs to be spread equitably over the whole economy as it cannot be borne solely by the enterprises and the wage-earners concerned.

This may require the use, hopefully of a temporary and degressive nature, of interventions by governments to counteract persistent instability in the trading system, and to guard against anti-competitive trade and restrictive business practices. The fact is that few world markets are free, and those that are free are no less disruptive than those which are not.

There is a noticeable absence of analysis in the background documents on trade protectionism in agriculture. This is a sector for which the national and community interest has been explicitly recognised by many governments, yet where the issues for consumers are equally if not more important than in the textiles and vehicles sectors, which have been extensively analysed in the documents.

The notion of the widest choice available to consumers should be explored further to see at what point it needs to be qualified. An attractive choice at any given moment may lead to an elimination of choices later: a product may be introduced into a market at an artificially low price, which is subsequently raised once a dominant market share has been secured and domestic competition eliminated. Increased competitive pressures may force enterprises, for the sake of survival, to reduce quality and increase prices on spare parts, with a deteriorating service to consumers.

Frequently the activities of enterprises, and in particular multinational enterprises, act against fair competition and consumer interests. In this respect, Chapter IB of the OECD publication "Competition and Trade Policies" is a useful guide. Cartels operating in the international arena may allocate markets for members of the cartel, and multinational enterprises which use transfer pricing and intra-firm trade may cross-subsidise their products to gain a dominant market position. There may be much more damage done to consumers in the private world of restrictive practices and inter-company deals than by the relatively open and well-known interventions of governments.

The TUAC supports moves towards more open and transparent trade interventions by governments and businesses. The present "closed" arrangements frequently exclude the views of trade unions, as well as those representing specifically the consumer interest, until after the event. Consultations with interested parties before trade negotiations are concluded could lead to a better functioning of trade interventions. Nevertheless, it remains the role of governments to negotiate their trade policies, and to assess the efficacy of each measure.

The cost-benefit analysis approach to trade intervention decisions has many methodological drawbacks which make the trade unions sceptical of its usefulness. It is very difficult to fully capture all of the short- and long-term negative and positive consequences of trade interventions in cost-benefit analysis. There tends to be systematic bias towards quantifying short-term costs and an inability to quantify the dynamic benefits, particularly as there may be multiplier advantages in other sectors. The picture is further complicated by the fact that many of the benefits accruing rely on government and business attitudes towards reinvestment and restructuring so as to regain international competitiveness.

The presumption that trade measures taken so far have led to gains for the few (i.e., some enterprises and the workers in them) and losses for the many ("consumers") is too sweeping a generalisation. It is not really very useful to proceed with an analysis by juxtaposing the consumer interest with those of industries and employees, or indeed with the interests of governments.

Protection of consumers, like protection of workers at the place of work, cannot be considered as "protectionism", even though consumer protection laws do have an impact on trade. Unsafe products should not enter into international trade without proper control and supervision. Harmonization of consumer protection laws upward to best-practice standards should be the aim, and not a downward erosion to the worst standards.

THE CONSUMER INTEREST IN TRADE MATTERS:
THE BUSINESS POINT OF VIEW

by

The Business and Industry Advisory Committee to the OECD (BIAC)

I. INTRODUCTION

BIAC affirms its support for the following basic principles:

1. Consumer interests are best served by the market economy system based on competitive enterprise. Competitive enterprise has a proven record as the most effective vehicle for maximising economic welfare and enlarging consumer choice;

2. There is a natural commonality of interests between business and consumers in a competitive market economy system, since the profitability and hence the very survival of enterprises depends on meeting consumers' requirements. It is clearly in business' own interest to offer consumers value for money in the goods and services it sells. To that end, business continuously studies consumer needs and wants, strives to find the lowest-cost methods of supplying a wide range of products to meet those needs and wants, and seeks to provide consumers with adequate relevant information about products to enable them to make their choices wisely;

3. The freedom of business to communicate with consumers through media and non-media advertising, and to provide commercial information generally, is an essential element of the free enterprise system and is in the interests of both business and consumers. It is of the utmost importance that that freedom should remain secure, within the framework of the relevant codes of the International Chamber of Commerce which are already recognised world-wide;

4. It is generally overlooked that business itself is a major consumer, albeit what may be termed an intermediate consumer. All companies are purchasers of materials and goods at various stages of processing, and all companies consume the services of other companies;

5. Given the rapid expansion of international trade since World War II, and the consequent interdependence today of national economies throughout the world, the ability of business to continue satisfying an ever-increasing range of consumer wants at prices consumers can afford to pay is closely linked to the maintenance, and indeed strengthening, of the open international trading system;

6. A fundamental role of governments is to promote the efficient functioning of the market economy and competitive enterprise system at both national and international levels. Their interventions should be primarily directed to preventing abuses like fraud and misrepresentation in those cases where these cannot be dealt with

90

effectively through business self-regulation and other non-legislative means. Where they are unavoidably necessary, government interventions must, however, be non-discriminatory and practical. Nevertheless, in addition to safeguards against unfair or illegal trade practices, the absence of effective, selective and workable GATT safeguards means that in some circumstances voluntary restraints fulfil a market need. The role of governments is also to create conditions in which business can prosper: this takes the form of setting the climate through the establishment of inter-nationally agreed rules of conduct to underpin liberal trade on an equitable basis. All nations have industries and employment to defend against blatant malpractice in trade (dumping, etc.) and/or the social costs of damage from totally unrestrained market forces. Governments furthermore have a role in keeping unsafe products off the market, an aim business shares with consumers;

7. The more that can be done to educate consumers to be more discerning in their choice of goods and services to purchase, the less will be the need for protective regulations which risk inhibiting and/or distorting business output and international trade.

II. THE EFFECT OF TRADE POLICY ON CONSUMER INTERESTS

As the ultimate purchasers of goods and services, consumers have a clear and direct interest in an open international trading system. Inter-national trade: a) affords consumers access to goods which are not produced domestically; b) enables them to buy at the internationally cheapest source of supply; and c) enlarges their choice of goods of different quality at internationally competitive prices.

By promoting international competition, an open trading system encou-rages countries to concentrate on producing what they produce best. It thus is conducive to the most efficient use of the world's scarce economic resour-ces. Moreover, by minimising the cost of producing innumerable goods and services, and by lessening the risk of market dominance, international com-petition helps contain inflation and protect the real purchasing power of consumers. Thus, in short, an open trading system plays a major role in raising living standards world-wide -- as post-war experience has un-ambiguously demonstrated.

BIAC strongly supports the open trading system, not merely because of business interest in exporting. As a major intermediate consumer, business also benefits from being able to buy in from suppliers anywhere in the world who offer the most internationally competitive mix of price and quality.

BIAC shares the OECD's evaluation of the dangers inherent in the increasing trend at the present time towards "managed trade agreements" established outside the GATT framework and which evade its disciplines. Such restraints on international trade damage consumers by raising prices, lowering quality, reducing choice, inhibiting technological advance and curbing economic efficiency generally.

91

BIAC emphasizes that discipline is maintained by international rules and the risk of retaliatory action. Cheap products, as a result of dumping, may be argued to be in the (short-term) interest of consumers, but in the long term the need for employment must predominate since consumers need employment and have a vested interest in employers staying in business. This involves acceptance of the controlled use of trade restraints in appropriate cases.

BIAC is profoundly concerned by the so-called "new protectionism" which, it believes, is exacerbating low economic growth in many countries and is seriously compounding the problems of heavily indebted developing countries. Business has in recent years repeatedly called upon governments to make a concerted effort to stem and then roll back the protectionist trend. Believing that unemployment as well as the instability of the international monetary system are important causes of the revival of protectionism, it has also been calling upon them to recognise the important linkage between trade and financial factors.

BIAC endorses the OECD statement that consumer interests sometimes do not receive adequate consideration by decision-makers in the area of trade policy. Partly, this is because the effects of trade policy measures on consumer interests are usually widely diffused and difficult to evaluate. Partly, it is because governments and consumer organisations have not always devoted sufficient time and effort to trying to evaluate them. And partly it is because consumers are often insufficiently informed about the benefits they derive from an open trading system and the overall losses they incur as a result of spreading protectionism.

III. THE IMPACT OF CONSUMER PROTECTION ON INTERNATIONAL TRADE

Consumer protection measures can curtail and distort international trade if they are vulnerable to abuse for protectionist purposes, or if they are excessively or unnecessarily restrictive. Consumer protection policies may also inhibit trade by adding to the uncertainty of the business environment. Such policies must therefore be carefully designed so as to ensure as far as possible that they do not inadvertently create barriers to trade.

The very heterogeneity of national consumer policies and regulations, even though not designed to restrict imports, may discriminate against exporters compared with domestic producers by obliging the former to conform with different product-related requirements in each national market where they seek to sell their products. This situation is exacerbated by a multi-tiered international regulatory framework with a proliferation of controls all ostensibly designed to protect the consumer. The adverse impact of these factors on international trade could, wherever possible, be substantially reduced through the introduction and recognition of harmonized international or regional standards and through harmonization of certification procedures, though some room must remain for national approaches to accommodate special local circumstances. International co-operation towards these ends should allow for the participation and contribution of business. A further essential requirement is to eliminate the duplicative consumer protection efforts of different United Nations bodies.

Consumer protection can often be achieved more effectively and at a lower economic cost through business self-regulation rather than by government legislation. Consumer protection measures, particularly when legislation is resorted to, should, however, all be designed on the basis of a thorough cost-benefit analysis prior to their introduction. The effects of their operation should also be kept under continuous review to monitor to what extent and at what cost they are achieving the objectives in pursuit of which they were introduced. If experience with the operation of particular measures demonstrates that their costs exceed their benefits, there should be a willingness to remove them or, at the very least, to attempt to beneficially modify them with the minimum of delay. It is, furthermore, essential to recognise that the importance attached to a range of economic and social costs and benefits will vary among countries with different cultures and at different stages of development.

IV. THE CONSIDERATION OF CONSUMER INTERESTS IN THE FORMULATION AND IMPLEMENTATION OF TRADE POLICY

BIAC supports the principle that, provided rigid institutional structures are avoided, consumers as well as business itself should enjoy access to consultations with intergovernmental organisations about the formulation and implementation of trade policy. Too lengthy or cumbersome consultations on proposed measures, leading to justifiable restraints on trade, where a clear breach of rules is evident (such as anti-dumping) should be avoided.

The difficulties of assuring the independence and representativeness of consumer organisations in Western countries are real and must be fully recognised. These organisations, representing the views of interest groups on the formulation of trade policy, can fulfil their proper task best if they work in harmony with the market economy system in which they operate.

THE ECONOMIC EFFECTS OF DIFFERENT TYPES OF TRADE
MEASURES AND THEIR IMPACT ON CONSUMERS

by

Richard Blackhurst
Director of Economic Research and Analysis,
General Agreement on Tariffs and Trade (GATT);
Part-time Faculty Member, Graduate Institute of International Studies,
Geneva, Switzerland

INTRODUCTION

The analysis of the impact of trade policies can be divided into two steps: identifying the effects of the trade policies, and attempting to quantify the costs and benefits stemming from those effects. This paper is concerned with the first step (1).

Three main themes are developed in the paper. One is that, because it is impossible to give net protection to the economy as a whole (only particular sectors can be protected, at the expense of other sectors), part of the analysis of restrictive trade policies should be carried out in an income redistribution framework. A second theme is that the harm inflicted on consumers by trade restrictions is not limited to higher prices and reduced variety of consumer goods (including a narrower quality range, as well as the unavailability of some products); trade restrictions also reduce consumers' income over time by causing the rate of economic growth to slow down, and it is by no means clear which effect -- the income redistribution effect or the efficiency effect -- is larger in any given situation. The third theme is that there are important differences between the usual analysis of the impact on the economy (including consumers) of a trade restriction on imports of a single product, and the analysis of the impact of the country's overall trade regime.

Trade policies affect, in different ways, three main groups: consumers, producers (that is, employees and shareholders) in both the protected and unprotected sectors, and taxpayers (the latter because different trade measures have different implications for government revenue). There is considerable overlap between the three groups, however, especially if we follow the common practice in economics of defining the household as the basic unit. Every household contains consumers and nearly all contain producers and taxpayers. Thus it is difficult to limit the analysis of the impact of trade policies to the effects on just one group -- say consumers -- because we are considering not the total impact on one group of people, but rather only a part of the overall impact on essentially everyone.

This is less of a problem when we are analysing the impact of trade measures applied to a particular product. While import restrictions on clothing affect all households, it is also true that households containing clothing producers are affected differently from other households because the "production" effect dominates the "consumption" and "taxpayer" effects in those particular households. However, as will be seen in Section III below, these distinctions are much less sharp when the impact of the overall trade regime is being considered.

In laying the groundwork for the analysis, there are certain other aspects which require some mention and/or clarification. One is the definition of a "trade measure". Until some time in the early 1970s, the standard practice was to identify trade measures (trade policies) with measures imposed at the border, such as tariffs, quotas, export subsidies, import subsidies, foreign exchange licensing, and so forth. All other (non-border) measures were considered to be "domestic measures" and therefore outside the realm of policies which a country feels obliged to discuss with its trading partners.

Whatever value the border/non-border distinction may have had in the past, it is now rapidly losing its analytical usefulness (2). A number of ostensibly domestic policies -- most notably production subsidies -- can have as important an effect on trade flows as the traditional border measures. The fact that a country's trade policies are not limited to border measures was recognised in the Tokyo Round trade negotiations (1973-79) by the decision to include domestic subsidies, technical standards and government procurement in the negotiations.

Another point which needs to be clarified is exactly which consumers are being referred to in any particular context. Consider the simple matrix in Figure 1. It includes foreign consumers, as well as domestic consumers in the country or countries whose trade measures are being evaluated. Being cosmopolitan organisations, the OECD and the GATT are precluded from the parochial joy of assuming that "consumers" means only "our consumers". Of course, when the trade policies of a single country are being analysed, the effects on foreign consumers will often be so small that they can be safely ignored. But other times, when we are interested in the impact of the trade policies of a large group of countries -- for example, the textile and clothing policies of the developed-country members of the Multifibre Arrangement (MFA), or the trade-related agricultural policies of the United States and Western Europe -- the assumption that the impact on foreign consumers is negligible may not be reasonable.

Figure 1

	Domestic Consumers	Foreign Consumers
Trade measure affecting product Z	(I)	(II)
The country's overall trade regime	(III)	(IV)

The first two elements in the matrix refer to a situation in which we are analysing the impact of trade measures applied to a particular product. In this case, only the consumers of the product in question are directly affected and often the analysis is largely partial equilibrium in nature (that is, most repercussions outside of the particular industry in question are ignored). Elements (III) and (IV) of the matrix, in contrast, refer to situations in which the analysis is concerned either with the impact on consumers of the country's entire trade regime, or with the impact on consumers of an across-the-board change in trade policies (for example, as the result of a major trade negotiating round or a decision to join a free trade area). In this instance, all consumers are affected and the analysis is necessarily general equilibrium.

Because the matrix in Figure 1 offers a convenient way of ordering the various situations in which, depending on the problem at hand, we are interested, I have used it as the basis for organising the discussion in this paper. Thus there are four main sections, corresponding to the four elements in the matrix.

I. THE IMPACT ON DOMESTIC CONSUMERS OF TRADE MEASURES APPLIED TO PRODUCT Z

Most of this section deals with measures that act to reduce imports of product Z. The effects on consumers of measures designed to stimulate imports of Z, to stimulate exports of Z and to restrict exports of Z are considered briefly in the latter part of the section.

Restrictions on imports of product Z

Measures which reduce imports of product Z redistribute domestic income and affect the efficiency of the economy. The decline in economic efficiency -- and thus in the rate of economic growth -- due to the trade restriction can be thought of as the cost of bringing about the income redistribution.

The beneficiaries of this particular way of redistributing income are the domestic producers of product Z and/or of close substitutes for Z, and (under certain conditions) taxpayers. In general, the size of the income transfer increases with the level of protection. As is explained below, the answer to the question "Who pays?" depends on the type of measure used. (At a more detailed level of analysis, the answer also depends on the particular products covered by the restrictions.) Thus when analysing trade measures, it is important to distinguish between: a) the level of protection given to domestic producers of Z, and b) the type of measure used.

The type of measure used also determines the degree of inefficiency (cost) involved in bringing about the income redistribution. Limiting the analysis to four basic types of trade measures (production subsidies, tariffs, global quantitative restrictions and voluntary export restraints), and setting aside for the time being certain "political economy" considerations, it is possible to make the following tentative ranking, from least inefficient to most inefficient (3):

1. A production subsidy

It is often argued that, of the various trade measures, a production subsidy (paid directly from the national treasury and/or in the form of special tax breaks) is the least inefficient way to redistribute income because the domestic price of Z is not distorted (that is, it remains equal to the world market price, provided of course that the subsidy is the only trade

96

measure being applied). In their role as consumers, households are unaffected; they are affected, however, in their role as taxpayers (or as consumers of public services if the subsidy is financed by reducing other government expenditures), since it is taxpayers who pay.

If three conditions are satisfied -- there is a valid externality/distortion at work, the subsidy is the correct size, and it is directed to the source of the distortion (for example, if it is a training-related labour market distortion, the subsidy should be a training-related employment subsidy) -- then the granting of the subsidy will result in an increase in efficiency (4). If these conditions are not met, granting the subsidy causes efficiency to decline (because resources are trapped in less productive occupations) and the income redistribution is not costless.

2. A tariff

Provided it is the only effective restriction being applied to imports of product Z, a tariff on Z will cause the domestic price of Z (that is, of both the imported version and of domestically produced close substitutes for the imported version) to be higher, by approximately the amount of the tariff, than it would have been in the absence of the tariff. This statement holds regardless of whether the domestic price of Z is rising faster than the general price level, rising more slowly, or even declining absolutely. For simplicity, however, the following discussion refers simply to the "higher price caused by the tariff".

If Z is a final consumption good, say television sets, the tariff causes income to be redistributed (a) from consumers of Z to producers of Z (via the price increase on domestically produced Z), and (b) from consumers to taxpayers (because government revenue is augmented by the tariff revenue on the imported units of Z). If Z is consumed relatively more by low-income families, the tariff is equivalent to a regressive consumption tax because the burden on low-income families is relatively heavier.

If Z is an intermediate good (that is, an input, such as sheet steel), the tariff will have no direct impact on consumers provided the final consumption goods which use that intermediate good continue to be freely traded. In this case, income is redistributed from the industries using Z to the domestic producers of Z. Alternatively, if the industries which use Z as an input are themselves granted protection, or if Z is used by an industry producing a non-traded final consumption good, they can pass the higher cost of Z on to their customers, in which case it is the consumers' income which is redistributed to domestic producers of Z (and to taxpayers).

3. A global quantitative restriction

As with a tariff, the imposition of a quantitative restriction (QR) raises the domestic price of product Z, with the result that income is redistributed from consumers of Z to producers of Z. However, other effects of a QR differ from those of a tariff in two important ways:

   -- Subsequent declines in the world market price have no impact on the level of imports and no impact on the price paid by consumers.

(Under such circumstances, a constant QR results in a rising level of protection, which is why industries demanding protection consider a QR much more effective than a tariff.) The same is true for increases in the world market price, up to the point at which the QR is no longer effectively restraining imports;

-- When a tariff is used, the spread between the world market price and the domestic market price is captured by the government as tariff revenue; when a QR is used, the issue of who captures the spread depends on how the system is administered.

Import licences connected with a binding quota have a value equal to the difference between (a) the domestic market wholesale price of the product in the importing country, and (b) the cost-insurance-freight (c.i.f.) supply price (inclusive of any tariff duties) of the imported version. The value of the licence is commonly referred to as the "quota premium" or "quota rent". If the import licences are given away free of charge, whoever receives the licences receives a windfall gain because they can import the product and pocket the "quota rent".

Under global QRs, the licences are typically distributed to domestic importers on the basis of historical market shares. Two points related to their receipt of the windfall gain may be noted. First, it has an equity aspect, in the sense that the importers are being compensated (to a greater or lesser degree) for the impact of the QR on the level of their business in the product in question. Second, there is a serious risk that this method of distributing the import licences will create a group with a vested interest in the continuation of the QR (or at least a vested disinterest in efforts to repeal the QR); not only do the established importers get the quota rents, but the entrance of new firms (competitors) into the importing business is made much more difficult by the lack (partial or total) of licences available for newcomers. The effect is similar to the creation of an importers' cartel.

Under these conditions, a global QR hits each household twice -- once as consumers via the higher price of Z, and a second time as taxpayers via the government's decision to forego revenue by giving away the import licences free of charge.

However, it is possible to administer a global QR in such a way that the second effect is avoided. If the import licences are sold at public auction, the quota rent is captured by the treasury, and there is no "taxpayer loss" (5). Auctioning of quota licences has two other important benefits: it makes the level of protection fully transparent, and it avoids the danger of creating another group (in addition to the domestic producers of Z) with a vested interest in the continuation of the QR.

Mention should also be made of global quotas which involve import licences that specify the exporting country from which the imports must be purchased. (In this instance, the label "global quota" is something of a misnomer.) The result is a bilateral monopoly situation, with the licence-holding importer on one side and the designated exporter on the other. Exactly how the quota rent will be divided between them cannot be predicted in advance.

4. A voluntary export restraint (VER)

VERs and other types of bilateral quantitative restraints (such as orderly marketing agreements, or OMAs) differ from global QRs in two important ways. One is that they are discriminatory, and thus inconsistent with Article I of the GATT (the most-favoured-nation principle) as well as with Article XIII (governing the use of QRs). The other is that VER agreements make the exporting country responsible for administering the quota system -- that is, the licences are export licences (rather than import licences) and they are distributed by the government of the exporting country to the exporting firms.

The effects of a VER differ from the effects of a global QR in various ways. Some of the more important differences are (briefly) as follows:

a) With a VER there is a terms-of-trade loss for the importing country because the exporting country -- more specifically, the established firms in the exporting country which receive the export licences free of charge -- capture the quota rents. As with a global QR system in which the import licences are given free of charge to the importers, consumers of Z lose twice, once as consumers because of the higher price and once as taxpayers because the treasury is not capturing as revenue the spread between the domestic and foreign prices (taxpayers who are not consumers of Z also lose on this count) (6);

b) Regarding the capture of the quota rents by the export firms, two points may be made. First, there is a compensation aspect, in that the quota rents are often viewed as more or less "compensating" exporters for the reduced level of their exports. Second, the receipt of the quota rents raises a serious danger of creating a vested interest among established exporters in the continuance of the VER -- especially when we add to the quota rents the exporters' opportunity to enjoy the respite from competition that comes with market sharing, and the awareness of established exporters that a distribution of export licences on the basis of historical export shares can create a serious barrier to the entry of new firms (competitors) in the exporting country;

c) Because the limitation under a VER is expressed in physical units (rather than value), exporters have an incentive to try to "squeeze" as much value added as possible into each unit exported under the VER. As a result, up-grading often occurs, that is, exports include a larger share of higher-priced versions of Z. This concentrates the import competition at the high-quality end of the scale. Since the industrial countries (the main users of VERs) are usually least efficient at producing items at the lower end of the quality scale, the result is a relatively greater reduction in availability -- and a relatively greater increase in prices -- confronting consumers of lower-quality versions of Z (7). And since the lower-quality versions are typically purchased by lower income households, the VER redistributes income from consumers to producers in a regressive way.

One important similarity between a VER and the traditional global QR scheme in which the licences are given to the importers is that both lack transparency. However, when there are provisions for the licences to be openly sold by the recipients -- as with petroleum import licences in the United States in the past and export licences for textiles and clothing in Hong Kong -- the public gets a glimpse of the level of protection being imposed.

Finally, mention should be made of a very worrisome practice that has surfaced in the last few years, namely the use of a threat of a countervailing duty action to induce "troublesome" exporting countries to agree to a VER. This can involve either of two undesirable situations: countries which are not subsidising production or exports of Z are induced to accept a VER by a combination of a desire to avoid costly litigation and the opportunity to capture the quota rents; and countries which are subsidising production or exports of Z are happy to be given a share of the importing country's market (along with a pledge that, in exchange for their agreement to limit exports, countervailing duties will not be imposed). The increased use of this tactic presumably results both from the search for new protectionist techniques that has accompanied increasing protectionist pressures, and from an awareness of the sharp increase in the level and frequency of government subsidies over the past decade.

5. A combination of two or more restrictive measures

There are numerous instances of two or more of the four measures described above being applied simultaneously to imports of a particular product, for example in the agriculture and steel areas. In some cases the impact on consumers and taxpayers is additive -- such as the case in which both production subsidies and tariff protection are granted. Other times they are not additive -- for example, if both a tariff and an effective VER are imposed on Z, the tariff has no effect on consumers (as such) and no impact on the price received by domestic producers of Z, since it is the VER which is the effective restraint on imports; however, the quota rent is reduced by the amount of the tariff and consumers (as taxpayers) benefit from the increase in treasury revenue.

Other trade-related measures applied to Z

Import restrictions are not, of course, the only type of trade measures. The impact on consumers of three other types of measures is considered very briefly below. (In general, each of the three measures also reduces economic efficiency by causing a misallocation of resources.)

Import subsidy on Z

Some countries subsidise certain imports, most often food. Such measures redistribute income from taxpayers and from domestic producers of Z, whose output is depressed by the artificially low price, to the consumers of Z. If administration costs are ignored, general cash grants to consumers of Z are unambiguously more efficient because they do not distort prices, and therefore do not distort production or consumption decisions; if administration costs are brought into the picture, the relative efficiency of the two ways of redistributing income is less obvious.

Export subsidy on Z

This measure has two income redistribution effects: the price paid by consumers of Z rises by the amount of the export subsidy (the domestic price must rise by the amount of the subsidy to induce exporters to sell part of their output at home), and the treasury pays out revenue on the units exported. Thus it resembles the QR and VER cases, where the consumer pays a higher price for Z and the treasury foregoes an amount of revenue equal to the difference between the domestic value of the imports and the world market value.

Export tax on Z

An export tax reduces the domestic price of Z by the amount of the tax. As such, it transfers income from domestic producers of Z to domestic consumers of Z. If the tax is not prohibitive, taxpayers gain from the addition to the treasury's revenue. When export taxes are applied to raw materials, the "consumers" which receive the income transfer are downstream manufacturers. Domestic consumers of tradable final consumption goods which use Z as an input are not likely to gain from the distorted price of Z because the prices of the final consumption goods in question are set in the world market, i.e., not affected by the artificially low price of input Z. Alternatively, if the export tax is applied to a final consumption good -- such as a food item -- the resulting price distortion causes income to be transferred from producers to consumers (also, of course, reducing efficiency and economic growth).

II. THE IMPACT ON FOREIGN CONSUMERS OF TRADE MEASURES APPLIED TO PRODUCT Z

Because we are considering a situation involving only one product, the impact of the trade measures on foreign consumers is likely to be slight. However, there are some effects that could be important in particular situations. For example:

a) A VER on Z could have a negative impact on consumers of Z in the exporting country/countries because the VER reduces competition in the exporting country by (i) drawing the established firms into a cartel-like agreement for the purpose of dividing up the export licences (an agreement which could be subsequently misused domestically), and/or (ii) reducing the ability of new or potential producers of Z (in the exporting country) to reach a level of output that would allow them to compete efficiently with the established producers (exporters) of Z;

b) A decision by country A to restrict imports from country B could benefit consumers in country C if B's exports are "deflected" from A to C and cause the price of product Z in country C to decline; how permanent such a price decline will be is a more complicated question, and of course there is a serious risk of a protectionist response in C;

c) Foreign consumers would benefit (at least in the short run) if a country pursued trade policies -- such as a production subsidy -- that resulted in "excess production" that was then dumped on the world market at less than the prevailing price (agricultural products come to mind). A similar conclusion holds in the case of export subsidies to the extent that they lower world market prices (as opposed to export subsidies that just offset above-world-market production costs).

III. THE IMPACT ON DOMESTIC CONSUMERS OF THE COUNTRY'S OVERALL TRADE REGIME

When we analyse the impact of a trade restriction on a single product -- say, colour television sets -- our attention focusses on the domestic consumers and domestic producers of colour television sets. Repercussions on the rest of the economy are generally ignored because colour television sets account for only a very small share of total domestic consumption, production and employment. And while passing reference usually is made to the efficiency implications of tying up capital and labour in an inefficient industry, the impact of the trade restriction on television sets on the growth rate of consumers' incomes is generally ignored (again, because the effect is proportionately very small). In this case, the concern of consumers is limited to the higher prices (and perhaps reduced selection) of colour television sets.

Once we reach the stage of trying to understand the impact on consumers of the country's overall trade regime (system of import restrictions), the analysis acquires a new dimension that goes well beyond a simple summation of the results obtained in the partial equilibrium analysis of the impact of each individual restriction. The new dimension encompasses the general equilibrium effects that, while small with respect to any single product, become important when import restrictions on a multitude of products are considered collectively.

In addition to the income redistribution effects emphasized in Section I above, the analysis of the overall trade regime highlights a major additional negative effect of protection on consumers in the protecting country, and that is the decline in the rate of growth of consumers' incomes caused by the protective measures (8). It also calls attention to the fact that the burden of the protection falls not just on consumers, but also on workers and shareholders in firms in the export sector.

Protection reduces economic growth in at least four partially overlapping ways. First, by interfering with the price mechanism (crippling the price mechanism in the case of global QRs and VERs), protection reduces the quality of the main type of information available to guide business investment decisions, namely changes in relative prices. The result is that scarce investment capital is wasted by being diverted into low-productivity projects.

Second, there is now both a well-developed theory and convincing empirical work supporting the proposition that a sizeable share of a country's import taxes get shifted onto the export sector -- in short, that "a tax on imports is a tax on exports" (9). Thus import restrictions not only reward inefficiency, but also tax the country's most efficient industries. This must lower the country's economic growth.

Third, protection reduces the degree of external competitive pressure on domestic industries. In the larger countries this is less of a problem because the domestic market is big enough for most industries to be fully competitive even in the absence of import competition. But with some industries, such as steel and automobiles, and with most industries in the medium- and smaller-size countries, import competition is needed to promote the efficiency and innovation required for healthy economic growth (10).

Fourth, protection -- especially the new protection in the form of subsidies and VERs -- reduces economic growth by undermining confidence in the trading system. The multilateral rules governing countries' trade policies stimulate trade and trade-related investment -- that is, international specialisation -- by substantially reducing the extra degree of uncertainty surrounding transactions across national frontiers. The rules are intended to make future commercial policies -- and thus future market access -- more predictable. Thus protection not only directs investment into less productive projects at home and abroad, but it depresses the overall level of world-wide trade-related investment by increasing the level of uncertainty about future market access. It is no exaggeration, therefore, to say that consumers depend heavily on the multilateral trading system not only for competitive prices and product variety, but also for growth of their income.

IV. THE IMPACT ON FOREIGN CONSUMERS OF THE COUNTRY'S OVERALL TRADE REGIME

Foreign consumers are affected in two ways by the country's overall trade regime. First, if the country in question is a relatively large participant in world markets, the reduction in its growth rate caused by its own protection measures could act as a drag (albeit a relatively minor one) on the rate of economic growth of its trading partners. Second, and more importantly, if the country's trade regime includes very many measures which are either inconsistent with GATT rules (e.g. VERs) or subject to considerable controversy (e.g. production subsidies), then foreign consumers will be harmed by the negative effects of such measures on both the degree of world-wide confidence in the trading rules, and the willingness of other countries to adhere to the trading rules. These two factors played a major role in the Great Depression of the 1930s. There are some disturbing parallels with that earlier period in the current situation, especially if we consider the trends in trade policies in recent years.

MAIN CONCLUSIONS

Ranking alternative import restrictions

When it comes to ranking the four types of import restrictions analysed in Section I, the usual textbook preference for subsidies over tariffs is less clear than appears at first glance (11). The principal advantage (in theory) of using a subsidy rather than a tariff to provide a given level of stimulus to a domestic industry is that a subsidy, as noted earlier, can be targeted on the source of the distortion which needs correcting and thus does not, for example, distort prices facing consumers. Other advantages include: (i) many subsidies require annual legislative review and approval, whereas the country's tariffs do not; (ii) assuming there is a valid social consensus in favour of aiding industry Z and that the country's tax system is considered equitable, subsidy aid can be considered more equitable (in an income distribution sense) than aid via a tariff; and (iii) when the goal is to aid only certain firms in industry Z (for example, the least efficient ones), a subsidy can be targeted on those firms, whereas a tariff does nothing to alleviate the competitive pressure on less efficient firms from their more efficient domestic competitors (that is, the more efficient domestic producers capture most of the benefits of undifferentiated protection) (12).

Economic policy is not made in a political or institutional vacuum, however, and it is not enough to limit the analysis to the question of which policy would be best from a theoretical point of view. It is also necessary to ask whether one type of policy lends itself more easily to abuse. It is at this stage -- when we consider how subsidy programmes operate in practice -- that the issue of subsidies versus tariffs becomes more complicated.

To begin with, not all subsidies -- perhaps not even a majority -- are direct cash grants that require annual legislative approval. Subsidies are also given in the form of "tax expenditures", that is, via tax exemptions, tax allowances, tax credits and special rate reliefs (13). Not surprisingly, tax expenditures are usually less transparent than direct payments by the treasury, since reporting requirements are generally much less strict and the cost of such assistance is more difficult to quantify. And tax expenditures are less likely to receive annual legislative review and approval than direct cash outlays.

It would also be very difficult to argue that many production subsidy programmes are appropriately targeted in practice, either in the sense of being tailored to correct an established and quantifiable specific market distortion, or in the sense of being given to a particular sub-group of "deserving" producers (consider, for example, the way in which most agricultural subsidy programmes operate).

Finally, there is the point that subsidies, as compared with tariffs, pose a much more serious challenge to international commercial relations. There is a clear legal framework governing the use of tariffs, which serves to minimise tariff-related frictions between countries. In contrast, there are no firm rules of conduct on the use of production subsidies; they are permitted, but the signatories of the GATT Code on Subsidies and Countervailing Duties are required to take into account "possible adverse effects on trade" (14). More generally, subsidies are a much more complex instrument than tariffs and give rise to a number of problems related to definition, transparency and potential for abuse.

These various "real world" characteristics of actual subsidy programmes are not necessarily sufficient to make tariffs a preferable form of assistance from the consumers' viewpoint. That is a matter of judgement. What is clear is that the choice is a good deal more complicated than it appears in the usual textbook discussion.

Quantitative restrictions are always more costly, from the viewpoint of domestic consumers, than subsidies or tariffs. Among the different types of QRs, a global QR with the import licences sold at public auction is the preferred measure on the bases of transparency (of the level of protection), of minimising the number of residents with a vested interest in the continuation of the QR, and (from the taxpayers' viewpoint) of its impact on treasury revenue.

The question of which is the lesser of two evils from the consumers' viewpoint -- a global QR with the import licences given free of charge to the importers, or a series of voluntary export restraint agreements with some or all of the principal foreign suppliers -- presents more of a challenge. One common argument is that a global QR is superior to a VER because the latter involves a terms-of-trade loss for the importing country (that is, foreign export firms, rather than domestic importers, capture the quota rents). But this argument is not likely to carry much weight with consumers unless nationalistic sentiments cause them to prefer that domestic importers get the rents, or they recognise that a part of the importers' added profits end up in the treasury as tax revenue. At the same time, it could be argued that in practice, reliance on VERs is often a "looser" and therefore less restrictive approach because the VER scheme does not cover all foreign suppliers of the product(s) in question (15).

There is, however, one decisive argument in favour of a global QR over a series of VERs. Provided that a global QR can be justified under GATT rules (for example, under the safeguard provisions of Article XIX), its use does not damage the trading system. VERs, in contrast, are by nature discriminatory and thus violate the non-discrimination principle in Articles I and XIII of the GATT. When rule violations are involved, there is of course less transparency as regards the precise nature and degree of restrictiveness of the measures. A much more important consideration is that actions in violation of the multilateral rules -- in particular of a rule as central to the trading system as that of non-discrimination -- inevitably weaken the trading system, and a weaker trading system will be less successful in providing consumers with competitive prices, product variety and rising incomes.

The "New Protection" is more costly

A common question is whether the new protection -- namely subsidies and VERs -- includes added costs for consumers. While it can be argued that any new measure extending existing protection can be said to involve added costs, the answer must depend on the "ranking" which consumers are likely to give each new type of measure. It is difficult on the basis of this analysis to give a firm answer. However, when one takes into account the facts that the new protection is more contagious and that VERs are "winning out" over production subsidies because of budgetary constraints, one may reasonably conclude that the new protection has indeed increased the burden on consumers.

Protection taxes consumers twice

At the beginning of the paper it was noted that it is by no means obvious which negative effect on consumers is larger -- the income redistribution effect due to higher prices for consumer goods, or the efficiency effect as reflected in the lower growth rate of consumers' incomes. In fact, the question of which effect is larger is not very important. The main point is that consumers have two good reasons, rather than one, for opposing protection.

More generally, we can conclude that:

1. All consumers, in their role as consumers, have a stake in fighting against trade barriers;

2. All consumers, in their role as taxpayers, have reason to oppose production subsidies, global QR systems in which the licences are given away free of charge, and VERs; as for tariffs, and global QR systems in which the licences are auctioned, taxpayers should find them less objectionable, but nonetheless undesirable since there are more efficient (less distorting) taxes available for raising government revenue;

   The growth-retarding effects of protection also have implications for taxpayers. To the extent that the slower growth of national income is not matched by a slow-down in the growth of government expenditure, taxes will eventually be raised. In the medium term, this is a particularly serious concern in light of the projected financial problems of many public social security systems;

3. All consumers involved, in their role as producers (that is, as employees and shareholders) in the export sector, in the non-traded goods sector and in import-competing industries with below-average levels of protection, are harmed by the country's overall level of protection (16);

4. And finally, the only consumers with a genuine personal stake in supporting protection are those whose household (as a collective unit) satisfies two criteria: a) as producers, they are involved primarily in import-competing industries with above-average levels of protection, and b) the negative effects of the country's protective trade policies which they experience in their role as consumers (and taxpayers), plus the negative effect of the lower rate of economic growth, are not sufficient to outweigh the benefits received in their role as producers. In any society the number of people who meet these requirements must be very small (17).

Many supporters of protectionist actions do not support "protection in general", but only protection against imports of products that compete directly with products which they themselves (as employees or shareholders) produce. But this is an untenable position because protectionist measures can never be confined to a single product. At least three "mechanisms" ensure the spread of protection in the protecting country: a) political precedent or demonstration effect -- "If them, why not us?" -- especially when the protective action violates the country's international commitments (as with a VER); b) granting higher protection to a primary or intermediate goods industry reduces the competitiveness of every industry that uses the protected input, thereby stimulating demands for similar "assistance"; and c) imposing protection on one product often deflects labour and capital in the exporting countries into the production of other export goods, thereby generating protectionist pressures in other import-competing industries. Account must also be taken of the likelihood that protection in one country will stimulate protectionist reactions in other countries.

Two suggestions for combating protectionism

From a political economy standpoint, the preceding analysis points to two important conclusions. One is the need to ensure that discussions of trade policies -- which, outside of the major negotiating rounds, usually take place on a piecemeal, individual product or industry basis -- do not lose sight of the impact of the country's overall trade regime. The costs, in terms of the income redistribution from consumers to producers, of any single protectionist action will generally be fairly small; the costs of that single action in terms of lower output/employment/wages/profits in the export sector (as a whole), and in terms of slower economic growth, are likely to appear even smaller. This surely is one important reason why it is so often diffi-cult to mount effective political counterpressure against proposals for extending/increasing restrictions on imports of a particular product (espe-cially in the absence of credible threats of retaliation by major trading partners). Yet countries' trade regimes, particularly the non-tariff parts, are by and large the cumulative result of such a piecemeal, one-product-at-a-time approach. And the cumulative effect of the multitude of protective actions on consumers, export industries and other unprotected groups is likely to be, even in a moderately protectionist country, very sizeable (18).

Second, the established consumer organisations need to explore oppor-tunities for co-operating with representatives from other groups which suffer conspicuously from the income redistribution and slower growth effects of pro-tection. These include not only export industries, but also taxpayers' and retirees' groups, and influential groups in the non-traded sector (for example, teachers' and civil servants' groups, unions representing plumbers, retail clerks and so forth). In terms of understanding their stake in liberal trade, the consumer organisations seem to be far ahead of the other groups, which means the initiative and much of the early work (in the form of educa-tion) would have to be provided by the consumer groups. But it could be well worth the effort.

NOTES AND REFERENCES

1.   The opinions and conclusions in this paper are my own and do not neces-sarily reflect the views of the GATT Secretariat. I would like to thank Jan Tumlir and Frank Wolter for comments on an earlier draft.

2.   For a more detailed discussion of this point, see Blackhurst (1981).

3.   In a more complete analysis of the impact of protection on consumers and taxpayers, it would be important to explore the nature and size of the costs associated with preferential government procurement practices (whereby foreign firms are either excluded entirely from bidding on

government contracts, or are awarded the contract only if their bid is at least a certain percentage below the bids of domestic firms). The burden of such procurement preferences -- which are particularly prevalent in the so-called high-technology area -- takes the form of higher taxes, reduced quantity and/or quality of public services, higher user fees (for example, as in the case of PTTs), or a combination of these.

4.   There are good reasons for being very sceptical about the likelihood that any of these conditions is ever satisfied (see Blackhurst, 1981, pp. 366-68 and the references cited therein). In other words (and to put it politely), real world subsidy programmes do not bear much resemblance to those advocated by the "optimal intervention" approach (as described, for example, in Corden, 1974).

5.   Portions of the Australian and New Zealand import licences for textiles and clothing are auctioned.

6.   VERs also alter the geographic origin of the country's imports of Z; in the typical case, the VERs cover imports from the most efficient suppliers, causing the import share of these countries to either decline or grow less rapidly. With production subsidies, tariffs and global QRs, exporters continue to compete for sales, and the restricting country continues to buy from the lowest cost exporters; with a VER, in contrast, the restricting country purposefully shifts part of its purchases to higher cost suppliers -- that is, trade diversion occurs only in the VER case. However, this trade diversion only affects the size of the quota rent (the less efficient the foreign producer, the smaller the quota rent -- that is, the smaller the margin between the wholesale price in the importing country and the tariff-inclusive foreign c.i.f. supply price). Since the foreigners capture the quota rents under a VER in any case, this trade diversion is of no direct interest to residents of the importing country.

7.   Talk about up-grading is much more common than rigorous empirical analysis of the extent to which it actually occurs. For an example of the latter which does support the up-grading hypothesis, see Feenstra (1984).

8.   To be more exact, there is first the static efficiency loss caused by the initial movement of some factors of production into the inefficient import-competing industries; this loss is then augmented over time by the negative impact of the protective policies on the future rate of economic growth. For ease of exposition, I have merged the first effect into the second.

9.   This conclusion has nothing to do with taxing imports of intermediate goods -- that is, it would hold fully even if trade were limited to final consumer goods. See Clements and Sjaastad (forthcoming).

An interesting result of the Clements and Sjaastad analysis is that in certain circumstances, protection can benefit consumers. This occurs when one or more of the country's export products is also a major item in the consumption basket of residents of the exporting country (beef in Argentina comes to mind). By causing exports to decline, the import restrictions cause the domestic prices of the export products to be lower than they would be under free trade, and domestic consumers benefit from these lower prices. The problem with the conclusion that consumers can benefit from protection is not just that it requires rather special circumstances, but much more importantly that it is static in that it ignores the impact of protection (that is, of reduced international specialisation) on the rate of growth of consumers' incomes.

10.   Such "dynamic" considerations are often invoked in support of demands for extended/increased protection. Thus it is argued that protection will give import-competing firms a breathing space to modernise, develop new business strategies and so forth (such arguments resemble those for infant-industry protection). The problem with this line of argument is the near-total absence of real world examples of industries which regained their competitiveness with a one-time dose of protection. Examples of virtually permanent dependence on protection, in contrast, abound. In other words, in the vast majority of cases protection is an opiate rather than an antibiotic.

11.   In the usual textbook analysis, the main exception to the preference for subsidies over tariffs concerns countries whose tax systems are so limited that they cannot afford to be indifferent to the fact that tariffs add to government revenue, while subsidies are a drain.

12.   The granting of assistance to particular firms is a graphic illustration of a more general aspect of all protective measures, namely that the resulting distortion of competition has important implications for property rights. See Tumlir (forthcoming).

13.   See Owens (1984).

14.   Quoting in full from Article 11 (2) of the Code: "Signatories recognize, however, that subsidies other than export subsidies, certain objectives and possible form of which are described, respectively, in paragraphs 1 and 3 of this Article, may cause or threaten to cause injury to a domestic industry of another signatory or serious prejudice to the interests of another signatory or may nullify or impair benefits accruing to another signatory under the General Agreement, in particular where such subsidies would adversely affect the conditions of normal competition. Signatories shall therefore seek to avoid causing such effects through the use of subsidies. In particular, signatories, when drawing up their policies and practices in this field, in addition to evaluating the essential internal objectives to be achieved, shall also weigh, as far as practicable, taking account of the nature of the particular case, possible adverse effects on trade. They shall also consider the conditions of world trade, production (e.g. price, capacity utilisation etc.) and supply in the product concerned".

15.   Other aspects of VERs would be worth considering in a more detailed analysis, in particular what might be called their "internal dynamism". Establishing a series of VERs on a particular product category is often the beginning of virtually continuous negotiations between the parties concerned. The result is not only substantial administrative costs, and a tendency for the agreements to become more restrictive, but also a tendency to move into new areas, such as

agreements on the location of new investment. Another question concerns the extent to which the technicalities of VERs are such that the government comes to rely more and more on expertise drawn from its own industry. These and other considerations suggest that VERs may bring markets closer to a pure cartel situation than is generally thought.

16.   One of the original insights of the "a tax on imports is a tax on exports" concept is that many industries which appear to be receiving protection are in fact being taxed by the country's overall trade regime. (This general equilibrium point is distinct from the partial equilibrium point that the effective rate of protection of value added in an industry can be negative, in that it does not depend on there being trade in intermediate goods.) For example, if three-quarters of the average level of protection is shifted onto exports, any import-competing industry whose level of protection is less than three-quarters of the national average is actually receiving negative protection -- that is, it is being taxed by the overall trade regime. Employment and output in such import-competing industries would, along with employment and output in the export industries, be stimulated by across-the-board trade liberalisation.

17.   The vast majority of people holding jobs that exist only because of protectionist measures would be able to find equivalent-wage employment following an across-the-board liberalisation, either in the export sector (which would be expanding as a result of the liberalisation) or in the non-traded goods sector (which would also be expanding as a result of the stimulus to economic growth provided by the liberalisation); in the case of low-skill workers in the developed countries, they could choose between retraining to upgrade their skills (and thus their wages) or moving horizontally into low-skill jobs in the non-traded sector (particularly into non-traded services).

18.   See, for example, Easton and Grubel (1982).

BIBLIOGRAPHY

Blackhurst, R. (1981) "The Twilight of Domestic Economic Policies", The World Economy, December.

Clements, K.W. and Sjaastad, L.A. (forthcoming) How Protection Taxes Exporters, Thames Essay No. 44 (London: Trade Policy Research Centre).

Corden, M. (1974) Trade Policy and Economic Welfare (Oxford: Clarendon Press).

Easton, S.T. and Grubel, H.G. (1982) "The Costs and Benefits of Protection in Growing World", Kyklos, Fasc. 2.

Feenstra, R. (1984) "Voluntary Export Restraint in U.S. Autos, 1980-1981: Quality, Employment and Welfare Effects" in R. Baldwin and A. Krueger (editors), The Structure and Evolution of Recent U.S. Trade Policy (Chicago: University of Chicago Press for the National Bureau of Economic Research).

Owens, J. (1984) "Spending Through the Tax System: A Review of the Issues", OECD Observer, May.

Tumlir, J. (forthcoming) "GATT Rules and Community Law" in Hilf, Jacobs and Petersmann (editors), GATT and the EC, Volume 4 in Studies in Transnational Economic Law (Kluwer Publishers).

THE EFFECT OF TRADE RESTRICTIONS IN SELECTED SECTORS -- WORKSHOP A

Part I: CONSUMER INTEREST IN THE AUTOMOBILE INDUSTRY

by

Dr. L.B.M. Mennes
Netherlands Economic Institute; Professor of Economics,
Erasmus University, Rotterdam

Dr. A. Krijger
Netherlands Economic Institute

I. PREFACE

This report presents the results of a study concerning the effects of trade restrictions in the automobile industry with special reference to the consumer point of view. Specifically, the study deals with passenger car trade barriers, with emphasis on mass-produced cars rather than specialist cars (Rolls Royce, Porsche, Volvo, BMW, etc.). It should be noted that the final results are closely related to assumptions regarding elasticities, productivity and the pricing process in the automobile sector.

The authors wish to acknowledge the co-operation of members of the supervising committee who contributed to the study with their advice and recommendations: Mrs. S. Höll (BEUC); Mr. L. Broch (IOCU); and Mr. J. Koopman, Mr. K. Köllen, Mr. P. van de Locht and Mr. H.H. Meeldijk (Ministry of Economic Affairs).

LIST OF SYMBOLS

P   price

Q^d total pre-liberalisation domestic consumption

Q^m total pre-liberalisation imports

Q^s total pre-liberalisation domestic supply

t   tariff percentage

r   adaptation coefficient between tariff percentage and price change

VER   volume of voluntary export restraint

η price elasticity of domestic demand

η_m price elasticity of import demand

η_v price elasticity with respect to change of VER

ε price elasticity of domestic supply

II. TRADE, PROTECTION AND THE AUTOMOBILE INDUSTRY

A. Trade and protection

Most of the post-war period has been marked by a process of progressive trade liberalisation which has significantly contributed to its record of rapid economic progress. The main advantages of trade liberalisation are well known: a more efficient allocation of resources, more competition and more stability in the general level of prices. For consumers, as the ultimate buyers of goods and services, trade barriers have a direct negative impact to the extent that the price, quantity and quality of goods and services, patterns of consumption and the distribution of income are affected. There is also an indirect negative impact for consumers to the extent that restrictive trade measures have a negative impact on the growth and dynamism of national economies.

Since the mid-1970s, there has been a revival of protectionism both in North-South trade and in trade relations among the industrial countries. It is usual to distinguish the present protectionism in developed countries from its previous forms. The "new protectionism" uses devices different from tariffs: mainly domestic subsidies, administrative and technical barriers and voluntary export restraints (VERs). It is characterised by the lack of transparency of the instruments employed, the shift from precise rules to administrative discretion and a return to bilateralism. A striking feature of the new protectionism is its concentration in the same sectors in various industrial countries: textiles and apparel, steel, television sets, footwear, shipbuilding and, more recently, automobiles (1).

Who is bearing the cost of protection? Protection in the form of subsidies is financed by means of tax revenues. Protection also leads to a change in the terms of trade between sectors at the expense of the non-protected sector. Further, protection leads to a redistribution of income. More specifically, from the consumer point of view, quantitative restrictions have a serious effect on income distribution if they induce importers to increase the unit value of the goods they sell, and the increase in cost is likely to fall on low-income consumers -- particularly if the product concerned is a basic necessity. In cases where protection leads to higher prices, the costs are obviously at the expense of the consumers. Such costs can be very high. In the late 1970s American consumers paid an estimated $58 000 annually per job saved by protection of speciality steel, television sets and footwear; the cost would amount to about double this figure at 1984 prices. European consumers paid approximately $11 billion yearly for the protection of European farm products ($17 billion at 1982 prices); American consumers pay an estimated $12 billion yearly for the protection of textiles and apparel (2). In another study by Munger, the annual cost of tariffs and quantitative restrictions to U.S. consumers is estimated at some $57 billion (1980 prices). For an average American family of four, the annual average cost is a hidden but very real tax burden of more than $1 000 (3).

The figures mentioned above show that the interests of consumers are significantly affected by the adoption of various trade policies (4). In fact, if protectionism rises, its negative effect on the cost and availability of imports leads to a decrease in the consumer's real income. Consumer

interests are usually served by competition policies aiming at economic efficiency by enhancing the effective functioning and competitiveness of markets.
Restrictive trade policy measures obviously will have a significant, negative
impact on the effective implementation of competition policy. In fact, trade
laws relating to unfair trade practices may be abused so as to either control
or exclude the presence of foreign competitors in domestic markets, leading to
harmful effects on consumer interests. Consumer policy considerations are
competing and sometimes conflicting with other aims of economic policy. Three
of these objectives, quite often entailing protectionist pressures, have
already been mentioned above: the fight against unemployment, often due to
insufficient adjustment; the promotion of specific -- high-technology --
industries; and national security interests. Thus far consumer interests
have had a rather limited impact on the formulation and implementation of
trade policies, while more sectoral concerns -- generally taken care of by
well-organised groups -- have tended to play a relatively important role in
the decision-making process.

In order to give proper consideration to consumer interest in designing
trade policies, and to enable decision-makers to make a rational choice, it is
recommendable to make visible the positive and negative effects of trade-
restrictive measures to the maximum extent possible. A useful method for this
purpose is the cost-benefit approach, which has been used increasingly in
other policy areas. In this paper an attempt is made to do a cost-benefit
analysis of trade-restrictive measures in one of the last major sectors where
they were introduced: the automobile industry. The major forces that have
brought protection into the sector are the following (5): first, the decline
in auto sales in the OECD countries due to the overall depression and high
interest rates; secondly, the high performance of Japanese auto producers;
thirdly, and partly related to the previous point, a considerable relocation
of production to semi-industrial countries. The U.S. share of world automobile production fell from 65 per cent in 1965 to 20 per cent in 1980, while
Japan's share has increased from near zero to 27 per cent, and that of semi-
industrial countries has risen from 2 to 15 per cent. The share of the EC
fluctuates around 30 per cent. These factors, but in particular the increased
competition from the Japanese, have led to a number of protectionist pressures
and measures in the auto trade policies in the industrial nations.

B. The automobile industry

Global production of passenger cars is still largely concentrated in
three areas: the EC, Japan and the U.S. with, respectively, 33 per cent,
25 per cent and 19 per cent of total world production in 1982. Production is
dominated by a restricted number of manufacturers: in the U.S., General
Motors and Ford; in Japan, Toyota and Nissan; and in the EC, Volkswagen-
Audi, Renault, Peugeot-Citroën-Talbot and Fiat. Although the automobile
industry made a remarkable recovery after the first oil crisis in 1973-1974,
the second oil crisis of 1978-1979, coupled with the deepening of the recession, affected it especially in the U.S. and the EC. Average annual growth
rates for 1978-1982 amount to -13.6 per cent for the U.S. and -2.7 per cent
for the EC. In Europe, only the Netherlands and Sweden are exceptions to this
negative trend. Japan, on the contrary, maintained a positive growth rate of
3.6 per cent. The turning point was reached in 1981; in 1982 most countries
registered again a positive production growth. In 1983 all countries -- in
particular the U.S. -- showed positive production growth figures.

The automobile industry is an important source of employment: in 1981 the automobile sector of the EC employed more than 1 800 000 people; in both the U.S. and Japan the automobile sector employed around 700 000 people. Employment growth during 1975-1981 amounted to -1.5 and -8.7 per cent in, respectively, the EC and the U.S. In Japan, on the contrary, it increased by 14.8 per cent. Within the EC the largest employers are Germany (36.3 per cent), France (25.0 per cent), the United Kingdom (20.2 per cent) and Italy (13.3 per cent), together accounting for almost 95 per cent of total employment in the EC automobile sector in 1981. Within the EC, employment growth was strongest in Germany (+11.2 per cent) and weakest in the United Kingdom (-23.5 per cent) during 1975-1981. Also, within the industrial sector, the automobile industry is an important employer, and its importance is growing: in 1975 it accounted for 4.8 per cent of total industrial employment in the EC; in 1981 it accounted for 5.1 per cent. In France and Germany employment in the automobile sector amounts to even more than 6 per cent of total industrial employment in 1981.

Japan is the world's largest exporter of passenger cars, with an export of almost 3.8 million vehicles in 1982. This is almost 55 per cent of Japanese passenger car production in 1982. Japan is followed by the EC at a distance with total extra-EC exports of almost 1.8 million vehicles (almost 20 per cent of 1982 production) and the U.S. with exports of 360 000 vehicles (around 7 per cent of 1982 production). Except for France, average annual export growth for the period 1980-1982 is negative. For 1983 export growth is positive again, except for the UK and Germany. In the latter country the decrease was, however, marginal.

The U.S. is the world's largest importer of passenger cars, with imports in 1982 amounting to almost 2.3 million; the EC is the second largest importer, with almost 1.5 million vehicles. Except for France, the average annual import growth is also negative during the period 1980-1982. For Japan, automobile imports are very small.

Expenditures for personal transport are an important item of the consumer budget. In the EC an average -- expressed as a percentage of gross domestic product (GDP) -- of about 2.5 per cent is spent on initial expenditures, and about 4 per cent on the operation of personal transport (6). It adds up to an average of around 6.5 per cent. Within the EC variance is high: from 3.6 per cent in Greece to 8.9 per cent in Luxembourg.

Prices for the same passenger car (in dealer prices and in prices net of tax) vary widely in the EC. In this respect the EC is still far away from being a common market. Most prominent is the wide divergence in tax rates. The value added tax (VAT) for instance is 10 per cent in Luxembourg, and can be as high as 38 per cent in Italy. In addition to the VAT other taxes are imposed, often based on engine capacity. However, different tax rates are not the only reason for the difference in car prices; prices net of tax also vary widely. Other factors such as customs rules, varying retail margins and market segmentation contribute to the price differences. Furthermore, the system of exclusive dealerships enables car companies to fix retail prices and limit effective competition within each national market. Maintaining differences in net-of-tax prices appears to be part of the marketing strategy of the car manufacturers (7). As a consequence of both the tax regime and the pricing policy, price differences for the same passenger car in the EC can be -- in prices net tax -- as high as 40 per cent.

In 1982 the total number of new registrations of passenger cars amounted to almost 9 million in the EC, almost 8 million in the U.S. and 3 million in Japan. Annual growth rates vary widely, also for 1983. In general, sales of passenger cars have been liable to the overall economic decline and high interest rates.

Recently the OECD published long-term automobile demand projections (8). Based on assumptions regarding car ownership levels, population estimates and scrapping rates, automobile demand for 1985, 1990, 1995 and 2000 was projected. Table 1 presents estimates for 1985 and 1990.

Table 1

AUTOMOBILE DEMAND IN 1985 AND 1990 (x 1 000 OF VEHICLES)

| Country | 1980 (actual) | 1985 | 1990 | Average annual growth (%) | |
				1980-85	1980-90
Germany	2 426	2 434	2 348	0.0	0.0
France	1 873	2 066	2 197	2.0	1.6
Netherlands	452	551	583	4.0	2.6
Italy	1 530	1 531	1 660	0.0	0.8
United Kingdom	1 514	1 639	1 718	1.6	1.3
Belgium/Luxembourg	430	444	477	0.6	1.0
Ireland	94	88	95	-1.3	0.0
Denmark	74	137	141	13.1	6.7
Greece	42	112	134	21.7	12.3
United States	8 761	11 338	11 460	5.3	2.7
Japan	2 854	4 410	4 262	9.1	4.1

Source: Verband der Automobilindustrie E.V. for 1980; OECD for 1985 and 1990.

For most EC countries demand is expected to grow less than 2 per cent per year because these markets are now approaching their mature phase (9). In Germany the growth in demand is expected to be very small because saturation levels are being approached and the population will decline (10). Growth rates of demand for the U.S. are biased due to the selected base year: sales in 1980 were extremely low.

Trade barriers can be classified into tariffs, quantitative restrictions and other trade barriers. Table 2 presents an overview of the trade barriers in force for the major car-producing countries.

Table 2

TRADE BARRIERS IN MAJOR CAR-PRODUCING NATIONS

| | Tariff Barrier | Non-tariff barriers | |
		Quantitative restrictions	Other non-tariff barriers
United States	3% (a)	Imports of Japanese cars limited to 1.85 million units (b)	(1) Strict safety, emission and fuel economy standards; (2) Fuel economy standards, embodied in Energy policy and Conservation Act of 1975, differentiate between North American-made (75 % or more value added in United States) and foreign-made vehicles in computing corporate average fuel economy
Japan	None	None	(1) Strict emission control standards; (2) Difficult compliance procedures; (3) Complex distribution system; (4) 15-20 % commodity tax on all cars, varying with size and weight; (5) High dealer margins on luxury (United States) cars
Germany	10.4 % EEC tariff	None	Safety and emission standards
France	10.4 % EEC tariff	Imports of Japanese cars limited to 3 % of market	(1) Emission standards; (2) Cars must be certified to be roadworthy (primarily to restrict Japanese imports); (3) Special taxes imposed on heavy passenger cars of foreign origin

Table 2 (continued)

United Kingdom	10.4 % EEC tariff	Imports of Japanese cars limited to about 10/11 % of the market	Surtax of 10 % on all vehicles
Italy	10.4 % EEC tariff	1982 quota for Japanese cars: 2 300 vehicles	Strict enforcement of "vehicle construction requirements"

a.   This table refers to passenger automobiles only, and therefore the recent reclassification of cab chassis as light trucks, with the resulting 25 % tariff rate, is not shown.

b.   This VER was renewed in March 1984 for one year.

Source: Business International quoted by Robert B. Cohen, "The Prospects for Trade and Protectionism in the Auto Industry" in: William C. Cline (ed.), Trade Policy in the 1980s, Washington, D.C., 1983. Data have been updated by the authors.

Tariffs and quantitative restrictions are mainly applied in the U.S. and the EC; in Japan a variety of non-tariff barriers are in force. The commodity tax on non-Japanese cars, for instance, is levied on imports value cost, insurance, freight (c.i.f.) rather than free on board (f.o.b.) as in other countries, while domestic cars are taxed on ex-factory value. Next the process of homologation -- the adjustment of cars to Japanese safety and environmental standards with an extensive list of requirements -- is a serious non-tariff barrier (11). In the U.S. during the last couple of years, there were discussions about the local content law. Such legislation would institute minimum "domestic content" requirements on firms selling at least 500 000 cars in the U.S. The renewal of the voluntary export restraint (VER) with Japan last March suggests that this local content discussion is not a topic for the moment. Except for Italy (the quota with Japan goes as far back as 1962), quantitative restrictions in the U.S. and the EC have been framed primarily as a response to the increased competition from Japan. Apart from the countries mentioned in Table 2, trade barriers in the automobile industry are known to exist in Spain, Portugal, Sweden, Brazil, Mexico, Argentina and Korea. It is safe to estimate that in 1982 more than 40 per cent of the world car market was affected by restrictions on Japanese exports (12). In the following sections the trade barriers applied by the EC will be elaborated in more detail.

There exists an EC customs duty, based on customs value, on imports of non-EC passenger cars. For 1984 this tariff is 10.4 per cent. Exceptions are the European Free Trade Association (EFTA) countries (zero-tariff) and Spain (4.2 per cent tariff). Furthermore, South Korea benefits from the Community's General System of Preferences allowing in 1983 a contingent of almost 53 million European Currency Units (ECUs) for small passenger cars for which customs duty is suspended. Annex 1 to Regulation (EEC) no. 288/82 presents a list of products for which free circulation is restricted by quantitative measures. Such measures are used by Italy and Ireland in the case of passenger cars. Italy has placed a quota on the import of cars from Japan and the

Soviet Union. It allows 2 300 passenger cars from Japan and 2 650 from the Soviet Union annually. For the last couple of years Italy received authorisation from the Commission to prevent indirect imports via other EC countries. Ireland is allowed a quota system during the transitional period -- expiring at the end of 1984 -- restricting the import of passenger cars. From the beginning of 1985 onwards Ireland has to ensure full compliance with EC rules. Since 1977 the French Government imposed a unilateral agreement on Japan to limit the Japanese car imports to 3 per cent of the car market. This is not an official import quota because it is suggested that Japan voluntarily limits its exports to France. Since 1976 informal arrangements exist in the United Kingdom between the British Society of Motor Manufacturers and the Japanese Automobile Manufacture Association to restrict the Japanese share in the UK car market to 10/11 per cent. In June 1982 Japan "voluntarily" promised to limit exports to the Benelux countries at the 1980 level and to limit exports to Germany at the 1980 level plus 10 per cent. Regular consultations are held between the Commission and Japan to discuss Japanese car imports to the Community. In February 1983 the Japanese Government renewed its intention to the effect that in 1983 exports to the EC of motor vehicles would be moderate.

Technical requirements are serious non-tariff barriers. In the area of technical harmonization, 59 EC directives have been effected covering almost all relevant automobile parts; three remaining directives are still pending. Until these are accepted, a uniform EC-type approval certificate will not come into force. The three remaining directives are still blocked because of different views within the EC about the access of vehicles from third countries to the type-approval system. It appears that nowadays further delay is related more to foreign trade policy than to technical issues (13).

Finally, measures to assist import-competing production should be mentioned. Reviewing national aids to the motor industry is both complicated, because of the many different financial flows, and delicate, because the matter is considered "sensitive". The public financial participation is of a comparatively widespread nature in the motor industry. A feature of the European automobile industry is state ownership: British Leyland, Renault and Alfa Romeo are state-controlled and Fiat (through Seat), Volvo and VW-Audi have an element of state ownership. Peugeot, Citroën, Talbot and Volvo have received direct government aid and Ford, GM, Fiat and Saab have received indirect aid (such as special capital investment grants) (14). According to Ford (15), Renault, British Leyland and Fiat are the major recipients of state aid. British Leyland has received since 1975 $3 billion from the United Kingdom in loan and equity stakes; Fiat received $1 billion and Renault (state-owned) was given $118 million in 1981 and $200 million in loans and equity in 1983, with $124 million requested for 1984. The Dutch Government promised Volvo in the Netherlands a loan of $166 million for the development of a new medium-range model; Alfa Romeo (state-owned) received in 1982 $140 million in equity and the Italian Government promised a further $624 million made up of loans and a government contribution. In 1981 the Commission of the EC took steps to initiate a monitoring system covering both specific national aids to the motor industry and other general aids (16), but not much progress seems to have been made. Also, the OECD -- aware of the growing public financial participation in the private sector -- initiated a study about government support to industry (17). Only four countries (Norway, Sweden, the United Kingdom and the Netherlands) were involved; consequently the study is descriptive rather than conclusive. It does not provide specific data about the car industry.

III. METHODOLOGY

A. Measuring costs and benefits

The economic consequences of trade policy can best be determined by comparing the corresponding streams of costs and benefits. When determining the costs and benefits of liberalisation or protection, one has to start with the short-term effects in a partial equilibrium framework. To what extent are prices influenced by different kinds and levels of trade restrictions? Prices paid by consumers for imports will normally be affected by import restrictions, but there will also be effects on the prices and profits of domestic producers. Measurement of these effects leads to an estimate of the change in consumer surplus due to a change in trade policy. The consumer surplus is the notional difference between what a consumer actually pays for a commodity or service and what he would be willing to pay for it. When trade liberalisation brings about a fall in price, the consumer surplus will rise. The rise includes both national welfare gains/losses and income transfers. The national welfare increases for two reasons: there is a consumption gain as more consumers enter the market; and the increased efficiency of domestic producers causes a production/efficiency gain. Insofar as (part of) the tariff is borne by overseas producers, there is also a welfare loss: the tariff-imposing authority loses the tariff revenues. Income transfers include two income redistribution flows to consumers from, respectively, domestic producers and government.

Trade liberalisation may also give rise to (adjustment) costs, particularly if a fall in price leads to a fall in domestic production resulting in a (temporary) redundancy of factors of production. Comparing the above-mentioned benefits and costs yields a first approximation of the economic consequences of a change in trade policy. Thus far, however, only static welfare effects were dealt with.

The dynamic effects of trade liberalisation -- including gains from economies of scale, stimuli to technical innovation and investment and output expansion resulting from reduced inflation -- may be both much stronger and more ambiguous than the static effects. Quantifying these dynamic and other macro-economic effects is obviously a very difficult task. In fact, it would require an additional study to produce any more than a highly speculative estimate. For this reason the present study will be confined to analysing the static welfare effects.

In this report the empirical measurement of the costs and benefits of trade liberalisation will be based on the concept of consumer and producer surplus. The well-known comparative static analysis underlying this concept may be outlined by referring to Figure 1. In theory (18) -- to assess the economic effects of tariff imposition -- two general cases are being distinguished: tariff imposition in a small open economy and tariff imposition in a large open economy. In the former, world prices are a given datum; in the latter they are not. This is the case for the automobile industry as in fact price formation appears to be regulated by the competition situation in each market (19). Figure 1 examines the case of a tariff effect on imports in a large open economy.

Figure 1

TARIFF IMPOSITION IN A LARGE OPEN ECONOMY

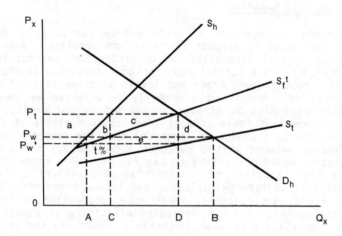

where: P_x =   price of product x;

Q_x =   quantity of product x;

S_h =   domestic supply curve;

S_f =   unrestricted total supply curve;

S_f^t =   restricted (by tariff) total supply curve;

D_h =   domestic demand curve;

P_t =   restricted domestic price; $P_t = P_w' (1+t)$;

P_w =   unrestricted import price;

P_w' =   restricted import price;

t =   tariff

P_t is the price where trade is restricted: domestic supply amounts to OC and imports to CD. P_w is the price where trade is not restricted: domestic supply decreases to OA and imports increase to AB. Assuming that (part of) the tariff is borne by foreign producers, the price of the importable on the domestic market does not decrease by the full amount of the tariff as the supply curve is assumed to shift from S_f^t to S_f in case of liberalisation.

The static welfare effects of the tariff can also be evaluated by reference to Figure 1. The lower price and consequent increase in demand generates a rise in consumer surplus equivalent to the areas a + b + c + d. However, this is not the net change in welfare. Part of this increase amounts to a redistribution from domestic producers to consumers (area a) and from government to consumers (area c). The net change in welfare is represented by areas b, d and e. Area b represents an efficiency gain because OA units are now provided by relatively efficient domestic producers; area d represents a consumption gain associated with DB, new consumers entering the market. Together the efficiency and consumer gain are the so-called dead-weight gains. Finally, area e represents the loss of income from foreign producers to the tariff-imposing authority. The less elastic the foreign supply curve, the greater the proportion of the tariff the foreign producers will bear. Apart from these welfare effects, trade liberalisation results in an -- at least temporary -- displacement of production factors. The cost of adjustment may be limited to the displacement of labour and depends on the length of the displacement and the social security benefits involved.

Costs and benefits of trade liberalisation may be more precisely described by the following set of formulae (20):

Dead-weight gains

Efficiency gain: $0.5 \cdot r \cdot t^2 \cdot \varepsilon \cdot Q^s$ (i)

where:

r   =   adaptation coefficient between tariff percentage and price change

t   =   tariff percentage

ε =   price elasticity of domestic supply

Q^s =   total pre-liberalisation domestic supply

Consumption gain: $0.5 \, r \cdot t^2 \cdot \eta \; Q^d$ (ii)

where:

η =   price elasticity of domestic demand

Q^d =   total pre-liberalisation domestic consumption

Redistribution of income:

from producers $(r.t.Q^s) - (0.5.r. t^2 . \varepsilon .Q^s)$ (iii)

from government $(r.t.Q^d) - (r.t.Q^s)$ (iv)

Costs

loss of income from foreign producers:

$[(1-r).t.Q^d] - [(1-r).t.Q^s]$ (v)

adjustment costs:

$r.t. \, \varepsilon .Q^s$ (vi)

It should be noted (21) that the dead-weight gains from liberalisation are a function of the square of the price change, whereas both the transfers from domestic producers and government to consumers and the cost of adjustment are proportional to the price change. This means that the net welfare gain is much more readily demonstrated when high tariffs are involved. In addition, it should be noted that the welfare gain is also greater in relation to both adjustment costs and redistribution gains/losses when elasticities are higher. Finally, it should be noted that the discounted present value of dead-weight gains easily exceeds the transitional social costs unless, in periods of high unemployment, the process of reabsorption of labour takes a relatively long time.

The presented set of formulae to measure the costs and benefits of trade liberalisation applies to countries with a domestic automobile industry. The following set of formulae applies to those countries without a domestic automobile industry. As domestic supply -- by definition -- does not exist, costs and benefits are directly related to imports.

<u>Dead-weight gains</u>: $0.5.r. \ t^2 . \eta_m \ Q^m$ (vii)

where: η_m = price elasticity of import demand

Q^m = total pre-liberalisation imports

<u>Redistribution from government</u>: $r.t.Q^m$ (viii)

<u>Loss of income from foreign producers</u>: $(1-r).t.Q^m$ (ix)

So far the analysis has dealt with the costs and benefits of tariff interventions. In case the analysis is extended to include the effects of abolishing VERs and quotas, one may use approximately the same set of formulae. Once the price change as a consequence of the abolishment of a VER/quota is estimated, the same procedure as for the abolishment of a tariff can be followed. However, there are two different assumptions, i.e., regarding tariffs and price policy. First of all we will abstract from tariffs. This assumption implies that the redistribution from government to consumers is substituted by a transfer from foreign producers to domestic consumers. Next, the estimated price change will be assumed to lead to a proportional change in the price level for passenger cars, because -- as will be seen later -- volume effects of the abolishment of VER/quota are more substantial than volume effects due to the abolishment of tariffs.

B. Estimating the price change of a VER/quota

Earlier, the tariff percentage could be used as an indication for the range of price changes. For the assessment of the price change as a consequence of the abolishment of a VER (22), there is far less to go by. Recently, Hamilton (23) has developed a methodology to estimate the price change as a consequence of a change in quantitative restrictions. It was applied to the textile industry in Sweden. According to this method, a price elasticity with respect to a change in a VER is formulated first:

$$\eta_v = -\frac{\Delta p}{\Delta \ VER} \cdot \frac{VER}{p} \qquad (x)$$

where: η_v = price elasticity with respect to a change in the VER

VER = volume of voluntary export restraint

p = price

It shows the decrease (increase) in price when the quantity supplied by the foreign country under a VER increases (decreases). η_v can be expressed in terms of supply, demand and corresponding elasticities, whose values are taken in relation to the size of the internal and external markets considered. The size of the markets is determined by the substitution possibilities in the export markets and the substitution possibilities for domestic products (24). Hamilton distinguishes four combinations and works out two of them. First he assumes the product to be a perfect substitute in export markets and a perfect substitute for domestic products. To assess the price change, both total world demand and world supply are taken into account. Secondly, he introduces a case where the product is a non-substitute in export markets and a perfect substitute for domestic products. In this case -- to assess the price change -- the quantities supplied by foreign VER countries and domestic suppliers as well as total demand in Sweden are taken into account. The logic is clear: depending on both the internal and external substitution possibilities, the size of the market -- and thus supply and demand relevant for the price change -- are determined.

Hamilton's second case comes very near to the situation in the automobile industry. As a consequence of type-approval regulations, passenger cars destined for one market cannot easily be transferred to another market. So the assumption of non-substitution in export markets appears plausible. Once inside a country, all cars have to comply with the same technical regulations, which implies that the assumption of substitution for domestic products appears plausible. The price elasticity with respect to a change in the VER can be expressed as (25):

$$\eta_v = \frac{1}{\dfrac{Q^s}{VER} \cdot \varepsilon + \dfrac{Q^s + VER}{VER} \cdot \eta} \qquad (xi)$$

Elasticity η_v and consequently $\Delta p/p$ [see (x)] will be relatively large if producers have difficulty in quickly increasing their output (ε is small) and if consumers are insensitive to price changes (η is small). Also if the country under VER is large, the impact on η_v of relaxing a VER will be relatively large. It should be noted that in this analysis the maximum impact of a change in VERs on the price of a domestically produced commodity is assessed to arrive at upper-limit estimates of the price effect and the employment effect.

In order to estimate the benefits and costs of abolishing the present EC trade restrictions -- that is, the EC customs duty, VERs and quotas -- in the automobile sector, the following sets of calculations will be presented. Costs and benefits of abolishing the EC customs duty in Germany, France, the Netherlands, Italy and the United Kingdom will be computed with the set of formulae presented in section III. A. (for countries with a domestic automobile industry). The same set -- slightly modified -- will be applied in the case of abolishment of the VERs/quotas in France, Italy and the United Kingdom. The set of formulae to evaluate the consequences of the abolishment

125

of the EC customs duty in Belgium/Luxembourg, Ireland and Denmark, countries without a domestic automobile industry, is presented at the end of section III. A.

The final results will depend to a large extent on assumptions regarding elasticities, productivity and tariff absorption of foreign producers. These main assumptions will be discussed at length in the following three sections. Section III. D. contains a note on the data used.

C. Main assumptions

Divergence in costs of purchasing and operating a passenger car, temporal shifts, special country situations (income levels, interest rates, used car market, replacement market, etc.) have led to wide differences in estimates for price elasticities of demand:

"For example, we see the following price elasticity estimates for the United States: -1.31 (Atkinson 1950), -1.0 (Suits, 1958), -0.1 to -1.8 (Wykoff, 1968) and -0.8 to -2.4 (Carlson, 1976); for the United Kingdom: -1.5 (Department of Industry, 1979) and -1 to -3 (Rhys, 1979); for France: -0.45 (quoted by Feeney and Tanner, 1980); for Australia: -0.3 (IAC, 1980)" (26).

Differences in estimates can also be attributed to different methodologies adopted in various studies. Because for most countries estimates for price elasticities are not available, and in order to employ a consistent methodology for all countries concerned, the following procedure is chosen to estimate price elasticities.

In a number of studies (27) estimating costs and benefits of trade barriers, price elasticities of domestic demand (η) and supply (ε) are derived from the price elasticity of import demand (η_m), because there exists a relationship between the price elasticity of import demand on the one hand and the price elasticities of domestic supply and demand on the other.

$$\eta_m = \eta \frac{Q^d}{Q^m} + \varepsilon \frac{Q^s}{Q^m} \qquad (xii)$$

Price elasticities of import demand are generally estimated with the help of trade statistics. Next, an assumption is made for the relationship between the price elasticities for domestic demand and supply, and the other two elasticities can be computed. Within the limited context of this study, it was not possible to make our own estimate for the price elasticity of import demand for passenger cars. Evidence (28), however, suggests an elasticity between -1.5 and -2.5, so we shall calculate the results for three possible values: -1.5, -2.0 and -2.5. As for the relationship between the price elasticities of domestic demand and supply, in general one may expect the first to be smaller than the second because it seems likely that there are greater substitution possibilities in production than in consumption. For Germany, for instance, it was found that as a consequence of the cut in tariffs in the 1950s, the increased imports resulted primarily in the contraction of domestic production rather than to an increase in consumption (29).

Therefore, following Magee and Fels (30), we assume the price elasticity of domestic demand to be half the price elasticity of domestic supply. After some manipulations (31) with (xii), the price elasticity of domestic supply can be expressed as:

$$\varepsilon = \frac{\eta_m}{1 - 1.5 \dfrac{Q^d}{Q^m}} \qquad \text{(xiii)}$$

where the price elasticity of domestic demand was assumed to be:

$$\eta = -0.5 \, \varepsilon \qquad \text{(xiv)}$$

Price elasticities of domestic demand and supply are higher if the price elasticity of import demand is higher. They will also be higher if imports are substantial compared to total demand.

Because $\eta = -0.5 \, \varepsilon$ is a rather straightforward assumption, computations will also be made assuming the price elasticity of demand to be equal to domestic supply. In that case the two price elasticities can be written as:

$$\varepsilon = \frac{\eta_m}{1 - 2 \dfrac{Q^d}{Q^m}} \qquad \text{(xv)}$$

and

$$\eta = - \varepsilon \qquad \text{(xvi)}$$

Summarising: Computations will be made for three different values of the price elasticity of import demand, each value combined with two different assumptions regarding the relationship between the price elasticities of domestic demand and supply. The results are presented in Table 3.

Table 3

PRICE ELASTICITIES FOR DOMESTIC DEMAND AND SUPPLY

| | $\eta_m = -1.5$ | | | | $\eta_m = -2.0$ | | | | $\eta_m = -2.5$ | | | |
| | $\eta = -0.5\varepsilon$ | | $\eta = -\varepsilon$ | | $\eta = -0.5\varepsilon$ | | $\eta = -\varepsilon$ | | $\eta = 0.5\varepsilon$ | | $\eta = -\varepsilon$ | |
	ε	η	ε	η	ε	η	ε	η	ε	η	ε	η
Germany	0.30	-0.15	0.22	-0.22	0.41	-0.20	0.29	-0.29	0.51	-0.25	0.36	-0.36
France	0.33	-0.17	0.24	-0.24	0.45	-0.22	0.32	-0.32	0.56	-0.28	0.40	-0.40
Netherlands	2.74	-1.37	1.40	-1.40	3.65	-1.82	1.90	-1.90	4.56	-2.28	2.30	-2.30
Italy	0.56	-0.28	0.38	-0.38	0.75	-0.37	0.51	-0.51	0.93	-0.47	0.64	-0.64
United Kingdom	0.88	-0.44	0.58	-0.58	1.17	-0.59	0.77	-0.77	1.47	-0.73	0.96	-0.96
EC (9)	0.60	-0.30	0.41	-0.41	0.80	-0.40	0.55	-0.55	1.00	-0.50	0.68	-0.68

Source: Own calculations based on data from the Verband der Automobil-industrie E.V.

These elasticity values are an important contribution to the rest of the study. As was to be expected, it shows that for those countries where imports are relatively more substantial -- Italy, the United Kingdom and, on the extreme end, the Netherlands -- elasticity values are higher.

Liberalisation of imports will generally lead to a decrease in production and, consequently, to a (temporary) redundancy of factors of production. We shall restrict ourselves in this analysis to the employment consequences. To what extent the employment loss will be affected is important, in order to assess the cost of adjustment. Straightforward data on the average productivity -- let alone the marginal productivity -- in the automobile industry in Europe are not available. American sources (32) suggest that about 200 hours are required per subcompact car: 60 hours directly in the automobile manufacturing company; 140 hours are provided indirectly by suppliers. Given an average of 1 700 working hours per year in the American automobile industry, this would result in an average productivity of about 8.5 subcompact cars per man per year for the whole sector. For Europe, similar detailed studies are not available. That leaves us with company reports and sectoral statistics on production and employment. However, data from company reports fail on at least two points. First, data to correct the product-mix is generally not given. Second, data to estimate the contribution of suppliers is also generally not presented. The first point is important in those cases where the production of commercial vehicles makes a substantial part of total production. The second point is important because information on the contribution of suppliers is needed to estimate total direct and indirect employment effects in case of trade liberalisation. This leaves everything but the sector statistics to make an estimate for productivity. Using NACE (Nomenclature générale des activités économiques dans les communautés européennes) 35 -- manufacture of motor vehicles and of motor vehicle parts -- the whole sector including suppliers is taken into account (33). In order to correct for the product-mix, the production statistics are corrected for the production of commercial vehicles assuming that the average labour input of a commercial vehicle is a factor 1.25 higher than the average labour input for a passenger car (34). Results are presented in Table 4.

Table 4

AVERAGE NUMBER OF PASSENGER CARS PER EMPLOYEE PER YEAR (CORRECTED FOR COMMERCIAL VEHICLES) (NACE 35) FOR 1974-1982

	Germany	France	Netherlands	Italy	United Kingdom
1974	4.99	7.64	3.74	7.13	4.09
1975	5.50	6.58	3.41	6.13	3.65
1976	6.70	7.57	4.17	6.74	4.01
1977	6.75	7.42	3.11	7.03	3.90
1978	6.59	7.38	3.48	7.24	3.67
1979	6.43	7.65	4.51	6.91	3.52
1980	5.73	7.29	4.12	6.34	3.28
1981	5.93	6.93	3.83	6.15	3.39
1982	6.21	7.47	4.62	6.89	3.82

Source: Own calculations based on data from Eurostat and Verband der Automobilindustrie E.V.

In the case of Germany and the United Kingdom, figures are biased due to the product-mix in these countries. Within the passenger car segment of the automobile industry, differences are made (35) between volume producers, who usually cover the whole model range from extra-small, small, light, medium and large passenger cars, and specialist producers such as BMW, Rolls Royce, Daimler-Benz, Porsche, etc. The interest of specialist producers in trade barriers is likely to be far less than the interest of volume producers, because Japanese producers compete mainly in the volume segment of the market. Specialist passenger cars generally require more labour per car than volume cars. Thus in the cases of Germany and the United Kingdom -- producing relatively more specialist cars -- the average number of passenger cars per employee is influenced negatively due to this product-mix.

At first sight results do not meet the expectation of a moderate and stable growth in productivity. This is probably due to the relatively short period considered. An American study (36) analysing statistics for domestic output and domestic employment of the Ford Motor Company for 1976-1980 found that much of the employment associated with automobile manufacturing does not vary directly with output and that much of the automobile industry employment would not change with normal fluctuations in output. Therefore, to arrive at an estimate for average productivity in 1985, we will use the long-term rate of productivity growth in the U.S. automobile industry of 3.3 per cent (37). Using 1978 -- a record world production year -- as a base year yields the following results: Germany: 8.27; France: 9.26; Netherlands: 4.37; Italy: 9.09; the United Kingdom: 4.61. The long-term growth rate may appear to be rather conservative because with the massive investment programmes in the automobile industry being initiated or being announced for the 1980s, productivity may rise well above its historical growth rate.

Determining the impact on car prices of liberalisation is crucial for the analysis, because it determines consumer behaviour and, consequently, sales and (thus) employment. In general it is correct to say that regarding the pricing policy of car manufacturers in Western Europe in those markets where national car manufacturers are in a dominant position (Germany, France, Italy and the United Kingdom), importers tend to follow the price movement of domestic producers (38). For the United Kingdom, for instance, it is concluded that the basic structure of car prices is determined by the dominant firms in the market (British Leyland and Ford) (39). In those markets where national car manufacturers are not in a dominant position, foreign producers will adapt to the behaviour of the leading competitor. In other words, the price policy of car manufacturers depends on market considerations rather than on considerations of cost structure, transport costs, tariffs, etc. To put it in extreme terms, it is even possible that the tariff is completely borne by foreign producers and does not have an impact on the consumer price. In the case of Japanese producers, for instance, the lower production costs enable them to overcome the 10.4 per cent tariff barrier without a problem (40). Following this line of reasoning to the extreme means that an abolishment of the EC customs duty will only imply a loss of tariff revenues (apart from a decrease in cost for Japanese producers). On the other hand, however, the existence of a tariff offers domestic producers the opportunity to raise their prices with the tariff percentage. Foreign producers will follow, passing on -- in this indirect way -- the customs duty. As real insight into the pricing policy is lacking, it is assumed that half of the tariff will be borne by foreign producers when calculating the effects of the abolishment of the EC customs duty.

This assumption does not hold in the case of an abolishment of VERs because in that case, sales of Japanese cars change not marginally but considerably. Therefore, the assumption concerned needs to be adapted. For this reason it is assumed that in that case, Japanese car manufacturers will play a far more prominent role in the process of price formation. The other manufacturers will adjust to the prices of the Japanese competitors, resulting in a general decrease in the price level for passenger cars proportional to the price change due to the abolishment of the VERs.

D. Note on data used

Data on new registrations of passenger cars (including station-wagons) -- split up into countries of origin -- from the Verband der Automobilindustrie E.V. in Germany are the point of departure for the empirical measurement of the costs and benefits from trade liberalisation. These statistics are chosen as a starting point above production and trade statistics for the following reasons. Statistics on new registrations of passenger cars use a definition of countries of origin conforming to common opinion of what is to be called a "German" or "Italian" car. Though there exist a lot of production and assembling activities in, for instance, Belgium (in 1982 Belgium produced more than 246 000 passenger cars but it exported almost 966 000 passenger cars due to assembling activities), "Belgian" cars are never heard of (41). Unfortunately this implies that all production and assembling activities outside the well-known car-producing EC countries are neglected and, consequently, that production in the car-producing EC countries is over-stated. Production and trade statistics provide an inadequate picture of the spatial spread of production and assembling activities in the European auto-mobile industry, so data are insufficient to correct for assembling activi-ties. The choice for new registrations of passenger cars implies that analyses are started from the demand side and that one neglects the building up of stocks. Total demand is equal to total new registrations in a certain year. Total domestic supply is equal to the domestically produced cars sold in the national market. Imports make for the balance. Initially, all com-putations are carried out in volume. Data on total demand, domestic supply and imports in order to calculate elasticities, market shares, price change due to VERs, etc. are based on a three-year average (1980-1982); average duration of unemployment is based on the 1981 situation and, with respect to the social security benefits, the situation of 1st July 1982 is taken. Computations will be made for 1985 using automobile demand projections from the OECD. In order to arrive at results in value terms in the case of tariffs, volumes are multiplied by the average import price (c.i.f.) in 1982 of imports subject to a tariff; in the case of quantitative restrictions, volumes are multiplied by the average import price (c.i.f.) in 1982. Conse-quently, the resulting values will be at 1982 prices. It should be noted that the difference between average prices net of tax and average import prices (c.i.f.) is estimated to vary between 30 and 50 per cent (42). The analysis will begin by country. Greece is not included because of lack of data.

IV. RESULTS

A. EC customs duty

In this section static welfare gains and losses when abolishing the EC customs duty for passenger cars are estimated. The analysis is based on the projected 1985 demand for passenger cars (43) and a tariff of 10.4 per cent (44); the values concerned are in 1982 U.S. dollars. Table 5 presents the share of total imports subject to the customs duty.

Table 5

SHARE OF TOTAL IMPORTS SUBJECT TO EC CUSTOMS DUTY (%) (a)

Germany	France	Netherlands	Italy (b)	United Kingdom	Belg./ Lux.	Ireland	Denmark	EC(9)
42.5	15.0	28.5	1.1	24.5	28.7	29.6	39.7	92.1

a. Based on three-year average (1980-1982). Because data on new registra-tions of passenger cars show a negligible number of "Spanish" cars, passenger cars of Spanish origin have been neglected.

b. Based on 1980 and 1981.

Source: Own calculation based on data from Verband der Automobilindustrie E.V.

In general, imports subject to the tariff vary between 20 and 30 per cent. Exceptions are: Germany, due to considerable imports from Japan; Denmark, due to substantial imports from Japan, Sweden and Eastern Europe; France, due to the VER imposed on Japan; and Italy, due to a quota regarding Japan. More than 92 per cent of total extra-EC imports are subject to the EC customs duty. As a consequence, the estimated change in price of the abolishment of the tariff very much depends on the share of the imports concerned and on the assumption that foreign car manufacturers bear half the tariff costs (see section III. C.). Table 6 presents the price decrease for the EC and its member countries as a consequence of the abolishment of the tariff.

Table 6

PRICE DECREASE AS A CONSEQUENCE OF THE ABOLISHMENT OF THE EC CUSTOMS DUTY
OF 10.4 % (%) (a)

Germany	France	Netherlands	Italy	United Kingdom	Belg./ Lux.	Ireland	Denmark	EC(9)
2.2	0.8	1.5	0.1	1.3	1.5	1.5	2.1	1.3

a.   For the individual countries estimated with: t x r x relevant import share; for the EC: a weighted average of the EC countries.

Except for Germany and Denmark, the estimated change in the domestic price level of passenger cars is not impressive.

Table 7 presents costs and benefits as a consequence of the abolishment of the EC customs duty. Results are shown for the case of a price elasticity of import demand of -2.0 and where the price elasticity of domestic demand is assumed to be half the price elasticity of domestic supply.

The increase in consumer surplus and the net welfare gain are both annual. Though the increase in consumer surplus for the EC is almost $500 million, the net welfare gain is negative and amounts to more than $-134 million. This is largely due to the assumption that the foreign car manufacturers bear half the tariff costs and consequently that in case of an abolishment of the customs duty these revenues are lost. The number of jobs protected in the EC car industry due to the customs duty is over 8 000 man-years. In the cases of Germany and the United Kingdom, results are biased due to the share of specialist cars in the product-mix. Assuming that workers remain unemployed for an average of between 6.4 months in Germany and 8.4 months in Italy, and given the social security benefits in the various EC countries, the adjustment costs amount to $29.5 million. Consumer surplus, net welfare gain and adjustment costs may vary for each country, due to the share of imports subject to the tariff (see Table 5). The main conclusion that can be drawn from Table 7 is that both redistribution effects and costs dominate the relatively small welfare gain from liberalisation.

Table 7

COSTS AND BENEFITS OF REMOVING THE EC CUSTOMS DUTY IN 1985 [IN MILLIONS OF 1982 U.S. DOLLARS (a)]

	Germany	France	Netherlands	Italy	UK	Belg./Lux.	Ireland	Denmark	EC(9)(b)
(1) Dead-weight Gains (annual)	4.7	1.3	2.4	0.1	4.5	2.1	0.5	0.7	21.0
efficiency gain	2.8	0.7	0.1	0.1	2.1				13.5
consumer gain	1.9	0.5	2.2	0.1	2.4				7.5
(2) Redistribution (annual)									
from domestic producers	131.6	33.0	0.6	1.6	32.3	19.9	4.3	6.3	310.0
from government	45.5	12.7	22.6	1.1	42.9				155.2
(3) Increase in Consumer Surplus (annual) (1) + (2)	181.8	47.0	25.6	2.8	79.7	22.0	4.8	7.0	486.2
(4) Costs (annual) Loss of income from foreign producers	45.5	12.7	22.6	1.1	42.9	19.9	4.3	6.3	155.2
(5) Net Welfare Gain (annual) [(1)-(4)]	-40.8	-11.4	-20.2	-1.0	-38.4	-17.8	-3.8	-5.6	-134.2
(6) Adjustment Costs (x 1 000)									
man-years	2.0	0.6	0.2	0.0	2.4				8.1
costs (c)	9.6	3.7	1.4	0.1	4.0				29.5

a. In order to arrive at the estimates in U.S. dollars, the set of formulae presented in section III. A. is multiplied by the average import price (c.i.f.) of relevant imports. As a consequence, taxes, wholesale and retail margins are not included, so in this respect the values in this table are underestimated (see also section III. D.)

b. Total sum of individual EC countries does not equal total EC (last column) because of different assumptions regarding total supply (for total EC: inclusive intra-trade) and imports (for total EC: only extra-EC imports). In other words, total EC supply consists of the sum of individual country supplies plus intra-trade.

c. Based on average duration of unemployment and social security benefits in the various EC countries.

Source: Own calculations based on data from: Verband der Automobilindustrie E.V.; Eurostat.

Except for the dead-weight gains and the adjustment costs, the results are practically the same for those alternatives where different assumptions regarding the elasticities are employed. In the case of a price elasticity of import demand of -1.5, and if the price elasticity of domestic demand is assumed to be equal to the price elasticity of domestic supply, dead-weight gains and adjustment costs are 50 per cent lower. In the case of a price elasticity of import demand of -2.5, and if the price elasticity of domestic demand is assumed to be half the price elasticity of domestic supply, results are 25 per cent higher for the EC.

The aforementioned results should not lead to the general conclusion that tariffs contribute to the welfare of a country under all circumstances. The specific situation in the automobile industry, reflected in the assumption that half the tariff is borne by foreign producers (r = 0.5), is responsible for these results. Different assumptions in this respect lead to entirely different welfare effects.

In the case of abolishment of the tariff -- and foreign producers bear the complete tariff cost -- the net welfare loss amounts to $310 million; in the case of abolishment of the tariff -- and consumers bear the tariff costs -- the welfare gain is $42 million.

B. Quantitative trade restrictions

In this section static welfare gains and losses are presented in the case of removal of the VERs in France and the United Kingdom and of the quota in Italy regarding passenger car imports from Japan. The abolishment of these quantitative restrictions will have effects on sales, prices and employment. In order to assess the magnitude of these effects, one needs to make an estimate of the market share of Japanese passenger cars in the case of no quantitative restrictions in the countries concerned. In this respect, sales of Japanese passenger cars in other EC countries with a more liberal trade regime may give a good indication. Table 8 presents Japanese penetration into the passenger car market in the various EC countries.

Table 8

JAPANESE PENETRATION INTO THE EC CAR MARKET (3-YEAR AVERAGE, 1980-1982) (%)

Germany	France	Netherlands	Italy	UK	Belg./Lux.	Ireland	Denmark
10.1	2.8	24.5	0.1	11.3	23.0	29.4	26.7

Source: Own calculations based on data from Verband der Automobilindustrie E.V. and l'Argus de l'automobile (for Italy 1982).

It clearly shows the impact of the quantitative restrictions in Italy and France: comparing the figures for Italy and France with those for the other EC countries leads to the conclusion that Japan would certainly have conquered a larger share of the car market without quantitative restrictions in Italy and France.

What would the market shares of Japan have been without restrictions? Table 8 shows that the upper limit of penetration is about 25 per cent. As a lower limit one may take the penetration ratio of Germany, being a country which, like the other countries concerned, has a national car industry, but is different with respect to trade policy. In fact, Germany is known for a more liberal trade regime. We assume that for Italy, France and the United Kingdom, the lower limit in the case of no quantitative restrictions would be at least equal to 10 per cent. So the possible market shares of Japanese cars are situated between 10 per cent and 25 per cent. In an article in the Financial Times, "Japanese Car Exports: The Brakes Stay On" (45), it is estimated that the Japanese would have captured 10 per cent of the French market, 15 per cent of the Italian market and 20 per cent of the British market without quantitative restrictions. Application of these upper-limit market shares to total demand in 1985 (46) yields the number of Japanese cars sold in the case of no quantitative trade restrictions. Table 9 presents sales of Japanese cars in both situations, with and without quantitative restrictions, for the three EC countries concerned.

Table 9

ESTIMATES OF JAPANESE CAR SALES WITH AND WITHOUT QUANTITATIVE
RESTRICTIONS IN 1985 (x 1000)

	With Quantitative Restrictions	Without Quantitative Restrictions	Difference
France	57.8	206.6	148.8
Italy	1.8	229.6	227.8
United Kindgom	185.7	327.8	143.1

Assuming that the total spending on new cars remains the same, the increased spending on Japanese cars results in an identical decrease in spending on non-Japanese cars. So far, price changes have been neglected. However, as imports of Japanese cars strongly increase in France, Italy and the United Kingdom, competition will increase in those countries. This will have its impact on prices and car sales.

A price elasticity with respect to a change in a VER is used to estimate the price changes as a consequence of trade liberalisation in the three EC countries. This procedure is described in section III. B. Here we present only the resulting price changes. Computations are made again with the aid of three values of the price elasticity of import demand, each combined with different assumptions regarding the relationship between the price elasticities of domestic supply and demand. Results are presented in Table 10.

Table 10

ESTIMATED PRICE DECREASES IN CASE OF AN ABOLISHMENT OF QUANTITATIVE TRADE
RESTRICTIONS IN FRANCE, ITALY AND THE UNITED KINGDOM (%)

	$\eta_m = -1.5$		$\eta_m = -2.0$		$\eta_m = -2.5$	
	$\eta = -0.5\epsilon$	$\eta = -\epsilon$	$\eta = -0.5\epsilon$	$\eta = -\epsilon$	$\eta = -0.5\epsilon$	$\eta = -\epsilon$
France	19.5	20.5	14.6	15.3	11.7	12.3
Italy	29.9	32.7	22.4	24.5	17.9	19.6
United Kingdom	13.7	15.1	10.3	11.3	8.2	9.1

The estimated price decrease varies between 18 and 33 per cent for Italy, between 12 and 23 per cent for France and between 8 and 15 per cent for the United Kingdom.

As indicated in section III. B. it will be assumed -- in contrast to the case of abolishing the EC customs duty -- that the estimated price decrease will lead to a proportional change in the domestic price level for passenger cars because of the magnitude of the volume changes due to trade liberalisation. Subsequently, Table 11 presents the costs and benefits of abolishing quantitative restrictions. Results are shown for the case of a price elasticity of import demand of -2.0, where the price elasticity of domestic demand is assumed to be half the price elasticity of domestic supply. The corresponding changes in the domestic price level for passenger cars are (see Table 10): for France -14.6; for Italy, -22.4; and for the United Kingdom, -10.3. It should be noted that throughout the whole analysis we compute the costs and benefits of the maximum price decrease.

The resulting increase in consumer surplus is large; where the increase in consumer surplus due to abolishing the customs duty hardly amounts to $0.5 billion for the EC, the increase in consumer surplus due to abolishing quantitative restrictions for Italy alone is more than $1.5 billion. The net welfare gain for France, Italy and the United Kingdom is $364 million, $741 million and $551 million, respectively. Due to the price decrease, new consumers will enter the passenger car market; the estimates show that in France almost 5 000 extra cars will be sold, in Italy more than 14 000 and in the United Kingdom over 5 000. But the cost of liberalisation is also large: a decrease in employment of over 10 000 man-years in France, almost 17 000 man-years in Italy and 19 000 man-years in the United Kingdom. The high employment loss in the United Kingdom is due to the relatively low productivity in that country, which can be explained partly by the share of specialist cars in the product-mix. Total employment in the industry (NACE 35) will decrease by 2.4 per cent in France, 7.5 per cent in Italy and 6.0 per cent in the United Kingdom. This loss of employment, coupled with the estimated average duration of unemployment and social security benefits, results in a loss to society of almost $70 million in France, $50 million in Italy and $32 million in the United Kingdom. The social costs in the United Kingdom are relatively low, due to the low level of social security benefits. The main conclusion to be drawn from Table 11 is that the increase in consumer surplus and the net welfare gain are large, and by far exceed adjustment costs.

Table 11

COSTS AND BENEFITS OF ABOLISHING QUANTITATIVE RESTRICTIONS IN FRANCE,
ITALY AND THE UNITED KINGDOM IN 1985
(in millions of 1982 U.S. dollars)(a)

	France	Italy	United Kingdom
(1) Dead-weight Gains (annual)	46.5	136.0	51.3
efficiency gain	27.6	73.7	24.2
consumer gain	19.0	62.2	27.1
(2) Gain from Foreign Producers (annual)	318.2	606.4	500.0
(3) Redistribution from Domestic Producers (annual)	817.3	807.1	376.9
(4) Increase in Consumer Surplus (annual)[(1) + (2) + (3)]	1 182.0	1 549.4	927.8
(5) Net Welfare Gain (annual) [(1) + (2)]	364.7	742.4	551.3
(6) Adjustment Costs			
man-years (x 1 000)	10.6	16.7	19.1
costs (c)	69.6	50.2	31.9

For notes see Table 7.

Source: Own calculations based on data from: Verband der Automobilindustrie
E.V.;   Eurostat.

Summing up, it is estimated that the annual net welfare gains for the three
countries together amount to some $1.6 billion. Total adjustment costs are
estimated to be some $150 million. In addition it should be noted that both
the increase in consumer surplus and the net welfare gain are annual amounts.
In the most extreme cases, benefits may be 50 to 60 per cent higher or 20 per
cent lower.

C. Main conclusions and prospects

The main conclusions for the EC car industry are as follows:

Abolishing the EC customs duty:

a) Would in most countries lead to very small decreases in the price
   level for passenger cars;

b) Would in all countries lead to a welfare loss, because the tariff
   revenue loss is much higher than the small welfare gain from lower
   prices;

c) Would for the EC as a whole result in a loss of more than 8 000 man-years and consequent adjustment costs of $29.5 million.

These results are clearly related to the assumption regarding the pricing policy in the automobile industry and should not lead to the general conclusion that tariffs contribute to the welfare of a country.

Abolishing the VERs in France and the United Kingdom and the quota in Italy:

a) Would lead to a large decrease in the price level of passenger cars of 14.6 per cent, 22.4 per cent and 10.3 per cent in France, Italy and the United Kingdom respectively;

b) Would consequently yield a large increase in consumer surplus of, for example, $1 182 million in France, $1 549.4 million in Italy and $927.8 million in the United Kingdom, in turn leading to 5 000, 14 000 and 5 000 new passenger car consumers in France, Italy and the United Kingdom respectively;

c) Would give a large net welfare gain of $365 million in France, $742 million in Italy and $551 million in the United Kingdom;

d) Would reduce total car employment in France by 11 000 man-years, in Italy by 17 000 man-years and by 19 000 man-years in the United Kingdom, with consequent adjustment costs of, respectively, $69.6 million, $50.2 million and $31.9 million.

As mentioned in section II, there has been a revival of protectionism in North-South trade as well as in the trade relations among industrial countries since the mid-1970s. This also affected the car industry. Apart from the negative impact on world trade, affecting global welfare, protectionism also gives rise to direct costs. Protection in the form of subsidies is financed by means of tax revenues. In cases of protection leading to higher prices (tariffs, VERs, quotas), the costs are at the expense of the consumer. The present study estimates that the EC consumers would save over at least $4 billion annually in the case of liberalisation (abolishing EC customs duty and VERs, quotas). If direct and indirect government aids (see last paragraph of section II) -- financed by the consumer as a taxpayer -- are also taken into account, the annual savings for consumers would even be considerably larger.

The quantitative restrictions in France, Italy and the United Kingdom are responsible for the greater part of these costs for consumers. It appears that this is a very expensive policy for protecting the automobile industry. Prices are kept high artificially to protect the domestic car industry at the cost of the consumer interest; this leads to higher profits per unit of output for the supplier countries under VERs or quotas, in exchange for a reduction in the number of units sold. This explains why foreign governments and producers "voluntarily" accept import restraints, certainly in a situation where they can easily sell passenger cars elsewhere.

Such a large transfer of income is not necessary because other protective measures producing the same result are available. Alternatives to a VER or quota are: direct subsidies for the sector, tariffs or Article XIX of the

General Agreement on Tariffs and Trade (GATT) emergency protective action.   In the latter case:

"...the exporting country will find itself faced with a tariff on its exports or by formal quota restrictions on them with the quota rights going to importers (probably implicitly) rather than to exporters" (47).

A point that all these measures have in common is that there is no un-necessary transfer of income to foreign producers as in the case of the quantitative measures dealt with in this report.

Apart from the pre-EC quota in the case of Italy, the VERs in France and the United Kingdom have a limited character. According to the Committee of Common Market Automobile Constructors, protection for the EC automobile industry should last until the end of 1985 (48). Also in March 1984 the existing VER in the U.S. was renewed for only one year until March 1985. The case for this type of protectionism -- on a temporary basis -- is founded on the argument in both the EC and the U.S. that the automobile industry must be given a fair chance to compete with the Japanese producers in the future. If the VERs are temporary, the high costs for consumers are also temporary. But will the VERs really be temporary? This depends on the question of whether the U.S. and the EC car manufacturers will be able to respond to the Japanese competition when they are facing stagnating domestic markets, declining exports and pressure from Japanese car manufacturers. In this context it is interesting to consider the reasons for the Japanese successes.

The successful penetration of overseas markets by Japanese car manu-facturers is entirely based on higher productivity and exploitation of economies of scale (49). The Japanese automobile industry is a fairly young industry. Therefore, production lines reflect higher technological stand-ards. Robots, for instance, are used on an increasing scale, particularly for welding and painting jobs. Apart from capital expenditure to achieve higher productivity, this is also due to a number of management practices, including just-in-time inventory systems, defect-prevention systems, an organisation pyramid with many fewer tiers between workers and executives and non-antago-nistic union and supplier relations (50). A further advantage of Japanese car manufacturers centres around economies of scale. Japan specialises in large model runs with consequent cost advantages. Finally, the Japanese passenger cars are considered to be of good quality (51), often delivered with many accessories considered as standard. This short overview stresses once again that the Japanese have advantages over the EC and U.S. car manufacturers. Table 12 illustrates Japan's superior position.

Will temporary protection bridge the gap between EC and U.S. car manu-facturers on the one hand and the Japanese car manufacturers on the other? We cannot answer this question but we can sum up some considerations.   The future of car manufacturing will depend largely on an increasing inter-nationalisation and co-operation.   Within the EC, arrangements among car manufacturers already exist, ranging from research and development sharing to joint production of engines and joint marketing (52).

Further co-operation will be necessary because EC car manufacturers have not yet achieved the economies of scale necessary to compete as volume producers in the future. Automobile manufacturers in the U.S. have started the production process of the so called "world car".   These cars are

Table 12

INDICES OF AVERAGE WAGES AND SALARIES, AVERAGE PRODUCTIVITY AND AVERAGE
WAGES AND SALARIES PER UNIT OF OUTPUT IN THE AUTOMOBILE INDUSTRY (NACE 35) OF
MAIN PRODUCERS (a)

Average Wages and Salaries							
Italy	Ireland	United Kingdom	France	Japan	Belgium	U.S.(b)	Germany
47	59	62	66	71	75	92	100

Average Productivity							
United Kingdom	Belgium	Italy	Germany	France	Ireland	U.S.(b)	Japan
20	33	36	37	46	64	72	100

Average Wages and Salaries Per Unit of Output							
Japan	Ireland	U.S.(b)	Italy	France	Belgium	Germany	United Kingdom
23	30	37	42	47	76	88	100

a.   Five-year average, 1978-1982.
b.   Based on 1978 and 1979.

Source: Own calculations based on data from Verband der Automobilindustrie
E.V.

single-design and will be produced and sold world-wide. The "world car"
represents the ultimate in scale economies of design, component production,
assembling and servicing. In the U.S. there is also a growing tendency
towards "offshore sourcing", which means purchasing from foreign makers and in
this way benefiting from low labour costs and government aids elsewhere.
One-third to one-half of the engines in the cars produced in the U.S. are
purchased abroad (53). In this respect the growing importance of the components industry should be mentioned. Japan -- traditionally more export-
oriented on complete cars and meeting an increasing number of trade
barriers -- is seeking co-operation with domestic producers.

The automobile industry invests large sums in modernisation and automation of their product processes in order to remain competitive. Last year
investments of between $120-130 billion were initiated or announced. U.S. car
manufacturers account for $75 billion. EC car manufacturers will spend
$35 billion and Japan $11 billion (54). The progress made in the adaptation
of the manufacturing process will be a determining factor of competitiveness.
In this respect, chances look more favourable for the U.S. than for the EC.
Whether the EC car manufacturers will be able to compete in a more liberal
trade situation will largely depend on further co-operation between EC car
manufacturers in order to reach scale advantages and to increase productivity. It is likely that the jobs that are now protected by trade barriers

will, notwithstanding the present protection, still be lost due to large productivity increases and growing "offshore sourcing".

NOTES AND REFERENCES

1. C. Fred Bergsten and William R. Cline, Trade Policy in the 1980s, Policy Analyses in International Economics 3, Institute for International Economics, Washington, D.C., 1982, p. 16.

2. C. Fred Bergsten and William R. Cline, 1982, op. cit., p. 11.

3. Michael C. Munger, "The Costs of Protectionism", Challenge, Vol. 26, no. 6, January/February 1984, pp. 54-58.

4. This issue is considered in detail in the report by the OECD Committee on Consumer Policy.

5. See Robert B. Cohen, "The Prospects for Trade and Protectionism in the Auto Industry", in William R. Cline (ed.), Trade Policy in the 1980s, Institute for International Economics, Washington, D.C., 1983, ch. 16.

6. It should be noted that these figures are not based on data from family budget surveys, but from national accounts.

7. See in this respect also: G. Locksly, Pricing Strategy of Car Manufacturers in the UK Compared with Some Other EEC Member States, London, 1983.

8. OECD, Long Term Outlook for the World Automobile Industry, Paris, 1983.

9. OECD, op. cit., p. 23.

10. Idem, p. 35.

11. Commission of the European Communities, Concentration, Competition and Competitiveness in the Automobile Industries and in the Automotive Components Industries of the European Community, Luxembourg, 1983 (A), p. 49. See also: K. Bhaskar, The Future of the World Motor Industry, Kogan Page, London/Nichols Publishing Company, New York, 1980, pp. 180 to 181.

12. "Towards a World Auto Industry" in: OECD Observer, no. 123, July 1983, p. 10.

13. Commission of the European Communities, Commission Activities and EC Rules for the Automobile Industry 1981/1983, COM (83) 633 final, Brussels, 21 December 1983 (B), p. 18a; European Research Associates (ERA), EC Protectionism: Present Practice and Future Trends, volume 1, Brussels, June 1981, p. 147, suggesting that it is being blocked

notably by France because of fear of the Japanese being the first to benefit.

14. Bhaskar, op. cit., p. 134.

15. Ford, Bulletin No. 14, February 1984.

16. Commission of the European Communities, 1983 (B), op. cit., p. 37.

17. Euromarkt-Nieuws, February 1983, p. 34.

18. See for instance: David Greenaway, International Trade Policy: From Tariffs to the New Protectionism, MacMillan, London, 1983, pp. 46-52.

19. See for instance: BEUC, Report on Car Prices and on the Private Import of Cars in the EEC Countries, Brussels, 1982, p. 7, and Commission of the European Communities, 1983 (A), op. cit., describing the oligopolistic market structure of the automobile industry in the various EC countries.

20. See: Greenaway, op. cit., p. 103 and V. Cable, Protectionism and Industrial Decline, Hodder and Stoughton, London, 1983, p. 113.

21. Cable, op. cit., p. 115.

22. For ease of exposition we restrict ourselves in the text to VERs, though quotas are also meant.

23. Carl Hamilton, Effects of Non-Tariff Barriers to Trade on Prices, Employment and Imports: The Case of the Swedish Textile and Clothing Industry, World Bank Staff Working Paper no. 429 (revised), Washington, D.C., 1980.

24. Hamilton, op. cit., p. 10.

25. For the derivation see Hamilton, op. cit., p. 54.

26. OECD, op. cit., p. 17.

27. See for instance: Gerhard Fels and Hans-Heinrich Glismann, "Adjustment Policy in the German Manufacturing Sector" in: Adjustment for Trade, OECD, Paris, 1975, and Hamilton, op. cit.

28. Robert M. Stern, Jonathan Francis and Bruce Schumacher, Price Elasticities in International Trade, an Annotated Bibliography, MacMillan, London, 1976.

29. J. Wemelsfelder, "The Short-Term Effect of the Lowering of Import Duties in Germany" in: The Economic Journal, Volume LXX, Cambridge University Press, 1960, p. 97.

30. Stephen P. Magee, "The Welfare Effects of Restrictions on U.S. Trade", in: Brookings Papers on Economic Activity, 1972, p. 665; Fels, op. cit., p. 70.

31. See: Gerhard Fels, op. cit., p. 70.

32. Congressional Budget Office, The Fair Practices in Automotive Products Act (H.R. 5133): An Economic Assessment, August 1982, p. 43.

33. NACE 35 comprises: NACE 351 -- Manufacture and assembly of motor vehicles and motor vehicle engines; NACE 352 -- Manufacture of bodies for motor vehicles and of motor-drawn trailers and caravans; NACE 353 -- Manufacture of parts and accessories for motor vehicles. Jobs involved in distribution, retailing, financing and insuring passenger cars are not included.

34. C. Pratten and A. Silberston, "International Comparison of Labour Productivity in the Automobile Industry" in: Bulletin of the Oxford University Institute of Economics and Statistics, 1967, vol. 29, no. 4, p. 375.

35. Bhaskar, op. cit., pp. 20-21.

36. Congressional Budget Office, op. cit., p. 37.

37. Congressional Budget Office, op. cit., p. 9.

38. Possibly excepting passenger cars from Eastern Europe.

39. Locksly, op. cit., p. 78. See also section II. B. on the price policy of car manufacturers.

40. ERA, op. cit., p. 145.

41. See also: Bhaskar, op. cit., p. 133.

42. Based on comparison of average import prices (c.i.f.) and a weighted average net price -- see Locksly, op. cit., p. 46.

43. See Table 1.

44. See section II. B.

45. Financial Times, 6th October 1982.

46. OECD, op. cit., p. 35.

47. Brian Hindley, "Voluntary Export Restraints and the GATT's Main Escape Clause" in: The World Economy, Vol. 3, 1980, p. 321.

48. ERA, op. cit., p. 159; In a letter to the EC Commission of April 1981.

49. Commission of the European Communities (1983) (A), op. cit., p. 45.

50. Congressional Budget Office, op. cit., p. 31.

51. Commission of the European Communities, 1983 (A), op. cit., p. 48 and Robert B. Cohen, op. cit., p. 557.

52.   Commission of the European Communities, 1983 (A), op. cit., p. 56.

53.   Robert B. Cohen, op. cit., p. 546.

54.   Commission of the European Communities, 1983 (A), p. 56.

Part II: CONSUMER INTEREST IN TEXTILE AND CLOTHING POLICY

by

Teresa Smallbone
Bureau Européen des Unions de Consommateurs (BEUC);
Research Manager, Public Affairs, Consumers' Association, United Kingdom

I. INTRODUCTION

Consumers are the residual beneficiaries of the open trading system and, at one remove, active participants in it. As world trade expanded dramatically in the post-war era, consumers in the industrialised countries experienced rapidly rising living standards. These were reflected in the vast increase in the choice and type of goods available to them, which they sought to acquire. Many consumer organisations were founded or grew rapidly in the late 1950s and 1960s in response to a desire for independent (i.e., not beholden to government or producers) sources of information to guide consumers in making purchasing decisions.

With the slowing down of the expansion of world trade after 1973, and the gradual retreat into protectionism, consumers have become aware that the continued existence of such a range of choice is threatened, and that they are seldom a party to decisions that affect them. Consumer organisations have become aware that too often the voice of the producer is the one that is heard, and that the consumer voice is weak and diffuse compared with the power of entrenched producer lobbies. So on food and food products, cars, colour televisions, footwear, clothing and textiles, video tape recorders and cutlery, consumer organisations have become active in lobbying their governments and international organisations, trying to persuade them to take account of the consumer case when making decisions on trade policy that directly affect consumer welfare.

After food and food products, textiles and textile products are probably the most heavily affected by protectionist measures of all items in international trade, certainly of those that are of direct interest to consumers. This paper looks at some of the measures that restrict the textile and clothing trade from the consumer angle. It begins by looking at what consumers expect from the textile and clothing trade, and then at some of the restrictive measures themselves in greater detail. It goes on to look at how the costs and benefits of these measures to consumers might be assessed, with a look at a number of studies on this subject carried out in various countries.

II. WHAT DO CONSUMERS WANT FROM TEXTILES AND TEXTILE PRODUCTS?

Compared with developing countries and with the (in some cases) quite recent past, most consumers in developed countries are fairly well dressed and have an adequate number of clothes.

Consumer spending on clothing in developed countries has risen in the last twenty years by about the same amount as expenditure on all other products: by around four-and-a-half per cent a year in real terms from 1963 to 1973, and about two-and-a-half per cent a year since then (1). Some countries have experienced lower growth: in Australia, for instance, demand for clothing declined as a proportion of total private consumption after 1973 (2). In the EC other than the UK, consumer expenditure on clothing increased less rapidly than total consumer expenditure after 1973, and in the UK more rapidly. Overall, suffice it to say that the growth in consumer demand for clothing and hence textiles has been fairly unexciting in the developed countries in recent years, and that the potential for future growth in the clothing market lies in developing countries.

With increased affluence, the clothing market in developed countries has also become fragmented. Only the very rich and the very poor might be said to shop exclusively at one end of the market, and even they might occasionally meet in one of the chain stores. Most consumers move up and down the ranges of price and quality when making their purchase decisions, many of which are taken in the context of the intended use of the garment. Cheaper merchandise of inferior quality may be all right for everyday clothes for both children and adults (3). More expensive, better-quality garments are almost always favoured for "best" or important occasions, or if it is intended that they should last a long time. Decisions as to what to purchase are complex and involve sophisticated trade-offs. At different times consumers will be looking for different combinations of quality, high fashion, durability, cheapness, conformity and so on. Thus clothing markets in the developed countries currently offer consumers a large variety of choice and price. Consumers with low incomes are able to exercise this choice only at one end of the market, while for the majority, purchases will be made at both the cheap and expensive ends of the market. The degree of substitution between the cheapest and most expensive ends is likely to be small, and influenced less by small price variations than by substantial changes in consumers' disposable incomes.

There is some evidence that price is by no means the most important consideration when making purchases for most consumers. Asked to nominate the most important considerations in choosing textiles, clothing and footwear, UK consumers in the National Consumer Council (NCC) study already cited mentioned appearance, style and fitting as the most important factors. A national sample survey of 1 733 adults who had recently bought textiles or clothing were asked to choose which of the nine following factors had most influenced their decision. More than one answer was possible and the results are summarised in Table 1.

Table 1

size/fitting	88 %
material/fibre content	75 %
price	70 %
washing/cleaning instructions	48 %
previous experience	48 %
brand name	35 %
country where made	21 %
recommendations from friends	8 %
independent reports	4 %

Source: National Consumer Council, op. cit.

Most trade restrictions such as the Multifibre Arrangement (MFA) (of which more later) have been based on the assumption that product categories (114 in the current MFA) are homogeneous, and that within these categories consumers buy the cheapest products available, regardless of origin, quality or composition. As far as these measures are concerned, a shirt is a shirt no matter what it is made of or how it is made. Since most trade restrictions do not take account of the sophistication of consumer purchasing decisions or the range of products on the market, their effect is clumsy and arbitrary. Most are directed at restricting imports from one source (low-cost countries) on the assumption that these produce low-cost products. Thus they aim to tax the cheap segment of the market only; the effects are not always what are predicted, and they may be the opposite of what is intended.

III. TRADE RESTRICTIONS ON TEXTILES AND TEXTILE PRODUCTS

Trade restrictions on textiles and textile products fall broadly into two categories: tariffs and non-tariff measures.

A. Tariffs

Tariffs are taxes levied on imports. They are collected by governments and form part of their revenue. In some countries where incomes are very low, taxes on imports may form a major part of government revenue. In developed countries they are generally much less important for their revenue-raising effect, but are used to raise the prices of imported goods vis-à-vis home-produced items. Though tariffs on manufactured goods in developed countries are generally low as a result of the various tariff-cutting rounds under the General Agreement on Tariffs and Trade (GATT), those on textiles and clothing have remained high. What is more, they tend to rise with the level of processing, so finished goods tend to carry the highest tariffs.

There are various problems with comparing countries' tariffs, which I do not propose to go into. The data presented here, taken from the GATT report, should be regarded as indicative only. Table 2 shows the post-Tokyo Round tariff figures, even though some of these have not yet been fully implemented.

Table 2

POST-TOKYO ROUND TARIFFS IN EIGHT DEVELOPED AREAS

	U.S.	CANADA	JAPAN	EC
Textiles (excl. fibres) & clothing				
weighted average (a)	19	21 1/2	11 1/2	11 1/2
simple average	10 1/2	14 1/2	10 1/2	10 1/2
Manufactures (excl. petroleum)				
weighted average (a)	5	8 1/2	5 1/2	6
simple average	6 1/2	7 1/2	6 1/2	6 1/2
	AUSTRIA	FINLAND	SWEDEN	SWITZERLAND
Textiles (excl. fibres) & clothing				
weighted average (a)	30	29	12 1/2	8 1/2
simple average	18 1/2	30	12	6 1/2
Manufactures (excl. petroleum)				
weighted average (a)	12 1/2	6	4 1/2	2 1/2
simple average	8 1/2	12	5	3

a.   Weighted by MFA imports.

Source: GATT report, op. cit., p. 67.

Table 2 shows that the tariffs on manufactured goods in these developed countries are only one-half to one-third of those on textiles and clothing.

The developing countries also levy tariffs, but their practices vary greatly. At one extreme, Hong Kong and Macao have no tariffs or quantity restrictions, and Singapore has none on textiles but a low tariff on cloth-ing. At the other extreme, five countries (Brazil, India, Pakistan, Tunisia and Turkey) have absolute prohibitions on the import of a wide range of tex-tile and clothing products.

The cost of tariffs is borne by consumers as a straight tax on imported goods. They form the main barrier to trade in textiles and clothing products between developed countries, though customs unions and free trade agreements mean that most trade in textiles and clothing between Western European coun-tries is tariff-free. Some calculation of the costs to consumers of tariffs is included in the later section on costs of protection.

B. Non-tariff measures

The 1982 GATT Ministerial meeting launched an examination by GATT of quantitative restrictions and other non-tariff measures operated by its con-tracting parties, and the GATT secretariat has been compiling an inventory of these. In the industrial sector they distinguish five categories of such measures (4):

1. State participation in trade and restrictive practices tolerated by governments, such as state aids, government procurement and counter-vailing duties;

2. Customs and administrative formalities that affect imports, such as customs valuation rules, rules of origin, anti-dumping duties, documents and consular formalities, etc.;

3. Technical barriers to trade, e.g. standards;

4. Specific limitations such as quotas, prohibitions, exchange control supply agreements that discriminate against other sources, price-control measures on the domestic market, export restrictions, etc.;

5. Import charges -- border taxes, surcharges, prior deposits, etc.

Consumers' interests are affected by such measures, but consumer organisations are rarely consulted when such measures are proposed or enacted. Nor are the effects of such measures on consumers or the industries they are trying to protect calculated in any systematic or coherent fashion. Trade in textiles and textile products is affected by non-tariff barriers which fall under each of the GATT's categories. One category of measures on which consumers are consulted, and which fall under Category 2, are those which are introduced in the name of protecting consumers from such perils as "T-shirts, origin unknown", or garments with an imprecisely named fibre content. Consumer organisations spend a lot of time commenting on such proposals. It is instructive to examine them in a little more detail if only to heighten the contrast between these and things deemed not to be of consumer concern.

Origin marking

Consumers are not excessively concerned about the origin of most of the goods they purchase, as the very limited success of national "Achetez Francais" and "Buy British/Irish/American" campaigns has shown. When they associate country of origin with quality, such information is deemed more useful. For instance, the NCC survey found that British consumers in 1979 associated Japanese goods with high quality when buying certain electrical goods. In the NCC survey, some of whose findings have been given above, the same 1 733 people who had recently bought a clothing or textile item were asked to rank which four of a number of pieces of information were most important to them. The first item mentioned was recorded separately:

Table 3

MOST IMPORTANT ITEM OF INFORMATION

	Rank
size/fitting	1
washing/cleaning instructions	2
price	3
material	4
brand name	5
country where made	6

Source: National Consumer Council, op. cit.

The NCC's recommendation was: "It is our view, therefore, that further legislation about origin marking should be given no greater priority, so far as consumers' interests are concerned, than other types of information labelling which may be more directly valuable to consumers" (5).

This lack of enthusiasm did not deter the UK Government which, in 1981, despite consumer representations that such a measure was unwanted and could constitute a trade barrier, introduced compulsory origin marking on four categories of goods in the Trade Descriptions (Origin Marking) (Miscellaneous Goods) Order 1981. The goods chosen were most textiles (including floor-coverings), clothing, footwear, cutlery and domestic electrical appliances. These are all products where UK manufacturers face intensified overseas competition, and were actively lobbying for protection. Other EC countries have since followed suit. In an effort to prevent these schemes forming an internal trade barrier, the Commission has now proposed a Regulation (6) which would lay down Community rules on this subject.

Consumers in the EC now have compulsory origin labelling of textiles and clothing in some member states (with the prospect of harmonization to all) which is the aspect of clothing in which the NCC survey showed they are least interested. This bit of consumer "protection" should really be seen as protectionism rather than protection.

Fibre content labelling

This is of more practical use to consumers as it gives them an indication of what textile products are made from and hence an indication of quality and durability, and may help with washing or cleaning. Unfortunately, the rules are of mind-boggling complexity. Within the European Community there have now been two main directives (Directive 71/307/EEC and 83/623/EEC) on the approximation of the laws of the member states relating to textile names, and several amendments to them. Consumer organisations have commented on them at various stages, stressing the point that "the first objective of a labelling directive must be to provide consumers in each of the member states with truthful and useful information which will help them to choose between competing products on a sound basis" (7). This principle has yet to be embodied in any of the multifarious EC laws relating to labelling, which leads one to suspect that their prime motive is not always to help the consumer. Consumer organisations continue to devote much effort to trying to establish how such laws should be interpreted.

Care labelling

Perhaps the most useful measure that could be adopted in the field of textiles and textile products which would benefit consumers would be standardized care labelling and washing instructions. Many countries use a voluntary system drawn up by manufacturers in international working parties. Three main systems are in use in Europe alone. Attempts to create an international system have failed, and consumers' desires for an easily understood system which correlated with symbols used on detergent packets, washing machines and garments have yet to be fulfilled.

Voluntary export restraints

The non-tariff measures which have the greatest impact on international trade are not, I can confidently assert, those such as I have outlined above, on which consumers are consulted. In textiles and textile products, voluntary export restraints under the auspices of the Multifibre Arrangement and similar agreements are undoubtedly the single greatest influence on the pattern of world trade in these products.

C. The Multifibre Arrangement

The most important feature of the Arrangement Regarding International Trade in Textiles (or MFA) (8), which was signed at Geneva in December 1973, is that it accords exceptional status to international trade in textiles and clothing. It is a derogation from the basic GATT rules of trade which must be on a non-discriminatory, multilateral basis. It permits eight developed countries -- the U.S., Canada, Austria, Sweden, Finland, Norway, Switzerland and Japan (though the last two do not apply the restrictions), as well as the EC -- to restrict imports of textiles and clothing from 31 developing countries. Australia and New Zealand are not MFA members but have made their own arrangements with developing-country exporters of textiles and clothing. Norway joined the MFA only from July 1984, and prior to that had its own restrictions.

The second feature of the MFA arises from the first: only the exports of "developing" or "low-cost" countries are restricted in this way. Trade between developed countries in textiles and clothing, which forms 70 per cent of total world trade in those products, continues under normal GATT procedures and rules. Yet textiles and clothing form 30 per cent of the manufactured exports of developing countries, and only around two per cent of developed countries' manufactured exports. Because imports from developing countries are restrained, and those from developed countries are not, one of the effects of the MFA is to divert trade from poor to rich countries.

In a BEUC study of the MFA in 1981 (9), an attempt was made to examine the trends of imports into the EC of the five most important clothing categories under the MFA. These are categories four through eight: respectively, T-shirts, jerseys, trousers, blouses and men's shirts. Using import figures by number of pieces, the study showed that the effects of the MFA since 1978

Table 4

VOLUME OF IMPORTS INTO THE EC BY CATEGORY IN 1978, 1980 AND 1983 IN MILLIONS OF PIECES

COUNTRY	CATEGORY 4 T-shirts			CATEGORY 5 Jerseys			CATEGORY 6 Trousers			CATEGORY 7 Blouses			CATEGORY 8 Shirts		
	1978	1980	1983	1978	1980	1983	1978	1980	1983	1978	1980	1983	1978	1980	1983
Italy	19.8	27.2	39.3	178.8	163.8	148.6	15.3	29.3	40.7	16.3	11.6	7.9	6.0	5.0	4.2
Germany	5.7	6.1	5.6	9.0	9.3	8.8	7.7	10.8	13.8	4.3	5.2	5.9	6.3	7.1	6.8
France	7.8	9.6	7.6	9.0	11.8	8.6	13.4	17.6	14.3	4.2	4.2	2.6	1.8	2.5	1.5
UK	3.2	4.6	6.5	10.6	14.5	13.5	4.9	5.5	8.1	3.5	4.0	4.5	2.6	2.4	2.5
Belgium-Lux.	2.4	2.6	3.2	3.6	3.8	5.4	25.2	28.7	27.7	2.3	2.3	2.5	3.0	1.9	1.8
Netherlands	5.5	7.9	8.8	5.1	5.8	7.4	7.7	9.0	10.8	2.9	3.8	2.5	3.8	5.0	4.6
Greece	38.3	36.7	40.2	13.9	20.7	12.1	4.6	6.4	5.7	6.4	5.8	7.3	0.9	1.6	0.5
Denmark	0.5	0.7	1.6	0.7	2.0	2.4	0.4	0.4	1.4	0.1	0.4	0.5	0.04	0.08	0.08
Ireland	1.4	2.4	3.3	2.3	1.4	0.7	2.5	2.7	5.4	0.5	0.5	0.5	1.3	1.0	0.6
Austria	0.7	0.7	1.1	1.7	2.3	2.9	1.1	1.9	2.5	0.6	1.0	0.9	1.2	2.0	1.7
U.S.	6.4	29.8	17.2	3.6	20.2	4.8	5.7	10.1	1.6	0.1	0.3	0.2	0.5	2.1	0.2
Portugal	27.1	36.8	38.0	6.9	12.1	17.1	4.5	4.4	6.8	2.4	3.2	4.1	5.5	7.4	10.0
India	8.1	7.6	7.5	1.0	1.9	2.1	0.5	1.5	1.5	22.3	20.7	15.9	14.0	14.8	10.8
South Korea	6.8	10.6	9.4	22.1	25.4	22.0	3.6	4.5	4.9	9.6	8.4	6.7	31.6	32.3	24.9
Hong Kong	17.5	24.7	22.3	30.4	28.6	29.5	57.9	48.6	52.7	36.1	29.1	24.3	56.6	46.3	48.7
Taiwan	8.8	5.7	5.6	15.9	17.6	17.1	3.0	3.2	3.4	4.2	3.6	2.2	11.8	8.8	9.1

<u>Note:</u> India, South Korea, Hong Kong and Taiwan are subject to MFA or MFA-type restraints.

<u>Source:</u> Eurostat.

had been to restrain imports from the major low-cost suppliers, but that other unrestrained, developed-country suppliers, principally the U.S. and Portugal, had taken up the slack. From Table 4, which revises and updates the earlier table, it can be seen that imports from the U.S. have fallen back quite considerably since 1980, almost certainly as a result of the increased strength of the U.S. dollar against European currencies. Since 1980 (a year of recession in the clothing industry), the EC economies have picked up and have traded more with each other. But the big low-cost suppliers have continued to experience a decline in exports of goods in these categories. Over the period 1978-83, Hong Kong exports in these five categories have declined by 11.8 per cent, South Korea by 8.5 per cent and Taiwan by 16.8 per cent. In contrast, imports of these products from Portugal (a candidate member of the EC, whose textile and clothing exports to the EC are restrained but much more lightly than countries subject to the MFA) have grown by 39 per cent, from the U.K. by 29 per cent, from Germany by 19 per cent, from Belgium-Luxembourg by 10 per cent, but from Italy, the biggest of them all, by only 1.9 per cent. Well might Hong Kong query why they have been restraining their exports to the benefit of Portugal!

The MFA has thus been a very effective protectionist measure and has controlled imports from developing countries very tightly. Far from allowing for the orderly run-down of developed-country industries, it has preserved for them a high share of their domestic markets, and helped other developed countries to increase their shares as well.

The third feature of the MFA that is unusual in terms of protectionist measures is that it operates almost entirely through the use of voluntary export restraints. The basic text of the MFA merely sets the framework within which the voluntary export restraints are concluded. Indeed the basic text is fairly liberal. Article 1 states that "the basic objectives shall be to achieve the expansion of trade, the reduction of barriers to such trade, and the progressive liberalisation of world trade in textile products, while at the same time ensuring the orderly and equitable development of this trade and avoidance of disruptive effects, in individual markets and on individual lines of production in both importing and exporting countries" (10).

As all consumers know, it is the small print of such agreements which contains the catches. The first bit of smaller print comes in Annex B to the MFA. This provides for restrictions on imports to be applied where the domestic market is being disrupted by imports and sales of domestic products are being seriously damaged or there is a threat of this occurring. In such a situation the importing country may conclude an agreement with the exporting country or countries who are causing the damage for the latter voluntarily to restrain their exports. The agreed level of restraint must not constitute a reduction of the volume imported from that supplier in the preceding twelve months, and, if it lasts longer than a year, must provide for an increase in imports in the following years of at least six per cent per annum for the products under restraint. So, the MFA provides for a minimum annual growth rate of six per cent of imports when consumption in developed countries is growing by two-and-a-half per cent a year? It would seem there is nothing to get excited about, except for the next bit of small print. This allows two exceptions to the six per cent growth rate. One, the so-called "Nordic clause", was inserted at Scandinavian insistence, as these countries were worried that their very small domestic markets would be swamped by a six per cent annual growth rate. Thus if "minimum viable production" would be threatened by a six per cent growth rate, a lower positive growth rate is permitted. Most significantly, "in exceptional cases, where there are clear grounds for holding that the situation of market disruption will recur if the above (i.e., six per cent) growth rate is implemented, a lower positive growth rate may be decided upon after consultation with the exporting country or countries concerned".

In practice, the bilateral agreements between each importing country and each of the exporting countries have been much more restrictive than the basic text allows. When the MFA was extended in December 1977 and again in December 1981, the protocols of extension ensured a much tighter regime (even smaller print). Both the EC and the U.S. were able to demand (and get) cutbacks in the level of imports from their major low-cost suppliers. Thus in 1981 the EC's aim was to achieve an overall growth rate of just 1.7 per cent per annum. The GATT report (11) found that the implementation of the current MFA (MFA 3) has been even stricter than in the past:

-- Unilateral measures have been taken more frequently;

-- There are new bilateral agreements with hitherto unrestrained countries;

-- More products are covered than ever before;

-- Agreements with the large suppliers are again more restrictive (under both MFA 2 and MFA 3 the quantities allowed in from the biggest suppliers have been cut back, ostensibly to permit greater growth for smaller exporters);

-- Growth rates and flexibility between quotas and levels shipped in different years have been cut back.

The fourth and final feature of the MFA that is of interest here is the way in which this massive retreat into protectionism has come about at the cost of some of, in human terms, the most deserving people in world trade -- the poorest producers and the poorest consumers. The political process involves the most significant interest groups being bought off. In the developed countries the textile producer lobby is very powerful. This power is disproportionate to the economic significance of the industry. Thus for textiles and clothing combined, in only three developed countries did output account for more than two per cent of gross domestic product in 1980 (Italy 3.1 per cent, Belgium-Luxembourg 2.3 per cent, Switzerland 2.1 per cent). However, the industry tends to be regionally concentrated, often in areas where governments are perceived to win or lose their majorities. Thus every tightening of textile protectionism can be traced in part to pledges given by U.S. presidential candidates to crucial potential supporters in the southeastern states and in New England. The Short-Term Arrangement (which lasted from 1961-62 and was followed by the Long-Term Arrangement and then the MFA) was a result of a Kennedy election pledge; the first MFA grew from promises made by President Nixon. Similarly, in the UK the "textile constituencies" in Yorkshire and Lancashire have been perceived as key areas for government support, and in Belgium support for textiles in French-speaking areas has become entangled with linguistic politics. In Sweden over half the labour force is concentrated in just one county, Alvsborg (12). In Australia, where textile protectionism, though outside the MFA, is very strong, the industry is regionally concentrated in the State of Victoria and New South Wales, and even more so in some parts of those areas, with clothing, footwear and textiles accounting for 44 per cent of employment in manufacturing in Warrnambool, 32 per cent in Wangaratta, and 26 per cent in Bendigo (13). In Canada, approximately 60 per cent of the textile and clothing industry is located in the province of Quebec, and it is heavily concentrated in single industry communities (14). The continuance and, if possible, strengthening of the MFA has become a powerful test of governments' sincerity for the producer lobbies.

The MFA also satisfies textile exporters from the most powerful countries in world trade, the developed countries. They are exempt from it. Developed countries trade mainly with each other in textiles. Eighty per cent of developed countries' imports of textiles in 1963 were from other developed countries. Despite the very rapid development of textile industries in developing countries in the intervening years, this figure was still 71 per cent in 1982. As a group, the developed countries had a trade surplus in textiles, textile fibres and textile machinery in 1981 with developing countries, though they had a deficit in clothing.

Paradoxically, and the MFA is riddled with paradoxes, some of the developing-country exporters have undoubtedly gained from the MFA. This has occurred because the MFA has, to a considerable extent, cartelised trade in the products it covers. Thus countries which were big exporters of MFA products back in 1973 have retained the lion's share of the quotas allocated for these products. As quotas for permitted imports have always been allocated on the basis of past performance, new, potentially cheaper and more efficient entrants to the market have been denied access to their biggest, likeliest customers. This is true both for new firms within countries, and for countries new to exporting textiles and textile products in large quantities. The GATT report concludes that "while market shares of exporting countries and exporting firms may not be frozen, they exhibit considerable stickiness" (15). For both the U.S. and the EC, the big increase in the number of supplying countries occurred under the old Long-Term Arrangement on Cotton Textiles, which lasted from October 1962 until December 1973.

The MFA has created its own group of people with vested interests in the continuation of the present system. Within governments both in developed and developing countries, there are now hundreds of officials who have built their careers around an ability to understand the intricacies of the system and to exploit its loopholes. They speak a language impenetrable to outsiders, dominated by terms such as "basket-exit mechanism", or "the surge clause", and share reminiscences about Geneva in 1977 (and 1981, and 1973). So entrenched have the producer lobbies become, that it has sometimes seemed that they have been dictating their countries' trade policies without regard to the interests of other sectors of the community. A consortium of American importer and retailer interests has summed up the whole process thus: "The U.S. textile and apparel program has, over the years, adversely affected the interests of importers, retailers, consumers, American farmers and industrial exporters. The administration of the program has not taken those interests into account". They concluded that "The lack of transparency and administrative due process has exposed civil servants to undue pressure and influence from the domestic textile and apparel industries. If textile and apparel imports are to be regulated in the national interest, government employees simply must be insulated from such pressure by sound procedures, transparency, deliberate decision-making, in accordance with rules and regulations, and government in the sunshine" (16).

IV. WHAT IS THE MFA TRYING TO ACHIEVE?

The MFA was allowed by GATT as an exceptional measure because many developed countries had been taking unilateral, _ad hoc_ actions against rising textile and clothing imports. At first these came from Japan, and then later from Hong Kong, India, Pakistan and many others (17). The fear was that there would be a general rush into protectionism, and the MFA and its predecessors were supposed to prevent this. The protectionist pressures stem from the fact that for many items of clothing and some textiles, comparative advantage has shifted to countries with low labour costs. Thus parts of the industries in developed countries have found it increasingly difficult to compete, firms have gone out of business and workers have lost their jobs. One of the original purposes of the MFA was to facilitate the adjustment process in developed countries, to enable companies to re-equip where necessary or to switch production, and to enable workers to learn new skills or find new jobs.

To a considerable extent this adjustment process has occurred. Table 5, taken from GATT report, shows that the relative importance of employment and output in Western European and U.S. textile and clothing industries has declined since the war, as new industries have grown up.

Table 5

RELATIVE IMPORTANCE OF EMPLOYMENT AND OUTPUT IN TEXTILES
AND CLOTHING INDUSTRIES IN WESTERN EUROPE AND THE U.S. -- 1953-80

	U.S.			WESTERN EUROPE		
	1953	1963	1980	1953	1963	1980
Employment in _textiles_ relative to: all manufacturing	6.7	5.4	5.1	11.4	8.5	5.8
total employment	2.0	1.4	1.1	3.3	2.6	1.6
Employment in _clothing_ relative to: all manufacturing	8.9	7.8	6.0	8.2	7.2	4.6
total employment	2.1	2.0	1.2	2.3	2.3	1.3

Source: GATT study, op. cit., p. 11.

In Western Europe in 1980, the textile industry accounted for only 1.6 per cent of total employment and a further 1.3 per cent in the clothing industry, a decline of nearly one-half since 1953. In the U.S. the corresponding figures were 1.1 per cent and 1.2 per cent. Nevertheless, the developed countries are among the world's top exporters in textiles and clothing, and still dominate world trade in these products. Table 6, taken from the GATT study, lists the world's top 15 exporters of textiles (accounting for

73 per cent of total trade in 1982) and of clothing (accounting for 71 per cent of total trade).

Table 6

WORLD'S TOP EXPORTERS OF TEXTILES AND CLOTHING IN 1982

Textiles	Clothing
1. Germany	1. Hong Kong
2. Japan	2. Italy
3. Italy	3. South Korea
4. U.S.	4. Taiwan
5. Belgium-Luxembourg	5. Germany
6. France	6. China
7. South Korea	7. France
8. China	8. UK
9. UK	9. U.S.
10. Netherlands	10. Belgium-Luxembourg
11. Taiwan	11. Romania
12. Switzerland	12. Netherlands
13. India	13. Finland
14. Austria	14. Portugal
15. Pakistan	15. Yugoslavia

Source: GATT study, op. cit., pp 42-43.

Company profits for those still in textiles and clothing are currently reported to be healthy, and this success has been attributed to investment in new technology, with the application of microprocessors to previously labour-intensive tasks, particularly in clothing (18).

The case for arguing for further time as a breathing-space for the industry in developed countries to adjust to overseas competition is weak.

V. EFFECTS OF THE MULTIFIBRE ARRANGEMENT

It follows from the above that those whose interests are damaged by the MFA are not taken into account when the policies are put into practice. Those adversely affected by it include:

1. Exporting industries in developed countries. The developed countries have a huge trade surplus on manufactured goods with developing countries: clothing is the only sector where there is a deficit. Restrictions on developing countries' ability to earn foreign exchange by selling clothing and textiles mean they can import less. In this context a tax (or restriction) on imports is a tax on exports. Sometimes the link is more direct: some developing countries have taken retaliatory action in response to restrictions on their exports of textiles and clothing. For instance, in January 1983, China retaliated against American farm exports in response to

harsh new restrictions on textile exports from China to the U.S. In 1980 Indonesia responded to new EC quotas on exports of clothing by cancelling or postponing some engineering contracts with the UK. The EC has also experienced periodic difficulties with Turkey because of attempts to restrict Turkish textile imports under the EC-Turkey Association agreement, and with Malta for similar reasons;

2. Smaller, poorer developing countries which have been late entrants to the international rag trade and have sometimes been hit disproportionately hard. Mauritius, Sri Lanka, Haiti, the Maldives -- among the world's poorest developing countries, with only a few clothing factories -- have been deemed a threat to the textile and clothing markets of developed countries, and have therefore had quotas imposed on them. This is very hard to justify on economic, humanitarian or political grounds;

3. Consumers in the developed countries who, as we have seen, are excluded from effective influence on decisions about trade restrictions, but who ultimately pay the price of protectionism in the form of dearer goods and less choice than would have been the case in the absence of protectionism.

For the purposes of analysing the order of magnitude of such costs to consumers, and perhaps contrasting them with benefits that protected producers might gain in the form of higher prices, profits and more employment, it is necessary to distinguish between the short- and long-term effects of protectionism.

In the short term, the prices that consumers pay for imports affected by restrictions will increase (or, where prices in general are falling, fail to fall as much as they would have) because import restrictions mean that imports are scarcer. If there is a tariff, the consumers will pay for this as well; if there is a quantity restriction or quota, this will have a price-raising effect similar to a tariff. Domestic producers will be able to obtain higher prices than would have otherwise been the case; this will increase their profits, and may be reflected in higher wage packets for their employees. Thus, in the short term, it is possible to work out the effects of restrictions on consumers, and to calculate the extent to which this cost is merely transferred to domestic producers or represents a loss to society as a whole. These costs are sometimes referred to as the static effects of protection. It is also possible to estimate the likely effect on output and employment in firms which are competing with imports when the restrictions are removed.

In the long term, the dynamic effects of import restrictions must be considered. While there is little argument that there are short-run costs which are borne by consumers, in the longer term many groups in favour of selective import restrictions argue that the dynamic benefits far outweigh the short-run costs. These dynamic effects include economies of scale which manufacturers might obtain from running their firms at a higher level of production than they were able to without import restrictions; greater incentive to invest in better technologies granted by the higher profits; and the opportunity for the industry to reorganise itself into better-sized, more productive units. Set against this are the cumulative effect on the economy of the transfer of resources from consumers to producers; the cost of investing in the protected sector when the interests of the economy might be better served by investing in other sectors; and the possible permanent loss of competitiveness of the protected sector.

Put like this it might seem surprising that anyone would have attempted to assess the costs and benefits of protectionism in textiles and clothing, let alone anything as complex as the MFA. In fact, various attempts have been made in a number of countries, the most important of which are summarised below.

As was shown in Table 2, tariffs on imports of textiles and clothing are generally high in developed countries. The advantage of tariffs from the government's point of view is that it collects the revenues, and so derives income from every imported unit. Tariffs may offer producers very high protection, as the effective tariff rate is often very much higher than the nominal one. Because tariffs impose no quantity restrictions, but permit all imports in as long as the duty is paid, domestic producers sometimes claim they offer inadequate protection. For instance, if import prices are very low, even a 50 per cent tariff may not bring the price up to domestic levels. In such a situation, which undoubtedly applies to some textiles and textile products, producers have successfully argued that what they require is the certainty which can be granted only by quantity restrictions or quotas on imports, so that they know in advance the maximum quantities of imports which will be allowed in. If quotas are imposed on imports, the domestic government may not derive any revenue from them unless they sell import licences to importers and retailers. Under the MFA the exporting countries arrange their own licences, so any income derived from their sale goes to them.

Several estimates have been made in the U.S. of the costs of tariffs on textiles and clothing, but they have tended to ignore possible dynamic effects. The most comprehensive study was made by the (since abolished) U.S. Council on Wage and Price Stability (COWPS) in 1978 (19). They calculated the cost to consumers in 1975 of U.S. tariffs on clothing. Their estimates showed a transfer to producers of $2.2 billion, with a total loss to consumers in 1975 of $2.7 billion. Morkre and Tarr, in a study for the U.S. Federal Trade Commission (20) again looked only at the costs of tariffs and ignored the costs of quantity restrictions and possible dynamic effects of protectionism. They investigated the costs over a four-year period and recorded values in terms of U.S. dollars in 1977. They tried to calculate the gains, if any, of removing tariffs altogether, by contrasting the benefits of such a move to consumers with the costs of greater unemployment. For their purposes the costs of unemployment were assumed to fall all in the first of a four-year tariff-free period, and in those four years the net gain to the U.S. economy of removing tariffs altogether was over $1.3 billion. Put another way, the cost to U.S. consumers of each job protected by tariffs was $13 200 in 1977, roughly double the average annual wages of workers in the textile and clothing industries. The total cost to U.S. consumers in 1977 of the tariffs alone was calculated to be $1.4 billion in one year.

Yet another U.S. study (21) attempts to summarise the studies on the costs of protecting the textile and clothing industries in the U.S. The most important conclusion is that only in clothing are the costs of tariffs very substantial, while for textiles the tariffs are more or less redundant. This can be explained by the strong trade performance of the American textile industry which is highly competitive internationally, even with the Far East.

The same study also notes that the effect of removing restrictions would be felt disproportionately in some regions of the U.S., particularly the south-eastern states (22). But it also points out that many jobs in these states are dependent on success in export markets, and the developing countries are major customers for U.S. manufactured goods. Thus, in Virginia 10 per cent of the manufacturing employment is dependent on exports, in South Carolina 10 per cent, and in North Carolina 8.4 per cent.

It is more difficult to estimate the costs of the quota restrictions to consumers (23). As the quotas interact with the tariffs, this problem is compounded. One very simple measure of the cost of quotas may be found by looking at the cost of obtaining licences to export from the Far East to the countries which operate the MFA restrictions. In a number of Far Eastern countries, licences are openly bought and sold with the tacit approval of the authorities who, having allocated quotas to their manufacturers mainly on the basis of past shipments, are anxious to ensure that unused quota is readily transferred to manufacturers who can use it. In Hong Kong the system has become so sophisticated that a market for quotas has grown up, with quota brokers offering to find export licences for manufacturers who need them and to off-load spare quotas for those who have too much. The price fluctuates throughout the year, according to the exigencies of demand and supply and the buying season for clothing.

The quota transfer price, or quota premium, is a measure of the value to exporters of export licences, and hence of the cost to importers and ultimately consumers in developed countries of the MFA quota restrictions. So institutionalised has the whole system become that there has even been a European Court judgement on whether the quota premium should be included in valuations for customs purposes. (They decided it should not.)

In 1979 the UK Consumers' Association collected a number of quotations of recent prices paid by importers in the UK for quota in Hong Kong and Taiwan. The results are summarised in Table 7. These charges exist only because of the MFA, and thus provide a rough indication, at any one time, of the costs of quotas to consumers.

In a forthcoming study for the Trade Policy Research Centre and the Consumers' Association in London, David Greenaway has made further calculations of the costs to UK consumers of some of the MFA clothing quotas. He found that, as might be expected, there was a cyclical element to quota premiums, and that in Hong Kong in 1982, the period he looked at, they were low because demand in the EC was low. Using quotations he obtained of the Hong Kong quota premium in 1982 for three garment categories exported to the UK (Category 6 -- trousers, Category 7 -- blouses and Category 8 -- shirts), Greenaway found that the ad valorem equivalent of the quota premium was 15 per cent of the unrestrained price. This, added to the 17 per cent EC tariff, yielded a UK landed price that was 34 per cent above the free trade price. From this he calculates the losses to consumers and the economy of protecting these three Hong Kong products, which in 1982 was £170 million. Of this figure the suppliers in Hong Kong gained £9 million, domestic producers £49 million, and other overseas suppliers of the same products £37.5 million. The present value of the net losses, extrapolated over all imported clothing, works out at £4.6 billion or £230 per household. More speculatively, the net cost per job saved in the clothing industry, assuming that protection is now permanent, is estimated to be around £170 000 -- over twenty times the average wage in the industry.

Table 7

QUOTA PREMIUMS FOR MFA PRODUCTS IMPORTED INTO THE UK IN MARCH 1979

Product	No. of quotations	Exporting country	Currency + quantity	Average	Range
Jeans	9	Hong Kong	HK$ per doz.	130	80-160
Men's and boys' shirts	7	Hong Kong	HK$ per doz.	65	40-90
Blouses	7	Hong Kong	HK$ per doz.	70	50-80
Knitwear	5	Hong Kong	HK$ per doz.	55	30-80
General	5	Taiwan	$ per doz.	15	5-24

Source: Consumers' Association, The Price of Protection, London, August 1979.

Two studies, one in Canada and one in the EC, have attempted to look at the costs of tariffs and quotas on imported clothing and textiles in both the short and long term, with an assessment of static and dynamic costs and benefits.

In his study of protectionism and its links to the decline of certain industries (24), Vincent Cable first considered the effects on landed prices in some EC countries of both MFA quotas and tariffs. Some of these findings are summarised in Table 8, which shows how the cost structure of some imported garments is affected by quotas and tariffs long before they reach the consumer.

Cable then goes on to consider what effect this level of protection has had on employment and investment in the textile and clothing industries. As we have seen, despite protection, employment in the textile and clothing industries in developed countries has fallen dramatically in the last twenty years. Work by Cable (25) and by Philip Hayes (26) has demonstrated that, for the UK at least, loss of jobs as a result of using imports has been relatively insignificant compared with the labour-displacing effects of improved labour productivity in a number of industries including textiles and clothing. The reasons for this are not hard to find. Both the textiles industry and, to an even greater extent, the clothing industry employ a not very skilled labour force, use technologies that have been around for a long time, and seem to operate most profitably with a small size of plant on average. It is these very characteristics that have made them so attractive to entrepreneurs and governments in developing countries. Taken together, they would seem to suggest that the dynamic benefits from operating at a higher rate of production or in bigger units in the industrialised countries are small. This is Cable's conclusion, and he cites a study of the Scottish jute industry, which enjoyed protection for over forty years from competition from the Indian subcontinent. The study, by the Overseas Development Institute and St. Andrews University (27), found that the higher profits gained from protection over a long period provided incentives and finance for investment in new technology (polypropylene) and in specialised end-uses. The new, high-technological industry flourishes but most of the labour force has gone as a result of adopting capital-intensive methods.

With the at least partial assistance of trade protection, which provided investment confidence together with a surplus for reinvestment, textile

Table 8

SOME APPROXIMATE ESTIMATES OF THE COST TO EC
CONSUMERS OF TARIFFS AND QUOTAS ON GARMENTS IN 1981

Protection Level	Product A	Product B	Product C	Product D
FOB price/unit (HK$)	14.8	32.0	25.2	68.0
Landed price (EC)	19.1	37.0	29.1	74.0
Tariff (17%)	3.2	6.3	4.9	12.6
Quota premium	5.0	19.0	12.0	9.0
Tariff and quota premium as % of landed price	43%	68%	58%	29%

Product A -- T-shirts exported from Hong Kong to Germany
Product B -- Knitted jerseys exported from Hong Kong to Germany
Product C -- Knitted jerseys exported from Hong Kong to Italy
Product D -- Parkas and anoraks exported from Hong Kong to Germany

Source: V. Cable, op. cit., p. 122.

companies in the EC have generally invested in labour-replacing machinery. The consequent rationalisation of the industry and increased productivity (especially in spinning and weaving) could, Cable argues, be counted among the dynamic benefits of protection. But the textile companies themselves still argue that they cannot be re-exposed to competition from low-cost countries, "and there is every reason to believe that greater benefits could have been achieved using scarce resources elsewhere" (28).

Professor Glenn Jenkins has carried out detailed calculations of the costs to Canadian consumers of tariff and quota protection. Unlike the EC, tariffs in Canada are changed on the basis of import prices which include the quota premium, so the two sets of protectionist measures interact even more closely than in the EC. Table 9, taken from Professor Jenkins' work, summarises his findings of the effects of tariffs and quotas on Canada's imports from Hong Kong, South Korea and Taiwan in 1979. As the table shows, the total protective effect ranges between 31 per cent, for foundation garments, and 74 per cent, for shirts with collars, of the total landed price.

Using these figures as a basis, Jenkins calculates the cost to consumers and the Canadian economy of the quotas and the tariffs. He estimates that in 1979 consumers paid C$198 million more for their clothing as a direct result of quotas, and with the tariffs as well a total of C$467 million more. Of this sum C$41.1 million was a direct gain to foreign manufacturers, the Canadian federal government received C$92.8 million in tariff revenue at consumers' expense, and Canadian manufacturers gained C$267 million.

He estimates that approximately 6 016 man-years of employment were created every year by this policy, at a cost to consumers of nearly C$33 000 per job per year. Some of this money of course is received by Canadian manufacturers in the form of higher profits, but the pure waste to Canada of this policy is of the order of C$14 000 per additional man-year of employment created. This compares with an average annual wage in the industry of less than C$10 000.

Though all the studies discussed above have their methodological drawbacks, and are based on some fairly major assumptions, the evidence does suggest that protection is a very wasteful and rather inefficient means of preserving jobs in textiles and clothing. Furthermore, there is quite substantial evidence to suggest that the MFA quotas are ɔre wasteful than tariffs and that the costs fall disproportionately on the poo. st consumers.

The evidence on the economic inefficiency of quotas as opposed to tariffs is quite clear. With a tariff, governments at least capture some of the revenue from protection, while with the MFA quotas they do not. As quotas seem to bite harder than tariffs, they are more protective and hence more expensive. Thus in Canada, while the tariffs transferred C$269.1 million from consumers and led to economic losses of C$20.9 million, the quotas transferred C$198.3 million at an economic cost of C$86.5 million, which was lost to the Canadian economy.

Quotas have other effects which may do further harm to the long-term prospects of the textile and clothing industries in the developed countries, but which these calculations do not measure. Over time producers, particularly those with large and established shares of developed-country markets, have sought to derive maximum use from their quotas by trading-up: moving their production up-market to more profitable lines on which their margins are greater. In Hong Kong this has been pursued as a deliberate policy. The Executive Director of the Hong Kong Trade Development Council explained in a recent interview: "In terms of quantity the (fashion) industry's growth rate is limited by quota systems and protectionist tariffs and even bans imposed by importing countries. At present growth is best sought by increasing the value of each item exported.

"In Hong Kong, free enterprise is not just something for the businessman. It applies to the workers too. They expect, quite rightly, to be rewarded for acquiring new skills and for working hard and well. So wages must go up and, to pay them, so must a company's sales. Faced with restrictions on quantity, the industry has been moving up-market at a fairly rapid pace. Now it is aiming for the top" (29).

In Taiwan the allocation of quota provides manufacturers with a strong incentive to move up-market. The Taiwan Textile Federation (TTF) allocates quotas on the basis of past performance, with 10 to 15 per cent of the total amount held back for manufacturers who are short of quota or for new exporters. Manufacturers requiring quotas take their orders to the TTF where the additional licences are assigned on the basis of free-on-board prices stated on the orders for goods in each category. The exporters who obtained the highest price per unit for their goods receive priority (30). According to Jenkins, this is part of a deliberate policy by the Taiwan authorities to force the exporters to move into higher added-value production, because of the quantity restrictions.

While there is an excellent industrial strategy for Hong Kong and Taiwan to follow, moving out of the production of basic lines and into designer clothes of higher quality means that they compete more intensely with the products of developed countries' clothing industries. With new entrants effectively kept out under the MFA, and with the present very low growth rates, the supply of basic, cheap imported clothing threatens to dry up.

Table 9

THE EFFECTS OF TARIFFS AND QUOTAS ON CANADA'S
IMPORTS FROM HONG KONG, SOUTH KOREA AND TAIWAN, 1979 (%)

Garment	Tariff protection	Quota	Total protective effect
Outerwear	26	34	60
Structured suits & blazers	25	18	43
Shirts with collars	20	54	74
Blouses & shirts	24	10	34
Jerseys & cardigans	23	10	33
T-shirts & sweatshirts	20	21	41
Men's & boys' trousers	22	11	33
Women's & girls' trousers	23	11	34
Overalls, coveralls	16	21	37
Dresses & skirts	24	8	32
Underwear	12	28	40
Shorts	19	18	37
Pyjamas, etc.	22	2	24
Foundation garments	24	7	31
Swimwear	20	15	35
Overcoats & rainwear	25	13	38

Source: Glenn Jenkins, Costs and Consequences of the New Protectionism. The Case of Canada's Clothing Sector, The North-South Institute, Ottawa, July 1980, pages 30 and 35.

One other effect of this is that under MFA 1, MFA 2 and MFA 3, retailers have consistently reported problems in obtaining children's clothing (31). Children's wear is counted in with adults' clothing in MFA quotas, and because it is more price-sensitive than adults' clothing (as children grow out of it so quickly), profit margins tend to be lower. Since an item of adults' clothing counts the same as an item of children's clothing for quota purposes, exporters tend increasingly to make only adults' clothing for export. Hence it is becoming more difficult to import basic children's clothing, with a consequent increase in price and diminution of choice in the importing countries. This evidence would add weight to the belief that the price of MFA protectionism hits the poor, including those with large families, harder than the better-off. As we discussed at the beginning of this paper, the poorest households do not shop in the same market for clothing as their wealthier compatriots. There is not much empirical evidence about the distribution of the costs of protectionism across classes. Jenkins (32) estimates that for households with income of less than C$10 000, the costs of tariffs and quotas per household in Canada in 1979 was C$86.06, rising to C$182.61 for households with incomes of over C$30 000. But for consumers in the lowest income group, the cost represents 1.3 per cent of income, while for those in the highest only 0.4 per cent. So proportionately the poor pay three times more than the rich.

The final piece of evidence on the costs and benefits of protecting textiles and clothing comes from Australia, a country which left the MFA in 1977 but nevertheless applies its own long-term protectionist policy to the import of textiles and clothing. In Australia tariff quotas have been used to restrict the import of textiles and clothing since 1974. Imports bearing a tariff are allowed in up to a certain level, after which a penurious tariff rate applies. In practice it is the quota which restrains imports. In Australia the Industries' Assistance Commission advises the Commonwealth Government on trade policy and industrial adjustment, taking evidence from all interested parties. In 1979 they published a controversial draft report on the textile clothing and footwear industries (33). In the event, their main conclusion -- that "in general, the long-term prospects of the textile, clothing and footwear industries in Australia are poor" (34) -- proved politically unacceptable, and their recommendations for a reduction in assistance to the industries were ignored. Their analysis of the costs of this policy was, however, telling. They calculated the nominal rate of assistance for 1977-78 as a percentage of the landed duty-free price of an import in 1977-78. For textiles this was estimated to be 44 per cent for items under quota, 17 per cent for those not under, yielding a total of 29 per cent for all textiles. For clothing the rates were much higher: 80 per cent, 31 per cent and 76 per cent respectively. The effective rate of assistance was still higher: 50 per cent for textiles and 135 per cent for clothing. If the government had paid the cost as a direct subsidy, the annual cost would have been about A$765 million, but as it was consumers bore most of the cost, estimated at A$200 per household per annum in 1977. Their loss, in welfare terms, of having to spend so much more of their incomes on clothing and hence less on other things was even greater.

VI. THE FUTURE OF THE MULTIFIBRE ARRANGEMENT

The GATT study concluded that the continuation of the MFA beyond July 1986 (when the current agreement expires) would lead in the developed countries to the following:

a) A continuation of past trends in textile production, which would be increasingly dependent on the growth of domestic clothing production;

b) Imports and domestic production would share any increases in domestic consumption, with the MFA growth rates determining the balance between them;

c) A continuing trend towards automation in the production of both textiles and clothing which would cause a further decline in labour input per unit of output;

d) Prices of clothing and household textiles would be higher, with a regressive effect on income distribution;

e) Because the level of clothing and textile imports would be lower, the developed countries' exports to developing countries would also be lower, thus reducing production and employment in these industries;

f) The entry of two major low-cost textile and clothing exporters (Spain and Portugal) into the EC could have a deleterious effect on other exporting countries.

165

VII. CONCLUSIONS

The Multifibre Arrangement has been in existence since 1974. Prior to that some form of textile protectionism seems to have almost always existed; certainly in Europe it goes back into the Middle Ages. These policies have not been framed with the consumer in mind. Rather, producers appear to have had it all their way for a very long time. At its meeting on 21st September 1984, the BEUC Council unanimously agreed that MFA number three should be the last, and that 1986 should mark the beginning of free trade in textiles and textile products. If a decision in principle is taken in 1986 to get rid of the MFA and not to replace it with other restrictions, given the high tariffs already imposed on the textiles trade, there would still be a need to chart a course out of the maze of restrictions and into the open seas. Below we make two suggestions as to how this might be achieved, as a starting point for discussion. But the most important principle to establish is that world-wide protectionism in the clothing and textiles trade must end now.

Seek to liberalise rather than to restrict

Many quite restrictive MFA quotas are on products which are scarcely manufactured in developed countries: grey cloth, for example, a basic raw material for the dyeing and finishing industries and ultimately for clothing, is no longer produced in quantity in the EC. T-shirts, again, are largely imported. Restricting imports of these products is pointless. As a first step towards complete liberalisation, a radical overhaul of quotas and removal of all quotas on goods where developed-country production supplies, say, less than 25 per cent of the domestic market would recognise the realities of current international specialisation.

Phase in radical departures according to a strict timetable

Consumers, producers, retailers, importers and exporters will require time to adjust to a changed trading environment. The MFA has gradually become more restrictive with each successive renewal. Now the process has to be turned round. The best means of achieving this is for a fixed date, say in 1991, to be established by which international trade in textiles and textile products will have returned to trade under the GATT. Starting with the removal of restrictions as suggested under 1) above, the MFA technical experts may then devise annual growth rates in quotas over the period to 1991 which would constitute a phased return to "free trade". During this period importing countries would be able to pursue adjustment policies which would help workers in industries whose livelihood was threatened to find other jobs, and which would enable firms who have sheltered behind the MFA protection to become more outward-looking and competitive. Growth rates would be known in advance and companies could plan their production accordingly.

NOTES AND REFERENCES

1. Figures are taken from the GATT study "Textiles and Clothing in the World Economy", GATT, Geneva, July 1984. Unless otherwise stated, all figures in this report are taken from the GATT study.

2. Industries Assistance Commission (1979), "Draft Reports on Textiles, Clothing and Footwear", Part A General, Canberra.

3. Some confirmation of this comes in a study made by the National Consumer Council in the UK. See: NCC Report on Country of Origin Marking for the Minister of State for Consumer Affairs, National Consumer Council, London, October 1979.

4. GATT Focus Newsletter, March-April 1984.

5. NCC report, op. cit.

6. Com. 81 (766), 15th December 1981.

7. Comments by Miss E. Roberts, Economic and Social Committee, R/CES 420/80 mb, April 1980.

8. The most comprehensive volumes written on the political economy and history of this trade agreement are: D. Keesing and M. Wolf, Textile Quotas Against Developing Countries, Trade Policy Research Centre, London, 1980 and the GATT study "Textiles and Clothing in the World Economy", Geneva, July 1984, op. cit.

9. The European Community, the Consumer, and the Multi-Fibre Arrangement, BEUC 91.81 rev. 1, November 1981.

10. Arrangement Regarding International Trade in Textiles, GATT, Geneva, 20th December 1973.

11. Op. cit.

12. Carl Hamilton, Effects of Non-Tariff Barriers to Trade, on Prices, Employment and Imports: The Case of the Swedish Textile and Clothing Industry, World Bank, 1980.

13. Industries Assistance Commission, Draft Report, op. cit., p. 12.

14. Glenn Jenkins, Costs and Consequences of the New Protectionism, The Case of Canada's Clothing Sector, North-South Institute, 1980.

15. Op. cit., p. 151.

16. Report of the National Retail Merchants' Association, American Retail Confederation, American Association of Importers -- Textile and Apparel Group to the White House Interagency Group on Textiles and Apparel, mimeo, 30th August 1983.

17. For a full history see: Textile Quotas Against Developing Countries by D. Keesing and M. Wolf, op. cit.

18. Economist, 15th September 1984, p. 78.

19. COWPS: Textiles/Apparel: A Study of the Textile and Apparel Industries, Washington, D.C., 1978.

20. M. Morkre and D. Tarr: The Effects of Restrictions on United States Imports: Five Case Studies and Theory, Federal Trade Commission, Washington, D.C., 1980.

21. J. Pelzman: Economic Cost of Tariffs and Quotas on Textile and Apparel Products Imported into the United States, Weltwirtschaftliches Archiv, 1983, vol. 119, part 3.

22. Ibid., p. 537.

23. For the purposes of this paper, I have ignored the numerous methodological problems with all these studies and discussion of the assumptions on which their calculations are based. We are definitely dealing with "ball-park" figures.

24. V. Cable (1983) Protectionism and Industrial Decline, London, Hodder and Stoughton.

25. Summarised in Cable (1983), op. cit.

26. Philip Hayes, The Newly Industrialising Countries and the Adjustment Problems, Government Economic Working Service Paper No. 18, London, 1978.

27. Cited in Cable, op. cit.: McDowall, Draper and McGuiness, Protection, Technological Change and Trade Adjustment: The Case of Jute in Britain, Overseas Development Institute Review, 1976.

28. Cable, op. cit., p. 146.

29. Interview with Brenda Polan in "The Guardian", London, 4th October 1984.

30. Jenkins, op. cit., p. 9.

31. See e.g. reports of the Foreign Trade Association, Retail Consortium and American Retail Federation.

32. Op. cit.

33. Op. cit.

34. Ibid., p. 38.

Part III: WORKSHOP CONCLUSIONS

by

John W. Hackett
Director, Financial, Fiscal and Enterprise Affairs, OECD

Two papers formed the basis for the Workshop discussion: the study by Professor Mennes and his colleague Dr. Krijger, which attempted to determine the consequences of the use of voluntary export restraints (VERs) in the automobile sector using cost/benefit analysis; and the paper by Mrs. Smallbone on the question of textiles and clothing, with particular reference to the functioning (or perhaps one should say, disfunctioning) of the Multifibre Agreement (MFA).

Professor Mennes' conclusion -- that the removal of VERs in Europe would greatly increase consumer welfare and that the present methods of restriction are especially costly -- was, for the most part, supported by Workshop participants. The major dissenting opinion came from the Trade Union representative, who voiced strong reservations regarding the analysis used. He felt that it was too static; that some of the basic parameters and data used were debatable; and that consequently, the costs of VERs were certainly not of the dimension suggested by Professor Mennes, if indeed they could be said to exist at all.

Discussion of the method used drew a number of useful, perceptive comments from participants regarding cost/benefit analysis. The BIAC representative, who spoke on behalf of the European Automobile Companies Federation, qualified his support of the study with the reservation that he thought that some of the basic data used by Professor Mennes did not really correspond to the kind that should be used when dealing with prices, e.g. elasticities. It was also suggested that price control in some European countries would in any case render the effects of the removal of VERs less than they would appear to be from Professor Mennes' paper. There is in fact always a margin of error contained in cost/benefit analysis, which can be quite considerable, in the choice of the actual level of any values incorporated; clearly, one could re-do the analysis using different figures and possibly come up with a different result. While he basically agreed with this last point, Professor Mennes nevertheless thought that the conclusion of his analysis would remain the same, whatever changes were made in the parameters and the data.

We devoted some time to discussion of this particular methodology. And, despite the reservations already mentioned, and recognition of additional problems such as the increasing difficulty of incorporating dynamic impact into this kind of method, there was in the end agreement among all participants that cost/benefit analysis helps to clarify the options, and thus aids in making more rational decisions. Further, it employs the sort of language which senior officials and ministers are growing increasingly accustomed to hearing. There was also, however, general agreement with the point made by the TUAC representative that one must be wary of the tendency, when employing

169

cost/benefit, to bandy about the figure arrived at as being "The Conclusion", with no further discussion possible.

Mrs. Smallbone's paper involved a rather heavy criticism of the way MFA has operated over the long period in which it has been in existence. Her main points were:

-- That it has become increasingly restrictive in practice, despite the occasional statement to the contrary made at the political level;

-- That it has had regressive effects from the point of view of income distribution in our countries, with children's clothing a particularly striking example;

-- That it has harmed the trade potential of a great number of developing, low-income countries, consequently producing internationally regressive effects as well.

There was certainly general agreement with Mrs. Smallbone that the MFA is a good example of the opaque nature of trade restrictions which can evolve over a period of years. The only disagreement voiced regarding the regressive income distribution impact of MFA came from the Trade Union representative, who expressed the opinion that the case for this had not really been made either for our countries or in a world context. Especially noteworthy were two interventions, one by Japanese businessmen and the other by a representative of the Swiss Government closely associated with international trade negotiations. They said that their respective countries had not been associated with MFA nor introduced quotas on imports of textiles and clothing; nevertheless, their industries had modernised themselves and were at the present time standing fully on their own feet without the support of MFA.

The remaining Workshop time was devoted to a discussion of the Consumer Policy Committee's proposal for a checklist. There was widespread agreement that this approach was a valid means of ensuring that when a restrictive measure is being envisaged or is being assessed, all·the relevant factors will be taken into consideration in an explicit manner. In this connection two points were made. One is that cost/benefit analysis can become a useful component of the checklist approach. The other point, which of course we all realise, is that in the end the decision taken is a political one which will not always inevitably go in the direction indicated (even strongly) by information obtained from using the checklist.

There were also some specific suggestions for amending the checklist which will be considered by the Committee in future meetings dealing with the results of the Symposium.

IMPROVING TRANSPARENCY AND CONSUMER INFORMATION ON
TRADE MATTERS -- WORKSHOP B

Summmary of contributions by

H.D. Lösenbeck, Chief Editor, Test, Germany
W.J. van Campen, Chief Editor, Consumentengids, Netherlands
David Watts, Chief Editor, Which?, United Kingdom

Conclusion by

Laurent Denis, Workshop Chairman
Director, National Consumer Institute, France

Information is undoubtedly the consumer's greatest asset in today's complex international market-place. Only accurately informed consumers are capable of a truly free choice in making purchase decisions, particularly when the best quality at the lowest price may well be found outside their own domestic markets. And one of the most valuable aids in making an informed choice is the comparative testing conducted by national consumer organisations around the world. As will be seen, the sphere of reporting -- and influence -- of such organisations and their respective publications can extend beyond product evaluation and into the domain of trade policy, guarding consumer interests against "protective" practices, "Buy National" prejudice and misrepresentation.

The Stiftung Warentest is a neutral organisation working in the interests of the consumer in the Federal Republic of Germany. Its most important publication, Test magazine, provides readers with the results of objective comparative testing of goods and services. And, as Germany's consumer market goods are characterised by a relatively large share of foreign products, imports undergo testing as well. Mr. H.D. Lösenbeck, the Editor of Test, points out that there are certain product groups in which foreign imports indeed have a considerably large market share (e.g. video recorders, home computers, cameras and cars). He stresses, however, that the same test criteria are applied to all products, whether produced domestically or abroad, in any given test, in order to arrive at a rating based on product quality, price and safety. He also points out that this objectivity, serving the interests of the consumer rather than those of domestic manufacturers, must be adhered to by all such testing organisations. Misuse of test criteria (and especially of safety norms) can lead to restrictive trade policies which hinder imports and consequently, the consumer's free choice. In those cases where products do fall short of safety requirements, testing organisations and their publications can actually help open the doors of exchange. Mr. Lösenbeck notes:

"Usually, due to their large influence on consumer demand, the publication of test results can often lead to foreign manufacturers quickly adopting domestic safety specifications and by doing so, can eliminate potential trade barriers".

In the UK, Consumers' Association and Which? magazine also test both foreign and domestic products. Adopting a philosophy in sharp contrast to the Buy-British lobby, Which? recommends the products it considers best value for money, regardless of where they are made. However, the magazine also does say where each product tested is from, allowing the readers to take that into account if they so desire. It is certainly not always the case that the "best buy" is produced domestically; in fact, for certain product groups it is indeed impossible to "Buy British". Moreover, in cases where it is more economical to buy a product abroad, the magazine will so inform its readers. For instance, in 1981 Which? produced an Importing A Car Action Kit.

There are, however, complications as regards a product's country of origin. Mr. David Watts, the Editor of Which?, points out:

"It's often a problem deciding where a product is made. For example, many cars are made in several countries, many electrical goods (e.g. videos) may be assembled in one country out of components made elsewhere, and so on".

This is a situation that can lead to misrepresentation in advertising, a point taken up by Consumentenbond, the Dutch national consumer organisation. Its comparative tests magazine, Consumentengids, has a long-standing policy never to mention where the products tested have been manufactured. Mr. W.J. van Campen, the Editor, further states that such information, quite apart from often being ambiguous, is irrelevant: "...from our own comparative testing we know for certain that the country of origin never contains any objective indication of the quality of a product".

Mr. van Campen's conclusion is that advertising which stresses such a correlation is misleading and restricts consumer choice through the establishment or support of prejudice. He cites the case of a supplier of bicycles which had printed on them "Made in Holland"; it was discovered that the minor bicycle part that bore those words was indeed the only part made in Holland. Mr. van Campen feels that such misleading claims and advertising call for agressive action: national consumer organisations should demand from advertisers proof, both of country of origin and of claims of special qualities linked to that origin.

That call for action can serve to introduce the second characteristic shared by these publications: all three further benefit the consumer by featuring articles on restrictive trade policies and practices. In Germany, for example, franchised automobile dealers were refusing to carry out the first free-of-charge inspection of cars purchased abroad. Once Test magazine printed statements made by automobile manufacturers attesting this basic right of the buyer, the situation improved. Consumentengids has published information on the existence of major price differences with neighbouring countries. The benefit to consumers here is twofold: at the same time that manufacturers and governments are pressured by the release of such information into reducing those price differences, the consumer can take advantage of existing price differences to buy more cheaply abroad. Mr. van Campen points out, however, that the improvement of international competition through the elimination of price differences can only happen if there is closer co-operation between national consumer organisations as regards the exchange of information on both prices and international trade procedures.

<u>Which?</u> has also published articles telling consumers how they are losing out because of trade restrictions and campaigning for changes on their behalf. Topics covered have included the Common Agricultural Policy -- how it works, what it costs consumers, and how it should be changed; Japan's agreement to limit exports and raise the prices of video recorders in the EC; and a discussion of import controls in general affecting a variety of products, which also considered the main argument in favour of any one country's import controls: the effect on employment. The magazine also has an ongoing campaign to get UK car prices reduced, financed in part by the proceeds from their <u>Importing A Car Action Kit</u>.

What is clear from the examples of all three magazines is that the key to best serving the interests of the consumer is indeed information. And getting that information takes a tremendous amount of work. Mr. Watts notes:

"Our campaigns on car prices and the Common Agricultural Policy, for example, have taken huge amounts of our scarce resources. And we can't throw the same resources at all the other areas which deserve it".

Consumers' Association has suggested that the UK Government set up "an independent body to analyse the pros and cons of each application for protection and to publish the results openly. It should also monitor the effects of measures currently in force. Then the public would know the costs and benefits of each protectionist measure. At the moment these costs are hidden".

CONCLUSION

The participants in this Workshop held very informal discussions and set out varied points of view. My report accordingly summarises the opinions that were expressed without claiming to reflect the consensus of the Workshop on every matter.

The Workshop made a number of observations on the role of consumer organisations and their publications in the area of international trade. The consumer media are concerned chiefly with comparative tests. These are designed to give consumers objective information about products and recommendations on the best buys, independent of the local or foreign origin of the products. Specialist reviews occasionally encourage their readers to buy abroad when price differences are significant, though they consider that this is not always easy. The organisations also endeavour to develop general consumer information, in particular with regard to the problems of foreign trade.

The participants identified a considerable number of obstacles to transparency in trade measures and to consumer information about international trade. First, there is the quite considerable lack of awareness of consumers on these matters. Even consumers' representatives are sometimes unable to evaluate trade measures on account of their number and complexity and the frequent lack of transparency, though some (such as anti-dumping procedures) are more transparent than others. It was further mentioned that some private measures to restrict imports, such as voluntary export restraints, were tolerated under certain competition laws.

The Workshop identified a lack of homogeneity among consumers and their organisations, which sometimes results in disaccord. In addition, the associations' shortage of financial resources was held to be a major handicap. When organisations use funds from public sources, their relative dependence may hamper their ability to criticise or make suggestions.

Some speakers stressed the relative lack of consumer interest in international trade questions; only when trade measures have direct and tangible consequences for their daily lives, and they are clearly aware of the relation, do consumers become concerned. In addition, it was mentioned that it is difficult to supply consumers with indications as to the consequences of given measures, since a proper idea can be formed only after the event (when it is too late for organisations to intervene). Finally, it is not always easy to identify the true consumer interest; a measure that appears favourable in the short term may turn out to be damaging in the long run, and vice versa. Can consumer representatives, for instance, wholly disregard questions of employment that may affect the purchasing power of considerable numbers of the population?

The fundamental suggestion put forward was to enhance general consumer knowledge about international trade. Such education should start in school, calls for continuing efforts and should be improved. One idea was that the OECD might take greater account of this concern for tangible consumer information when publishing its trade statistics. Governments should inform consumers of the foreseeable consequences of the trade measures that they adopt. In cases where this is difficult, they at least need to explain the reasons for their decisions. In fact, for the more important measures, consumer organisations should be associated at an early stage in the decision-making process in order to have the opportunity of stating their views before the trade measures are actually applied.

Lastly, it was considered that co-operation among consumer organisations should be encouraged, both nationally and internationally. The participants did not all share the view that an independent international agency could do useful work by collecting specialised information and statistics in this area and circulating them to member organisations. Some participants were more in favour of informal exchanges among consumer organisations.

Theme II

THE IMPACT OF CONSUMER PROTECTION ON INTERNATIONAL TRADE

SUMMARY

by

Nils Ringstedt
Deputy Director-General, National Board for Consumer Policy, Sweden

The papers contained in Theme II present concrete suggestions of possible ways to avoid barriers to trade and will, in my opinion, serve as a good basis for future work within the Consumer Policy Committee, particularly in the field of product safety. We now have a clearer picture of the connections between OECD consumer policy work and the work going on in other international organisations.

The Committee has already recognised that enhancing competition, improving the means of providing consumers with information and minimising safety hazards of products and services are among the basic requirements for an efficient functioning of the market and an open international trading system.

On the basis of what has been said in this Theme, I think it is necessary to take into account -- among other things -- the need to monitor developments in product-related measures at the international level with regard to both product safety and labelling requirements.

The contributions to Theme II very much supported the ongoing considerations in the Committee's Working Party on Product Safety regarding future work activities and priorities. To improve product safety while at the same time avoiding barriers to trade, it is -- in my opinion -- important to consider making the existing informal notification system more effective, to discuss possible improvements and, not least, to follow up the measures taken in Member countries as a result of the notifications. A continued exchange of information will hopefully in the long run lead to the adoption of similar measures in Member countries, benefiting both consumers and international trade.

With regard to the different regulations in Member countries, I believe it is essential for the Committee to continue discussions regarding measures to cope with the problem of export of hazardous products. It is necessary to find a common solution which takes into account the consumer's need of protection without at the same time disrupting international trade.

Many speakers have stressed the importance of reaching common international standards. That, of course, is a matter for the international standardization organisations. However, an aspect of international harmonization which has been and must, I believe, remain a part of the Committee's work is the need for reaching common principles on which methods and policy are to be based. Further work could be done in the OECD to encourage international co-operation in the area of product safety rules. This work could be concentrated on some selected product areas where there is particular international interest that regulations in Member countries become harmonized in order to avoid barriers to trade.

The Working Party on Product Safety has already suggested that work be undertaken to examine different product fields which are important from a safety point of view, studying them with the purpose of long-term harmonization of Member countries' measures. OECD Recommendations regarding investigated product fields could then support the work going on in international standardization bodies, for example by including suggestions that countries consider the possibility of adopting similar rules based on international standards once these are established. That need not necessarily result, as some may fear, in Member countries with a high level of consumer protection reducing their safety efforts. Rather, we should encourage other countries to harmonize their consumer protection in accordance with a higher level.

And perhaps we in the Committee should also consider taking up a more systematic discussion concerning regulations unrelated to product safety which also create trade barriers under the guise of consumer protection. I am not suggesting an extension of the notification system to regulations other than those regarding product safety, because that would duplicate work going on, i.e., in GATT. But the Committee could again consider the development in different countries of, for example, standardization, labelling, regulations, etc. and investigate the possibilities of harmonization in order to facilitate the situation of exporters in Member countries. In certain cases, self-regulation on the part of business as an alternative to government intervention should be explored further.

To sum up, I think the Committee has an urgent task to give increased attention to the trade aspect when considering consumer problems. In that way we can contribute internationally both to the protection of consumers and to the proper functioning of markets at the national and international levels.

PRODUCT SAFETY, TRADE BARRIERS AND PROTECTION OF CONSUMERS

by

Sverre Roed Larsen
Head of Division, State Pollution Control Authority, Norway

I. CONSUMER PROTECTION AND TRADE: HARMONY OR CONFLICT?

In its "Consumer Protection Charter of 1973", the Council of Europe has described one of the consumer rights thus: "the right of consumers to protection and assistance including both protection against typical physical damage due to unsafe products and protection against damage to the economic interest of the consumer".

Historically speaking, many examples can be cited of public efforts to safeguard the health of the individual member of the community, in particular by imposing requirements concerning, and controlling products such as, foods and beverages, housing conditions, sanitary conditions, etc. Following the technological development which led to new groups of products such as electrical appliances, motorised transport, etc., the protection of the individual was extended to these areas as well. But in this century, the mass manufacture of consumer goods and general economic progress in many countries have made it possible for a very large number of goods to be spread to the greater part of the population. In this explosive development in the standard of living, the efforts to ensure product safety and protect the health of the individual have lagged behind. In many countries there seems to be a similar sluggishness as regards regulations for and control of public and private service to consumers -- for example, authorisation for the installation and repair of products involving a serious potential hazard (lifts, electrical installations, safety requirements to hotels, restaurants, cinemas, etc.).

In the industrial countries, protection of the consumer as citizen or employee is the aspect of consumer safety which has been developed to the greatest degree in the form of legislation, institutional arrangements and specific functions. In some countries, the development of a public product control apparatus has meant that certain groups of products and services are now regulated from the point of view of safety. The production, import, sale and use of all such products must satisfy specific requirements as to properties, labelling, packaging, etc. Product safety considerations are also taken care of through various voluntary agreements between the authorities and industry and through internal arrangements within branches of industry producing certain groups of products. But there are great variations from country to country and region to region. The greatest differences are found between the various industrial countries themselves as regards the establishment and extent of the measures to ensure physical protection of the consumer.

In modern society, the consumer can choose between hundreds of thousands of different products within a very large number of product groups; however, only a very few types of products are subject to public control and regulation with a view to increased safety. The U.S. Consumer Product Safety Commission (CPSC) estimates, for example, that its area of responsibility covers about 15 000 different products, and only 220 of these are subject to one form or another of safety regulation. The OECD analysis of measures to increase children's safety also showed that many countries had not introduced specific measures against the hazardous products which appear frequently in the child's material environment.

The Norwegian Product Control Act imposes safety requirements for only four or five groups of products, other than chemical substances and products. In a number of areas the producer, importer and safety authorities have not acquired adequate knowledge about the harmful effects on the life and health of the consumer, and this may be why only few consumer products are regulated from the point of view of safety. It is not uncommon that the consumer version of a tool has a lower safety specification than the comparable tool manufactured for professional use.

It is only in the last ten years that the occurrence and extent of product-related accidents in the home and during leisure have been documented in any detail. The establishment at hospitals and outpatient clinics of a system for the collection of data on such accidents has played an important part in this connection. More systems of this kind and the increased application of them, for example for special in-depth analyses, will help to bring to light the extent to which the design and properties of the product are responsible for or are a contributory factor to the injury. Such knowledge is necessary both for further product development in industry, and for the formulation of suitable product-regulating measures on the part of the authorities.

A review of the percentage of controlled trade for all types of products in the years 1974 and 1980 shows that in the OECD countries, such trade increased from 36.3 to 44.3 per cent, and on a global basis from 40.1 to 47.8 per cent. In Norway the increase was from 16.3 to 33.7 per cent.

The trade pattern shows that more than two-thirds of the trade of the industrialised countries occurs with other industrialised countries, while the developing countries are becoming a steadily growing market for North America, Western Europe and Japan. In both the industrialised and the developing countries, manufactured goods are an important part of both exports and imports. The control of trade is especially widespread for textile products. Only a few countries, however, have introduced special safety regulations for textiles (e.g. the U.S., Canada, the UK, Australia, New Zealand and Norway), and the nature and extent of these safety regulations are such that the obstacles to trade in absolute terms should be minimal and, in relation to other restrictions to trade (quotas, labelling showing the country of origin, etc.), probably of negligible importance. At the same time, the public authorities give considerable support to different ways of maintaining and giving preferential treatment to the national textile industries. This example serves to illustrate how trade in a category of products of major importance to the consumers from the point of view of both comfort and economy, as well as safety, is strongly regulated in many countries, but where the regulations are very largely based on interests connected with the commercial and industrial policies.

It has not been possible to collect data to show just how much of the world trade is concerned with products that are subject to national restrictions relating to the safety of the individual. If specially regulated categories of products such as foodstuffs, transport and medicines and drugs are excluded, it seems reasonable to estimate that the number of other groups of safety-regulated, similarly specific products is small, and that the amount of trade in these products is also small. Even if today the actual safety regulation of consumer goods is not very widespread, this situation will certainly change in the future. Unless there is a clear shift over to true free trade, there is further reason to assume that the authorities will try to legitimise protectionist action with reference to the necessity for measures to safeguard the life and health of the consumer. The use of consumer protection in this way as an excuse for protectionism may easily lead to the loss of political goodwill in this sector, perhaps even to a general weakening of consumer safety protection.

In many countries, however, there seems to be a tendency to make a greater effort to encourage broader regional or even global co-operation. The focus on consumer protection as a special topic in the work of the United Nations, extended co-operation within such organisations as the International Organisation for Standardization (ISO) [including the Council Committee on Consumer Policy (COPOLCO)] and the International Electrotechnical Commission (IEC), the General Agreement on Tariffs and Trade (GATT) and the growth of activity of the International Organisation of Consumers Unions (IOCU) are examples of this global trend. Nevertheless, it would be an illusion to assume that the further development of the physical protection of the consumer and additional reductions in trade barriers can occur simultaneously without conflict. This is demonstrated clearly by experience from regional efforts. In a global perspective the problems will be much greater.

Uninhibited efforts to increase free trade will give the consumer a wider range of products and services at reasonable prices. But what in the short term may seem to be an economic gain for the consumer may also in certain cases result in both damage to health and economic loss over a longer period of time. This aspect will seldom be obvious, or present the consumer with a dilemma when he makes his purchase, partly because the risk connected with the product will usually be unknown, not properly elucidated, or difficult to assess.

Both for the consumer and the authorities, imported products can present special problems, sometimes more serious than the conflict with domestic production. These may relate to conditions connected with the product itself -- for example, properties, product information, etc. -- or conditions related to import and sale, such as complete lists of importers and dealers, possibilities for repair and procurement of spare parts, guarantee obligations, continuity of import, feedback of experience from the consumers, etc. To what extent these conditions may involve safety problems for the consumers and the authorities will depend, for example, on the foreign manufacturer's ability to participate as a serious partner in the trade arrangements, either directly through national sales departments, or indirectly through agents and importers with a responsible attitude towards product hazard.

Within the regional organisations involving close co-operation on economic policy, such as the EC, this conflict may often take another form, namely the possible clash between the desire to develop the physical protection of the consumer and the obligation to follow one's own directives. The decision of the EC Court in the so-called "Cassis de Dijon" case is important in this connection, because it establishes the principle that a product that is legally manufactured and sold in one of the member countries can be sold freely in the other member countries. In special, important cases such as the protection of health and safety, for example, national standards and technical regulations may be used to prevent imports.

In order to achieve greater harmony between the considerations relating to consumer protection and the interests of free trade, it is furthermore a prerequisite that the persons making the important decisions in industry, the administration and politics are all thoroughly acquainted with the interests of the different parties and of the consequences, both economic and from the point of view of health, of the different alternatives. To choose a high level of safety of products should be more attractive -- for manufacturers and consumers alike.

II. MEASURES TO ENSURE THE PHYSICAL PROTECTION OF THE CONSUMER, AND THE IMPACT ON INTERNATIONAL TRADE

The internationalisation and sale of consumer goods creates a number of problems, both for the consumers who purchase the goods, and for manufacturers and the various links in the chain of trade. Experience from the last ten years has shown that the sale and use of a particular type of product in an industrialised country may fit in well with the general needs of the consumer, while the similar sale in a developing country may have drastic, even fatal consequences for the consumers. A whole series of examples can be cited in connection with the sales of medicines, baby foods, pesticides and tobacco products and other stimulants, where the disregard or deliberate exploitation of social and economic conditions and/or the legal and political situation, etc. has led to the sale of products which have represented a direct threat to the life and health of the consumer. Therefore, seen from the point of view of many consumers, the very development of various product safety regulations which may unintentionally imply an obstacle to trade, e.g. for international concerns, may be the best possible guarantee of protection of life and health.

There seems to be a trend towards a world community divided into two: on the one hand, countries where consumer protection, both formally and in actual terms, is well developed through legislation, control authorities, etc.; and on the other, countries which do not have the resources to build up an effective system for the physical protection of the consumer. This gap in the actual protection of the consumer between different kinds of countries may lead to a distortion of the flow of trade, so that products that are declared dangerous, prohibited products, products with hidden hazardous properties, etc. are turned towards countries with minimum means of stopping the sale and use of these kinds of products.

Most agreements contain exceptions to the principle of free trade for reasons of national security. Furthermore, many international agreements confirm the right to national protection of the life and health of the citizens (personal safety).

In the European Free Trade Association (EFTA) Agreement, to which Norway is a party, it is stated that the Convention shall not prevent a country from implementing the measures necessary to protect the life or health of human beings, animals or plants. Article 36 of the Rome Treaty excludes, inter alia, prohibitions or restrictions on trade which are justified out of consideration for the protection of human beings, their life and health.

The interpretation of what may be a threat to national security or to the safety of the individual may vary considerably from country to country. Trade restrictions which in one country are motivated out of consideration for the safety of the consumer may in another country be regarded as protectionist measures, at least when applied to important articles of trade. The prohibition on the import of skateboards to Norway, implemented in 1978, can hardly be misinterpreted. As in the case of other prohibitions imposed for reasons of personal safety, this prohibition obviously applied also to domestic manufacture and marketing. When the same principle applies for domestic and foreign trade -- which is the case for the vast majority of prohibitions imposed for reasons of personal safety -- this is not a barrier to trade in the true sense.

The notifications exchanged between the different EFTA countries on trade barriers unconnected with tariffs are characteristic in that:

-- They almost never refer to conditions affecting the physical protection of the consumer;

-- The problem is usually connected with the requirement for labelling showing the country of origin, other labelling requirements, import duties and taxes, delays in connection with licences, foreign tests and analyses, registration of products, etc.;

-- Some of the notifications applied to consumer goods, but referred especially to foods, medicines, textiles and footwear.

With respect to trade between EFTA countries and EC countries, the notifications from the former to the latter indicate certain problems:

-- The EC directive concerning testing/type approval, which is often expensive, time-consuming and required for all the EC countries. Other countries' own tests, certificates, approvals and labelling are not accepted;

-- Various aspects of the consumers' safety are referred to more frequently, particularly those regarding building materials and fittings and transport. A Swedish report to France, based on the French Act of 1978 relating to consumer protection and information, in principle covers all consumer goods.

Since the GATT arrangement for notification of regulations which may imply technical obstacles to trade entered into force on 1st January 1980, a total of 851 such notifications were recorded (in the period 1980-1983). An analysis of these showed that in the period 1981-83, 752 notifications were issued, 131 of them from the U.S. and 17 from Norway. Of the notifications from the U.S., 13 related to product regulations implemented by the Consumer Product Safety Commission. More than half of the Norwegian notifications related to measures to ensure personal safety. A review of all the GATT notifications for the last three years brings to light the following typical characteristics:

-- The number of notifications from the different countries varies considerably. In the period 1981-83, five countries alone were responsible for as many as 478 of the total of 752 notifications. Thirteen of the 37 GATT Member countries did not issue any notifications in the period;

-- The notifications relating to personal safety play a noticeable but not, generally speaking, dominant part in the picture;

-- The period for comment is often relatively short. In 1983, only four countries on average allowed a period of comment exceeding the recommended 60 days.

The specific product safety requirements issued by the authorities will often be expressed in the form of references to international, national or regional standards, test methods or technical specifications. To date, relatively few standards have been issued by the ISO which deal in whole or in part with the safety aspects of consumer products. The proportion of safety standards/test methods is probably greater in the electrotechnical sector, where the international standards are prepared by IEC. The situation is probably the same in Europe in respect of standards issued by CEN (Comité Européen de Normalisation) and CENELEC (the equivalent body for electrical standards). As regards CEN, it is estimated that about 30 per cent of the total number of European Standards (EN) and Harmonization Documents (HD) issued to date are concerned with safety. At the national level there seem to be great variations from country to country. For example, Sweden has developed far more national safety standards in the consumer goods sector than Norway, where there are exceptionally few.

A large number of technical specifications and test methods are developed outside the framework of the usual standardization organisations, partly by special organisations and partly by industry itself. Often the manufacturer alone will decide the different properties of his own products. This development of numerous and often very different technical specifications as regards safety from the different manufacturers may thus lead to a situation where the market offers several products of the same kind, but with very different properties from the point of view of safety. In such cases the consumer will find it either very difficult or impossible to assess the safety of one product as against another and make a deliberate and calculated evaluation of the risk. In this way the safety of the consumer is reduced particularly in connection with the purchase and use of products which obviously involve a hazard, such as bicycles and motorised products for hobby and leisure purposes, and of products intended to give special protection against obvious risk, such as helmets, life-jackets and crampons. In many cases the consumer will make his purchase out of a "false feeling of safety", either in the belief that there must obviously be official requirements for a certain minimum standard of safety, or professional faith in the branch of industry itself on the basis of previous experience. In Norway there are no official requirements, for example, concerning most forms of personal protection equipment in the consumer sector. Another example is the bicycle trade, which previously mainly sold Norwegian-manufactured products of high quality. In recent years, however, the large imports of low-price bicycles has led to more varied standards of safety as regards design, manufacture and equipment. In this and many other product sectors the different branches have shown little ability to exercise internal control and develop common standards on a voluntary basis.

In many areas, from the Norwegian point of view at any rate, there is a need for increased effort toward greater harmonization of safety requirements for consumer products. Regional co-operation is appropriate for many reasons; in the case of Norway, this would involve both Nordic and European co-operation.

NORDTEST and INSTA are two of the collaborative organisations established within the Nordic countries.

One of the aims of NORDTEST is to promote the development of product testing, thus facilitating Nordic trade collaboration and contact as well as improving the ability of Nordic industry to compete on the international market. NORDTEST has developed a whole series of test methods, some of them directed purely at safety. A special expert group for consumer goods was established in 1980.

The importance of NORDTEST and other similar organisations for the reduction of trade barriers can be summarised as follows:

1. The development of common methods of testing helps to reduce or prevent technical obstacles to trade occurring already in the first phase of product regulation;

2. The need for test methods is considered of major importance in connection with the work going on or planned to formulate regulations, and in deciding which test methods should be given priority;

3. The general effect of the regulations will increase in step with the increase in the number of NORDTEST methods;

4. The effect of the work of harmonization can be increased by using the methods, standards of co-operation and experience from the ordinary work of standardization.

The effect of NORDTEST on the preparation of regulations in the Nordic countries has been greatest in connection with building and construction, fire, the mechanical industry and noise.

INSTA is a Nordic co-operation agreement in the field of standardization to which all the national standardization organisations are a party except for the electrotechnical sector, which has its own organisation, NOREK. INSTA does not issue any special standards of its own. The results of INSTA's work are published as national standards in each country.

Assessed as a whole, the co-operation through NORDTEST and INSTA has so far had little influence on the national work to ensure product safety, at least in Norway. Resources have been limited, and the work has not been co-ordinated to any extent with national long-term programmes.

In the field of product safety, there is a clear tendency towards an increase in the number of regulations concerning a product's properties, labelling, etc. Such regulations will often be put into effect in spite of the lack of international or national standardization, lack of test methods, etc. Therefore, in order to prevent the establishment of new trade barriers, it will be necessary to achieve a far greater degree of co-operation at an early stage in the preparation than occurs today in the best of cases. The present systems of notification -- both the formal systems like the GATT arrangement which exists in the EFTA and EC countries, and the informal arrangements existing within the OECD, the Nordic Council of Ministers, etc. -- at present function more as channels of information on the regulations, rather than co-operative efforts aimed at making the regulations more uniform. It seems that real international co-operation on product regulation will have to be founded on quite different organisational or institutional arrangements than those established at present.

In some countries, there is a total lack of safety regulations in many product areas. A firm exporting to such countries is therefore confronted not with specific requirements as to the safety of the product, but instead with a situation of "non-regulation". A consequence of this may be that the exporter complies with the standard or regulations having the most optimal effects for safety. In this way he will be able to achieve a uniform production series for export to several countries while taking into account the safety of the consumer. This standpoint was put forward when the Working Party No. 3 discussed the OECD report on safety requirements for toys in 1973. An argument in this connection is that because national markets for these particular products (toys) have very similar features, more stringent safety requirements in the one country will thus make it possible to improve the standard of safety for toys in other countries. For example, strict Swedish requirements regarding toys will have a positive effect on the quality of the toys imported to Norway. Obviously, another possible consequence is the widespread export of poor quality and hazardous products to such countries, because there are no official regulations or control; countries with no safety regulations in a particular product sector may risk becoming a dumping ground for batches of goods rejected in a neighbouring country. This happened in the case of a large batch of toys (Magic Eggs) which were ruled forbidden in Sweden in summer 1983, and which the Swedish importers immediately tried to resell in Norway. Similar (more lasting) situations exist in more traditional, regulated fields where either the regulations have not been brought up to date or there is inadequate control. In the case of foods and cosmetics as well, Norway risks being used as the recipient of products which have been rejected in the other Nordic countries.

Even if experience shows that in certain sectors it is necessary to maintain and further develop the public protection of the consumer, greater emphasis should at the same time be placed on developing industry's ability to exercise internal control. In the Norwegian Product Control Act this is expressed as a general requirement for care which is the special responsibility of the manufacturer and the importer, and imposes the obligation to obtain adequate knowledge concerning the products manufactured or sold. The intention is to prevent injury.

Due to the enormous range of products found in modern society, widespread international trade and rapid changes in the products themselves, there are several factors which will have the effect of substantially restricting the ability of the authorities to ensure the protection of the consumer. This should, therefore, be primarily the responsibility of industry itself -- in all phases of production, from product development through manufacture, marketing and sale. The main function of the authorities will then be to stimulate an awareness of the risk, promote a positive attitude towards the efforts to prevent accidents, and to give practical advice and concrete support towards product development and testing.

III. PRODUCT CONTROL IN PRACTICE -- NORWEGIAN EXAMPLES FROM FOUR PRODUCT AREAS

Norway has stringent public health legislation in respect to foods, medicines and stimulants of various kinds. There is also strict regulation of special products such as electrical appliances. The general Product Control Act dates only from 1976, and so far has been applied to very few products. The standards prepared in this connection are to a large degree adapted to already existing standards in other countries. Therefore the Norwegian Product Control Act should not result in noticeable trade barriers on imports to Norway. Norway imports a substantial proportion of its consumer goods, and is thus extremely dependent on trade.

Example 1: Electrical appliances

Electrical equipment is potentially very dangerous. The control of such equipment varies. In some cases the control is the responsibility of the supplier of electricity. In Norway the control is exercised by a public agency, the Norwegian Board for Testing and Approval of Electrical Equipment (NEMKO). What distinguishes NEMKO and similar control arrangements from the system practised in most other countries is the obligation for control. This obligation applies to heavy-current and weak-current equipment which may cause radio interference or which generates high voltages, e.g. fluorescent hand-lamps. The Norwegian control does not apply to electrical wiring or cables which can be approved on the basis of tests in other West European countries.

The obligation for control works in that the Norwegian representative of a company must submit a product for testing. If the product is approved, it may be sold and the representative is responsible for ensuring that the product sold is the same as the product approved. There is a similar arrangement in Sweden. Several importers may obtain approval for the same product, but in order to ensure full control, each importer's product is registered separately and given a different type of labelling. NEMKO's fee is partly a fixed (one-time) fee and partly a tax on the value after sale. In the Nordic countries, there is an arrangement where approval may be granted on the basis of documentation of tests carried out in another of the Nordic countries.

The problems relating to international trade and the NEMKO arrangement are primarily connected with two factors: 1) representation in Norway and 2) different rules. Representation in Norway is connected with the necessity for control. A responsible agency in Norway will make the control more effective.

Different rules are an obstacle to trade which apply to many different measures. In the electrical sector, strenuous efforts have been made to harmonize requirements. But the requirements still differ for good reasons. In some cases the same product will nevertheless be sold in two countries having different requirements. For example, there is reason to believe that stoves sold in Norway and Sweden are the same, in spite of different requirements. Simplification, including common testing and approval on the basis of documentation, helps to make the most stringent rules the ones actually applied in several countries. Many of the problems of consumer protection can already be solved at the design stage. In such cases, it will not necessarily be more expensive to use the same standard for several countries, and the consumer in one country will benefit from the improved consumer protection introduced in other countries. Since large countries usually mean a larger market, the standards applying in these countries will be more easily accepted in other countries. To the extent that the requirements are more stringent, the consumers in the other countries will benefit from this protection without these countries having introduced such strict regulations themselves.

Import by consumers themselves, or the possibility for such import, may lead to lesser increases in prices, due to segmentation of the market. In the case of electrical products, in Norway it is permitted to import single examples of a product without a control by NEMKO. The use of such products shall be approved only by the local Electricity Board. NEMKO approval must be obtained, however, for products used in connection with hair and the skin. The reason is that several serious accidents have occurred from the use of products imported directly in this way. There are examples of cases where consumers have bought household appliances cheaper in another country which looked exactly the same as those sold in Norway. But these machines have been shown to have a far lower level of consumer protection, because a special series was manufactured in order to conform with Norwegian requirements.

A recent example illustrates some important aspects of protection of the consumer against dangerous electrical products. An electric lamp manufactured in a European country was submitted for control, but could not be approved because the temperature in the holder, the flex and the base was too high. After the lamp had been improved by using, among other things, a ceramic holder, it was approved. It was found, however, that none of the sold examples complied with the requirements, or were of the same standard as the lamp which was originally submitted for approval. This illustration shows the need for follow-up inspection, and responsible representation in Norway. Furthermore, the variations in the requirements can be explained by conditions peculiar to the different countries -- in this case, different building traditions and the different use of the lamps. The well-insulated wooden ceilings common in Norway require greater protection against heat from roof lamps; also, lamps in Norway are used for a longer time per day and for more months of the year.

Example 2: Highly flammable textiles

In the last fifteen to twenty years, most industrial countries have given steadily increasing attention to flammable textiles. The growing interest in efforts to prevent accidents and the research activity performed in many countries has led to much greater knowledge of the part played by textiles in accidents caused by fire. The Norwegian authorities want to reduce the potential risk to which consumers are exposed by removing from the market products which present an unreasonable risk of catching fire and causing injury from burns.

Textile products are consumer commodities which are largely sold across national boundaries. The Norwegian authorities have therefore tried to harmonize their rules as far as possible with those of other countries, particularly the Nordic countries. This must not, however, in any way reduce the desired safety for the consumer.

Regulations concerning the Prohibiting of Highly Flammable Textile Products entered into force in Norway on 13th February 1984. The main intention of the regulations is to prevent easily ignitable and flammable textiles from being used in children's clothing, but requirements are also imposed for wearing apparel for adults and piece-goods used for clothing. The textiles are tested in accordance with a well-known American standard method, ASTM 1230-83.

The total prohibition on extremely flammable textiles will probably only to a small extent represent a real barrier to trade. It will have very little effect on Norwegian-manufactured goods, and little effect on imports. With a little extra effort it will be possible to manufacture textiles which meet the requirements of the Norwegian regulations, and are therefore also safer products for the consumer.

Example 3: Metal in food containers

Containers for the preparation, storage or intake of food may be dangerous in that some metals could dissolve into the food. In the past, examples have been found in Norway of imported ceramic products where the glaze, in particular, contained heavy metals which the food absorbed. In more recent years, there have been several examples of cooking pans which have released too much nickel or lead into the food. These vessels came from France, Portugal and Korea.

There is no system of approval for these products. However, both the legislation relating to foodstuffs and the product control legislation give government the authority to interfere. Relevant initiatives are recall, pro-hibition, agreement, injunction and negotiation. The responsible authorities are the Directorate of the Health Services and the local Boards of Health. Trade barriers, if any, will have their foundation in the regulations issued by the Ministry of Health and Social Affairs. When these regulations vary from country to country, certain products will not be able to be imported. The protection of the consumer is weakened, however, in that the problems have to be discovered by the consumers themselves. Sometimes this does not happen until somebody has been injured by the products.

Prohibition and similar measures directed at specific products and batches of goods may prevent other countries with less stringent requirements, or no requirements at all in this sector, from being burdened with products which are dangerous and rejected elsewhere. In the case of cooking vessels, there are examples of a prohibition on sales which only applies locally, because it has been imposed by the local Board of Health. With respect to the actual cooking vessels concerned, it is known that one batch has been returned to the manufacturer in France, and it is possible that the product can be sold there.

Example 4: Toys -- safety guidelines

Various kinds of accidents occur in connection with the use of toys of poor quality. In the toys sector, Norway is lagging far behind most of the OECD countries as regards both accident statistics and measures by the authorities. Through the special Nordic system of notification, the product control authorities came to know of several toys which had been prohibited in other countries, and were then dumped on the Norwegian market. Through the efforts of the Inter-Ministerial Committee to Prevent Accidents to Children in the two-year period 1st July 1981 to 1st July 1983, children's safety was finally given high priority by the Norwegian Administration. At the end of its term of office, the Committee distributed diverse recommendations to the authorities concerned.

Toys are commodities which in Norway are largely imported. The Norwegian authorities therefore try to impose requirements regarding the toys which harmonize to the greatest degree possible with the provisions in other countries, especially the Nordic countries.

A Norwegian Standard for mechanical and physical properties of toys was published in 1983. In 1984 a Norwegian Standard was published for chemical and flammable properties of toys. The standards, which are based on European requirements, are the co-operative effort of branch representatives, consumers and the product control authorities. The new "Safety Guidelines for Toys" describe how the product control authorities consider that the requirement for care, as expressed in the Product Control Act of 11 June 1976, should be complied with. The guidelines are intended as advice to the manufacturer, importer and others concerned with the requirements which the authorities consider it reasonable to impose for this type of product. If experience shows that the guidelines are not followed, then the product control authorities will consider proposing binding regulations in this sector. The guidelines are very largely based on the existing Norwegian standards, but also address the problem of noise from toys of such a level as may damage hearing.

IV. INCREASED CONSUMER PROTECTION WITH MINIMAL BARRIERS TO TRADE

The measures which may serve to harmonize the national formulation of regulations concerning product safety include the following:

-- Property specifications, test methods and regulations should as far as possible be international;

-- When regulating specific products/groups of products, the requirements as to properties and the test methods should be specified in one and the same set of regulations;

-- In sectors where internationally accepted rules for the approval of test institutions have been developed, tests conducted at an approved test institution should be accepted by the regulating authorities of another country;

-- Co-operation on regional and international measures to promote product safety should be directed to a far greater degree at practical co-ordination of the development of regulations with associated requirements, test methods, rules for certification, labelling, etc.

Relevant measures on the part of the authorities to facilitate the import of consumer goods can include:

-- Advising importers concerning the course of action open to them if
their products are declared prohibited or as having hazardous properties, i.e., if they do not comply with stipulated standards or
regulations, or other requirements for care;

-- Making the control mechanism connected with import and sampling of
specimens of products for testing, and the testing itself, simpler
and more effective.

V. CONCLUSION

It is generally accepted and expressed internationally, nationally and
regionally in different connections that the right to safety of life and
health is one of the most fundamental rights of the consumer. The formal and
institutional protection of the individual varies considerably, however, from
country to country and among industrialised and developing countries in
particular.

Historically speaking, the individual countries have made the greatest
effort to protect the health of the individual in his capacity as employee,
and in connection with the basic functions of the role of the consumer, such
as nutrition, housing and sanitary conditions. Mass production and the
development of the welfare society has meant that the safety regulation of
many consumer products has not managed to keep up with events. In many countries the incidence of accidents in the home is higher than that of accidents
at work or in traffic.

The development of new, general product control legislation and exten-
sions to the traditional special legislation, very different administrative
structures, resources, consumer patterns and patterns of risk, collectively
give an extremely varied picture of the efforts to limit the occurrence and
use of hazardous consumer products in many industrial countries. The picture
is further complicated by the fact that the national authorities have often
introduced different safety measures for one and the same product (and the
same type of injury). This gives rise to varying safety profiles for the consumers in the different countries.

In the course of the last three to five years, the long-term tendency
towards free trade has been weakened. The protectionist measures span over a
wide range, and often the real measures of consumer protection are the least
significant for the occurrence of trade barriers. Even if the degree of
protection, and thus the occurrence of trade barriers, varies substantially
from country to country, the main overall impression is that the obstacles to
trade are few and insignificant, and the benefit to the consumer far exceeds
the costs in terms of trade policy. Without international harmonization, however, increased protection of the consumer may involve a possibility for the
development of more technical barriers to trade in the future.

The growth of the multinational companies, the tendency for internationalisation and the increased marketing of proprietary brands known the
world over have changed the status of the traditional domestic industry on the
consumer market. Consumers have in a sense become global: every day

commodities and capital goods alike contain a high proportion of products manufactured abroad. This is further reflected in the import statistics. A dominant feature, however, is trade within regions and among the industrial countries themselves. The developing countries are still to a large extent suppliers of raw materials and receivers of manufactured goods.

Norway has fairly stringent public health regulations in the traditional areas of foods, medicine and drugs (stimulants). There is also strict control in other specific consumer sectors, especially of electrical equipment. But the general Product Control Act only dates from 1976, and so far has resulted in very few cases of regulation of products. Therefore with respect to Norway's import, which is very large, the product control measures should present few problems. Norwegian export, on the other hand, is confronted with various national safety requirements in certain other countries. But these usually cause only minor or unimportant problems for Norwegian export compared with other kinds of discriminating arrangements.

"Globally" speaking, the resources do not exist to provide reasonably good protection of the life and health of the consumer against injury from hazardous products, without having to resort to product regulation of the kind which can result in obstacles to trade. Compared with the need, no international standards, test methods, certification arrangements, etc. exist which can form the basis for uniform requirements in all important areas of consumer goods. Nor are there any global institutions or procedures adequate to provide an effective harmonization of national measures to ensure safety. At the present stage, the strongly expressed requirement for harmonization may in fact lead to a weakening of the protection of the health of the consumer nationally. In the short term, stronger regional co-ordination may lead to a better balance between consumer protection and the prevention or reduction of technical barriers to trade.

CONSUMER PROTECTION AND PROTECTIONISM

by

Tony Venables
Director, Bureau Européen des Unions de Consommateurs (BEUC),
Brussels, Belgium

I. INTRODUCTION

BEUC appreciates the holding of this Symposium by the OECD. For years, we have been asking the EC to take consumer interests into account in trade relations, and particularly to calculate the impact of trade barriers on consumers. We will now be able to put forward the same demands with the support of the OECD and the proposals contained in the Committee on Consumer Policy Report "to give greater weight to consumer policy considerations in trade and related measures". The recommendations as they stand are somewhat general and are not binding. The next stage should be for governments and international organisations to take them up and make them binding. This would be an important step forward, since mechanisms to take consumer interests into account in trade questions are non-existent in the vast majority of countries.

In this report, I will show that such mechanisms are badly needed. This is not only because the consumer protection argument is absent from trade negotiations, but also because it is already being used and, more frequently, misused. It is a justification both for maintaining barriers to trade on health, safety and quality grounds and for abolishing them (access to a wider choice of goods at lower prices). In fact, both "sides" of the same trade dispute often make contradictory appeals to the interests of consumers, invariably the only group whose opinions are not sought. National producer and manufacturer associations often receive the support of governments in resorting to false consumer protection arguments to justify trade barriers, which in fact are nothing but a disguised loss of consumer choice and purchasing power. In this way, the currency of consumer protection is devalued and, in turn, legitimate consumer protection measures are wrongly criticised as protectionist. I will examine this problem by referring to the case-law of the European Court of Justice. This case-law is of interest beyond the EC, because it serves as a model for exposing false consumer protection arguments and identifying consumers' real interests.

A. Definition of the consumer interest in trade

Before examining how consumer interests can be taken into account on a specific case-by-case basis, there has to be an agreed general definition. Consumers are best served by a wide choice of goods and services, at reasonable prices and corresponding to accepted safety and health standards. If this definition is self-evident, so too is the scope for confusing consumer interests and indeed creating a false opposition between a safe market and a free market. Safety objectives and economic objectives are reverse sides of the same coin, requiring different policies.

Consumer organisations have drawn attention to a number of measures required to improve the safety of products in trade:

-- Alert systems to ensure not only that information is circulated among the responsible authorities about dangerous products or substances in trade, but also that these items are withdrawn from the market;

-- Requirements in national and EC regulations to ensure that products withdrawn from the domestic market for health and safety reasons are not exported;

-- A regime of "strict liability" to make manufacturers responsible for injury or death caused by defective products proposed for all countries, to avoid double standards in safety and in the treatment of victims in different countries.

Consumer interests are clearly identical to the anti-protectionist interest, but a number of measures are necessary to take them into account explicitly:

-- Mechanisms are needed to qualify the loss to consumers from tariff or non-tariff barriers, which often exceed the gains to the workers or employers of the particular industry protected by them. As long as it remains invisible, this loss will remain underestimated (1);

-- The losses to consumers are spread over the broad mass of the population, so even when quantified they may appear acceptable compared with the gains to a particular sector or regime hard pressed by unemployment. Often though, the resulting hidden tax on consumers hits the least-well-off consumers hardest (e.g. when it is applied to clothing, food), and reduces their purchasing power and living standards.

Taking consumer interests into account in trade questions requires policies which are both regulatory and deregulatory. Ideally, there should be no contradiction or confusion between the interests in safety and in price, because the corresponding policies would be applied at different stages in the manufacture and distribution of products. Consumer interests are best served by regulatory efforts to ensure that products are safe before they are put on the market, but by the maximum degree of free trade and competition once they are distributed.

B. The problem of priorities

Besides seeing their interests represented on a case-by-case basis, it is equally if not more important for consumers to ensure that policies to eliminate trade barriers are based on clear priorities. It is often said that neo-protectionism is particularly insidious because it is difficult to detect. It is rarely admitted though in the general rhetoric about the "fight against protectionism" that trade barriers are complex and choosing the right priorities to eliminate them is therefore difficult. For example, "frontier formalities" is the current fashion in the EC, but while their elimination would be of undoubted wider symbolic importance, this should not be presented as the only means of creating a "Citizen's Europe". Delays at frontiers are a soft and visible target, but other restrictions on trade -- for example in the services sector -- which are more difficult to assess and dismantle represent a more substantial burden on the consumer. If trade policy were pursued in the consumer interest, dismantling of barriers to trade would concentrate on goods and services which are important items in the household budget (i.e., cars, basic foodstuffs, etc.). This is not the case, for example, where specific action is taken largely in response to complaints from traders with a vested interest. Despite its importance, the action by the European Court of Justice has not yet had an impact on some of the most protected areas, like air fares.

Consumer interests are not met either when the "fight against protectionism" is seen only in terms of the elimination of disparities in national legislation and the removal of obstacles to trade under government control while ignoring the contribution manufacturers can make to maintaining or reducing trade barriers. In the car sector, BEUC's price surveys have raised discussion and further research about the extent to which price differences for the same models in the EC are due to differences in tax regimes and technical standards, or rather, to the desire of manufacturers to insulate national markets. Parallel progress is therefore often needed under instruments to remove barriers to trade and antitrust laws (2).

C. Protectionism in the EC's other policies and in trade relations with the rest of the world

I should also like to mention briefly some of the wider trade problems before examining the case history of the European Court. It is necessary to make it clear that there are other policies where the consumer interest in trade liberalisation is being ignored totally, and that like national authorities, the EEC does not always practice what it preaches about protectionism.

The Common Agricultural Policy (CAP) has discriminated against consumers, and never so clearly as when it came to deciding how to reduce the two-million-ton dairy surplus. Faced with the option of cutting farm prices, which would be to the advantage of consumers, or introducing milk quotas, EC agricultural ministers opted for the latter. Quotas inevitably become an umbrella for putting up farm and food prices, while limiting the financial liability of the EC budget for disposing of surpluses. Quantitative limits in production amount to transforming part of the visible budgetary burden of the CAP into an additional burden on the consumer in the form of higher food prices, a cost which remains conveniently hidden (3). A short-term emergency programme to reduce budget expenditure, including quotas and other proposals, may have pushed the CAP irrevocably in a more protectionist direction. In fact, consumers and taxpayers on both sides of the Atlantic now have a clear common interest in limiting the protectionist pressures on imported food as well as the race for subsidised export markets, which are the options preferred to domestic consumer subsidies, cheaper food at home and less expensive ways of meeting the social objectives of agricultural policy, such as direct income support to small farmers.

Agreements between the EC and Japan on video tape recorders provide another example. In theory, there might be an advantage for consumers if the various bilateral and voluntary restraint agreements between European countries and Japan were put on an EEC footing. In practice, however, the Tokyo agreement between the EC and Japan on video tape recorders in 1983 is a very dangerous precedent: it contains not only a quantitative arrangement, but also an undertaking by Japanese producers to respect a floor price. Recently the agreement has been renewed despite evidence that it did not succeed in its objective of protecting the European Video 2000 system. It has had the effect of maintaining prices higher than they might otherwise be, given the increase in demand. BEUC has carried out two price surveys in this area which show large price differences for the same models.

The third example is textiles. BEUC in 1981 demanded a phasing out of the Multifibre Arrangement (MFA) governing textile imports. We will be asking the same, with a better chance of success, when the MFA negotiations start again.

The reason this paper focusses on barriers to intra-Community trade is simply that the consumer protection argument is being constantly used as a justification in specific cases -- the theme of our contribution to this Symposium. The consumer protection argument is largely absent from trade negotiations between the EC and the rest of the world, but of course that does not mean that they are of any less importance to consumers. International trade restrictions on food and clothing in fact probably have a bigger impact on consumer welfare than many of the examples discussed here.

II. CASE STUDIES

A. Background to the case-law of the European Court

In this section, the use and abuse of consumer protection is examined in relation to "campaigns to buy national", protecting consumers against unfair "commercial practices" and "health and safety". The consumer protection argument is often central to case-law on intra-EC trade, although it goes unrepresented. This is because it is inherent in the provisions of the Treaty, the interplay of arguments between articles 30 to 36 and their interpretation by the Court and the Commission.

The widest possible interpretation is given to "measures having an equivalent effect" (to tariffs or quantitative restrictions which have been eliminated in the Common Market) under article 30 as "any national measure capable of hindering, directly or indirectly, actually or potentially, intra-Community trade" (Case 8/74, "Dassonville"). This was reaffirmed in the "Cassis de Dijon" case (Case 120/78), the importance of which was recognised by the Commission in a special communication on the judgement (OJ C256/2 of 3/10/1980). The case-law underlined the principle that products lawfully produced and marketed in one of the member states can be introduced to any other member state, at least as far as commercial and technical regulations are concerned. The principle also applies where such regulations do not discriminate against foreign products.

Although not specifically mentioned as one of the potentially legitimate justifications for maintaining a barrier to trade in article 36, "Cassis de Dijon" introduces consumer protection, and gives it a wider interpretation than protection of public health. The Court rules that "Obstacles to movement within the Community resulting from disparities between the national laws relating to the marketing of the products in question must be accepted insofar as those provisions may be recognised as being necessary in order to satisfy mandatory requirements relating in particular to the effectiveness of fiscal supervision, the protection of public health, the fairness of commercial transactions and the defence of the consumer".

In its communication, the Commission went further than the Court in drawing general conclusions and attempting to lay down "very strict criteria" in order to assess claims that a national measure is a "mandatory require- ment": it must be necessary, correspond to a general and compelling interest, be coherent and least likely to hinder trade. This application of general criteria, placing the burden of proof on member states to justify consumer protection measures (i.e., as "necessary" rather than just "desirable"), naturally caused concern to consumer organisations at the time, and might indeed have led to existing national rules being undermined, or could have been used as a pretext not to introduce new measures [see opinion of the Consumers Consultative Committee (CCC 29/81 rev 4)]. Fortunately, this initial anxiety over the role of the Court in eliminating trade barriers has not been borne out in practice. Rather than using general criteria, the Court has applied a reasonableness test on a case-by-case basis.

With the deep and prolonged recession, the threats to consumer inte- rests have in reality been the protectionist pressures exerted by producers, manufacturers and their national associations rather than attempts to under- mine genuine consumer protection measures. Between 1980 and 1983, possible infringements of the EC Treaty rules increased from 28 to 192 and complaints from 180 to 399 (4). The Commission comments as follows on this increase: "The trend is not only quantitative: the infringements are taking more sophisticated forms and are often deliberate. The public is becoming in- creasingly aware of this. Consequently, the Commission is taking stronger measures, as failure to take action, or belated action, against such infringe- ments might, especially in the present difficult economic climate, encourage proliferation, or even retaliatory action". What the public sees is only the tip of the iceberg, but it is enough to make a mockery of the concept of a common market -- farmers taking the law into their own hands to stop imports from other countries, and periodic outbreaks of long-standing disputes (e.g. Franco-Italian over wine; Anglo-French over milk and lamb; dubious use of import controls for public and animal health reasons, etc.). The irony is that such health checks, if they are not excessive, may well be justified in the absence of agreed EC methods of controls in areas such as pesticides or hormones; often, however, clear retaliatory motives are revealed because they are introduced when there are trade disputes in other areas.

Rather than keeping their distance and taking the broader public inte- rest into account, government ministers have in many instances lent public and vocal support to the protectionist demands of national producer associations, even when they must have known that their claims stood no chance at all of being accepted in the European Court. Apparently even if the legal case is weak, it can still be strong politically and at any rate receives widespread press coverage. When health reasons fail, governments and producer associa- tions often resort to appeals to xenophobia and make false allegations about other countries' products which, if made by a consumer organisation, would probably lead to libel action. Declarations by British ministers concerning UHT milk, and those of their German counterparts concerning other countries'

beer, are good examples. Legitimate measures to protect health and safety
standards and consumers against dishonest trading often become enforced with a
deliberately protectionist intent as part of commercial policy. It would be
too easy to dismiss those issues which attract public attention as exceptional; they reveal the protectionist climate of the recession and the
"guiding principles" which lie behind such non-tariff barriers to trade: the
chauvinistic attitudes that the quality of domestically produced goods is
naturally superior to that of foreign goods; that the consumer is ignorant of
this and therefore paternalistic government intervention is deemed necessary;
and that the "efficient" domestic producer needs to be protected from these
"substandard" products (5).

B. Campaigns to buy national

BEUC represents organisations which for the most part derive their
revenue from providing objective advice to consumers on the whole range of
products on the market, whether domestic or foreign. Advice to consumers
through comparative testing and surveys helps to provide information to
counter the various schemes to "buy national", "quality labelling" and appeals
to brand loyalty through advertising, etc. "Buy national" campaigns mislead
consumers because they appeal to patriotism but the products and the firms are
rarely purely "national"; a brand name often says nothing about the
nationality of the product. Cars and domestic appliances in particular are
increasingly multinational products. It is debatable whether EC Treaty rules
can be applied to non-governmental campaigns to buy national; there has to be
a degree of government support or complicity. In one of the few cases to be
dealt with by the Court (Case 249/81 -- Commission against Ireland), the Court
found that a programme covering the economy as a whole aiming to slow down
intra-EC trade by a national advertising campaign to promote the purchase of
national products was against article 30 of the Treaty. In reality, this
particular campaign did not succeed in its objective. Fortunately many authorities are beginning to realise that although people may support the idea of
"buying national" as citizens, they may not as consumers. Consumers claim
that their reduced purchasing power does not allow them to buy more expensive
or superior-quality products, or that they might buy more nationally if only
the products they wanted were manufactured nationally.

It is because the direct appeal to "buy national" has little lasting
impact that some authorities experiment from time to time with more sophisticated indirect appeals, using the language of consumer protection itself to
persuade the consumer to concentrate on domestic products.

In February 1983, BEUC introduced a complaint, together with l'Union
Fédérale des Consommateurs (UFC) in France, against a quality labelling scheme
promoted by the Minister for Consumer Affairs whereby a (national) manufacturer would sign a quality contract with one or more consumer organisations, backed by a publicly funded advertising campaign. In the preparatory
discussions, it became evident that it was enough for a manufacturer to add a
few improvements to an existing product or service. This therefore had
nothing to do with the concept of quality, which must, by definition, cover
all aspects of a product. "This sort of label...may be contradicted at any
time by our own comparative tests or by our surveys. It is the negation of
the serious studies we make to improve quality. There is therefore a very
serious risk that these quality contracts will harm the credibility of

consumer organisations" (Note to the BEUC Council by UFC). The way this scheme was devised obviously went further than most towards attempting to "recuperate" the consumer organisations and promote national manufacturers (6).

And this is by no means an isolated example. There is an abundance of quality labelling schemes of all kinds in all countries; seals of approval by national standards organisations; and symbols used by manufacturers' associations. Some are quite genuine and honest attempts to protect a certain quality product. But the more they proliferate, the more they reveal protectionist purposes, and are often misleading as to the quality of the products and the guarantee service.

The Court of Justice sees no objection to quality labelling provided it does not infringe the Treaty rules, i.e., it must correspond to objective characteristics inherent in the product which make it better than others, and not to geographical location (Case 13/78, "Egger"). In another judgement (Case 222/82 -- "Apple and Pear Development Council"), the Court ruled that such a body set up by a member state can organise promotional campaigns for specific varieties of fruit even if they are typical of the national products, provided this does not lead to advising people against buying competing products from other member states.

Similarly, information about the country of origin, while useful to consumers, can easily be distorted to become a protectionist measure. In the UK the National Consumer Council (NCC) was asked by the government to undertake a survey on country-of-origin marking. The survey, published in May 1980, concentrated on domestic electrical appliances, clothing, shoes and cutlery. It showed that although the vast majority of consumers were in favour of country-of-origin marking (as a rough guide to quality), they were equally, if not more, concerned about receiving information on labels regarding safety and durability. Both France and the UK have introduced country-of-origin marking for textiles. While such national laws could have been challenged by the Commission under article 30, draft EC legislation was put forward instead. In theory this regulation might reduce distortion of trade within the Community, but it would also be used in addition to quantitative restrictions under the MFA to discourage imports from textile-producing countries in the rest of the world. BEUC is therefore against a scheme limited to country-of-origin marking, but there is a case for better and more uniform textile and clothing labelling covering this as well as all the other information required by the consumer.

The European Court has sought to avoid importers' obligations to declare the origin of products, leading to excessive administrative controls (Cases 41/76 and 52/77). The Court has also ruled that a national law requiring "souvenirs" and jewellery imported from other member states to have a country-of-origin label or be termed "foreign" is against the Treaty provisions on the free circulation of goods. Consumers are sufficiently protected if national manufacturers use their own origin label (Case 113/80 -- EC against Ireland). One may assume that the Court will therefore give a negative answer to the question of whether a member state may impose the indication of the country of origin for products originating from another member state. "As to the right of a member state to reserve specific denominations for specific domestic products the Court has (very rightly) decided that an appellation of origin or indication of provenance can only benefit from the protection of article 36 if there is a link between quality and provenance and that the definition of the provenance in function of the national territory could never be justified" (7).

C. Protecting the consumer against unfair commercial practices

In a number of other judgements, the Court has effectively rejected false consumer protection arguments put forward by member states. In fact, the position of the governments concerned has often showed a patronising attitude towards consumers, arguing that since imports could confuse choice, they should be denied that choice in the first place. The Court judgements do, however, create some new problems. They presuppose that consumers are sufficiently aware to compare domestic and foreign products. The judgements also imply far better EC labelling schemes than actually exist. The following examples show the kinds of arguments put forward, and the attitude of the Court to them:

-- In the "Cassis de Dijon" affair, a firm was not allowed to import French "Cassis de Dijon" because there is a provision of German law which fixes a minimum alcohol content of 25 per cent for fruit liquors. The Court rejected the argument (indeed a paradoxical one) that the 25 per cent standard meant that less strong alcoholic drinks should not be admitted on public health and consumer protection grounds; a labelling requirement would be sufficient;

-- In the wine vinegar affair (Case 788/79 -- "Gilli"), the Court rejected the arguments put forward by the Italian Government that because for their consumers all vinegar, by tradition, is made from wine, they would be misled by imports of apple vinegar. The Court pointed out that apple vinegar contained no health risks, and was easily distinguishable in form, labelling and price from the traditional product. It would be incompatible with the EC Treaty for a country to reserve a generic term for its own products as a means of excluding competing products from other member states;

-- On compositional standards for bread (Case 130/80 -- "Kelderman"), the Dutch Government set out to justify the ban on imports of French "brioches" which did not conform to the Broodbesluit (Bread Order), on the grounds that this rule "introduced a clear delimitation between the various shapes and weights of bread and thus helps to prevent consumers from being misled...". The Court rejected this since consumers could easily be informed by other means "such as requiring labelling showing, for example, the weight and specific composition of an imported product";

-- In the margarine affair (Case 261/81 -- Rau v. De Smedt), the government justified the rule that margarine must be sold in cubic form as "rooted" in the habits of Belgian consumers, and therefore as necessary to avoid confusion with butter. The Court pointed out that although a packaging requirement is not an absolute barrier, it makes imports more expensive and difficult and that although prices in Belgium were higher than in other member states, there was practically no "margarine of foreign origin" to be found on the market. Consumers could be protected against confusion by rules on labelling which are less of a hindrance to the free movement of goods. However, it cannot be concluded from the case-law that the Court rules out the possibility of consumers being misled in some circumstances by imported products, or that labelling is always the solution;

-- In Case 6/81 (Industrie Dienster Goep v. Beele), the Court ruled that a trader who has traditionally marketed a distinct product can obtain an injunction against an imitation product "coming from another member state in which it is lawfully marketed, but which for no compelling reason is almost identical to the first-named product and therefore needlessly causes confusion between the two products";

-- Similarly, in Case 286/81, the Court ruled against an importer who invoked article 30 to use premium offers as a promotional technique, pointing out that it was contrary to Belgian legislation which was justified to protect consumers and fair trading;

-- A number of other judgements expose advertising rules which discriminate against foreign products (i.e., those which allow advertising for nationally produced alcoholic drinks, but ban advertising of similar products from other EC countries). But these judgements in no way challenge the competence of member states to introduce rules to protect the consumer, even to ban certain types of advertising.

D. Health and safety

In the same way that it has exposed and rejected a number of national measures which were said by member states to prevent consumers from being misled, the Court has been equally vigilant in exposing false health reasons to justify trade barriers while explaining the commercial pressures behind them. But again, this does not mean that the Court has been insensitive to genuine consumer protection arguments on health grounds; on the contrary, the judgements have shown an extremely prudent attitude (the Commission probably thinks excessively so) by avoiding any decision which might overrule a national measure justified on health grounds. Even where there is doubt about the validity of a particular measure (i.e., a ban on the use of a particular additive), because scientific opinion is divided, it is likely that the Court will allow national rules to be maintained. The following examples will again show therefore how the decision may vary depending on the merits of the particular case:

-- In the UHT affair (Case 124/81), the United Kingdom argued that because of disparities in national laws, only a system of specific import licences enabled it to impose conditions "according to the disease status of the exporting country", and to trace consignments which might be infected with foot-and-mouth disease. The Court rejected this by pointing out that these regulations meant a second heat treatment for imports, and this "constitutes, owing to its economic effects, the equivalent of a total prohibition on imports". The Court also noted that the UK has accepted imports of UHT cream and flavoured UHT milk without requiring a second treatment, whereas "according to its own arguments, those products theoretically represented the same risks to humans". The Court rejected such measures under article 36 on the grounds that the alleged differences in law and even more in practice for producing UHT milk were more apparent than real. It was pointed out that since UHT milk can be preserved for long periods, control over the whole production cycle is not needed if the necessary precautions are taken at the time of heat treatment. In a report, Consumers' Association came to the conclusion that there were no real health risks. The real motive for the import ban was to protect doorstep deliveries of fresh milk in the UK;

-- Similarly, the import ban on poultry and eggs (8) (Case 40/82), which the United Kingdom attempted to justify under article 36 in order to go over from a policy of vaccination to one of compulsory slaughter in the event of an outbreak of Newcastle disease, was rejected by the Court. The Court went on to declare: "Certain established facts suggest that the real aim of the 1981 measures was to block, for commercial and economic reasons, imports of poultry products from other member states, in particular from France. The United Kingdom Government had been subject to pressure from British poultry producers to block these imports. It hurriedly introduced its new policy with the result that the French Christmas turkeys were excluded from the British market for the 1981 season". The Court considered that less restrictive measures were possible and that "the manner in which the Danish authorities deal with imports of poultry products from other member states -- even from those where recent outbreaks of Newcastle disease have been recorded -- suggests that it is possible to preserve the highest standard of freedom from Newcastle disease without completely blocking imports from countries where vaccine is still in use";

-- In Case 53/80 ("Eyssen"), on the other hand, the ban on the use of nisin (a preservative) in processed cheese in the Netherlands was upheld by the Court. The Court noted the disparity of national rules and upheld the Dutch law since "the issue of the addition of preservatives to foodstuffs is embraced by the more general issue of health protection" and studies have not yet reached certain conclusions regarding the health risks and the maximum permissible daily intake. The Court also appeared to accept that requirements for the protection of health may be different in different countries depending on consumer habits;

-- In another case concerning the Netherlands (174/82, "Sandoz"), the Court also upheld the Dutch prohibition on the addition of vitamins to foodstuffs under certain conditions. It noted the contradictory points put forward on the one hand by Sandoz and the Commission -- vitamins may only have harmful effects in the event of excessive consumption -- and on the other by the Dutch and Danish Governments that "the harmfulness of vitamins depends on the quantity absorbed with the whole nutrition of a person". The Court accepted that in the current state of uncertainty, it is for member states to decide about the degree of public health protection: "Those principles also apply to substances such as vitamins which are not as a general rule harmful in themselves but may have special harmful effects solely if taken to excess as part of the general nutrition, the composition of which is unforeseeable and cannot be monitored. In view of the uncertainties inherent in the scientific assessment, national rules prohibiting, without prior authorisation, the marketing of foodstuffs to which vitamins have been added are justified on principle within the meaning of article 36 of the Treaty on grounds of the protection of human health".

E. <u>The lessons to be drawn from the case-law of the European Court</u>

The first conclusion is the obvious one that the Court is a model, because of its independence, of how the consumer interest can be correctly interpreted in trade issues. In a genuine common market, consumers should accept imports which are presented differently from traditional domestic products under national rules. There is no evidence to suggest that this has resulted in bad products chasing good off the market, or of a threat to food quality generally. But the Court has also shown far greater prudence than many expected when it comes to health questions, even in cases of doubt. It is important that a conflict which was presumed to exist before the case-law developed between free trade principles and consumer protection legislation has been shown not to exist in practice. On the contrary, many consumer protection arguments have been revealed as false and simply excuses for protecting national interests. The real lesson is that consumers should beware of their would-be protectors, especially when the protector is a government intervening in a conflict over imports of products from other parts of the EC.

Secondly, there is a need for better enforcement of Court judgements. It will be argued that it may not matter if governments put forward false arguments, since it is what the Court decides that counts. Unfortunately it does matter because the Court decisions, when taken on a reference from a national court, are of a procedural nature and merely give guidance about how restrictions on trade could be lifted. Their implementation depends on the good will of national authorities. More seriously, many of the cases brought by the Commission have still not been implemented or are implemented too late after the Court decision. New cases have been brought, and old problems have appeared in new forms. There is scope for delay in applying the decisions; for example, many judgements call on member states not to abandon health controls or administrative checks on imports, but to replace them with measures which are less of a barrier to trade. Thus not only were the procedures too slow to prevent turkey imports to the UK in 1981, but the ban was still in force in practice for the Christmas of 1982! There are new cases on UHT milk, wine vinegar and margarine, because of non-implementation of Court judgements. No wonder the Commission, in the report to the European Parliament already mentioned, states that it will "pay closer attention to the implementation of the Court judgements".

Thirdly, the EC must redefine priorities for harmonization. The case-law of the Court is also self-limiting because of the prudence shown with regard to health issues, particularly additives. It will be interesting to see how the Court rules in the German beer case in the light of earlier judgements, and in particular how easily applicable its decision will be. While the Commission had hoped, as its 1980 Communication showed, that more issues would be dealt with under article 30 than through the harmonization process which requires unanimity in the Council of Ministers, it apparently has now come to accept that the process of approximation of national laws will have to be reassessed and begun again.

From the consumer viewpoint, it would not be desirable to return to earlier attempts to harmonize rules for specific product sectors (except perhaps the few that are central to people's diet, such as dairy products or meat), but rather to introduce EC rules applying to all products. This means a broader legislative approach covering such areas as food additives and their conditions of use, and safety standards for cars and domestic electrical appliances. The implication of "Cassis de Dijon" is that the EC should have a legislative policy on consumer health, safety and information. In the absence of such a policy, member states will constantly make use of the possibilities for exemption under article 36 or under the case-law of the Court, and find their requests accepted.

In a number of judgements the Court has ruled that labelling should suffice to avoid confusing consumers and replace measures which restrict trade more seriously. This approach though does come up against the fact that EC labelling schemes have not succeeded in providing clear comparable information to consumers over the whole range of products. They contain too many exceptions and open options for varied application, and are too uneasily married with existing national requirements. This was the main finding of a BEUC survey of the implementation by member states of the EC directive on food labelling (BEUC/82/82). The tendency of the Court to suggest relying on labelling to eliminate trade barriers underlines the need for revision of the EC food labelling directive as soon as possible to eliminate exceptions and to provide for more information on imported products such as the percentage declaration of ingredients. The EC should also draw up standards on nutritional labelling to avoid a proliferation of national schemes creating new barriers to trade.

III. CONCLUSIONS

Although trade policy is having an increasingly important impact on prices, choice, and health and safety standards for products marketed in different countries, there is no mechanism for consulting consumer interests. There is a strong case for providing adequate means of representation when, as is normal in international trade relations, consumers are simply ignored. But the case is even stronger when, as this report shows, consumer interests are constantly being used and more often than not misused, both to justify and to maintain non-tariff barriers to trade. In many cases, consumers are being deliberately misled as to where their interest lies. In the light of BEUC's own experience in taking up consumer issues in relation to rules on the free circulation of goods and the EC's relations with the rest of the world, I should like to offer some comments on "the proposals to give greater weight to consumer policy consideration in trade and related matters", particularly on the recommendations which relate to consumer organisations. There is an invitation to the consumer movement: "Consumer organisations in member states are encouraged to take a continuing interest in trade policy issues of significant impact on consumer interests and to keep consumers informed on such issues". It has to be admitted that this interest is insufficient. The main obstacle to fulfilling this role is the lack of resources for consumer organisations, even more than the lack of an institutional and representational framework for putting forward their views.

To strengthen the consumer voice in trade issues, the following steps are necessary.

A. Strengthening resources

Consumer organisations could play a stronger role in trade matters because of the knowledge of the market which is available to them from comparative tests and surveys. The tests and surveys are of course designed for the members of the association, to guide their choice over the range of products and services available on the domestic market. Extra resources would be needed to adapt the findings to enable consumer organisations to offer more than general comments on trade issues. Consumer organisations can best contribute by extending domestic tests and surveys to the European and international scale. Policies to remove barriers to trade should concentrate on areas where there are large unexplained price differences.

It is evident though that surveys (except in a few areas such as car prices) present serious problems. Often local and regional price differences are bigger than the differences between countries, and the lack of market transparency (i.e., for white goods) makes it difficult even to draw up a list of generally available basic models, since technically similar machines may be sold under different brand names in different countries. In many countries too, extra resources are needed if consumer organisations are to comment on whether non-tariff barriers to trade are justified on health and safety grounds.

It is for public authorities to realise that the built-in imbalance in resources between industry and consumers is particularly acute in trade policy issues. For consumer organisations, European or international trade negotiations are remote and complex; for the industry demanding protection they are of immediate concern, and there are by comparison no limits on the resources devoted to putting forward its case. For example, the textile industry must make it its business to concentrate on the MFA, whereas consumers, retailers and importers cannot afford to compete as single-issue interest groups. Inevitably they arrive on the scene less well prepared.

B. The need for objective analysis of the costs of import controls

While the recommendations do not sufficiently recognise the need to enable consumer organisations to prepare their own evidence to back up their positions on trade problems, they go much further when it comes to the role of governments and consumer policy authorities and the need for "transparency" in trade policies. It is stated that "efforts should be made to ensure that consumers have adequate information on trade policy measures", a checklist for such evaluations is suggested, and member countries are asked to encourage independent analysis of trade policy measures.

Within the EC, no bodies exist corresponding to those in the U.S. or Australia for this purpose. They should be set up, and there is a strong case, because of the EC Treaty rules on the free circulation of goods and the common commercial policy, that they should be set up at the European level. The OECD Recommendations cover objective analysis of the costs of barriers to trade, but we would like to see objective analysis of the health and safety aspects as well, particularly since it is there that consumers are being most often misled as to their true interests.

The following suggestions could be examined by national authorities, as well as the EC and the OECD:

1. Departments involved in trade issues should set up a joint economic unit to analyse the costs and justification of any proposed measure to restrict trade. Such a body should be independent from the process of trade negotiations, and its reports should be published. In particular, it should:

   -- Assess the impact of economic policies on the industries concerned, importers and consumers. The impact of the CAP on food prices or of the MFA on the market for clothing are obvious examples. Particular attention should be paid to the impact on low-income consumers;

   -- Regularly publish up-to-date price surveys for the same products traded on a European or international scale. This could help stimulate competition and parallel imports by importers and individual consumers;

   -- Prepare background analyses, i.e., reasons for excessive price differences, the costs to industry of adapting to different technical standards.

2. As mentioned in the introduction, the consumer interest is best served by separating the health and safety aspects from the commercial interests in trade liberalisation or trade restraint. Scientific committees whose role has so far been limited to the legislative process should be asked to examine the justification of health and safety or other claims in relation to trade barriers. Objective scientific analysis could help defuse many trade disputes. It could also ensure that legitimate health and safety rules are not overridden by purely commercial objectives (9).

3. Although the consumer protection argument is central to trade disputes involving non-tariff barriers, consumer organisations are often not consulted on the grounds of commercial and administrative secrecy. But many of the issues to be considered relate to national consumer or health protection laws, which are in the public domain and so inevitably are the issues surrounding the cases. Consultative mechanisms are needed to ask consumer organisations whether or not they find a particular measure constituting a non-tariff barrier to trade justified or not on consumer protection grounds. This could help defuse the misuse of consumer protection arguments by producers or governments. It should finally be recognised that many of the problems that used to be dealt with under the legislative process with consultation of consumers in advisory committees, and consultation of scientific committees, are now being handled to an increasing extent in trade policy negotiations. The result is that consumers might, for example, be consulted on origin marking for textiles, or care-labelling schemes and other "technical" aspects, but not on the trade policies which actually influence the prices

and choice on the market. Consumer organisations should also bring these arguments to the attention of parliaments which have a role to play in defending the right to representation. Indeed, in our experience, parliamentary circles are often more aware of consumer problems than government authorities.

4. Finally, the possibility of access for consumers to legal remedies against trade barriers should be mentioned, although the scope for this approach is probably very limited. BEUC has submitted a number of requests to the Commission to investigate intra-EC trade barriers, but the question of whether consumers could intervene in the European Court of Justice has not yet been tested, as it has under the competition rules. Consumer oganisations should also take advantage of the possibility of intervening in hearings on anti-dumping cases. The EC Commission recognises the potential scope in its report on the application of Community law in pointing out that "the possibilities of action by private citizens have been greatly extended by the consistent decisions of the Court recognising the direct effect of numerous provisions of the Treaty and of secondary legislation". What are the possibilities more generally for legal remedy under national law against the loss to consumers from import controls? We hope that further investigation will be undertaken by the OECD to answer this question.

I should end by repeating that the recommendations contained in the report by the Committee on Consumer Policy are welcomed by BEUC and its member organisations. The task now is to implement them in all OECD countries.

NOTES AND REFERENCES

1.   Cost-benefit analysis of import controls is carried out to some extent in the U.S., Canada, Australia and New Zealand, but not at all by European governments.

2.   In the final outcome of EC discussions on a block exemption for cars from the competition rules, however, it is difficult to see what the benefits of the regime will be for consumers, except for those prepared to buy cars abroad.

3.   BEUC report on the EC dairy surplus and options for reform (BEUC/101/83). In our comments on the annual farm price review, BEUC has published calculations of the impact on consumers.

4.   First annual report to the European Parliament on Commission monitoring of the application of Community law [COM(84)181 final]. This report shows that although most of the public issues and Court cases have concerned food and drink, the Commission is in fact dealing with just as many cases in other areas.

5. Paper by Diana Welch on barriers to trade in agricultural and food products, 4th European Congress of Agricultural Economists held 3rd-7th September 1981.

6. Recently, the scheme has been revised and extended despite a statement of objections sent to the French Government by the EC Commission.

7. Jules Stuyck, "Free Movement of Goods and Consumer Protection", University of Leuven.

8. This led to a complaint by BEUC and Consumers' Association.

9. In this connection, BEUC raised the issue of the changes which were made in European wine regulations without consultation of consumers or scientific committees because of the commercial interest in maintaining exports to the U.S.

PRODUCT SAFETY, TRADE BARRIERS AND CONSUMER PROTECTION --
THE SITUATION IN SWITZERLAND

by

Josef Moser
Counsellor, Federal Office of Consumer Affairs, Switzerland

Switzerland, with only 6.4 million inhabitants and practically no raw materials, is a country that relies heavily on foreign trade. Its central position within Europe and its linguistic diversity in fact make it a kind of test market, a very open one, for the Swiss consumer. And, while Switzerland lays claim to a high degree of freedom of trade and industry, consumer protection is rooted in its Constitution. The country's five consumer organisations seek dialogue with producers and suppliers.

The consumer's fundamental right to safety is hardly a new idea: for decades the law has set down strict health and safety conditions for both foodstuff and everyday products -- conditions adhered to through a series of controls extending all the way to the local store. The consumer's day-to-day existence is facilitated by an ever-increasing number of appliances and technical devices, and here too Swiss law covers operations at home and at work.

The consumer wants the freedom to choose goods suited to his particular use. Levels of product safety, quality, price and packaging should conform to the normal criteria of his country. For domestic as well as imported goods, he demands a suitable warranty, easy access to spare/replacement parts and good after-sales service. Finally, he wants a fixed standardization of products.

There is no such thing as absolute safety for any consumer product. Thus, safety requires the government to establish general rules, sales people to be aware of their own responsibility, and consumers to be careful. Switzerland has opted for two means of product control: a purely state control for food products and articles of everyday use, and a larger co-responsibility between state and seller for appliances and technical devices. Regarding food products, state intervention undeniably goes beyond the bounds of health and quality control. The market for agricultural products is influenced by various regulatory measures of economic policy. This is the domain where consumers need most to be on their guard as concerns the limiting of their freedom of choice through reduced competition.

As regards the control of appliances and technical devices, close collaboration has been established between the state and the private sector. General product safety surveillance is the responsibility of the federal authorities. They alone can order sequestration or prohibit sale. They have also established a commission with the participation of consumers to ensure co-ordination on safety matters. The enforcement body is made up of the Swiss Bureau of Accident Prevention (a private institution), certain cantonal agencies and private specialist organisations appointed by the government. Enforcement bodies can initiate investigations and are entitled to compel manufacturers and importers to adopt safety measures. Safety law enforcement is based on sanctions for violations and not on prevention -- that is to say, the enforcement body intervenes only if a routine inspection, an inquiry or an accident establishes that safety requirements are not being met.

This second kind of control involving collaboration between government and business has indeed proven itself. Cases of patently dangerous products are relatively rare. Moreover, this method has not necessitated the establishment of an extensive state control system.

Switzerland centres on export trade and thus desires freedom of world trade. Its protection of consumers springs from a constitutional mandate which prescribes a respect for freedom of trade and industry and does not favour protectionist measures. Even voluntary country-of-origin labelling on non-food products is viewed with a critical eye, because it is often difficult to establish with any certainty a product's actual country of origin and because, moreover, the quality and price of a product are more important than its origin.

It would be inadmissible for a false or exaggerated notion of product safety to bring about unwarranted impediments to trade, to the detriment of the consumer. Reasonable risk evaluation, notification systems such as those of GATT (on new regulations) or of the OECD (on dangerous products), as well as harmonization through the creation of standards, contribute to the free movement of goods without neglecting the safety factor. Nevertheless, closer international collaboration is still necessary in the matter of safety.

The consumer should be free to make his own decisions. A well-conceived policy of consumer protection need not limit this freedom. That is why, in order to guarantee his security and retain freedom of choice, the consumer has the following expectations:

-- Closer collaboration among governments, manufacturers and consumers on safety matters;

-- A wide choice of reliable articles and products, as well as good after-sales service. In general, best value for money is of prime importance, whether the product is domestic or imported;

-- Increased competition between domestic and foreign products push producers toward innovation, product improvement and (thus) an increase in product safety;

-- Standardization is in the consumer's interest. He wants generally applicable safety provisions. Differences in norms render use and repair irksome;

-- The consumer does not want artificial price hikes due to repeated safety inspection. There should be further mutual acknowledgement of inspection certificates;

-- The consumer favours more extensive international harmonization in safety matters. He opposes the tendency to transform well-intentioned safety provisions into trade barriers;

-- The consumer does not wish to be "overprotected"; responsibility should fall just as much on the consumer as on the supplier.

As a wage-earner and as a taxpayer, the consumer should know that protectionist measures in the long run detract from his well-being, while free trade and free competition contribute positively.

STANDARDS HARMONIZATION IN INTERNATIONAL TRADE

by

G.M. Ashworth
Chairman, International Organisation for Standardization (ISO)'s
Consumer Policy Committee;
Director, Public Affairs, British Standards Institution

Modern industrial production, from watchmaking to shipbuilding, depends on an intricate flow of standard interchangeable parts. With the expansion of industrial production networks beyond national boundaries, international standardization became essential to a broad range of manufacturing industries. The need was first evident in the electrotechnical areas and led to the establishment of the International Electrotechnical Commission (IEC) in 1906. National standards bodies collaborated to form the International Organisation for Standardization (ISO) in 1947 to take responsibility for international standardization in all other areas. Now ISO is supported by the standards bodies of 90 countries representing more than 95 per cent of the world's industrial production and, with IEC as its sister organisation, forms the world nucleus for technical harmonization.

The impact of international standards

International standards are today the hidden hand of the world economy: taken for granted, or not even guessed at, perhaps still imperfect in coverage and content but, through voluntary world-wide effort and regular review, providing a stable foundation on which to build a better society.

International standards support international trade. They underpin the assessment of raw materials with test methods and grading systems and define transport, containerisation, storage and handling requirements. Their range extends beyond manufacture and trade to other areas crucial to human survival. They help to secure the world's food supply by clarifying complex technical and commercial requirements in agriculture and food production. They provide methods of identifying and quantifying environmental hazards such as toxic chemicals or radioactive waste. They offer specifications for medical, surgical and laboratory procedures and apparatus. They speed communications across national boundaries in information, banking and commerce. Components made in one country can be tested and assembled in another. And, of course, products themselves can be readily traded on a basis of harmonized specifications detailing relevant requirements.

The impediments to trade

The role of IEC and ISO as sources of technical agreement which help world trade has long been recognised by intergovernmental agencies and within the United Nations, and in particular by the General Agreement on Tariffs and Trade (GATT). What then are the difficulties? First is the sheer magnitude of the task. There are today 7 000 published IEC and ISO standards. Major work programmes are in hand. But at the national level, agreements may meanwhile be reached which differ from each other and may become more or less market requirements because of different national testing and certification procedures, and of course through differing national regulations which invoke standards.

It can be argued that a voluntary national standard, without obligations attached to it, is a useful indication of local market preference. Home producer and importer can both gear themselves to meet that preference. But where other formal and restrictive acts attach themselves to the standard, the costs of market entry rise, the home market is protected, the free flow of trade is impeded and customer choice is restricted. The fact is that successful international harmonization of standards depends in the first place on an acceptance of the need to harmonize, on the support and participation of governmental interests in standards work, and on a readiness to look equally closely at government-controlled restrictions in the technical field which may impede trade.

Test and certification procedures: some progress

The interrelationship between standards and regulations, whether at the national or international level, is both exceedingly important -- for the impetus which standards derive from being linked with regulations is immense -- and highly complex. But notable progress is being made internationally to achieve a broad measure of international consensus about other activities which can help or hinder trade: testing, inspection and certification procedures.

Through an ISO policy committee, CERTICO, in which IEC participates, a series of guides has now been endorsed by ISO and IEC for world use. They set out common criteria for the acceptance of testing laboratories, the acceptance of inspection bodies and the acceptance of certification bodies. The potential impact of these agreements for the freeing of trade is significant. They mean that products tested and/or certified in one country against common criteria, and through common procedures, can be accepted with confidence in another market with minimal formalities. If we add to that the work now being done in the ISO technical committee on quality assurance to specify the elements by which the capability of a manufacturing unit to produce a consistent quality level can be assessed, we begin to see a world-wide quality system in the making. A "long-term objective" certainly, but a major contribution to world trade and economic development.

The consumer interest

How is the consumer interest brought into these technical developments in the standards world? International standards are drafted by technical committees where, through delegations from national standards bodies, many nations and interests are represented. Where standards are to provide technical criteria relating to consumer products (materials, tests, levels of performance and safety, packaging, labelling...), consumer views need to be brought into the discussion via the national standards body. In matters affecting personal safety, the consumer view is a vital element of the debate. From a legal standpoint, the committee responsible for a standard should always reflect with care and foresight upon the level of safety the man or woman in the street is reasonably entitled to expect. The consumer representative's task is to convey precisely what that reasonable expectation requires from a standard.

In many countries of the world, the structure for consumer representation now exists and a national delegation to IEC or ISO may well include a consumer representative for relevant projects. Both bodies encourage full consumer involvement. Seven years ago the ISO Council Committee on Consumer Policy (COPOLCO), in which IEC also takes part, was set up to study ways of assisting consumers to benefit from standardization. One of its objectives is to improve their participation in the development of national and international standards, where their experience of products in use is invaluable. COPOLCO also provides a forum for the exchange of information between consumers of different countries and allows scrutiny of ISO and IEC's technical programme from the consumer's point of view. New work items may also be proposed; several ISO projects were started in this way.

Standards bodies stimulated by the opportunity to hear about other countries' problems with consumer participation, and the solutions devised to meet them, have responded well to the policy lead given by COPOLCO, and are developing strategies to allow consumers to express their views on the technical content and policy direction of standards. The main difficulties identified by COPOLCO are not insuperable, and representation could be much increased if financial assistance to cover travel costs were available. Quite small sums can make a difference, and I commend to government representatives at this Symposium the thought that an economical way to make standards work responsive to consumers' needs is to offer some basic funding to encourage consumer participation in their drafting.

International standardization is an investment in the future, based on a belief in the rational application of technology for the benefit of all the people of the world.

THE USE OF PRODUCT STANDARDS IN INTERNATIONAL TRADE

by

Jacques Nusbaumer
Director, Technical and Other Barriers to Trade,
General Agreement on Tariffs and Trade (GATT)

The title of this item of the agenda would be misleading if it were meant to convey the idea that product standards as such have a particular usefulness for international trade. Common standards indeed can and do facilitate trade, but divergent standards in different countries rather hamper it. From the trade point of view, therefore, the right question to ask is: which standards should be used so as to minimise obstacles to the international exchange of goods and services? Put in economic language, the question is: which standards can be considered as "public goods", as distinct from "collective goods" (or standards) which benefit various interest groups, or "private goods" (or standards) which benefit only the "owner" of the standard by entrenching his monopoly position in the market.

In other words, the question is whether the objective of standardization is to facilitate trade for all producers in a competitive market or to restrict trade to a few or one. Basically, the rationale for standardization rests on the gains from comparability and interchangeability of products, which permit an efficient operation of market mechanisms for the benefit of producers and consumers alike. In an international trade setting, international standards perform this function. That is the reason why the GATT Agreement on Technical Barriers to Trade (also known as the GATT Standards Code), whose principal objective is to reduce or eliminate obstacles to trade arising from differences in product standards among countries, encourages the use of existing international standards and the development of such standards as behavioural norms, under certain conditions to be discussed below.

The GATT Standards Code covers the whole range of standardizing activity, both public and private, though the level of obligations of Member governments differs with regard to the two types of activity and to some specific standards-making methods. Since only central governments are GATT contracting parties, they can only assume full obligations in respect of their own activities. However, under the Standards Code, they have undertaken to ensure to the best of their ability that local government and private sector bodies conduct their standardizing activities in accordance with the principles and objectives of the Code.

While the use of existing international standards is the norm, the Agreement on Technical Barriers to Trade recognises that governments may need to deviate from such standards to meet specific conditions regarding consumer health, security, etc. prevailing in their respective countries. Apart from climatic conditions, the best way to describe the rationale for such deviations is differences in "cultural" conditions. For example, in some countries there is a higher degree of concern for the physical environment than in others, standards of hygiene also differ, or food may be required to present certain characteristics for religious reasons. These are matters of sovereign concern for each government, but the Agreement makes it clear that any deviations on such grounds must not create unnecessary obstacles to trade and imposes the obligation to justify them on request. In addition, recourse to the dispute settlement provisions of the Agreement is available to any party that considers that the national regulations of another party are not in conformity with these principles. In practice, it should be noted that national standards do continue to differ among countries party to the Agreement where climatic and "cultural" conditions are very similar, though these differences are not necessarily considered as giving rise to unnecessary obstacles to trade by the parties concerned.

One reason why these differences persist is the lack of adequate international standards, that is, standards which suit the regulatory requirements of all or at least most members of the GATT Standards Code. Why should this be so?

The answer lies in the definition of an international standard. This can be one of two things: a standard that is effectively applied internationally, or a standard that has been decided upon at the international level. Most standards produced by international standardizing bodies are adopted by consensus among technical experts with different economic backgrounds and cultural horizons, and often they do not completely fill any one country's particular needs. While world standards are international public goods, they tend to be disregarded by producers who can raise the level of technological performance above the standard without loss of market, and superior standards will be preferred by consumers if they incur no loss of real income as a result. Conversely, standards that surpass the technological capacity of domestic producers will tend to be ignored by governments, and the temptation of consumers to turn to better-quality imported goods and services will be resisted through different kinds of trade restrictions.

The protection of consumers therefore involves higher standards only if these can be applied without giving rise to monopoly profits for producers on the one hand, or without imposing undue strains on the competitiveness of national producers on the other. However, in a free market setting, where profits and market shares are rewards for efficiency, successful firms only enjoy scarcity rents from their superior technological performance until their innovations spread by imitation. The interests of producers and consumers in applying superior performance standards set by leading enterprises may therefore be less antagonistic in the long run than in the short run, unless these standards are recorded in mandatory regulations adopted by governments dependent on supplies from such enterprises (de facto or "captive" standards). At the international level, mutual recognition of superior performance standards could conceivably constitute an approach to the reduction of unnecessary obstacles to trade complementary to the development and application of international consensus standards.

Standards, when they are observed and, a fortiori, when they are mandatory, eliminate shoddy goods from the market. By analogy with a regressive tax, they limit the choice of consumers in the lower income brackets. From a distribution point of view, high standards may therefore be the converse of a "public good", i.e., a "public bad", or at least appear elitist. Indeed, in practice, considerations of social justice are not without influence on governments' attitudes towards standardization in general, or on their determination to ensure compliance with existing standards. The low priority given to enforcement of domestic standards in many developing countries is a case in point.

For developing countries generally, the development and enforcement of appropriate domestic standards for consumer protection is only one and, as indicated, not necessarily the most urgent problem in this field. In order to be competitive, their industries must produce goods to the standards of their main, primarily developed, markets. In many instances this poses insurmountable technological difficulties unless the required technology is imported by foreign enterprises or transferred by foreign governments in the form of technical assistance. An additional complication is the existence of different standards in different markets. Clearly, from the point of view of these countries, the establishment of widely acceptable and attainable international standards would be a distinct advantage. Provided adequate technical assistance is provided, they could achieve the technological performance implied by high international standards, bringing great secondary benefits to their economies. Hence, consensus standards need not be low standards.

The shape of future international co-operation in the field of standards will depend on the balance that will be struck between the sometimes complementary, sometimes conflicting factors outlined above. From the point of view of consumer protection, a watchful eye must be kept on the adaptation of standards to the real needs being catered to, in order to avoid over-regulation to the detriment of consumer choice and, ultimately, of free international trade. In this regard, the technical performance criterion laid down in article 2.4 of the GATT Standards Code provides a sound basis for reducing or eliminating trade barriers that arise from the technological parochialism of governments. In addition to the harmonization of standards, the mutual recognition of methods of testing for conformity with standards and of the results of such tests would constitute a major advance in this direction. Any future efforts to strengthen existing international commitments should accord a high priority to this issue.

Theme III

THE CONSIDERATION OF CONSUMER INTERESTS IN THE FORMULATION AND IMPLEMENTATION OF TRADE POLICY

SUMMARY

by

D.L. Gatland
Assistant Secretary, Consumer Affairs Division,
Department of Trade and Industry,
London, United Kingdom

It needs to be recognised that in this field, as well as in most others, the best way of getting what one wants is to persuade the person or people who will make the relevant decisions that doing what you want them to do is in their own interests. But to do this successfully one has to make three sets of decisions oneself: what it is that one wants to achieve; who it is that one needs to persuade; and how to achieve that persuasion, both the methods to be used and the timing. It was with the third category that the discussion in Theme III was mainly concerned.

To aid our discussions four papers had been circulated and the four speakers drew attention to the particularly relevant points in those papers.

Mr. Maddern summarised the main action that governments could take: create an appropriate climate; consider the general principles which should be followed; and consider what role might be played by existing organisational structures or those to be created. He went on to list the general principles that should be considered, although not all of them would need to be followed in every instance. He also drew attention to the fact that his paper had described some possible institutional arrangements.

Mr. Corbet illustrated a number of the issues involved by criticising the way international trade policy had developed through the GATT. He emphasized that governments had a central role both to inform themselves, in such a way as to have the necessary information in advance rather than having to make urgent decisions in crisis circumstances, and to create understanding in the public sector. He stressed the need for transparency to be a central feature of government policy, with detailed and public analysis showing the costs of all aspects of the problem and of proposed remedies. He drew attention to the need for this action to be taken at both the national and the international level.

Mr. Stegemann set his comments against the background of his analysis of anti-dumping policy. He drew attention to some weaknesses in the way that policy had been formulated and applied, and emphasized the need for consumer organisations to participate on the side of those making sure that anti-dumping procedures were properly argued out in a transparent way. He, too, emphasized the need for action at both the national and international levels, suggesting some rather radical changes.

Mr. McCarty, Assistant Director, Bureau of Competition, Federal Trade Commission (introducing Mrs. Crawford's paper in her absence), described the activities of the Federal Trade Commission in the U.S., an example of a body already working within an existing system, advising those who make decisions on trade policy. In view of the many references in other parts of the discussion to the importance of adequate resources, it was interesting to learn that the FTC's staff includes about 85 economists engaged in this work. We also noted that when a trade policy decision was announced, no indication was given about the extent to which the FTC's advice had influenced the decision, even where that decision was much in line with what the FTC had recommended.

The following points came up in the course of the ensuing general discussion.

The problem of limited resources for those wishing to strengthen the presentation of the consumer case in trade policy matters was emphasized. A suggestion was made that some form of "people's council" should be set up, possibly along the lines of ombudsman arrangements which had been found to work well in some countries. Other speakers emphasized that the problem of getting public finance for such an arrangement would be very difficult in many countries.

Attention was drawn to the fact that many decisions in this field were made on what appeared to be purely political grounds, so that whatever arrangements were established would need to provide an avenue for influencing those political decisions.

It must be recognised that when making these political decisions, governments face high-pressure demands from industry. In this context some form of agreed trade rules could be a useful safety-valve, but it is important that those rules be narrow, clearly defined and internationally agreed.

Other speakers were in support of the need to tighten the criteria used in international trade agreements, and the point was made that these international rules should be sharpened to ensure that all nations were competing on the same basis.

In relation to the timing of efforts to influence trade policy decisions, the point was made that speed was often vital when some form of trade protection action was under consideration. In these circumstances, it was suggested, although a separate body providing independent assessments might be a good idea for background material, it would not be the best practical route to a decision. It was suggested that it would be better for those in the government department who were going to be responsible for advising government ministers on the policy decision to be required to maintain regular contacts. This would ensure that they were fully appraised of all ideas and opinions so as to present a properly balanced view to the decision-makers.

The general impression to emerge from discussions in Theme III was that there were a number of steps which could be taken, but that it would be wrong to suppose that there was one common ideal solution which would be applicable in all countries of the OECD. It would be for each Member country to consider which of the various ideas put forward were most applicable to the political, legal and institutional arrangements applying in that country.

THE INSTITUTIONAL FRAMEWORK FOR TRADE POLICY MEASURES AND THE REPRESENTATION OF CONSUMER INTERESTS

by

D.I. Maddern
Assistant Secretary, Consumer Policy Branch,
Department of Home Affairs and Environment, Australia

INTRODUCTION

In a symposium on consumer policy and international trade, some discussion about institutional matters is appropriate, and probably unavoidable given the number and nature of existing institutions, national and international, which operate in both areas. In a sense, however, such a discussion is about a topic of secondary importance. It is also a discussion which runs the risk of focussing too much attention on organisational structures and relationships, and not enough upon the objectives those organisations seek to achieve or upon the role of non-institutional factors.

In saying institutional aspects are secondary, it is not suggested that they are unimportant or that there are not third or fourth-order issues below them. Rather, it is suggested that a sound institutional framework for representing consumer interests in international trade policy is unlikely to be effective unless certain pre-conditions are present. Chief among these would seem to be a recognition that consumer considerations are important, an ability to identify consumer interests, a determined desire (particularly on the part of governments) to evaluate consumer interests in particular instances, and adequate resources within the institutions.

Assuming these pre-conditions are present, or can be encouraged within a reasonable time, appropriate institutional structures can perform a vital function. They can, for example, facilitate the making of informed decisions, encourage community debate about major economic issues, assist institutions engaged in related areas of activity, and undertake research into important topics. They also represent tangible evidence of a perceived need to address a significant issue in a formal way.

The institutional implications of consumer policy and international trade involve both government and private organisations. While there is a perhaps understandable tendency to focus upon government institutions in the present context, it should not be forgotten that the nature and effectiveness of private organisations -- consumer, business, trade union -- have an important influence on decisions made about international trade issues. As with government organisations, the sphere of operations of private organisations can be either national or international.

For a number of reasons, it is unlikely that any one institutional framework is the best for all countries at any given time. A federal system of government is likely to require a different set of institutions from that appropriate for a country with a unitary system of government. A country with few statutory bodies separate from the departments of State may be able to accommodate appropriate organisations and procedures within those departments, whereas other countries may derive benefits from an organisation separate from mainstream departments. An open economy in which international trade has a minor role in influencing the level of domestic economic activity is less likely to require elaborate, formal institutional structures than an economy where international trade plays a major influencing role.

The approach of this paper, therefore, is to suggest some desirable general principles and to sketch out some institutional alternatives which could be considered by countries desiring to afford consumer issues greater significance in international trade policy.

INTERACTION BETWEEN CONSUMER AND TRADE POLICIES

Before directly addressing institutional issues, it seems sensible to briefly examine the interaction between consumer and trade policies, if for no other reason than to seek an explanation as to why a need is felt by some to increase the influence of the former on the latter.

Policies in both areas do not exist in isolation. Typically, international trade policy influences, and is influenced by, other specific policies for industry, employment, health, defence and fiscal matters, as well as general policies in such areas as foreign affairs. Many issues need careful consideration when decisions are made in international trade. The scope of consumer policy is potentially wide, but in many countries the actual focus is narrower, being concerned mainly with protecting individual citizens from "unfair" trading practices, with product information and safety issues, legal redress and consumer education.

International trade directly influences the economic situation of some citizens, particularly those engaged in import, competing or export industries, but indirectly exerts a much wider influence on the population. For example, at the micro-economic level it influences the range, quality and price of goods available in domestic markets, and at the macro-economic level it influences such areas as balance of payments and monetary policy. Because of the complexity and dynamic nature of international trade, the danger exists that in considering individual aspects or products, sight will be lost of the wider impact of decisions on the community at large or upon community groups which are less able to advance arguments and evidence than groups directly representing specific industry groups. The temptation may be to resolve particular issues by adopting a short-term solution which "oils the door which squeaks the most".

A reply to this last point may be that governments, through the legislative or executive arms, are responsible for considering overall community interests, and take into account such broader issues when considering and deciding international trade issues. As a broad comment this is no doubt true, but often there is an inequality between the information, research and informed advice furnished to decision-makers by the general community and that furnished by industry. Appropriate institutional arrangements can help redress this inequality and assist decision-makers in making informed judgements and in raising the level of general community awareness about the issues involved.

SOME GENERAL PRINCIPLES

In considering the creation of new institutions, or modifications to existing institutions, to increase the representation of consumer interests, regard should be paid to principles most likely to achieve the desired result. Not all need to be slavishly followed, but adoption of a mix of principles appropriate for local conditions is likely to foster a constructive climate for change.

The following is a list, certainly not exhaustive, of such general principles. Some refer to procedures, others to structures and general attitudes:

-- Information disclosure. Authorities and private organisations at the national and international levels should provide statistical data, analysis and comment to foster informed debate;

-- Public debate. In addition to publicly providing information and inviting submissions on specific topics, authorities could consider other means of encouraging public debate. Such means could include convening conferences, providing assistance for academic institutions, publishing discussion papers and encouraging the involvement of professional bodies;

-- Composition of bodies. With certain institutions, particularly those charged with tendering independent advice, the composition of the decision-making level is an important consideration. At least two approaches are possible. One is to select individuals with high levels of general competence but without necessarily possessing specialist experience or knowledge of particular sectors. The second is to choose a blend of persons with technical skills, policy appreciation, and industry and consumer knowledge. The second approach may lead to a form of representation of sectional interests, in which case careful balance would be required;

-- <u>Personnel</u>. To be effective, institutions should have staff resources which are technically qualified, recruited on merit, provided with suitable training and adequate in number. Opportunities should be provided for exchanges and short-term placements for specialist tasks;

-- <u>Research</u>. Research into both particular issues and broad approaches by as wide a range of qualified persons as possible, and within limits of reasonable expenditure, should be encouraged. The results of research should be given appropriately wide distribution;

-- <u>Inviting submissions</u>. Authorities should invite interested parties to lodge submissions about trade issues. Submissions could be oral or written, with the latter perhaps preferred to ensure certainty and assist distribution. Provisions should exist for submissions to be treated as confidential where appropriate;

-- <u>Publicity</u>. Secrecy is not conducive to widespread consultation and debate. Some confidentiality is unavoidable and appropriate, for example during the negotiation of multilateral trade agreements, but as a rule broad publicity should be given to matters such as overall trade policy, particular trade issues currently under examination, and decisions taken;

-- <u>Encouraging consumer participation</u>. Not all representative bodies or individual organisations with legitimate interests in trade issues have the resources, human and financial, to adequately represent those interests. Encouragement should be given by authorities, to the extent their own resources permit, in such circumstances. Such encouragement could take the forms of providing advice about key issues and preparation of submissions, the provision of non-confidential information, access to research, and financial assistance to increase participation;

-- <u>Public scrutiny</u>. The views of private interested parties should be subject to careful scrutiny by authorities, and the various interested parties should be provided with the opportunity to respond, preferably publicly, to the views of others. Substantiation of claims should be required and expressions of opinion clearly identified;

-- <u>Avoiding excessive legalism</u>. While there should be some safeguards against dishonesty, falsehood and intimidation in the giving and consideration of submissions, etc. by interested parties, resort to procedures which are valid in courts of law may be inimical to reasonably free exchanges of information and opinion about essentially economic and commercial matters. Strict rules of evidence are an example;

-- <u>Consultation between officials</u>. To ensure that proper consideration is given to all relevant aspects, including consumer implications, officials should consult among themselves before advice and recommendations are formulated and submitted for decision;

-- <u>Access to decision-makers</u>. To the extent feasible, the various levels of decision-making within governments should permit access to interested parties. Such access provides not only a mechanism of exchanging information, but also an opportunity to influence attitudes and bring about realistic change. Access of this kind should not, however, be seen as an alternative to public scrutiny and debate;

-- <u>Ministerial decision-making</u>. When decisions are made by ministers, either collectively or individually, it is desirable that the minister responsible for consumer matters be present, or at least that the minister's views be known. Such a procedure provides the opportunity for greater balance in consideration of issues. It may also facilitate greater public acceptance of decisions made;

-- <u>Decision explanation</u>. Publicity about decisions taken should include some explanation of the rationale behind the decisions. This could involve reference to the weight assigned particular views, to the need for further review, to consistency with overall policy and to international implications;

-- <u>Periodic review</u>. The opportunity for periodic review of past decisions can be valuable to assess achievement of desired objectives and to consider the impact of changed circumstances. The reviews should be conducted after a period of time sufficient to properly assess the impact of past decisions, and there may be merit in mandatory reviews of all decisions after, say, ten years.

INSTITUTIONAL OPTIONS

The level of decision-making about international trade matters varies from country to country, and may depend upon the gravity of the particular issue. Major matters, such as the formation of regional economic groups, bilateral agreements, significant commodity agreements and the handling of multilateral trade agreements, are likely to be decided collectively by ministers of State. Other matters of intermediate significance, such as the imposition of anti-dumping duties or variations of tariff preferences, may be settled by individual ministers, perhaps with an obligation to later inform, or obtain confirmation from, parliaments. Lesser matters may be handled by officials, sometimes exercising authority delegated by ministers.

To advise and support these decision-makers, a number of organisational structures can be employed. The more significant of these are: departments of State, interdepartmental committees of officials, independent statutory bodies, committees of inquiry, professional associations, international organisations, private interest groups and universities.

These structures are not mutually exclusive, and indeed it is not uncommon to find many of them operating simultaneously. Brief comments about the characteristics of some of these organisations may be helpful.

The main features of departments of State are reasonably well known. They provide advice and assistance to elected ministers who are assigned responsibility for major governmental areas of activity. Typically, they are large organisations staffed with a mixture of managerial, technical and administrative people organised into functional groups which often compete for resources and influence. Often they are the repositories of considerable data and knowledge about particular industries, commodities or activities.

Because departments are responsible for directly assisting ministers, they usually are influenced more immediately by the policies of the government of the day than are official bodies with some independence, private groups or international organisations. Such influence is normal and proper, but it may be that the overall process of giving advice to decision-makers is enhanced by providing the opportunity for additional advice of a more disinterested nature.

Interdepartmental committees bring together officials from different areas of government to focus on a particular matter. As such, they represent a subgroup whose conclusions often reflect the attitudes and policies of particular departments. They may provide a useful mechanism for co-ordinating information and advice, but an inability to agree upon advice can occur. This can lead to the adoption of "the lowest common denominator" approach to reaching conclusions, where compromises are made -- perhaps undesirably -- in order to secure agreement.

Independent statutory bodies enjoy official status and are often seen as providing disinterested advice not forthcoming from departments, and a convenient means of assembling professional expertise. In the eyes of some, the separation can be a mixed blessing. Distance from decision-making in a political climate may aid objectivity in some circumstances, but at the same time runs the risk of loss of relevance in the provision of practical advice.

Official committees of inquiry are usually established to examine and report upon specific matters and, once that task is achieved, are then disbanded. Terms of reference for these committees are set by governments, and may be broad where a matter of major policy is involved, or narrow where individual products or issues are involved. Other matters which must be settled for each committee include the size and composition of the committee, its ability to invite submissions, and the reporting date, costs and support facilities, both research and administrative. Lags in establishment are often considerable.

Professional associations can provide a valuable source of expert alternative advice which transcends occupational divisions between, say, the government and private sectors. Law and economics are two examples of professions which operate in this way. Associations are likely to vary as to the extent of their activities beyond the immediate interests of their members and into the domain of public issues. The frequency with which associations want, or are able because of resource restraints, to participate in such broader issues is also likely to vary.

At this point it may be salutary to consider which of the above official institutional options are most likely to embody at least the majority of relevant desirable general principles mentioned earlier in this paper. Because committees of inquiry usually have a limited purpose and life, and interdepartmental committees are really in the nature of an organisational sidecar, the focus narrows to departments of State and independent statutory bodies.

Both organisational options are theoretically capable of satisfying many of the principles, in particular those concerned with publicity, inviting submissions, encouraging participation, scrutiny, information disclosure and decision explanation. Independent statutory bodies are more likely, in certain circumstances, to be able to accommodate some principles than departments because of their more limited range of responsibilities and greater distance from day-to-day political pressures. For example, they may be better placed than departments to encourage participation by non-government organisations, undertake research (including short-term research by academics or specialists), conduct periodic reviews of decisions, engage in public debate and have a broadly based composition.

A choice need not be made between these two options. A few countries, including Australia, have decided to have both in the form of a battery of departments with general and special economic and social interests, and a statutory authority currently known as the Industries Assistance Commission, or IAC (before 1974 called the Tariff Board). [For further discussion of IAC, see "The Representation of Consumer Views in the Formulation and Implementation of Trade Policy" in Theme III of this publication.] Various reviews over the years have seen changes in the authority's charter and procedures, but its continued existence is testimony to its valuable role. Perhaps other countries without similar authorities may also find such bodies worthwhile in seeking to give greater weight to consumer considerations in international trade.

A POSSIBLE PRESCRIPTION

This paper has adopted a very general approach to a broad topic with several elements and various applications -- some procedural, some structural. For a country seeking an institutional framework conducive to giving consumer interests proper weight in international trade matters, its suggestion is threefold:

-- Firstly, create an appropriate climate to ensure that institutional factors are given an opportunity to operate effectively;

-- Secondly, critically examine the general principles that should apply and select those most suited to local conditions;

-- Thirdly, carefully consider the role of institutional structures, the desirability of modifications to existing structures and the creation of new and different structures which encourage public debate, undertake research and provide independent advice.

PUBLIC SCRUTINY OF PROTECTION: TRADE POLICY AND THE INVESTIGATIVE BRANCH OF GOVERNMENT

by

Hugh Corbet
Director, Trade Policy Research Centre, London, United Kingdom

Economic development is largely the outcome of domestic policies. But domestic policies, in an integrating world economy, can be profoundly affected by how the institutional environment of international economic relations evolves. That is why the multilateral framework of principles and rules for regulating change in a dynamic world economy has become more important with the growing interdependence of national economies. The international economic order, as established after World War II, is based on the liberal principles associated with open markets and private enterprise. Reliance on markets, with private initiative bringing about adjustment, is the only way -- consistent with the rights of the individual -- to ensure peaceful and prosperous co-existence, both within a society and between societies. Simply stated, that is the thinking underlying the institutions of the international economic order, particularly the General Agreement on Tariffs and Trade (GATT) (1).

Since the late 1960s, if not earlier, the international economic order has been subject to mounting strains, much of which can be traced back to the growth of government intervention in the market process (2). Increasingly, government measures have been introduced in industrialised countries to postpone, "correct" or offset adjustment to changing economic circumstances. One consequence has been that the institutional environment in which governments make policies and take decisions on industry support and protection has got murkier and murkier. There is only one ship which does not slow down in a fog and that is the ship of state. Governments have become more closely involved in the detailed structure of their countries' economies than many of them would wish, so much so that they now have difficulty in discharging their proper function, which in a market economy is to provide a stable institutional environment, which in turn provides continuity and "predictability" so that firms can plan for expansion or if need be for adjustment, enabling economic development to proceed as smoothly as possible (3).

In the economies of Western Europe, more than in those of North America and the Western Pacific, structural adjustment problems are compelling periodic reviews of government intervention in the market process. In the major intergovernmental organisations -- the GATT, the International Monetary Fund (IMF) and the World Bank -- annual reports and occasional studies have argued in recent years that government intervention in the market process has been carried too far, that the trend has to be reversed and that, more specifically, the adjustment process of the market has to be allowed to work (4).

In June 1981, the GATT's Consultative Group of Eighteen, a representative group of officials with responsibilities for their countries' trade policies, solemnly decided that a ministerial conference should be convened in November 1982. The communiqué issued at the time noted that "trade relations are beset by a number of complex and potentially disruptive problems, reflecting growing protectionist pressures, and that there is a need for improved international co-operation to solve these problems", adding that "it would be useful to consider at a _political_ level the overall condition of the [international] trading system" (emphasis added) (5). In the preparations for the GATT ministerial conference in November 1982 it became all too clear that multilateral commercial diplomacy has come to be perceived as a form of "crisis management" rather than the joint administration of a body of internationally accepted rules governing trade relations between market-oriented countries.

Successive intergovernmental meetings since November 1982 have agreed that "something has to be done" about the difficulties in the world economy. But it is not as if governments are at a complete loss what to do. They know full well, as a steady flow of _communiqués_ attest, that inflation has to be stopped and protectionism has to be reversed. They know that the achievement of these two goals involves resolving the debt crisis and securing both a sustained recovery and thence stable growth in the world economy. They also know though that halting inflation and protectionism will be painful in the short run and, still worse, that public opinion has not been made aware of the necessity for either.

It is too simple to say that there is a lack of political will to deal with the difficulties in the world economy. What is more fundamentally lacking is political leadership and control. That, however, requires political understanding. Only when economic issues are properly understood at political level can ministers exercise political leadership and control. Generating political understanding is thus the task which lies ahead.

This is a part of the task which is being undertaken by a study group established by the Trade Policy Research Centre early in 1983 under the chairmanship of Olivier Long, the former Director-General of the GATT, to investigate ways of achieving "transparency" in the administration of trade restrictions. It is sometimes said that there are four branches of government: the executive, the legislative, the judicial and the investigative. The study group, like this paper, is focussing on the last, drawing attention to what F.A. Hayek calls the "information function of government" in facilitating the adjustment process in market-oriented economies (6). Getting the adjustment process of the market working properly in both developed and developing countries could be the overall objective of a new GATT round.

"TRANSPARENCY" ON THE GATT AGENDA

For a decade and a half, as previously mentioned, serious tensions have been developing in the international system of trade and payments. Some of them relate to differing rates of interest in the major industrialised countries, reflecting differing rates of inflation, which give rise to fluctuating rates of exchange between their currencies. On the "real" side of the world economy, the sources of tension relate to structural rigidities in the major industrialised countries. These hamper adjustment in industries that are having difficulty coping with advances in technology, with changes in patterns of demand, with shifts in comparative advantage and with other developments in their economic circumstances, these difficulties giving rise to requests from those industries for protection against foreign competition (7).

The "new protectionism" has also been described as "creeping protectionism", given the surreptitious nature of the instruments of policy used, namely "hidden" non-tariff measures against imports and "voluntary" export-restraint agreements (VERs) with other countries (or their producers), these last being negotiated on a bilateral basis, in camera and outside the disciplines of the GATT system. The danger with creeping protectionism has always been that it might stand up and run. With the advent of "slow growth" in the industrialised countries, governments have begun to recognise the danger, but they have made it hard for others to do so by hiding from public scrutiny the size and scope of public assistance being extended to troubled industries (8), fooling themselves as much as anybody.

With the insidious spread of protectionism, the incidence and effects of which are not readily identified, "transparency" has become a fashionable word in the lexicon of commercial diplomacy. What trade negotiators are talking about in their use of the term is the murkiness which surrounds the different ways and means by which international trade i) is restricted now that tariffs have been reduced to very low levels, at least in the major industrialised countries, or ii) is otherwise distorted through incentives to production and export as an alternative approach to "saving jobs" and so on. They appreciate the need for light to be shed on that murkiness and for "hidden" non-tariff measures and "informal" export restraints to be rendered transparent, subject to public scrutiny and investigation.

The term "transparency" itself is not clearly defined. Its use in this paper, however, refers to much more than the visibility of particular impediments to trade and adjustment. It refers to the visibility of the effects -- the costs and benefits -- of those impediments, not only to an economy as a whole but also to allied producers, to exporters, to consumers, to retailers and to other affected interests.

NON-TARIFF INSTRUMENTS OF POLICY

Non-tariff measures involving discrimination against foreign suppliers in favour of domestic ones, thereby distorting competition, come in a wide variety of shapes and forms ranging from import licences, customs-valuation procedures and anti-dumping actions to public subsidies to production and export, public procurement policies and public health and safety standards (9). Many non-tariff measures, especially subsidies and procurement, are instruments of what, in domestic circles, is called industrial policy (or agricultural policy).

Trade policy, with which border measures are traditionally associated, and industrial policy are virtually synonymous terms, both bearing on investment, on the structure of production in an economy and on the international allocation of resources. Because governments now intervene in the market process in so many different ways, there is less point than before in distinguishing between border and non-border instruments of policy; what is crucial is to distinguish between the purposes of government interventions. Most instruments of industrial policy appear to have a protectionist purpose, being aimed at preserving existing structures of production regardless of their economic efficiency. It is because of their protectionist purpose that the instruments of industrial policy and the "informal" trade-restrictive arrangements required to sustain them are together labelled the "new protectionism".

The architects of the international economic order, who began their meetings when the United States entered World War II, anticipated the possibility of governments frustrating by other means the benefits expected from the tariff reductions which would be pursued in successive rounds of multilateral trade negotiations. They wrote into the GATT a number, of provisions on non-tariff measures. The first six rounds of GATT negotiations, spanning twenty years, were devoted to the reduction of tariffs. In the preparations for a seventh round, however, it was realised that with tariffs on industrial products traded among industrialised countries getting down to very low levels, the time had come for GATT disciplines on the use of non-tariff measures to be tightened up, the articles dealing with them in Part II of the GATT being only skeletal.

Since the effects of non-tariff measures are difficult if not impossible to quantify, the "reduction" or modification of them could not be negotiated like the reduction of tariffs, the effects of which can be quantified for the purpose of achieving a balance of "concessions", enabling the GATT's multilateral concept of "reciprocity" to be satisfied. Instead it was conceded that the principle of reciprocity would have to be satisfied by an equal commitment by Member countries to codes of conduct containing specific principles and rules, consistent with general GATT principles and rules, regulating government use of the different types of non-tariff intervention in the market process.

Thus, unlike previous GATT rounds, the seventh round of multilateral trade negotiations, formally launched in Tokyo in September 1973, was concerned with more than the further liberalisation of trade within an accepted framework of rules. The Tokyo Round negotiations were concerned with the rules as well. Governments accordingly set about negotiating codes of conduct on non-tariff measures. By then, alas, certain non-tariff measures were being actively deployed, by the major industrialised countries in particular, as instruments of industrial policy (10).

As a result, a number of unresolved problems, within and among industrialised countries, which had to do with public assistance to troubled industries were reflected in the codes of conduct that were finally negotiated. The governments of the major industrialised countries each tried to retain a degree of freedom of national action which, in an interdependent world, was incompatible with their international obligations as "contracting parties" to the GATT. Most conspicuously, the code on subsidies and countervailing duties (11) is deemed by many commentators to have weakened the relevant GATT articles, while the code on public procurement (12), although tightly drafted, is limited to the public procurement of listed "entities" (governmental agencies) which do not yet include those bearing on industries where public procurement is actually a significant instrument of industrial policy (13).

When the Tokyo Round negotiations were getting under way it was quipped that if they succeeded they would never end. By this it was meant that the codes on non-tariff measures, once they were agreed, would have to be implemented by a process of more or less continuous consultation and negotiation. Since the Tokyo Round negotiations were concluded in 1979, however, governments have been experiencing great difficulty (much more than expected) in implementing the new GATT codes. In discussions in the GATT committees formed to oversee the codes, the question of how to achieve greater transparency in the administration of public assistance to troubled industries is being considered, for public scrutiny and discussion of the costs and benefits of non-tariff measures is probably the only way to have them critically assessed and eventually modified by governments acting, in the fullest sense, "in the national interest" of their respective countries.

CONCERN OVER "GREY AREA" MEASURES

Transparency is also being discussed in the GATT forum in relation to the effort of the European Community to induce "small" countries to accept a "selectivity" provision in a new safeguard code, elaborating the GATT's Article XIX, which provides for emergency action against a sudden surge of imports of a particular product. What a "selectivity" provision would do is allow a country, in exceptional circumstances, to impose selective (i.e. discriminatory) emergency protection against imports from one, two or maybe three countries, rather than against imports from all supplying countries. This proposed (further) departure from the principle of non-discrimination, which is meant to be the guiding principle of the GATT system, has been widely seen as an attempt to legitimise the host of VERs which have been negotiated "outside GATT disciplines" (14) since the late 1960s -- and are euphemistically referred to as "grey area" measures. In fact, the United States and Japan, which have mainly been fence-sitting on the issue, have argued from time to time in favour of a "selectivity" provision on the grounds that it would be a way of bringing VERs within the ambit of the GATT, subjecting them to multilateral discipline and surveillance, in the process rendering them transparent, all with a view to phasing them out in the course of time.

The question of transparency comes up in connection with another possible feature of a new safeguard code. Article XIX provides for emergency action against imports of a particular product which cause, or threaten to cause, "serious injury" to domestic suppliers of the competing product. Since "serious injury" is a subjective term, and since securing international agreement on appropriate objective criteria for determining when it is being caused or threatened has proved to be very elusive, it has been suggested that it might suffice as far as the GATT is concerned if a successful plea for emergency protection has been submitted to a public enquiry in which not only the complainant has been heard but also representatives of allied industries, importers, retailers and consumers -- besides the foreign suppliers of the product in question. At least then, it is argued, the decision by the responsible minister to take emergency action could be seen to have been subjected to public scrutiny (and investigation) by all interested parties (15).

PERCEIVED NEED FOR PUBLIC ENQUIRIES

In a number of countries, the implementation of regulatory trade measures -- anti-dumping actions, subsidy-countervailing duties, emergency protection -- involves public enquiries in one form or another, affording other interested parties, apart from the "plaintiff" and the "respondent", an opportunity to be heard. The country which is most conspicuous in this respect is the United States, where public hearings are a significant part not only of the policy-making process but also of the decision-taking process. And the role of public hearings in Australia has also been attracting attention, especially in respect of public assistance on a discriminatory basis to particular industries. Indeed, the Industries Assistance Commission in Australia is being seen abroad as a model, one worth emulating as far as possible in different constitutional circumstances.

Interest in the United Kingdom

In April 1982, for example, the Consumers' Association in the United Kingdom proposed to the National Economic Development Council that the British Government establish a system to monitor the costs and benefits of VERs and other arrangements -- outside the purview of the European Community -- for restricting imports (16).

Soon after, in a speech on 9th June 1982, the British Minister for Trade, then Peter Rees, said that he welcomed recent "moves towards achieving greater transparency in international trade relations, particularly the idea that the less formal intergovernmental and inter-industry voluntary export-restraint arrangements should be exposed to some kind of international scrutiny in the GATT", both to reduce suspicion and to make the costs of subsidies and protection clearer.

"Similarly", Mr. Rees went on to say, "there might also be a case in a domestic context for a body, drawing on the experience of the trade commissions of the United States and Australia, to study and publish the wider costs of any proposed new protectionist measure, not only to consumers, whose voice would be more widely heard, but also to other sectors of industry which would be adversely if indirectly affected. In this way we would, I believe, generate a more balanced debate on given measures and the narrow sectoral or regional case could be judged against a wider national or international background" (17).

In spite of opposition from the Confederation of British Industry, or perhaps because of it, Mr. Rees submitted a proposal to Mrs. Thatcher's Cabinet for the establishment of an import advisory commission having a small staff. At that time, however, the British Government was adamant (as it remains) on closing down "quangos" -- quasi-autonomous, non-governmental organisations -- and therefore the proposal got short shrift. But the idea is by no means dead. [Of the 2 165 or so quangos, including nationalised industries, that existed in 1979, the Thatcher Government has eliminated about 600, although 115 new ones have been created in their place (18).]

TRADE POLICY IN AN AGE OF UNCERTAINTY

In considering the place of public enquiries in the administration of measures affecting industrial structure and international competition, it might help to consider briefly what trade policy embraces nowadays, for there is still a tendency to think of it as simply being concerned with the means by which on the one hand exports are encouraged and on the other imports are discouraged -- by tariffs and a range of non-tariff measures.

Scope of trade policy

Essentially, trade policy bears on investment, as noted earlier. Subsidies to and taxes on production and international trade have effects on industrial structure. These tariffs and non-tariff interventions in the market also affect the international allocation of production. Therefore, trade policy is not only virtually synonymous with industrial policy; it is also a key factor in international investment decisions. But trade-cum-industrial policy has become vastly more complicated since government intervention in the market process began to escalate in the 1960s.

Since the end of World War II, there have been growing electoral pressures on governments to assume more and more responsibilities towards the social and economic welfare of their peoples through policies for full employment, price stability, economic growth, income distribution, regional balance and environmental control, as well as industrial organisation (involving the promotion of high-technology industries and the protection of low-technology ones), the "encouragement" of exports and the regulation of investment flows.

Such responsibilities have been easier to assume than to discharge. One reason for this relates to the international forces to which individual economies are subjected. Intense competition, large-scale capital flows, technological advances in industry and agriculture as well as in transport and communications, together with new and expanding markets and suppliers, are having profound and continuing effects on international production and trading patterns. Indeed, the rapid integration of the world economy has resulted in a high level of interdependence between national economies, especially between the more industrialised ones. Economic interdependence combined with the wider obligations assumed by governments in the conduct of domestic affairs has meant that economic measures in one country are liable to affect economic conditions in other countries.

To elaborate, the policies by which governments have sought to achieve their multitudinous objectives are seriously impairing the ability of the economic system in each country to maintain economic growth, which is only to be expected. It stands to reason that when government objectives become so large in number, the actual effects of individual policies implemented in their pursuit become indeterminate. Since policies interact, their combination will produce unanticipated results; therefore, their combined effect is bound to inhibit economic growth by increasing uncertainty. A study by the GATT Secretariat, published in 1978, concluded that the economic difficulties now being experienced by the industrialised countries are reducible to a single cause: increased policy-induced uncertainty (19).

Impact of uncertainty on adjustment

The conditions of economic activity are in a constant state of flux. And it is in this unceasing, uncontrollable and sometimes radical change that

societies seek some overall stability. Such "overall stability" as they hope
to attain may only be reached through prompt adjustment by those affected --
individual firms, maybe whole sectors of industry, the employees in them and
the capital market -- by each consequence of economic change.

Only approximate "overall stability" is attainable because, as mentioned, change is sometimes radical and adjustment to it is then rough. But
attempts to postpone, "correct" or offset that adjustment -- in the illusion
that it is possible to avoid the social and political strains which it implies
-- only makes the society and economy more vulnerable to the continuing change
and sets the stage for more violent instability later on. Such attempts are
also the main, if not the sole, source of international friction in economic
relations between countries. International economic order can be said to
exist only when adjustments can proceed unobstructed.

We live in an imperfect world, they say: the international economic
order is imperfect, but it cannot be improved, the degree of stability it provides cannot be increased, by manipulating the rate of change to which society
is exposed. Social and economic change, especially in a free society, results
from a process so complex that nobody can comprehend it in its entirety. For
an improvement in the international economic order to be brought about, it is
necessary to increase the predictability of change. If change can be anticipated over a longer period, the adjustment can be better prepared; it need
not be precipitous.

That in turn presupposes a need to limit the number of key variables
which those directly responsible for adjustment -- firms themselves, that is,
and the institutions of the capital market -- have to treat as uncertain. The
state of demand facing any firm, and certain elements of its costs, may have
to be regarded as essentially, and inescapably, uncertain. But needless uncertainty is added when the decision-maker in the firm, or in the capital
market, must also try to guess the future rate of inflation, the future
pattern of rates of exchange, future access to foreign markets for the
products of the firm and the future of such other conditions of business as
are affected by government policies.

ADJUSTMENT, UNDERSTANDING AND CONSENT

Policy-induced uncertainty inhibits the investment which is necessary
for adjustment to proceed. Adjustment, a continuous part of the process of
economic growth, is an exercise in foresight (20). Market pressures make certain activities unprofitable. New and better uses for the productive factors
that are so released have to be sought. The concept of "anticipatory adjustment policy" derives from this need for foresight. Governments, however,
cannot exercise on behalf of industry the detailed foresight that is needed
for anticipating which particular lines of production will eventually have to
be abandoned and which particular lines will grow. But in helping society at
large to anticipate and face change, governments have an essential role, one
that gets very little attention in policy-making circles.

The need for adjustment in the developed countries is not disputed.
There has accumulated during the 1960s and 1970s a substantial backlog of

much-needed adjustment which goes a long way towards explaining the "slow growth" being experienced in industrialised countries (21). In the final analysis, this lag in adjustment reflects an inadequate public understanding of the nature of change creating the need for adjustment; and, too, an inadequate understanding of the policies needed to prevent this change from becoming disruptive. When little is known about prospective changes in the economic environment, it is not surprising that uncertainty, or fear, prompts and mobilises widespread resistance to those prospective changes (22).

"Public awareness of the costs and benefits of adjustment, and of the inevitability of change", the Industries Assistance Commission in Australia remarked in 1977, "seems to be an imperative if we are to develop the community attitudes and political environment necessary to achieve worthwhile progress in redressing the serious imbalances in [Australia's] industrial structure" (23).

The information function of government has two aspects. First, the government must inform itself: it must improve its own foresight. It must be able to anticipate crises in industries. In crisis conditions, analysis is usually narrow, coming from those immediately concerned with the particular area of concern. In the nature of things, the analysis is hardly ever put in an economy-wide context, taking into account the impact of "crisis" measures on other industries. When decisions are made under crisis conditions, there is simply not the time to consider all the repercussions which a "crisis" policy will generate and transmit through the pervasive interdependence of economic relationships within a country and between countries.

Consequently, policy-making tends to assume the form of ad hoc reactions to unanticipated changes, implying frequent and abrupt changes in the "rules of the game", whether domestic or international. As a result, policy-induced uncertainty is enhanced and the pattern of expectations on which businesses plan their investments is disrupted further, discouraging risk-taking still more.

The second aspect of the information function of government is still more important. Many have observed that policies of adjustment assistance have amounted in practice to policies of adjustment resistance. Accordingly, any policies which accepted the inevitability of constant change in the economic environment, reflecting shifts in comparative advantage or technological advances or whatever, and the resultant need for continuous adjustment, would require quite a noticeable change in direction from what was witnessed throughout the 1970s. Such a change in direction, however, is not likely to be implemented without the understanding and consent, in representative democracies, of the electorate at large. Only government can create such an understanding and mobilise the necessary consent. It can do so only by inducing and cultivating a continuous and informed public discussion of the costs and benefits of adjustment and, too, of the costs and benefits of protection. Societies, as argued earlier, can be prepared for change.

Attention might be drawn to three more specific reasons for promoting public discussion of economic policy issues. First, by encouraging contributions from the relevant specialist fields of enquiry, public discussion should lead not only to the generation of "better" information but also to the creation of new knowledge, which is sorely needed in improving the conduct of economic policy in most countries. Secondly, the development of public discussion would oblige governments to articulate their view of the desirable and attainable longer-term future for the economies for which they are, for the time being, responsible. This would ensure a better co-ordination of the detailed policies being pursued by the different departments of government, and it would help to reduce the policy-induced uncertainty which firms face in planning their activities. Finally, such a discussion of economic policy issues would help governments secure the political backing for refusals on their part to grant protection to industries which prefer to resist change rather than adjust to change, thereby obliging the energies of firms to be directed towards more productive purposes than those of lobbying.

SIGNIFICANCE OF THE TRANSPARENCY ISSUE

In view of the widely perceived need to get the adjustment process of the market working again, both in developed and developing countries, a focus for GATT deliberations could be finding ways of promoting greater public awareness (that is, increased public knowledge) of the costs and benefits of the means whereby governments try to support and protect particular industries. Constitutionally appropriate ways have to be found, at least in the major industrialised countries, for generating information to provide a basis for public scrutiny of domestic "industry policies". Viewed from this perspective, those ways -- be they through a commission or tribunal or whatever -- should not be concerned directly with the formulation of policy or with making policy recommendations, although they would inevitably be concerned with the evaluation of policy options. Their chief purpose should be concerned with the information function of government.

If discussion on "transparency" in the GATT system were limited to standard and generally acceptable ground rules for promoting public awareness and understanding of the consequences of industry-support measures, it could not be seen as posing a threat to governments -- promoting something which could usurp their role -- in the conduct of domestic policies. Indeed, it might be quite difficult for any GATT Member country to find a reason for refusing to allow such an issue to be put on the negotiating agenda, for if a government were to object, it would be signalling to its constituents a desire to continue keeping them in the dark. In the longer run, as the costs and benefits of public assistance to industries are better understood, the introduction of methods of conducting public enquiries would render rational policies less of a political liability to governments.

Doubts over how to proceed with a new GATT round reflect deep-seated concerns about the erosion of the GATT system. When the principles and rules of the GATT are no longer effective, when they are rarely invoked in trade disputes between the major trading powers, when they no longer enjoy the confidence of the smaller countries whose interests they are supposed to safeguard, it is hardly reasonable to argue, as some do, that the present incoherent state of the GATT system is not too bad in the circumstances, what with the world economy struggling out of a prolonged period of slow growth and with conflicts among so many of its Member countries. Nor is it reasonable to expect serious attention to be paid to "new" items on the GATT agenda (24).

Thus it is necessary to think through, once again, what constitutes a viable framework of principles and rules for the conduct of international trade. The purpose of those principles and rules, and of the procedures embodying them, should be to ensure i) that there is a minimal degree of coherence in the policies of the major trading countries, ii) that the participating countries are encouraged and helped to adjust to change and iii) that there will be growth and prosperity in the world economy. How can these objectives be achieved?

The GATT system embraces ends and means. It has a method, reciprocal bargaining, for agreeing on ends, namely levels of protection. But it is mostly concerned with means, criteria and procedures for conducting trade policy. The attempt to agree on ends has not held very well. This has partly been because reciprocal bargaining has concentrated in practice on reducing levels of protection on goods of export interest to industrialised countries. But it has mainly been because changing circumstances in the world economy also changed the domestic view in the industrialised countries of what should be the levels of protection accorded to particular industries.

An agreement on ends is difficult to sustain in the long run. What might be sustained, however, is an agreement on the means, criteria and procedures that would oblige governments to take decisions on questions of public assistance to industries in a public, transparent and rational way. The education of public opinion could be strengthened thereby and, in consequence, the decisions ultimately taken would be far more likely to be rational.

It is necessary, then, to consider what needs to be done to ensure that decisions on public assistance to industries are less likely to be against the interests of a national economy as a whole, let alone the world economy as a whole. On this the OECD Report "Consumer Policy and International Trade" clarifies many of the issues. If governments continue to find it easy to resist change through the imposition of discriminatory trade restrictions (via import quotas or export restraints) because their constituents find it easier to lobby than to adjust, there will be little to prevent the continued erosion of the GATT system, leading eventually to its demise.

IN SHORT

The need for greater transparency in the conduct of trade policy is not merely a reflection of current calls for more open government. Transparency should be a fundamental element in the conduct of good trade policy.

There are three reasons why trade should be formed in public, should be justified in public and should be evaluated in public:

a) First, it is very difficult, almost impossible, for governments to resist demands for protection from producer interests if they are not required both to notify those who may be harmed by those demands and to justify to the public any decision to meet those demands;

b) Secondly, enterprises cannot plan their business, they cannot make decisions on investment and marketing and so on, if the policy environment is both unknown and unpredictable;

c) Thirdly, the public cannot be informed or educated about what is, or is not, a good policy -- a policy that should be accepted -- if it is not acquainted both with the thrust of the policy and with how it is determined and implemented (25).

The increasingly common practice of granting favours to particular sectional interests in society, often behind closed doors, smacks of arbitrary despotism. Actions by governments which transfer income from one section of society to another can be distinguished from theft only by the procedures that are followed. Protection, whatever form it takes, is a form of taxation. When protection is given in secret it amounts to taxation without representation.

NOTES AND REFERENCES

1. For a succinct discussion of the thinking of those present at the creation of the international economic order after World War II, see Lord McFadzean of Kelvinside et al., Global Strategy for Growth: Report on North-South Issues, Special Report No. 1 (London: Trade Policy Research Centre, 1981), ch. 3.

2. Throughout this paper the phrase "government intervention in the market process" is used in order to avoid implying criticism of government intervention of any kind.

3. In this connection, see Hugh Corbet, "What Happens After the Tokyo Round Negotiations?", Asia Pacific Community, Tokyo, Summer 1979.

4. This conclusion is traced in Richard Blackhurst, "The Twilight of Domestic Economic Policies", The World Economy, London, December 1981.

5. "Fifteenth Meeting of the Consultative Group of Eighteen", GATT Press Release, GATT Secretariat, Geneva, No. 1201, 26th June 1981.

6. Much of this paper draws on two articles by the present writer, namely "Ordre international, 'transparence' et aides publique à l'industrie", Politique Etrangère, Paris, No. 1, 1984, and "Public Scrutiny of the Costs and Benefits of Public Assistance to Industries", Australian Outlook, Canberra, April 1985. In addition, the author has benefited from discussions with Gary Banks, Michael Calhoun, W.B. Carmichael, Gerhard Fels, Rodney de C. Grey, Jan Tumlir, Clayton Yeutter and Martin Wolf.

7. This point is elaborated in Lydia Dunn et al., In the Kingdom of the Blind: Report on Protectionism and the Asian-Pacific Region, Special Report No. 3 (London: Trade Policy Research Centre, 1983) ch. 3.

8. On this point, see Helen Hughes and Jean Waelbroeck, "Can Developing-country Exports Keep Growing in the 1980s?", The World Economy, June 1981.

9.   For early analyses of non-tariff measures, see Gerard and Victoria Curzon, <u>Hidden Barriers to International Trade</u>, Thames Essay No. 1 (London: Trade Policy Research Centre, 1970), and Robert E. Baldwin, <u>Non-tariff Distortions of International Trade</u> (Washington, D.C.: Brookings Institution, 1970).

10.   Non-tariff measures as instruments of industrial policy are reviewed in Victoria Curzon Price, <u>Industrial Policies in the European Community</u> (London: Macmillan, for the Trade Policy Research Centre, 1982).

11.   <u>Agreement on Interpretation and Application of Articles VI, XVI and XXXIII of the General Agreement on Tariffs and Trade</u> (Geneva, GATT Secretariat, 1979). For a succinct analysis of the subsidies issue, see Harald B. Malmgren, <u>International Order for Public Subsidies</u>, Thames Essay No. 11 (London: Trade Policy Research Centre, 1977).

12.   <u>Agreement on Government Procurement</u> (Geneva: GATT Secretariat, 1979). For a discussion of the economic issues, see Brian Hindley, "The Economics of an Accord on Public Procurement Policies", <u>The World Economy</u>, June 1978.

13.   For brief assessments of the Tokyo Round agreements, see Curzon Price, op. cit., ch. 1 on "What the Tokyo Round Negotiations Failed to Settle".

14.   The phrase comes from the Ministerial Declaration issued after the GATT ministerial conference in Geneva in November 1982. See <u>GATT Press Release</u>, 1328, 29 November 1982, p. 2.

15.   See David Robertson, <u>Fail Safe Systems for Trade Liberalisation</u>, Thames Essay No. 12 (London: Trade Policy Research Centre, 1977). Dr. Robertson, now a senior official in the Australian Prime Minister's Department, prepared this paper while a Senior Research Associate of the Trade Policy Research Centre.

16.   "Monitoring the Costs and Benefits of Selective Import Controls", Memorandum by the Consumers' Association, NEDC(82)26 (London: National Economic Development Council, 1982).

17.   Address by the British Minister for Trade, then Peter Rees, to the Wilton Park Conference on "Protectionism versus a Free Trade World", Wiston House, near Steyning, Sussex, 9th June 1982. See <u>Press Notice</u>, Department of Trade, London, No. 278, 9th June 1982.

18.   <u>The Sunday Times</u>, London, 18th November 1984.

19.   Blackhurst, Nicholas Marian and Jan Tumlir, <u>Adjustment, Trade and Growth in Developed and Developing Countries</u>, GATT Studies in International Trade No. 6 (Geneva: GATT Secretariat, 1978).

20.   This section draws on Gary Banks and Tumlir, <u>Industrial Evolution as a Policy Problem</u> (London: Trade Policy Research Centre, forthcoming).

21.   Blackhurst, "The Outlook for World Trade", <u>Business Economist</u>, London, Summer 1981.

22. Dunn et al., op. cit., p. 117.

23. Industries Assistance Commission, Annual Report (Canberra: Australian Government Publishing Service, 1977).

24. By "new" items on the GATT agenda are meant trade in services, export criteria for foreign investments and trade in high-technology products.

25. Brian Scott et al., Has the Cavalry Arrived? A Report on Trade Liberalisation and Economic Recovery, Special Report No. 6 (London: Trade Policy Research Centre, 1984), ch. 6.

THE CONSIDERATION OF CONSUMER INTERESTS IN THE IMPLEMENTATION
OF ANTI-DUMPING POLICY (1)

by

Klaus Stegemann
Professor of Economics, Queen's University, Kingston, Canada

I. INTRODUCTION

When Canada adopted its new anti-dumping law in 1984, Parliament approved at least one new provision that is designed to permit the consideration of consumer interests in the implementation of anti-dumping policy: Section 45 of the Special Import Measures Act (Canada, 1984a) now authorises the Canadian Import Tribunal to consider the concerns of consumers and of other groups opposed to the imposition of anti-dumping duties, and to make a recommendation for total or partial remission of anti-dumping duty if the Tribunal finds this to be in the "public interest" [ibid., Section 45 (1)]. The introduction of a public interest clause into Canadian anti-dumping law may be justly celebrated as a breakthrough for consumer interests and concerns of competition policy. Yet, the real battle still lies ahead.

The new provision (or others like it) will become an active instrument only if there is strong political support for consumer interests. To achieve such support, the public's attitude towards anti-dumping policy will have to be turned around dramatically. In spite of a growing incidence of anti-dumping measures, the public's current attitude is characterised by benevolent indifference. Except for import-competing producers (who increasingly make use of mechanisms offering special protection) and directly affected importers, not many people appear to know or care what anti-dumping policy does to their interests. There can be no question that such measures protect the interests of import-competing producers at the expense of consumers. The reason for so little apparent consumer protest is that the true nature and effect of anti-dumping policy are hidden behind an ideological smoke-screen (Stegemann, 1982a, pp. 51-61).

This study is an attempt to expose three common misconceptions that make it difficult to win political support for changes in anti-dumping proceedings that would increase the weight of consumer interests. It is often assumed that:

a) The GATT rules on dumping do not permit the consideration of consumer interests in the implementation of national anti-dumping policies when dumping causes injury to domestic producers;

b) Anti-dumping policy is essentially an "extension" of domestic competition policy, in the sense that it contains international price discrimination for the same reasons as antitrust policy supposedly contains domestic price discrimination;

c) Anti-dumping policy defends the national interest of the importing country, and the elaborate two-stage investigation process required for the imposition of anti-dumping duties is designed to determine whether for the particular case such measures are, indeed, in the national interest.

Sections II-IV below focus on these misconceptions; Section IV, moreover, suggests practical ways of introducing the consideration of consumer interests into the anti-dumping proceedings of various jurisdictions.

II. THE GATT DOES NOT CONDEMN DUMPING

The GATT provisions on dumping and anti-dumping policy are contained in Article VI of the General Agreement (GATT, 1952) and in a supplementary Agreement on Implementation of Article VI, known as the "Anti-Dumping Code" (GATT, 1968 and 1980). The Code was first drawn up during the Kennedy Round of GATT negotiations (1964-1967); a revised and expanded version became part of the Tokyo Round trade agreements in 1979. The Anti-Dumping Code constitutes the mutually agreed interpretation of the anti-dumping provisions of the GATT. It is the reason why we observe a good measure of uniformity in signatories' anti-dumping laws, regulations, and administrative procedures. The 1979 Code also established a specific consultation, conciliation and dispute settlement procedure for anti-dumping matters (GATT, 1980).

Neither the General Agreement nor the Anti-Dumping Code ever refers to consumer interests. Yet, it can be demonstrated that the GATT rules do not stand in the way of an explicit consideration of consumer interests. Indeed, the strengthening of consumer interests in the implementation of anti-dumping policies would tend to complement the thrust of the internationally agreed interpretation of Article VI that is embodied in the Code.

1. The GATT does not establish an obligation for the contracting parties to counteract dumping.

This statement, at first sight, seems to be at odds with the wording in Article VI which says that dumping "is to be condemned if it causes or threatens material injury to an established industry in the territory of a contracting party or materially retards the establishment of a domestic industry" (GATT, 1952, Article VI, paragraph 1). Understandably, the phrase "to be condemned" also appears in statements by representatives of import-competing industries who lobby for tougher anti-dumping policies (Canada, 1981-1982, No. 4, p. 9; No. 11, p. 6). Yet, it is quite clear from the context of the provision and the subsequent interpretation of Article VI that the GATT does not establish an obligation for the contracting parties to counteract dumping, even if such dumping causes injury to domestic producers. What Article VI does establish is a right to use anti-dumping duties in certain narrowly defined circumstances (2).

It must be remembered that the GATT originally was an agreement on tariffs and on the negotiation of tariff reductions (Dam, 1970, chapters 2 and 3). Article I of the General Agreement stipulates the principle of "Most-Favoured-Nation Treatment" and Article II requires that the contracting parties "bind" their tariff rates at mutually agreed levels. A tariff for a bound item may not be raised above the level of binding. Furthermore, a contracting party making a tariff concession is committed, except as otherwise specifically provided, not to increase or introduce other duties or charges that would tend to undercut the binding of agreed tariff rates. The right to impose anti-dumping duties is an exception to the general provisions of Article II. Thus, any contracting party is entitled to apply anti-dumping duties (and countervailing duties) as long as such duties are "applied consistently with the provisions of Article VI" [GATT, 1952, Article II, paragraph 2(b)].

The exception for anti-dumping measures is more generous than other GATT provisions that permit contracting parties to increase protection in special circumstances, in that anti-dumping (and countervailing) duties may be imposed selectively and unilaterally, without international consultation, compensation, or fear of retaliation from affected trading partners. The special treatment of these duties reflects the widely held view that such duties should be regarded as defensive measures against "unfair" trading practices (Barcelo, 1980). Still, the fact remains that the GATT provides a right for contracting parties to protect domestic producers from injurious dumping, rather than an obligation for anyone to counteract or refrain from dumping.

Article VI does, however, contain an obligation of a different sort for contracting parties: to observe the GATT constraints on anti-dumping policy if they apply anti-dumping measures. Accordingly, it has been said that the GATT provisions deal not with the regulation of dumping, but with the regulation of anti-dumping measures (de Jong, 1968, p. 186; Grey, 1973, p. 4; Lloyd, 1977, p. 4).

2. <u>Article VI and the Anti-Dumping Code are intended to <u>constrain, and not to</u> encourage, the use of anti-dumping measures</u>.

As has been pointed out, the right to impose anti-dumping duties must be regarded as an exception to the fundamental principles of the GATT. Article VI is intended to keep the exception narrow, to ensure that contracting parties avail themselves of this exception only for bona fide anti-dumping measures. A GATT group of experts concluded as early as 1961:

> "That it was essential that countries should avoid immoderate use of anti-dumping and countervailing duties, since this would reduce the value of the efforts that had been made since the war to remove barriers to trade. These duties were to be regarded as <u>exceptional</u> and <u>temporary</u> measures to deal with <u>specific cases</u> of injurious dumping or subsidisation" (GATT, 1961, emphasis added).

Yet, Article VI alone was not sufficiently specific or comprehensive and therefore had to be supplemented by the Anti-Dumping Code (Dam, 1970, pp. 172-177). The Code emphasizes provisions that limit the scope of anti-dumping policies and tries to make the anti-dumping proceedings of the signatories more predictable. In particular, the Code provides more precise definitions of critical concepts; emphasizes the triple requirement of determination of dumping, of material injury, and of a causal link between them; includes detailed procedural rules; and limits the scope and duration of anti-dumping remedies (GATT, 1980, Articles 1-11). Because of Article I of the General Agreement, the signatories must apply the provisions of the Code on a most-favoured-nation basis (Grey, 1973, p. 39).

3. <u>The GATT constraints for the implementation of anti-dumping policy are intended to protect the interests of exporters, although those constraints serve simultaneously to protect the interests of consumers in the importing country</u>.

As an international agreement on trade liberalisation, the GATT asserts the rights of exporters vis-à-vis import-restricting policies of the contracting parties. It is, therefore, not surprising that the language of the Anti-Dumping Code in its more "rhetorical" passages "is the language of the dumpers, not of the dumped upon" (Grey, 1973, p. 40). The Code protects the rights of alleged dumpers, and one might have expected this emphasis to be expressed also in the anti-dumping laws of the signatories to the Code (Van Bael, 1979, pp. 404-407). The interests of consumers in the importing country are not identical with the interests of foreign suppliers whose rights are protected by the GATT anti-dumping rules (3). However, in the majority of cases consumers in the importing country benefit from rules that protect the interests of alleged dumpers, particularly when the rules prevent the imposition of anti-dumping duties on imports that are not dumped or that do not cause material injury to domestic producers. Consumers also benefit if the procedures do not permit harassment of foreign suppliers or importers, if implementation has to occur on a case-by-case basis, and if the anti-dumping remedies are limited in scope and duration. The stricter the internationally agreed constraints on the implementation of anti-dumping policies, the more consumers can expect to retain the advantages of active and potential import competition. Thus, to a certain extent, the GATT rules protect the interests of consumers even if consumer interests are not considered explicitly in the implementation of anti-dumping measures.

4. <u>There is a tendency for import-competing producers to appeal to "our rights under the GATT" and for national lawmakers to respond to such pressure by moving towards making maximum use of restrictions permissible under the Anti-Dumping Code</u>.

Thus international law that was intended as a ceiling tends to become a floor for national policies. When the United States, the EC and Canada adjusted their anti-dumping law after the Code had been revised by the Tokyo Round negotiations, the thrust of the new provisions was to increase protection for domestic producers; the adjustment to more precisely defined constraints of the Code appeared to be secondary (4). At the same time, the United States, Canada and the EC responded to the prolonged world-wide recession by increasing the frequency of use of anti-dumping measures and by adopting semi-automatic enforcement systems, such as the "trigger-price mechanism" for steel products (Stegemann, 1978; Adams, 1979). In spite of the GATT rules, the signatories' new legal provisions, new procedures, and more frequent use thereof provide opportunities for harassment and procedural protectionism going beyond bona fide anti-dumping action (Jacobs and Hove, 1980, p. 13; Caine, 1981; Thomas, 1981; Stegemann, 1984a). Furthermore, the increasing "legalisation" or "judicialisation" of anti-dumping policy tends to give an advantage to domestic producers, although the legalistic system may have been designed to protect equally the rights of foreign suppliers and importers (Jackson, 1984).

There is a tendency in all countries to equate the interests of import-competing producers with the interests of the country as a whole. In the case of anti-dumping policy, it seems almost natural to assume that the national interest is served automatically when domestic producers are protected from the injury of dumped imports. Would it not be natural for any signatory "to take full advantage of its rights under the GATT" (Canada, 1980, p. 1) and make maximum use of any leeway for protecting domestic producers? Why aren't we doing what other countries do? (Lazar, 1981; Canada, 1981-1982; Martin, 1984). Let's not try to be "the Boy Scouts of the World!" (Canada, 1981-1982, No. 28, p. 15). Add to these sentiments the use of a value-charged language and further elements of camouflage (Stegemann, 1982a, pp. 51-61), and it is not really surprising why we observe anti-dumping policies that pursue the interests of import-competing producers in the name of the national interest (5).

5. <u>The GATT rules in no way prevent countries from adopting procedures that would give greater weight to consumer interests in the implementation of anti-dumping policy</u>.

Unquestionably, the signatories are permitted to pursue their national interests within the boundaries of the Code. A policy intended to promote the national interest (which is not automatically the same as that of domestic producers) must consider both costs and benefits of intervention. The benefits of anti-dumping intervention accrue to import-competing domestic producers; the costs are borne by domestic consumers (6). To serve the national interest, anti-dumping policy has to determine a trade-off between the interests of affected domestic groups; countries could find it in their interest to abstain from import-restricting intervention in certain cases or types of cases.

While it made sense for the GATT rules to define the conditions under which countries may protect the interests of import-competing domestic producers, it is clearly not implied that the contracting parties are under an obligation to ignore the interests of all other domestic groups (7).

III. THERE EXISTS A CONFLICT BETWEEN ANTI-DUMPING AND ANTITRUST POLICIES

For readers who are closely familiar with both anti-dumping and anti-trust policies, it must be quite obvious that the enforcement of existing anti-dumping laws is largely inconsistent with the objectives of domestic policies directed at promoting competition (8). The conflict has been documented in the United States by numerous interventions in anti-dumping proceedings by the Antitrust Division of the Department of Justice (Applebaum, 1974, pp. 602-603; ABA, 1974, p. 689; U.S. Department of Justice, 1981 and various years) and similar submissions by the Federal Trade Commission (Crawford, 1984) (9). In Canada, the Director of Investigation and Research, Combines Investigation Act has recently begun to take an interest in anti-dumping proceedings by intervening in the refined sugar case (Canada, 1984c), and also intervened in the legislative process leading to the 1984 changes in Canadian anti-dumping law (Canada, 1981-1982, No. 23, pp. 4-25; No. 27, pp. 4-30; Canada, 1982, p. 76). Furthermore, the conflict between anti-dumping and antitrust policies has been acknowledged by the majority of lawyers and legal scholars writing on this subject (Barcelo, 1972; Dickey, 1979, p. 4; Metzger, 1982, p. 159; Victor, 1983, p. 350).

Still, the fact that this conflict exists has not yet become public knowledge. Anti-dumping policy is not in the same category as, say, agricultural supply management, where there is some recognition that the "stabilization" of producer income (which is the predominant policy objective) tends to conflict with the consumers' interest in low prices. Anti-dumping policy is not yet at a stage where widespread recognition of the policy conflict could lead to reforms that would eliminate inconsistencies with pro-competitive policies, or would permit a rational trade-off between conflicting policy objectives. Under the existing regime, anti-dumping and antitrust policies frequently operate at cross purposes, i.e., anti-dumping measures restrict (or even eliminate) import competition for the same industries for which antitrust tries to promote domestic competition.

Lack of information concerning crucial institutional details of anti-dumping proceedings appears to be the main reason why the conflict with domestic competition policy has not been recognised by the media, non-specialist lawyers, and the economics profession. Why, in particular, would most academic economists, who generally favour free trade and pro-competitive policies, be so uncommonly tolerant of anti-dumping policies that obviously reduce import competition? They appear to take it for granted that anti-dumping policies prevent mainly undesirable forms of import competition; to them, dumping necessarily represents price discrimination, which in turn requires monopoly power (in this case in the exporting producers' home markets). Furthermore, price discrimination can be used by monopolists to extend their market power in space and/or in time. On the surface, it is therefore tempting to conclude that "anti-dumping is a consistent extension of antitrust" (Epstein, 1973, p. 2) or that "anti-dumping legislation is in a broad sense a counterpart in commercial policy to legislation penalising damaging price discrimination in domestic commerce" (Grey, 1973, p. 2). Yet, both these statements are grossly misleading.

1. Price discrimination is not a prerequisite for the imposition of anti-dumping measures.

GATT law permits a definition of dumping that is considerably broader than the definition commonly found in economics textbooks. The initial definition in Article VI of the General Agreement and in Article 2 of the Code corresponds to the textbook definition:

> "A product is to be considered as being dumped ... if the export price of the product exported from one country to another is less than the comparable price, in the ordinary course of trade, for the like product when destined for consumption in the exporting country (GATT, 1980, Article 2, paragraph 1)".

But Article VI provides alternatives which also have been spelled out, in slightly modified form, in Article 2 of the Code. This provision distinguishes two cases in which a so-called "constructed value" may be used to determine the margin of dumping. Either there are no comparable sales in the foreign suppliers' home markets or "because of the particular market situation, such sales do not permit a proper comparison". In neither case does the textbook definition of dumping apply; both cases allow two ways of constructing the normal value of the goods in question. The importing country may use a comparable price of the like product exported to a third country or it may use "the cost of production in the country of origin plus a reasonable amount for administrative, selling and any other costs and for profits".

The largest divergence from the textbook definition of dumping is attained by a combination of the case of home-market sales that are deemed not to permit a proper comparison and the cost-based method of determining a constructed value. This combination allows signatories to disregard the prices of like products in the domestic market of the exporting country and to substitute a constructed value that equals the full cost of production and selling, plus general overhead and profits. Thus, under this rule, dumping is defined as selling in export markets at less than full cost; no evidence of price discrimination is required to establish a margin of dumping.

The U.S. statute [Title VII of the Tariff Act of 1930, 19 U.S.C. ss. 1673 et seq. (1980), as amended by the Trade Agreements Act of 1979, Pub. L. No. 96-39, 93 Stat. 144] makes it very plain in what circumstances the prices for sales in the exporting country should be disregarded. A cost-based constructed value may be applied whenever it is found that sales in the exporters' home market have been made below full cost "over an extended period of time and in substantial quantities" [Tariff Act of 1930, Section 773 (b)(1)]. Thus the purpose of the broader definition of dumping is to shelter domestic producers from aggressive import competition when prices in foreign markets are depressed. It is not the element of international price discrimination (based on foreign monopoly), but the abnormally low level of foreign prices that anti-dumping measures are meant to offset. When active competition in foreign markets at times of weak demand results in substantial home-market sales below full cost and in below-cost export prices, such export prices are considered just as "unfair" as export prices below profitable home-market prices, whenever import competition causes injury to U.S. producers (10).

It should be pointed out that the businessmen's view of "fair" competition has not penetrated antitrust laws to nearly the same extent as it has penetrated dumping laws. There have been many attempts to legislate "fair trade" or "non-discrimination" laws that would make selling below cost illegal. Yet currently, no important statutes exist that producers could use to stop domestic competitors from selling below full cost in the same way that they can stop foreign competitors.

2. <u>The regulation of price discrimination in domestic markets is much more narrowly conceived than anti-dumping policy</u>.

Several groups of experts and individual scholars have compared United States anti-dumping law to the Robinson-Patman Act, the principal U.S. statute dealing with domestic price discrimination. Most authors would agree with Applebaum (1974, p. 599) that "in terms of both language and enforcement, the Anti-Dumping Act is not basically analogous to the Robinson-Patman Act". A subcommittee of the American Bar Association found significant "inconsistencies" between the two laws (ABA, 1974, pp. 682 and 686) and concluded that anti-dumping policy "operates to deter price discrimination to a much greater extent" than does the Robinson-Patman Act in comparable domestic circumstances (ibid., p. 689). Others have pointed out that anti-dumping law uses a "tariff approach" rather than an "antitrust approach" (Yale L.J., 1965 and Metzger, 1982, pp. 154-155), where the fundamental principle of the tariff approach is described as "protection of American competitors regardless of the cost in higher prices or reduced availability of goods to the American consumer" (Yale L.J., 1965, p. 712).

3. <u>Anti-dumping policy would be redundant if it were aimed exclusively at the prevention of predatory pricing</u>.

There is no evidence suggesting that dumping cases tend to concern practices that would fulfil the conditions required for predatory pricing under domestic competition law. On the contrary, we have convincing testimony to the effect that dumping does not typically, if ever, involve practices that would meet the narrower (non-colloquial) definition of predatory behaviour (11). At a recent conference on Canadian anti-dumping policy (Stegemann, 1984a), there was a consensus among experts from government, industry and the legal profession that predatory dumping was an extremely rare, almost non-existent phenomenon, represented by possibly one case in a total of over 150 cases that have flowed through the Anti-Dumping Tribunal since 1969.

Obviously, there cannot exist an official confirmation of such views since the issue of predatory behaviour is not investigated under either U.S. or Canadian anti-dumping law. Yet in most cases the evidence adduced for other purposes permits the conclusion that a charge of predation would not make sense. Predation can be ruled out, for example, whenever the domestic industry remains basically healthy and suffers injury from dumping only in the form of reduced sales or reduced profits. Predation can also be ruled out when dumpers account for only a small share of the world market and would be prevented by international competition from attaining and abusing significant market power in any importing country (Dickey, 1979). The complainants themselves frequently supply the evidence that makes their case inconsistent with predatory dumping when they contend that in addition to current injury there exists a threat of future injury from dumping. This type of argument is usually based on evidence suggesting that the world market for the product in question will be excessively competitive for many years to come. It would be inconsistent to argue in the same case that the elimination of domestic production would leave buyers exposed to exploitation by a foreign monopoly (Stegemann, 1982c, p. 344).

If prevention of predatory dumping were the true and only objective of anti-dumping laws, such laws would be redundant for two reasons. First, since genuine predatory dumping cases appear to be extremely rare, there would be no justification for maintaining a costly anti-dumping mechanism. Second, separate anti-dumping laws would be redundant even if the number of predatory dumping cases were potentially substantial, because the general antitrust laws could be used to deal with predatory behaviour of foreign suppliers. Indeed, John Barcelo (1979) and others (Metzger, 1974) have argued convincingly that for the United States, relying on Section 2 of the Sherman Act would be preferable to any other form of anti-dumping protection if protection against genuinely predatory dumping were the objective (12).

As a "second-best" solution, these writers recommend a revision of existing anti-dumping law "to ensure that it applies only to predatory dumping or threats thereof and is only minimally restrictive of healthy price competition from imports" (Barcelo, 1979, p. 67). In fact, the initial attempt by the United States to enact a separate anti-dumping statute, the Anti-Dumping Act of 1916, was focussed narrowly on the prevention of predatory dumping. Jacob Viner (1966, pp. 244-245) and others (Marks, 1974, pp. 581-582; Victor, 1983) have argued that the Anti-Dumping Act of 1916 has been ineffective because as a criminal law statute it must be strictly construed. Yet, the fact that few cases were brought under the 1916 Act and that none involved convictions might simply confirm the judgement of all the experts that genuine predatory dumping is an extremely rare occurrence. A revised anti-dumping statute need not require proof of predatory intent. The revised law, which would not be criminal law, could establish a presumption of predatory dumping with the burden of rebuttal falling on the alleged dumper (Barcelo, 1979, p. 68). As has been said above, the circumstances of most observed anti-dumping cases would make it relatively easy to refute an allegation of predatory behaviour, because such behaviour just would not make sense under the given market conditions. Presumably, most of the observed cases would not proceed even to the preliminary investigation stage if a revised statute allowed anti-dumping measures only in cases of predatory behaviour.

4. The European Economic Community (EC) does not have an anti-dumping law or an anti-dumping policy for trade between member countries, relying instead on general competition law to deal with predatory pricing and related practices in so far as they affect trade between member states.

The EC Treaty or "Treaty of Rome" (EC, 1957) contains a provision, Article 91, dealing with intra-Community dumping. But this provision applied only "during the transitional period" [ibid., Article 91, paragraph (1)], i.e., at a time when trade barriers between member states had not been fully removed. In order to reduce opportunities for international price differentiation even during the transitional period, paragraph (2) of Article 91 provides that member countries cannot restrict the re-importation of products that have been exported to another member state. The Treaty provisions are intended to make anti-dumping measures redundant and to avoid giving member states the opportunity to reintroduce trade barriers in the guise of anti-dumping measures as other restrictions on intra-Community trade were coming down.

The EC competition law that may be considered to fill the place of intra-Community anti-dumping law is contained in Article 86 of the Treaty, which prohibits the abuse of a dominant position by one or more enterprises in the Common Market. More specifically, the Treaty names as one type of prohibited abuse "directly or indirectly imposing unfair purchase or selling prices or other unfair trading conditions" (13).

5. Anti-dumping measures restrict import competition just as much as do so-called "orderly marketing agreements" (OMAs).

Anti-dumping measures force foreign suppliers to raise their export prices and/or to restrict their shipments to the importing country. Such effects can occur at different stages of the implementation process. After imports have been found to be dumped and to cause (or threaten to cause) material injury to domestic production, foreign suppliers will cease dumping, which usually means they raise their export prices. The reason is, of course, that foreign suppliers could only be worse off if they left it to the importing country to eliminate the margin of dumping by collecting anti-dumping duty. A successful anti-dumping complaint thus tends to contain or remove the most aggressive foreign competitors who might be the only ones to disturb a peaceful oligopoly in the importing country.

Essentially the same result is obtained if an anti-dumping investigation is suspended at an earlier stage because foreign suppliers agree to give an "undertaking" that they will either cease exporting, cease dumping, or will restrain themselves to eliminate the injurious effects of dumping. In the United States and Canada (14), each undertaking must include exporters who account for substantially all of the imports that are subject to the investigation. The foreign suppliers are thus encouraged or even required to agree among themselves, as well as with the importing country (and at least indirectly with producers in the importing country), on how import competition should be reduced to a level that is acceptable under anti-dumping law. In the EC (15), where comprehensive coverage is not required, the Commission appears to negotiate undertakings with individual exporting countries. In fact, the majority of EC anti-dumping cases have been settled by voluntary undertakings to "revise prices" (16).

Finally, the existence of anti-dumping laws and certain enforcement procedures can have a "chilling effect" on import competition even without proceedings being officially initiated (Caine, 1981). Foreign suppliers and their potential domestic customers shy away from getting caught in costly and protracted anti-dumping cases. Rather than risk these costs and long-term exclusion from a market, foreign suppliers apply "anticipatory and preventive considerations" (Thomas, 1981, pp. 327-336), which means they compete less aggressively than they would in the absence of the anti-dumping threat. The chilling effects of anti-dumping policy can be enhanced considerably if importing countries establish special import-monitoring systems for certain products, as happened in the case of steel in the late 1970s, when the United States, the EC and Canada introduced their "trigger-price mechanisms" (17). As Walter Adams (1979, pp. 42-43) has reported, the trigger-price mechanism established a new floor for domestic steel prices in the U.S. market, while foreign steel suppliers were not displeased with the system either as the intercession of government helped steelmakers everywhere to achieve better results.

In sum, I agree with John Barcelo's conclusion (1980, p. 258):

"That through their acceptance of countervailing duty and anti-dumping laws, the GATT countries have, in effect, entered a market sharing arrangement under which, for protectionist purposes, they have restricted the share accorded to subsidised and dumped goods in their respective markets".

One cannot rule out the possibility that "protectionist purposes" might be sound reasons for government intervention from a national point of view (18). Still, anti-dumping policy can be shown to be unnecessarily wasteful (Stegemann, 1982a and 1982c).

IV. HOW TO INCREASE THE WEIGHT OF CONSUMER INTERESTS IN THE IMPLEMENTATION OF ANTI-DUMPING POLICY

Consumer interests would be best served if anti-dumping laws were repealed, or were revised to cover only genuine cases of predatory dumping. Assuming that such a radical policy shift is not within reach, the consideration of consumer interests can be strengthened by making use of several opportunities that either exist already or could be created via relatively minor amendments to national anti-dumping laws.

1. <u>In the absence of a public interest clause, consumer interests can be furthered mainly by participation in anti-dumping proceedings on the side of foreign suppliers or domestic importers</u>.

The existence or absence of an effectual public interest clause or an override provision determines the purpose of the participation of consumer representatives in the basic anti-dumping proceedings by which the authorities of the importing country determine the three factors that are critical for the implementation of anti-dumping protection under the GATT rules: the margin of dumping, the existence or threat of material injury, and the causal link between dumping and injury. If the national law has an effectual public interest clause, participation by consumer representatives is essential, because the decision to invoke the public interest clause or to consider an override may be influenced decisively by the evidence and argument that is presented during the basic proceedings. If a public interest clause does not exist, or if it is practically irrelevant because it is applied only in rare circumstances, the participation of consumers and antitrust authorities in anti-dumping proceedings can only have a much narrower purpose. The public interest is not an issue of investigation during routine anti-dumping proceedings. All that matters is whether dumping has caused (or threatens to cause) material injury to import-competing domestic producers. If these conditions are found to exist, the remedy is automatic: anti-dumping duties are imposed, unless (alternatively) foreign suppliers have chosen to offer a price undertaking that has been accepted by the domestic authorities. The cost of intervention, i.e., the effect of the proceedings and of the remedy on other groups in society is never an issue in a formal sense. In the absence of a public interest clause, there is no room for a compromise or a trade-off between legislated policy objectives which may be in conflict.

Therefore, consumer interests or antitrust considerations cannot be presented as such in routine anti-dumping proceedings, as for example was the case under Canada's old Anti-Dumping Act (Canadian Consumer Council, 1973, p. 14; Richardson, 1973, pp. 34-38; Slayton, 1979a, p. 59). All that consumers and antitrust authorities can formally do is to intervene on behalf of foreign suppliers and domestic importers whose interests are protected by the GATT Code and corresponding national anti-dumping laws. Thus, consumers and antitrust authorities can help by adducing evidence and argument to refute the allegation of dumping (the size of the alleged margin of dumping), the allegation of material injury (or threat of future injury) and the alleged existence of a causal link between injury and dumping.

In practice, we find that major domestic buyers or users of imports do intervene in anti-dumping proceedings on the side of importers or act as witnesses on behalf of importers. Yet, it appears that in the majority of anti-dumping cases, domestic buyers or users of imports do not participate actively in the proceedings. In some cases, no doubt, it is known in advance that the testimony of buyers could not possibly make a difference for the outcome. In other cases, buyers may be reluctant to become involved because they fear that appearing on the side of sellers of dumped imports might do harm to their business reputation, or they are afraid of antagonising their domestic suppliers on whom they depend for the major part of their requirements, and who will remember in times of short supply (19). Finally, there must be at least some cases in which the buyers of imports are not large enough or well organised enough to regard participation in anti-dumping proceedings as profitable, even if their intervention on the side of importers could affect the outcome; in some of these cases, the participation of organised consumer groups and/or antitrust authorities could be most useful. Crawford (1984) has reported how the U.S. Federal Trade Commission has assumed the role of consumer advocate in various trade law proceedings.

In Canada, neither the consumer groups nor the antitrust (anti-combines) authorities have demonstrated more than a casual interest in anti-dumping proceedings. The Canadian Consumers Association appeared in a single case, that of the tetanus immune globulin from the United States (ADT-3-74). The Director of Investigation and Research, Combines Investigation Act, i.e., Canada's antitrust authority, was also represented in exactly one case: refined sugar from the United States (ADT-8-84) (20). This case was unquestionably important from a competition policy point of view and the Director made a useful contribution by intervening on the side of the importers (21). Yet, it seems surprising that the Director let pass unnoticed the previous 150 anti-dumping cases. Section 27.1 of the Combines Investigation Act (Canada, 1976), on which the Director's intervention is based, has existed since the Act was last amended in 1975. It is known that the Director was concerned about other cases in which anti-dumping measures eliminated all active competition for a domestic monopoly (22). The Director's decision to intervene in the 1984 sugar case might be seen as the first step to gain experience for a role that the Director will have to play more regularly under Canada's revised anti-dumping law. Indeed, the so-called "public interest clause" of the new legislation (Canada, 1984a, Section 45) might dramatically improve the opportunity for the Director to influence the outcome of anti-dumping proceedings, because the Tribunal has been given a mandate to consider interests and policy objectives that conflict with the narrowly conceived objective of anti-dumping protection.

2. Major domestic buyers of imports, consumer representatives, and antitrust authorities should insist that the government make use of public interest clauses or override provisions that permit the waiving of anti-dumping duties or the reduction or remission of such duties in individual cases. Where override provisions do not exist, consumer representatives and anti-trust authorities should insist that the law be amended.

As concerns existing law, this consideration is relevant for Canada and the European Community. The external anti-dumping law of the European Community requires that anti-dumping duties be imposed only if "the interests of the Community" call for an intervention (Stanbrook, 1980, pp. 33-34). EC anti-dumping law thus contains a fourth requirement that must be fulfilled before anti-dumping duties are imposed. In addition to dumping, injury, and causation, the Commission's investigation must establish that the interests of the Community (meaning the EC or ECSC, respectively) call for intervention to protect import-competing producers from injury. Furthermore, the Commission may determine that the anti-dumping duty (if applicable) should be less than the margin of dumping (Didier, 1980, p. 366). EC anti-dumping law does not define the "interests of the Community". As the Head of the Commission's Anti-Dumping Service has observed, "the public interest element in dumping is a tacit acknowledgement of the overlap of political and legal considerations" (EC European Parliament, 1981, point G-19). This is to say that the interests of import-competing producers are treated as identical with the interests of the Community, unless other interests mount sufficient political pressure to prevent the imposition of anti-dumping duties. The opposing Community interests include the interests of consumers, import-using industries, and exporting industries (which might suffer from de facto retaliation by trading partners). Whether or not the opposing interests are represented and considered in all cases is not known. The Commission's comprehensive report on its anti-dumping activities during the years 1980-1982 (EC Commission, 1983) does not discuss the application of the trade-off provision. Competent observers agree that the Community interests clause "has only been a significant factor on very few occasions" (EC European Parliament, 1981, point F-17).

Section 45 of Canada's new Special Import Measures Act, also called "SIMA" (Canada, 1984a), reads as follows:

"45. 1. Where, as a result of an inquiry referred to in section 42 arising out of the dumping or subsidising of any goods, the Tribunal makes an order or finding described in any of sections 3 to 6 with respect to those goods and the Tribunal is of the opinion that the imposition of an anti-dumping or countervailing duty, or the imposition of such a duty in the full amount provided for by any of those sections, in respect of the goods would not or might not be in the public interest, the Tribunal shall, forthwith after making the order or finding:

a) Report to the Minister of Finance that it is of such opinion and provide him with a statement of the facts and reasons that caused it to be of that opinion; and

b) Cause a copy of the report to be published in the Canada Gazette.

2. Where any person interested in an inquiry referred to in subsection (1) makes a request to the Tribunal for an opportunity to make representations to the Tribunal on the questions whether the Tribunal should, if it makes an order described in any of sections 3 to 6 with respect to any goods in respect of which the inquiry is being made, make a report pursuant to paragraph (1 a) with respect to those goods, the Tribunal shall afford such person an opportunity to make representations to the Tribunal on that question orally or in writing, or both, as the Tribunal directs in the case of that inquiry".

This is one of seven sections under the title "Inquiries by Tribunal", starting with the routine procedure in Section 42. The Tribunal's orders or findings "described in any of sections 3 to 6" are orders or findings that normally result in the imposition of an anti-dumping or countervailing duty equal to the margin of dumping or the amount of the subsidy, respectively.

The phrase "any person interested in an inquiry" that occurs in paragraph 2 of the above provision has been defined in the Special Import Measures Regulations (Canada, 1984b). The definition in addition to exporters, importers and producers "includes any person required or authorised by any Act of Parliament or the legislature of a province to make representations to the Tribunal", any user of goods that are of the same description as goods that are the subject of proceedings, as well as "any association whose purpose is to advocate the interests of consumers in Canada" (ibid., Section 41). The Act does not say what the Minister of Finance is supposed to do after receiving the Tribunal's report. Presumably, the Minister has to decide whether or not the government should issue an Order in Council under Section 17 of the Financial Administration Act (Canada, R.S. c.116, s.1) to permit the total or partial remission of anti-dumping duties for the goods in question.

The Canadian Government did not propose a public interest clause in the July 1980 "discussion paper" (Canada, 1980), which initiated the four-year process that led to the adoption of SIMA. The proposal for such a clause was formally introduced in the Final Report of the Subcommittee on Import Policy (Canada, 1981-82, No. 31, pp. 27-28). The Subcommittee had been persuaded by strong representations by officials from the Department of Consumer and Corporate Affairs (ibid., Nos. 23 and 27) and other witnesses (ibid., Nos. 26 and 29) "that the concentration on producer interests alone is too narrow a focus and the consumer interest must be considered" [ibid., No. 31 (Final Report), p. 27]. The Subcommittee's recommendation was:

"The Tariff Board should be empowered to undertake a review of decisions made by the Anti-Dumping Tribunal, when so requested by consumer advocates, and when in the opinion of the Board it is in the national interest to do so" (ibid.).

This proposal still differed from Section 45 of SIMA in two important respects: the Subcommittee appeared to open the door only for the consideration of consumer interests, narrowly defined, and it recommended a separate review by the Tariff Board, rather than a review that would form an integral part of the Tribunal's investigation.

From the context of the recommendation, one can infer that the Subcommittee was concerned primarily with opening up an avenue that would permit reducing the conflict between anti-dumping policy and competition policy in certain cases. The cases that had been brought to the Subcommittee's attention (ibid., Nos. 23 and 27) involved highly concentrated domestic industries for which anti-dumping measures had practically eliminated all import competition. The Subcommittee's definition of consumer interests presumably would have included the interests of downstream industries such as furniture producers in the case of hardboard panels (ADT-4-81); its definition of "consumer advocates" might have covered the Director of Investigation and Research, Combines Investigation Act. Still, the Subcommittee did not mention other opposing interests that might be covered by the public interest clause in Section 45 of SIMA, as for example the interests of exporting industries which might suffer from the de facto retaliation by trading partners, other foreign policy repercussions of anti-dumping policy, or repercussions affecting federal-provincial relations.

As regards the procedural discrepancy between Section 45 of SIMA and the Subcommittee's recommendation, the Subcommittee had considered expanding the Tribunal's mandate to include a review of consumer interests among its criteria (Canada, 1981-82, No. 31, pp. 27-28), but decided to recommend locating the review procedure in the Tariff Board to indicate that the consideration of consumer concerns would be an exceptional matter.

> "Such a reference, to the Tariff Board, would be an explicit recognition of the legitimate protection Canadian business is entitled to from unfair competition and, in exceptional circumstances, would allow consumer concerns to be heard" (ibid., p. 2).

By adopting the procedure provided in Section 45, Parliament thus appears to have acknowledged that the review of consumer concerns (the public interest) ought to be part of the Tribunal's regular mandate and that the application of the new provision might become less exceptional than it would have been if the Subcommittee's recommendation had been adopted.

One should assume that for Section 45 cases the Tribunal will receive assistance from relevant branches of the government. In cases that involve a serious conflict between anti-dumping policy and competition policy, the Tribunal presumably will receive extensive input from the Director of Investigation and Research, Combines Investigation Act. The Director is expressly authorised to provide such input under Section 27.1 of the Act, and has intervened in numerous proceedings before federal and provincial regulatory bodies and authorities like the Tariff Board (23). It stands to reason that, for cases where Section 45 of SIMA should apply, the Director generally will have at hand evidence and argument that were prepared in the course of the Director's principal activities under the Combines Investigation Act.

3. Consumer representatives and antitrust authorities should insist that governments make use of existing provisions permitting the statutory exemption of certain products from the application of anti-dumping law, or should insist that the law be amended to make such exemptions possible.

In the case of Canada, Section 14 of SIMA provides:

> "The Governor in Council may, on the recommendation of the Minister of Finance, make regulations exempting any goods or class of goods from the application of this Act" (Canada, 1984a, Section 14).

Essentially the same provision was contained in Section 7 of the old Anti-Dumping Act (Canada, 1969). This provision has been used infrequently. During the lifetime of the old Act (1969-1984) there existed only one exemption under Section 7 that is relevant in the present context: "pharmaceutical products of a kind not made or produced in Canada" (Canada, 1972, Regulation 23).

Whereas one might envisage the public interest clause in Section 45 of SIMA being used to make ad hoc adjustments to anti-dumping policy to account for temporary or regional shortages, strikes and other short-term concerns, exemptions under Section 14 of SIMA would seem more appropriate for situations where the application of anti-dumping measures would conflict with important objectives of government policy, such as maintaining competition in the domestic market on a long-term basis. For this purpose, a statutory exemption under Section 14 would have significant advantages as compared to a Section 45 recommendation. All parties concerned would know in advance that anti-dumping measures cannot be applied for imports of the exempted goods. There could be no "chilling effects", no threats with anti-dumping actions, nor any moral hazard effects (Stegemann, 1982c, pp. 337-341), and nobody would have to incur the costs and delays of anti-dumping proceedings.

The procedure for implementing Section 14 should be flexible. In some cases it could follow the pattern that was established with the exemption of pharmaceutical products in the 1960s, when the government introduced the required regulation as part of a package of measures designed to decrease the cost of drugs to consumers. In other cases, an exemption order may derive from an anti-dumping proceeding, e.g. when it has been established that a highly concentrated industry is using anti-dumping protection to facilitate monopolistic conduct in the domestic market. It is also conceivable that an exemption order would be issued as a consequence or integral part of an anti-combines decision.

V. CONCLUSION

In the final analysis, any attempt to utilise opportunities for the consideration of consumer interests provided under national anti-dumping laws can succeed only to the extent that there exists sufficiently strong political support for consumer interests and for the objectives of competition policy generally. The strength of such political support can be increased by educating the public about the nature and effects of existing anti-dumping procedures. Consumer representatives and antitrust authorities should make a greater effort to monitor anti-dumping proceedings and to expose the costs of anti-dumping measures in terms of national welfare. The monitoring is particularly important for "hidden" import restrictions such as price under-takings. Furthermore, major domestic buyers, consumer organisations and anti-trust authorities should more regularly make use of appeal procedures and review provisions, and should insist on the introduction of "sunset" clauses that automatically limit the duration of anti-dumping measures. As a long-term objective, consumer representatives and antitrust authorities should persuade legislators to harmonize anti-dumping proceedings with escape clause proceedings. Anti-dumping law would thus require more stringent tests for injury and causation, and would permit more discretion in the choice of reme-dies. This long-term objective would be consistent with the recent proposal by two OECD Committees of Experts that Member countries develop improved evaluation procedures for trade policy measures (OECD, 1984a and 1984b). In principle, the assessment procedure which has become known as the "checklist" (ibid., pp. 88-90 and 27-28, respectively) ought to be followed in each individual anti-dumping case.

NOTES AND REFERENCES

1. This study has been sponsored by the Department of Consumer and Corporate Affairs Canada in order to foster informed discussion and debate. The opinions expressed herein should not be construed as those of Consumer and Corporate Affairs Canada or the Government of Canada. The author is also indebted to the Social Sciences and Humanities Research Council of Canada for funding a larger research project on anti-dumping policy of which this paper forms a part and gratefully acknowledges exceptionally competent research assistance by William G. Gilliland.

2. "In order to offset or prevent dumping, a contracting party may levy on any dumped product an anti-dumping duty not greater in amount than the margin of dumping..." (GATT, 1952, Article VI, paragraph 2, emphasis added).

3. For example, a conflict between the interests of consumers and foreign suppliers may occur in the case of "price undertakings", regulated in Article 7 of the Anti-Dumping Code, if such undertakings permit foreign producers to restrict international competition more severely or for a longer period than anti-dumping duties would.

4. For Canada, this tendency can be documented with reference to the 1980 Discussion Paper (Canada, 1980, pp. 11-13), the Minutes of the Subcommittee on Import Policy (Canada, 1981-1982, No. 29, p. 21) and views on the new Special Import Measures Act (Stegemann, 1984a). For the U.S., see Ehrenhaft (1979), Barcelo (1980), Metzger (1982), and Jackson (1984). For the EC, see Didier (1980).

5. Producers are defined to include all owners of inputs affected, including the employees of import-competing industries (Stegemann, 1982a, p. 24).

6. Consumers defined in a wider sense, including all buyers or potential buyers and users of dumped imports.

7. Also see Gupta (1967, pp. 128-129).

8. Throughout this paper, antitrust policy will be used in the general sense of pro-competitive policy; it will be evident when reference is made to U.S. antitrust in a narrower sense.

9. The interventions are generally prepared jointly by the FTC's Bureau of Competition, Bureau of Consumer Protection, and Bureau of Economics. For an up-to-date survey see Crawford (1984), who includes a list of trade intervention briefs (ibid., pp. 23-25).

10. While the GATT Anti-Dumping Code first introduces the textbook definition of dumping and appears to treat the constructed-value methods as
exceptions, the U.S. Department of Commerce (1982, p. 3) is presumably
right in claiming that the "Code does not indicate a preference for
either of these alternatives".

11. See Marks (1974), who defines predatory dumping as:

"The possibility that the lower price will be employed to drive competition out of the market of the importing country. Once this is
achieved, the foreign producer would then be theoretically free to
raise his prices to an exorbitantly high level" (ibid., p. 580).

12. "The domestic Robinson-Patman Act would not be a good surrogate both
because it is still an anti-price discrimination law and because it
might not be available on jurisdictional grounds for use against predatory dumping. There would be no such difficulty, however, with the
Sherman Act section 2 provisions against monopolisation or attempts to
monopolise 'any part of the trade or commerce among the several States,
or with foreign nations...' The Sherman Act has long been applied
against all forms of predatory pricing, not just discriminatory predation, and there would be no difficulty in obtaining personal jurisdic-
tion over a foreign supplier against whom a colorable case could be
made of seeking through predatory dumping to monopolise an American
market. Moreover, as a general antimonopoly law, the Sherman Act would
counter predatory dumping without chilling all price rivalry"
(Barcelo, 1979, p. 67).

13. EC Treaty (EC, 1957), Article 86(a). One of the few relevant cases (if
not the only relevant case) concerning predatory pricing in the Common
Market is ECS.AKZO (O.J. No. L252 of 13th September 1983, pp. 13-21).

14. See Section 734 of the U.S. Tariff Act, 1930, as amended by the Trade
Agreements Act, 1979, Section 101, 19 U.S.C. 1673c and the new provisions on undertakings in Canada's Special Import Measures Act (Canada,
1984a, Sections 49-54 and Section 2 giving the definition of an undertaking).

15. See Article 10 of the EC Anti-Dumping Regulation (EC Council of
Ministers, 1979); also Stanbrook (1980, pp. 47-49) and Van Bael (1978,
p. 533).

16. See list in Stanbrook (1980, pp. 71-86) and EC Commission (1983).

17. Canada used the term "benchmark price". See Canada, 1981-1982, No. 10,
pp. 6-7.

18. See my earlier paper (Stegemann, 1982a, pp. 22-45), which distinguished
the following reasons that might justify government intervention when
import prices are abnormally low: a) a distortion of the domestic income distribution; b) short-sightedness of domestic buyers; c) overpriced domestic inputs (low social opportunity cost of inputs);
d) overpriced domestic outputs (monopolistic conduct of import-
competing domestic producers). The last reason is treated in more
detail in a recent paper (Stegemann, 1984b).

19. On the other hand, there is evidence suggesting that some potential anti-dumping cases are not initiated because the potential complainants fear they will antagonise powerful customers. See Canada, 1981-1982 No. 13, pp. 11-12 and 19-20.

20. For details, see Canada, 1984c and 1984d.

21. The domestic buyers of refined sugar tend to be very large firms, yet none was represented at the Tribunal's hearing (Canada, 1984d).

22. Canada 1981-1982, especially testimony by Director and associates, ibid., Nos. 23 and 27.

23. For example, see the Director's Annual Reports, chapters entitled "Regulated Sector Branch" (e.g. Canada, 1982, pp. 60-82).

BIBLIOGRAPHY

ABA (1974) "Report of the Ad Hoc Subcommittee on Antitrust and Anti-dumping", Reprinted in Antitrust Law Journal, 43: 653-698.

Adams, Walter (1979) "Import Restraints and Industrial Performance: The Dilemma of Protectionism", Anti-dumping Law: Policy and Implementation, Michigan Yearbook of International Legal Studies Volume I (Ann Arbor: The University of Michigan Press), pp. 34-52.

Applebaum, Harvey M. (1974) "The Antidumping Laws -- Impact on the Competitive Process", Antitrust Law Journal, 43: 590-607.

Barcelo, John J. III (1972) "Antidumping Laws as Barriers to Trade - The United States and the International Antidumping Code", Cornell Law Review, 57: 491-560.

Barcelo, John J. III (1979) "The Antidumping Law: Repeal It or Revise It", Antidumping Law: Policy and Implementation, Michigan Yearbook of International Legal Studies Volume I (Ann Arbor: The University of Michigan Press), pp. 53-93.

Barcelo, John J. III (1980) "Subsidies, Countervailing Duties and Antidumping After the Tokyo Round", Cornell International Law Journal, 13: 257-288.

Caine, Wesley K. (1981) "A Case for Repealing the Antidumping Provisions of the Tariff Act of 1930", Law and Policy in International Business, 13: 681-726.

Canada (1969) Anti-Dumping Act, R.S., c. A-15 (1970), amended by c.1, 10 (2nd Supp.), 1970-71-72, cc. 43, 63.

Canada (1972) Anti-dumping Regulations, P.C. 1968-2349 of 31st December 1968, as amended by P.C. 1969-544, P.C. 1972-1305 (SOR/72-191).

Canada (1974) Anti-Dumping Tribunal, Rules of Procedure, pursuant to Section 25(1) of the Anti-Dumping Act (Ottawa: ADT).

Canada (1976) Combines Investigation Act, R.S., c. C-23 amended by c. 10 (1st Supp.), c. 10 (2nd Supp.), 1974-75-76, c. 76.

Canada (1980) Department of Finance, Proposals on Import Policy, a discussion paper proposing changes to Canadian import legislation (Ottawa: Supply and Services, Cat. No. F2-50/1980E).

Canada (1981-1982) Minutes of Proceedings and Evidence of the Subcommittee on Import Policy, Standing Committee on Finance, Trade and Economic Affairs, House of Commons, First Session, Thirty-second Parliament, Nos. 1-31 (Ottawa: Supply and Services).

Canada (1982) Department of Consumer and Corporate Affairs, Annual Report of the Director of Investigation and Research, Combines Investigation Act (Ottawa: Supply and Services, Cat. No. RG 51-1982E).

Canada (1984a) Special Import Measures Act, s.c. 1983-84, c.25 (proclaimed to come into effect 1st December 1984).

Canada (1984b) Special Import Measures Regulations, P.C. 1984-3728 of 22nd November 1984 (SOR/84-927).

Canada (1984c) Director of Investigation and Research, Combines Investigation Act "Submission in the Matter of an Inquiry under Section 16 of the Anti-Dumping Act Respecting: Refined Sugar originating in or exported from the United States of America, ADT-8-84" (Ottawa: mimeo, June 1984).

Canada (1984d) Anti-Dumping Tribunal, "Refined sugar, refined from sugar cane or sugar beets, originating in or exported from the United States of America", Finding of the Anti-Dumping Tribunal in Inquiry No. ADT-8-84 (Ottawa: ADT).

Canadian Consumer Council (1973) Report on the Consumer Interest in Regulatory Boards and Agencies (Ottawa: Canadian Consumer Council).

Crawford, Carol T. (1984) "Trade Policy and the Consumer: The Consumer Advocacy Role of the FTC in Trade Law Proceedings", paper presented at the OECD Symposium on Consumer Policy and International Trade, 27th-29th November 1984 (Paris: OECD mimeo 25.186).

Dam, Kenneth W. (1970) The GATT: Law and International Economic Organisation (Chicago: University of Chicago Press).

de Jong, H.W. (1968) "The Significance of Dumping in International Trade", Journal of World Trade Law, 2: 162-188.

Dickey, William L. (1979) "Prevalent 'Myth' of Unfair Dumping Practices Challenged", The Journal of Commerce and Commercial, 339: 24,389 (1st February 1979), 4 and 29.

Didier, P. (1980) "EEC Antidumping Rules and Practices", Common Market Law Review, 17: 349-369.

EC Commission (1983) First annual report of the Commission of the European Communities on the Community's anti-dumping and anti-subsidy activities, Documents, COM(83) 519/final/2 (Microfiche No. EN-83-175).

EC Council of Ministers (1979) Council Regulation (EC) No. 3017/79 of 20th December 1979 (O.J. No. L339/1 1979), as amended by Council Regulation (EC) No. 1580/82 of 14th June 1982 (O.J. No. L178 of 22nd June 1982).

EC European Parliament (1981) "Report on the Community's Anti-Dumping Activities", Working Documents, 1-422/81.

EEC (1957) Treaty establishing the European Economic Community (Treaty of Rome), Reprinted in Treaties establishing the European Communities (Luxembourg: European Communities, 1973).

Ehrenhaft, Peter D. (1979) "What the Antidumping and Countervailing Duty Provision of the Trade Agreements Act [Can] [Will] [Should] Mean for U.S. Trade Policy", Law and Policy in International Business, 11: 1361-1404.

Epstein, Barbara (1973) "The Illusory Conflict Between Antidumping and Antitrust", Antitrust Bulletin 18: 1-22.

GATT (1952) "The General Agreement on Tariffs and Trade", reprinted in Basic Instruments and Selected Documents, Volume I (Geneva: GATT).

GATT (1961) Antidumping and Countervailing Duties, Report of Group of Experts (Geneva: GATT).

GATT (1966) Analytical Index, Notes on the drafting, interpretation and application of the Articles of the General Agreement (Geneva: GATT).

GATT (1968) "Agreement on Implementation of Article VI of the General Agreement on Tariffs and Trade", reprinted in Basic Instruments and Selected Documents, Fifteenth Supplement (Geneva: GATT).

GATT (1970) Anti-Dumping Legislation, Anti-Dumping Laws and Regulations of Parties to the Agreement on the Implementation of Article VI of GATT (Geneva: GATT).

GATT (1979) "A Legal Guide to the Tokyo Round", Journal of World Trade Law, 13: 436-447.

GATT (1980) "Agreement on Implementation of Article VI of the General Agreement on Tariffs and Trade", Reprinted in Basic Instruments and Selected Documents, Twenty-sixth Supplement (Geneva: GATT).

Grey, Rodney de C. (1973) The Development of the Canadian Anti-Dumping System (Montreal: Private Planning Association).

Gupta, K.R. (1967) A Study of the General Agreement on Tariffs and Trade (New Delhi: S. Chand and Co.).

Jackson, John H. (1984) "Perspectives on the Jurisprudence of International Trade", American Economic Review, 74: 277-281.

Jacobs, Leslie W. and Randall A. Hove (1980) "Remedies for Unfair Import Competition in the U.S.", Cornell International Law Journal, 13: 1-32.

Lazar, Fred (1981) The New Protectionism (Ottawa: Canadian Institute for Economic Policy).

Lloyd, Peter (1977) Anti-Dumping Actions and the GATT System, Thames Essay No. 9 (London: Trade Policy Research Centre).

Marks, Matthew J. (1974) "United States Antidumping Laws -- A Government Overview", Antitrust Law Journal, 43: 580-589.

Martin, R.J. (1984) "Background and Main Elements of the Special Import Measures Act", in Klaus Stegemann, rapporteur, Report of the Policy Forum on Special Import Measures Legislation (Kingston, Ontario: John Deutsch Institute).

Metzger, Stanley D. (1974) Lowering Non-Tariff Barriers (Washington, D.C.: The Brookings Institution).

Metzger, Stanley D. (1982) "The Amended Anti-Dumping Code and the Trade Agreements Act of 1979", In Non-Tariff Barriers After the Tokyo Round, eds. John Quinn and Philip Slayton (Montreal: The Institute for Research on Public Policy).

OECD (1984a) Competition and Trade Policies: Their Interaction, report by the Committee of Experts on Restrictive Business Practices (Paris: OECD).

OECD (1984b) Consumer Policy and International Trade, report by the Committee on Consumer Policy (Paris: OECD mimeo 23.637).

Richardson, Ellen (1973) Consumer Interest Representation: Three Case Studies (Ottawa: Canadian Consumer Council).

Slayton, Philip (1979a) The Anti-Dumping Tribunal, a study prepared for the Law Reform Commission of Canada (Ottawa: Supply and Services Cat. J32-3/21).

Slayton, Philip (1979b) "The Canadian Legal Response to Steel Dumping", Canada-United States Law Journal, 2: 81-100.

Stanbrook, Clive (1980) Dumping: A Manual on the EEC Anti-Dumping Law and Procedure (Chequers, Sharrington: European Business Publications).

Stegemann, Klaus (1977) Price Competition and Output Adjustment in the European Steel Market (Tubingen: J.C.B. Mohr).

Stegemann, Klaus (1978) "The Rationale of Anti-Dumping Protection for the Steel Industry", Proceedings of the Eighth Annual Meeting of the Illinois Economic Association (Springfield: Illinois Economic Association), pp. 77-90.

Stegemann, Klaus (1982a) "The Efficiency Rationale of Anti-Dumping Policy and Other Measures of Contingency Protection", John Quinn and Philip Slayton, eds. Non-Tariff Barriers After the Tokyo Round (Montreal: Institute for Research on Public Policy), pp. 21-69.

Stegemann, Klaus (1982b) "Special Import Measures Legislation: Deterring Dumping of Capital Goods", Canadian Public Policy, 8: 573-585.

Stegemann, Klaus (1982c) "The Net National Burden of Canadian Anti-Dumping Policy: Turbines and Generators", Cornell International Law Journal, 15: 293-351.

Stegemann, Klaus (1984a) Report of the Policy Forum on Special Import Measures Legislation (Kingston, Ontario: John Deutsch Institute).

Stegemann, Klaus (1984b) "The Social Cost of Monopoly in an Open Economy", Canadian Journal of Economics, 17: 718-730.

Thomas, R. Keith (1981) "The New U.S. Antidumping Law: Some Advice to Exporters", Journal of World Trade Law, 15: 323-336.

U.S. Department of Commerce (1982) Anti-Dumping Duties: The Tokyo Round Trade Agreements, Volume 5 (Washington, D.C.).

U.S. Department of Justice (1981) Submission to the ITC in the Antidumping Investigation of Truck Trailer-Axles-and-Brake Assemblies from Hungary, ITC Inv. No. 731-TA-38 (Preliminary).

U.S. Department of Justice (Various Years) Annual Report of the Attorney-General of the United States (Washington, D.C.).

Van Bael, Ivo (1978) "The EEC Anti-Dumping Rules -- A Practical Approach", International Lawyer, 12: 523-546.

Van Bael, Ivo (1979) "Ten Years of EEC Anti-Dumping Enforcement", Journal of World Trade Law, 5: 395-408.

Victor, A. Paul (1983) "Antidumping and Antitrust: Can the Inconsistencies be Resolved?", New York University Journal of International Law and Politics, 15: 339-50.

Viner, Jacob (1966) Dumping: A Problem in International Trade (New York: A.M. Kelly Reprint, original 1923).

Yale Law Journal (1965) "The Antidumping Act, Tariff or Antitrust Laws", Yale Law Journal, 74: 707-724.

TRADE POLICY AND THE CONSUMER:
THE CONSUMER ADVOCACY ROLE OF THE FEDERAL TRADE COMMISSION IN TRADE LAW PROCEEDINGS

by

Carol T. Crawford
Director, Bureau of Consumer Protection, Federal Trade Commission,
United States

I. INTRODUCTION

This paper deals with "Trade Policy and the Consumer" and, more specifically, the role of the Federal Trade Commission (the "Commission" or the "FTC") in recent years in attempting to identify and define the real "social costs" to the consumer and the free-world economy of protectionist trade law measures (1). This is not a new area of concern for the OECD; as early as 1960, this Organisation recognised the economic dangers inherent in barriers to free trade. Member countries stated in the OECD's 1960 Convention that they agreed "to pursue their efforts to reduce or abolish obstacles to the exchange of goods and services and current payments and maintain and extend the liberalisation of capital movements". Twenty-four years later, this concern remains; as recently as last year, in a communiqué following the 1983 Ministerial Council meetings, the OECD Ministers stated, in pertinent part, that:

> "They... agreed that the economic recovery, as it proceeds, provides favourable conditions which Member countries should use, individually and collectively, to reverse protectionist trends and to relax and dismantle progressively trade restrictions and trade distorting domestic measures, particularly those introduced over the recent period of poor growth performance" (2).

Inherent in both these pronouncements, made more than two decades apart, is the concern of this collective multinational body over the negative impact of such trade policies upon the free world's economies and, indeed, the ultimate consumer. Given this historical and continuing concern, it is quite fitting that the Committee on Consumer Policy sponsor this Symposium; the issues being addressed have perhaps never been more timely.

The current Administration has been, and remains, committed to promoting free and open world trade. During the last four years, working within the constraints of the existing trade laws of the United States as well as the practical realities of the frequently overheated political climate surrounding trade issues, the current Administration has sought to implement its commitment to free trade on the principle that such open and unfettered trade is essential to a healthy, vigorously competitive free-world economy which enhances the welfare of all consumers. Recently the FTC, under the Chairmanship of James C. Miller III, has played an increasingly active role in the governmental process related to the enforcement of the United States' trade laws. This paper describes the FTC's efforts in this area: the attempt to underscore and dramatise to the appropriate trade agencies the demonstrable "social costs" of protectionism by presenting both legal and economic analyses of the issues presented by particular cases and estimates of the proposed import relief's effect on both consumers and the domestic economy.

There is bipartisan support among the FTC's Commissioners for these efforts, even though the current five Commissioners have been appointed by two different Administrations and belong to both major political parties. Indeed, there has not been a single dissenting vote on any of the Commission's trade briefs, which are discussed below.

II. THE PRINCIPAL ENFORCEMENT AGENCIES AND THE PRINCIPAL TRADE LAWS

It may be useful to begin by providing a brief summary of the U.S. trade laws and the principal enforcement agencies charged with their administration.

The President and several agencies administer U.S. foreign trade laws. The principal agencies are the United States Trade Representative ("USTR"), the Department of Commerce ("DOC"), and the International Trade Commission ("ITC") (3). In addition, the Trade Policy Committee ("TPC") -- which includes the USTR (who is its Chairman), the Secretary of State, the Secretary of the Treasury, the Secretary of Defense, the Attorney-General, the Secretary of the Interior, the Secretary of Agriculture, the Secretary of Commerce, and the Secretary of Labour (4) -- plays an important role in the trade policy area. Some U.S. trade laws -- countervailing duty and anti-dumping -- require decisions by both the DOC and the ITC. The DOC determines the amount of the foreign subsidy or dumping, and the ITC determines whether the domestic industry is injured. Some U.S. trade laws -- such as unfair practices and the "escape clause" -- explicitly give the President the final decision; in these situations he is advised by the TPC.

While U.S. trade laws cover numerous fields, this paper concentrates on those four areas in which the FTC has recently played a role: countervailing duties, anti-dumping, unfair practices, and the escape clause.

Countervailing duties are imposed when the DOC determines that a "subsidy" is being provided to goods imported into the U.S. and the ITC determines that a U.S. industry is materially injured, or threatened by injury, by reason of imports of the subsidised merchandise (5). Anti-dumping duties are imposed when the DOC determines that imports are being sold at "less than fair value" and the ITC determines that a U.S. industry is materially injured, or threatened by injury, by reason of imports of the dumped goods (6). There is judicial review by the Court of International Trade of both countervailing duty and anti-dumping decisions.

The ITC also investigates whether unfair methods of competition or unfair acts in the importation of articles into the U.S. are destroying or substantially injuring an efficiently operating industry in the U.S., preventing the establishment of such an industry or restraining or monopolising trade in the U.S. (7). If such a violation is found, the ITC may order the exclusion of such articles from the U.S. The President, however, may disapprove such an order by the ITC. The Court of International Trade reviews decisions by the ITC under this provision as well.

Under the "escape clause", the ITC determines if rising imports are a substantial cause of injury to a domestic industry (8). If so, the ITC may recommend adjustment assistance for the workers and firms in that industry, higher tariffs, or import quotas. The President receives a recommendation from the Trade Policy Committee following its review of the ITC's decision, and then decides what relief, if any, to order. If the President takes action different from what the ITC recommends, then Congress may override the President by passing a concurrent resolution directing the President to proclaim the relief recommended by the ITC (9). The Court of International Trade reviews the action taken by the ITC and the President (10).

III. THE CONGRESSIONAL PERCEPTION OF THE LINK BETWEEN THE TRADE LAWS AND THE ANTITRUST LAWS

A brief review of the legislative history related to the enactment of the U.S. trade laws demonstrates that the United States Congress believed that the goals of the countervailing duty, anti-dumping, and unfair practices provisions of our trade laws are intimately connected with the goals of our antitrust laws. The first countervailing duty statute was passed in 1890, the same year as the Sherman Antitrust Act. In 1916 Congress passed the first anti-dumping statute (11), two years after passing the Clayton Antitrust Act and the Federal Trade Commission Act. The stated purpose of this first anti-dumping law was to place foreign firms selling in the U.S. in the same position "with reference to unfair competition" as domestic firms (12). In 1921 Congress passed another anti-dumping law -- the predecessor of the current anti-dumping law administered by the ITC and DOC -- to prevent foreign firms from engaging in what it called "predatory pricing" in the U.S. (13). In 1922 Congress made minor changes to the countervailing duty law and also enacted legislation prohibiting imports associated with "unfair methods of competition" (14). Senator Smoot, one of the sponsors of the 1922 tariff legislation, said that these provisions were an extension of the existing anti-dumping and countervailing duty laws, intended to protect U.S. firms against "unfair competition" (15).

Congress enacted two specific statutory provisions dealing with links between the FTC and the ITC. In its investigations of unfair practices in import trade, the ITC is directed to consult with, and seek advice and information from, the FTC and other agencies (16). More generally, the FTC and other agencies are directed to "co-operate fully with the (ITC) for the purposes of aiding and assisting in its work" (17).

Additionally, the "escape clause" statute states that the President, in determining whether to provide import relief, shall take into account, inter alia, "the effect of import relief on consumers...and on competition in the domestic markets for such articles" (18). The unfair practices provision states that, in deciding whether to exclude an article, the ITC shall consider the effects of such exclusion "upon...competitive conditions in the United States economy...and United States consumers" (19).

Given this historical statutory linkage of trade policy to competition policy, the FTC in recent years has undertaken analyses designed to determine in specific cases the economic impact of trade relief on competition and the consumer (20). The Commission's analyses are then shared with the agencies with which the individual proceedings are pending. The typical trade proceeding involves the domestic firms and the unions representing their workers on the one hand, and U.S. importers and foreign exporters on the other. Individual consumers rarely appear (21) and organisations representing consumers have not appeared in any of the proceedings in which the FTC has been involved. The Commission's so-called "intervention" programme therefore has allowed the FTC to assume the role of consumer advocate before the agencies holding the proceedings (22).

IV. THE FTC'S RECENT INTERVENTION IN TRADE CASES (22)

Countervailing duties and dumping: carbon steel

In January 1982, seven major United States steel firms filed anti-dumping and countervailing duty petitions covering nine major steel products imported from Belgium, Brazil, the Federal Republic of Germany, France, Italy, Luxembourg, the Netherlands, Romania, South Africa, Spain and the United Kingdom. The FTC filed briefs, presented oral testimony, and cross-examined other parties' witnesses at both the DOC and the ITC.

The FTC's principal brief to the DOC on countervailing duties stated that a major purpose of the Trade Agreements Act of 1979 (which enacted the current countervailing duty law) is to promote world trade based on efficiency or long-run comparative advantage. The brief then applied this general principle to three of the principal alleged subsidies involving imported carbon steel.

It was alleged by petitioners that European steel firms received subsidies because of payments by the respective European governments to their domestic coal firms. The Commission said that the legislative history and judicial precedent interpreting the countervailing duty law indicate that payments to local coal companies are not subsidies to the steel companies to the extent these payments merely reduce the difference between the price of local coal -- which the steel companies are forced by their governments to buy even though foreign coal is cheaper -- and the price of imported coal; the Commission also said that there is no subsidy to the steel firms if they buy the coal at the same price as other users of coal.

A second major alleged subsidy involved the acquisition of equity and the provision of grants, loans, and loan guarantees by governments to steel firms as part of the "financial restructuring" of these firms. The FTC observed that in bankruptcy proceedings in the U.S., private creditors frequently take equity or give new loans to private debtors, and the Commission noted that in many cases the foreign government was a creditor of the foreign steel firm prior to the "restructuring". The Commission concluded that the foreign government's acquisition of equity or provision of additional grants, loans, or loan guarantees was not a subsidy if it was consistent with rational policies of private lenders in similar circumstances.

Another major alleged subsidy dealt with government payments for research and development. The FTC said that such payments are not a subsidy if they are financed out of a special tax on steel earmarked for research and development, or if they are for basic research.

Finally, the Commission proffered estimates prepared by our Bureau of Economics of the costs to the economy and the consumer of imposing a countervailing duty. For example, if a uniform countervailing duty of 15 per cent were imposed, this would then impose an annual cost to U.S. consumers of $480 million and an annual inefficiency loss to the U.S. economy of between $238 million and $257 million.

The FTC's brief to the DOC on the dumping aspects of the carbon steel cases again began by stating that in both the anti-dumping law and the anti-trust laws, Congress sought to create a legal environment in which the most efficient firms would survive. Thus, while prohibiting "unfair" competition from foreign imports, the anti-dumping law should not be interpreted so as to deny the United States' consumers the benefits of fair competition by efficient foreign firms. The FTC then turned to some of the particular problems raised by these petitions. The dumping law provides that the DOC shall compare the price in the U.S. with an estimate of foreign production costs -- "constructed value" -- if the price in the foreign market does not cover the foreign firm's total costs over "a reasonable period of time". The Commission suggested that a "reasonable period of time" would be the entire business cycle and not just the recession period argued by petitioners. Noting that the DOC adjusts the price in the foreign market to reflect physical differences in the product, the FTC suggested that the DOC should also adjust the foreign price downward to allow for certain important non-physical differences between sales to customers in the foreign country and sales to customers in the U.S. (e.g. foreign steel firms may give their local customers prompter service, more reliable and timely deliveries and better technical assistance than they give their U.S. customers).

Following the DOC's findings that most of the foreign steel firms were receiving subsidies and were dumping, the FTC submitted briefs to the ITC on the injury phase of the proceedings. The Commission asserted that there is no injury to domestic steel firms if competitive conditions in the U.S. would be unchanged even with subsidised imports. The FTC suggested that that might be the case here because a majority of steel imports came from low-cost-producing countries, such as Japan and Canada, which were not found to have been sub-sidising their steel exports, and these countries had substantial unused steel capacity available. The Commission also stated that there was no injury if the foreign subsidies did not have the effect of increasing sales of foreign steel in the U.S. Since most of the subsidies found by the DOC related to the financial restructuring of foreign steel firms, the Commission suggested that some of this restructuring may simply have affected the steel firms' fixed costs and so had no impact on their sales in the U.S. The FTC also said that some, if not all, of the alleged margin by which foreign steel sold below domestic steel in the U.S. might be due to differences in non-physical aspects of the two products, such as reliability of delivery, promptness of delivery, and service. Finally, at the request of the FTC, the staff of the ITC, using confidential data they had collected, calculated Hirschman-Herfindahl indices for the various steel products, and the Commission observed that some of the product markets -- hot-rolled plate and structurals -- were so concentrated that elimination of the challenged imports might result in an increase in concentration sufficient to attract attention if such an increase were to result from a merger (23).

While the cases against the EEC steel firms were settled in the fall of 1982 by an agreement between the EEC and the U.S. Government setting quotas on EEC steel exports to the U.S., the U.S. steel companies challenged in the Court of International Trade the DOC's findings about the magnitude of the subsidies for Brazil, South Africa and Spain. The FTC was granted permission by the Court to be an amicus curiae in these cases; it then filed, in 1983, briefs that presented essentially the same analysis concerning financial restructuring that the FTC had made to the DOC. The FTC pointed out to the Court that the DOC had adopted our analytical framework about restructuring in the case of a Luxembourg steel firm; we therefore suggested that it would be appropriate to apply the same legal standard to the restructuring that had occurred in the cases of Brazil, South Africa and Spain. Following a settlement between the U.S. steel companies and the DOC in early 1984, these cases were voluntarily dismissed by the Court prior to any ruling on the issues the FTC had raised.

Softwood lumber products from Canada

In April 1983 the FTC filed with the DOC a brief concerning alleged subsidies given by the Canadian national and provincial governments to exporters of softwood lumber products. The alleged subsidy concerned the fee charged by the governments for the right to cut trees on land owned by the governments ("the stumpage fee"). The FTC endorsed the DOC's preliminary finding that the stumpage fee was not a countervailable subsidy, noting that petitioners' request, if granted, might raise the cost of a single-family house by as much as 6.5 per cent.

The FTC stated that the language and legislative history of the countervailing duty statute both indicate that not every government payment or benefit to a private party is a countervailable subsidy; only those payments that distort trade and resource allocation by affecting the price or quantity of the good produced should be subject to countervailing duties. The FTC then provided a detailed economic analysis which showed that the benefit, if any, realised by timber owners in Canada from the stumpage fee did not affect the quantity or price of Canadian lumber sold in the U.S., and so was not a countervailable duty subsidy to lumber. The FTC's analysis also indicated that the appropriate benchmark by which to determine whether there is a subsidy would not be, as alleged by petitioners, the stumpage price in the U.S., but rather the stumpage price that would exist in Canada under a different system. The DOC's final determination used a framework similar to that proposed by the FTC and held that there was no subsidy.

Colour television receivers from the Republic of Korea and Taiwan

Reflecting the ever-increasing internationalisation of trade, many foreign firms have established manufacturing facilities in the United States on a "grass roots basis" or through acquisitions and joint ventures. The status of such firms became an issue in a recent trade proceeding. Foreign companies had established several plants in the U.S. to produce colour television receivers. In May 1983 the FTC filed a brief with the ITC on the issue

266

of whether plants owned by Japanese, Korean, and Taiwanese firms should be considered by the ITC as part of the U.S. industry in determining whether, under the applicable trade law, the U.S. industry was being injured by allegedly dumped imports from the Republic of Korea and Taiwan. The petitioners argued that the U.S. industry consisted of only five U.S.-owned companies and -- without explanation -- one Dutch-owned company. The FTC presented a broader definition, which included eight Japanese plants, a Korean plant and two Taiwanese plants (24). The FTC stated that the legislative history, the ITC's own precedents, and the nature of competition in the U.S. market between foreign and domestic television receivers all indicated that the ITC should consider all producers located in the U.S. as part of the U.S. industry. The ITC eventually agreed with the FTC's analysis on this issue (25).

Vertical milling machines from Taiwan

In January 1984 the FTC filed with the ITC a brief concerning alleged unfair practices by 43 Taiwanese manufacturers and importers of vertical milling machines, a type of machine tool. The petitioner argued, in part, that the general shape of its "Bridgeport"-brand vertical milling machine was a common-law trademark and that the Taiwanese firms' products should be excluded from the U.S. because they were infringing on that trademark and thus were engaging in an "unfair method of competition". The Commission stated that there was a strong national interest in encouraging competition in the production and sale of unpatented products, and that the public interest in preventing consumer confusion and deception can be adequately protected by ensuring that imported products are truthfully labelled as to their origins. The Commission suggested that in determining what constitutes an "unfair" trade practice, the ITC should be guided by domestic law so that foreign producers are not held to a higher standard of conduct than their domestic competitors. Where the purchasers of milling machines were knowledgeable and exercised a high degree of care in buying the expensive machines, the Commission concluded that accurate labelling as to the machines' manufacturer was sufficient to prevent any consumer deception. The ITC dismissed this portion of the petition.

"Escape clause" petitions on carbon steel, copper and canned tuna fish

In early 1984, "escape clause" petitions were filed with the ITC seeking relief from imports of footwear, carbon steel, copper, and canned tuna fish. The FTC participated fully in the ITC's proceedings on all of these items except footwear (26). Following affirmative findings of injury or threat of injury by the ITC on carbon steel and copper, the FTC also filed briefs with the USTR and the Trade Policy Committee on these two matters. In each of these three escape clause proceedings, the FTC presented identical analyses concerning the appropriate analytical framework for determining if there was injury and, if so, what remedy should be recommended to the President. The Commission also presented in each ITC proceeding an estimate of the cost to the U.S. consumer and the economy of the relief requested by the petitioners (27).

In the injury phase of each ITC investigation, the FTC asserted that the statutory language and legislative history both suggest that escape clause relief should not be based on long-term shifts in comparative advantage, declines in domestic demand, or increases in the costs of a domestic industry. The FTC then applied this analytical framework to each of the three investigations.

For carbon steel, the Commission stated that available information raised questions regarding petitioners' entitlement to escape clause relief, since many of the import-related problems appear to have had their origins in long-term trends, and increased imports appear to be only one of many factors contributing to the decline of the domestic steel industry.

For copper the FTC suggested that while a recurring decline in domestic demand may be the most important cause of injury to the domestic industry, the ITC should also consider depressed copper demand outside the U.S. and foreign currency devaluations as other possible causes of injury which might entitle the petitioners to relief.

For canned tuna fish, the Commission indicated that according to available information, the shift in domestic demand from tuna canned in oil to tuna canned in water is the most important cause of actual or threatened injury, and that there was reason to doubt whether the domestic tuna industry could become competitive with foreign tuna industries within the limited time period -- five years -- for which escape relief would be available if injury were found.

In each of these proceedings the FTC also proffered to the ITC estimates of the costs to the consumer and the economy over five years if the requested relief were granted (28):

	Cost to consumers and economy of requested relief		Cost of adjustment assistance to workers
	Consumers	Economy	
	($ Million)		
carbon steel	3 368	615	114
copper	1 718	228	NA
canned tuna fish	783	46-74	15

In the remedy phase of each ITC investigation, the Commission stated that adjustment assistance to workers whose jobs would be lost because of rising imports was preferable to restricting imports. The Commission said that if imports were to be restricted, then tariffs were preferable to quotas. If quotas were to be imposed, the Commission suggested that the quotas should be global rather than country by country, and that they should be allocated to U.S. citizens, perhaps through an auction, rather than to foreigners.

The Commission's briefs to the USTR and the Trade Policy Committee on carbon steel and copper (29) presented essentially the same analysis that the Commission had presented to the ITC concerning the appropriate remedy; the

FTC also provided estimates of the costs to consumers and the economy of the specific remedies recommended to the President by the majority of the ITC.

V. EVALUATING THE IMPACT OF THE FTC'S PARTICIPATION

It is difficult, if not impossible, to evaluate the impact of the FTC's participation in the proceedings described above. In some of these proceedings there were numerous other parties (30) who sometimes presented the same (or similar) analysis that the Commission made. In some of these proceedings, the formal decision was consistent with our analysis (31). Some decisions stated that the analysis relied upon had been developed in the Commission's brief (32); others did not. In some cases there has been no discussion whatsoever of the issues raised by the FTC.

One aspect of the FTC's role, however, has been rather unique. In all these proceedings the FTC has blended fundamental economic analysis with legal arguments derived from the statutory language, the legislative history, and the precedents. The FTC has been the only party to present estimates of the costs to the consumer and the economy of the relief requested by the petitioners in the proceedings, as well as the only party to cross-examine the economists presented by the other parties.

The FTC has also been cited in both the general press (33) and the trade press (34), and it is, of course, possible that these articles have influenced the final decisions in the settlement of the carbon steel countervailing duty and anti-dumping cases; they may have influenced the President in the escape clause cases involving copper and carbon steel as well. Given these possibilities of positive impact upon the trade proceedings in the United States, the Commission believes that this voice for competitive markets should be heard, and the Commission remains committed to representing consumers in future trade proceedings.

LIST OF TRADE INTERVENTION BRIEFS

A. Carbon steel: countervailing duties and anti-dumping

Department of Commerce

Comment by the Federal Trade Commission's Bureau of Competition, Bureau of Consumer Protection, and Bureau of Economics on Countervailing Duty Investigations (28th May 1982).

Post-hearing Brief by the Federal Trade Commission's Bureau of Competition, Bureau of Consumer Protection, and Bureau of Economics on Countervailing Duty Investigations (21st July 1982).

Post-hearing Brief by the Federal Trade Commission's Bureau of Competition, Bureau of Consumer Protection, and Bureau of Economics on the

Issue of Financial Restructuring in the Countervailing Duty Investigations (26th July 1982).

Comment by the Federal Trade Commission on Anti-dumping Investigations (28th July 1982).

International Trade Commission

Comment by the Federal Trade Commission on the Countervailing Duty Investigations (11th August 1982).

Pre-hearing Brief of the Federal Trade Commission (27th August 1982).

The Federal Trade Commission's Post-hearing Brief and Responses to Commissioner's Questions and Requests (14th September 1982).

Court of International Trade

Brief by the Federal Trade Commission as Amicus Curiae on Plaintiffs' Motions Concerning Creditworthiness and Equity Infusions of ISCOR, USIMINAS and COSIPA (14th June 1983).

Brief by the Federal Trade Commission as Amicus Curiae on Plaintiffs' Motions Concerning Carbon Steel Products from Spain (2nd December 1983).

B. Softwood lumber products from Canada: countervailing duty

Department of Commerce

Pre-hearing Brief by the Federal Trade Commission (7th April 1983).

C. Colour television receivers from the Republic of Korea and Taiwan: anti-dumping

International Trade Commission

Brief by the Federal Trade Commission (31st May 1983).

D. Certain vertical milling machines and parts, attachments and accessories thereto: unfair practices

International Trade Commission

Comment by the Federal Trade Commission Opposing an Exclusion Order (9th January 1984).

E. Carbon and certain alloy steel products: escape clause

International Trade Commission

Pre-hearing Brief by the Federal Trade Commission (3rd May 1984).

Post-hearing Brief by the Federal Trade Commission (18th May 1984).

Pre-hearing Brief on Remedy, the Federal Trade Commission (15th June 1984).

Post-hearing Brief on Remedy, the Federal Trade Commission (29th June 1984).

Office of the United States Trade Representative, Trade Policy Committee, and Trade Policy Staff Committee

Brief by the Federal Trade Commission on Section 201 Investigation Regarding Imports of Carbon and Alloy Steel (10th August 1984).

F. Unwrought copper: escape clause

International Trade Commission

Pre-hearing Brief by the Federal Trade Commission (8th May 1984).

Post-hearing Brief by the Federal Trade Commission (23rd May 1984).

Trade Policy Staff Committee

Brief by the Federal Trade Commission Regarding Recommendations of the International Trade Commission on Unwrought Copper, Investigation No. TA-201-52 (2nd August 1984).

G. Certain canned tuna fish: escape clause

International Trade Commission

Pre-hearing Brief by the Federal Trade Commission (29th May 1984).

Post-hearing Brief by the Federal Trade Commission (18th June 1984).

NOTES AND REFERENCES

1. The opinions expressed are solely those of the Director of the Bureau of Consumer Protection of the Federal Trade Commission and do not represent the views of the Commission itself or any individual Commissioner; however, the Commission has voted to authorise the presentation of this paper.

2. C(83)77; paragraph 14, as cited in Report on Issues Arising at the Frontier of Competition and Trade Policies, RBP(84)9, Part II at 72.

3. The ITC is an "independent" agency like the FTC. The other agencies are part of the Executive Branch. The Customs Service, also part of the Executive Branch, classifies and values imports, determines the proper rate of duty applicable to imports, and assesses and collects the duty.

4. 15 C.F.R. Section 2002.0.

5. 19 U.S.C. Subsection 1671 et seq. If a foreign country has not signed the International Agreement on Subsidies and Countervailing Measures, or an equivalent agreement, then countervailing duties are imposed even if there is no injury [19 U.S.C. Section 1303 (a)(1)]. If a country is a signatory of the General Agreement on Tariffs and Trade (GATT) and if the imported item is duty-free, then countervailing duties can be imposed only if the ITC makes an affirmative injury determination [19 U.S.C. Section 1303 (a)(2)].

6. 19 U.S.C. Subsection 1673 et seq. "Less than fair value" is a technical term; roughly speaking, it means selling in the U.S. at a price that either is below the price in the domestic market or is below the cost of production.

7. 19 U.S.C. Section 1337.

8. 19 U.S.C. Subsection 2251 et seq.

9. 19 U.S.C. Section 2253 (c)(1). This part of the law may no longer be valid in light of the Supreme Court's recent decision involving a similar provision in our immigration law. Immigration and Naturalisation Service v. Chadha, 103 S. Ct. 2764 (1983).

10. Maple Leaf Fish Co. v. U.S., 566 F. Supp. 889 (Ct. International Trade 1983) and 6 ITRD 1019 (Ct. International Trade 1984).

11. 15 U.S.C. Section 72.

12. H.R. Rep. No. 922, 64th Congress, 1st Session 9-10 (1916).

13. H.R. Rep. No. 1, 67th Congress, 1st Session 23-24 (1921).

14. 19 U.S.C. Section 1337.

15. 62 Congressional Record 5874 (1922). See S. Rep. No. 595, 67th Congress, 2d Session 2-3 (1922).

16. 19 U.S.C. Section 1337 (b)(2).

17. 19 U.S.C. Section 1334.

18. 19 U.S.C. Section 2252 (c)(4).

19. 19 U.S.C. Section 1337 (d).

20. The organisation of the Commission is divided into three Bureaus which carry out its two principal Congressional mandates: maintaining competition in the market-place and policing unfair and deceptive trade practices. The separate but complementary duties, responsibilities, and expertise of its three Bureaus facilitate this goal. The FTC's participation in foreign trade proceedings is a product of the joint efforts of the Bureaus of Consumer Protection, Competition and Economics. The principal mission of the Bureau of Consumer Protection is to eliminate unfair or deceptive acts or practices in or affecting commerce, with an emphasis on those practices that may unreasonably restrict or inhibit the free exercise of consumer choice. The Bureau enforces the consumer protection laws administered by the FTC. The principal mission of the Bureau of Competition is to enhance the welfare of consumers by maintaining competitive operation of our economic system of private enterprise through enforcement of our antitrust laws. Lastly, the Bureau of Economics' principal mission is to provide economic support to the FTC's consumer protection and antitrust activities.

21. Individual consumers did participate in the carbon steel escape clause case.

22. The FTC's first major involvement in a trade proceeding was in the "escape clause" case in 1980 dealing with imported automobiles. In that case our Bureau of Economics presented to the ITC a model which analysed the likely impact of the proposed tariffs and quotas on sales, prices, profits, employment, competition and costs to the consumer.

23. For further development of this concept, see Benjamin I. Cohen (1983) "A Method for Analysing the Effect on Competition of Restricting Imports", Northwestern Journal of International Law & Business, 510 (Autumn).

24. These plants were built following numerous successful efforts by U.S. producers of television receivers to limit imports from these countries. These efforts include a major anti-dumping proceeding in 1971, claims of unfair trade practices, and an escape clause proceeding in 1977. The President negotiated Orderly Marketing Agreements with Japan in 1977 and with Korea and Taiwan in 1979.

25. The FTC did not participate in the "injury" issue in this case.

26. On 20th March 1984 the FTC notified the ITC that it wished to partici-
    pate in the ITC's hearing on remedy in the footwear case. The ITC
    ultimately determined that there was no injury in this case, and so
    there was no remedy hearing.

27. Recently the USTR specifically requested the ITC to furnish the
    Administration with estimates of the likely cost of import relief to
    consumer industries and the ultimate consumer in these types of pro-
    ceedings. Letter from Hon. William E. Brock to Hon. Alfred Eckes,
    Chairman, ITC, 6th April 1984.

28. These costs were discounted using a discount rate of 7 per cent.

29. The ITC determined there was no injury in the tuna fish case, and so
    the investigation ended. On 6th September 1984, the President decided
    that he would not impose import restraints on foreign copper, and on
    18th September the President decided he would not unilaterally limit
    imports of carbon steel.

30. For example, in the carbon steel escape clause case, there were 79
    other parties.

31. For example, our arguments about financial restructuring in the carbon
    steel countervailing duty cases were cited in other parties' post-
    hearing briefs, and in one case -- Luxembourg -- the DOC used our
    approach.

32. See opinions of ITC Vice-Chairman Liebeler in "Unwrought Copper", ITC
    No. 1549 (July 1984) and "Carbon and Certain Alloy Steel Products", ITC
    No. 1553 (July 1984).

33. See e.g. news stories in The Economist (16th June 1984) at 64,
    Washington Post (22nd June 1984) at D-7, New York Times (8th May 1984)
    at D-15. See also editorial in Wall Street Journal (13th June 1984),
    reprinted as part of Senator Chafee's remarks in Congressional Record
    (18th June 1984) at S 7527.

34. See e.g. American Metal Market (8th May 1984) at 1.

THE REPRESENTATION OF CONSUMER VIEWS IN THE FORMULATION AND IMPLEMENTATION OF TRADE POLICY -- WORKSHOP C

by

Frederic Davidson
Senior Staff Economist, Office of the U.S. Trade Representative,
United States

D.I. Maddern
Assistant Secretary, Consumer Policy Branch, Department of Home Affairs
and Environment, Australia

N. Nagy
Deputy Permanent Representative to the OECD, Switzerland

J.P. Olivier
State Secretariat for Consumer Affairs, France

Jeremy Sheehan
Director, Consumer Affairs, Commission of the European Communities, Belgium

Conclusion by
Gerhard af Schulten, Workshop Chairman, Consumer Ombudsman, Helsinki, Finland

I. INTRODUCTION

The primary task of the Workshop was to assess the existing procedures for taking into account consumer interests in the decision-making process on trade matters. The presentations and subsequent comments by participants reflected experience in several Member countries, highlighting the following institutional approaches:

a) Review of trade measures by an independent expert body (Australia);

b) Consultative procedure, either of a formal or informal nature, where interested groups such as producers, employees and consumer representatives are brought together and given the opportunity to give their advice on domestic policy formulation involving trade matters (France, Switzerland, Australia);

c) Institutionalised consultation mechanisms at the level of regional or international organisations dealing with trade matters (the EEC);

d) Consumer involvement in international trade negotiations (the U.S. advisory committee structure for discussion of negotiating positions within GATT);

e) The consumer advocacy role of government bodies such as competition authorities (see "Trade Policy and the Consumer: The Consumer Advocacy Role of the FTC in Trade Law Proceedings" by Carol T. Crawford, in Theme III of this publication).

II. AUSTRALIA

Like many countries, Australia's import regime is a mixture of tariff and non-tariff barriers to trade. Unlike some countries, however, the principal instrument for assisting import-competing industries is the Customs Tariff, which publicly indicates the nominal assistance provided to particular products. This degree of transparency facilitates the representation of consumer (and other) views about assistance to particular industries. Apart from the Customs Tariff, Australia's manufacturing industry assistance measures have been based (to a much lesser extent) on quantitative import restrictions, subsidies and bounties, export incentives, local content schemes and customs by-law arrangements.

The Industries Assistance Commission (IAC), which is an independent statutory authority established in 1973, is required by law to conduct public inquiries into industry assistance matters, so that all interested parties have an opportunity to put forward their views. The IAC then advises the government on the nature and extent of government assistance granted to all sectors of industry. In the exercise of its functions, the Commission is required to have regard to the government's desire, inter alia, "to recognise the interests of consumers and consuming industries likely to be affected by measures proposed by the Commission". Its conclusions appear in draft reports, which are open to public scrutiny and comment before final recommendations are presented to the government.

It should be noted that not all instances of industry assistance require an IAC report before the government takes decisions. For example, the government is not required by the Industries Assistance Commission Act to obtain a report from the Commission before acting in areas such as bilateral or multilateral trade agreements or tariff preferences for developing countries. Nor are they so obliged regarding changes to the tax system, e.g. preferential taxation arrangements for industry; changes in certain forms of assistance per established sectoral monitoring procedures (e.g. the Textiles, Clothing and Footwear Advisory Committee reviews the operations of the existing assistance package for these industries and can recommend, within certain limits, changes to the operations of the package); changes resulting from administrative decisions, e.g. for dumping and tariff concessions.

The Economic Planning Advisory Council (EPAC), established in 1983, provides the government with independent advice from the representatives of state and local governments, industry, unions and other community groups, to be utilised in the formulation of economic policy. A member of the Executive Committee of the Australian Federation of Consumer Organisations was appointed as one of the seventeen inaugural members of EPAC to represent consumers and community groups. And this consumer representation is noteworthy as EPAC is considered to be an extremely important advisory body in the economic policy formulation area, whose deliberations could well extend beyond domestic economic matters and possibly have an influence in the trade policy field.

In addition, consumers are represented on Australia's highest industry advisory council, the Australian Manufacturing Council, established in the mid-1970s by the government to facilitate consultation with industry, trade unions and consumers on developments in trade policy.

Information contained in the 1982-83 Annual Report of the IAC (Australian Government Publishing Service, Canberra, 1983, page 52) indicates that average assistance levels to the Australian manufacturing sector have remained largely unchanged, with a slight upward trend, from 1977-78 to 1981-82. Assistance has generally declined for tariff-protected manufacturing industries, but has increased for quota-assisted industries with the overall effect of the latter outweighing the former. (It should be noted, however, that industries which received substantial increases in assistance were a relatively small group.) In seeking reasons why assistance levels have not been further reduced, the following may provide at least a partial explanation:

-- Subdued general economic conditions are not, according to some, the appropriate time to effect major reductions;

-- The employment and social effects of reducing assistance levels have not always been adequately addressed in IAC reports;

-- Insufficient attention and explanation has been given to developing optional strategies for assisting industries;

-- Advice provided on essentially economic grounds may not be the most appropriate on practical or political grounds, particularly in the short term;

-- The assumptions behind logical economic advice may be unrealistic or may not be shared by significant sections of the community;

-- Absence of reciprocity by other countries in reducing assistance may make reductions by any one country harder to achieve, even though in some instances unilateral reductions can ultimately bring benefits.

Against this background it may be tempting to conclude that consumer representations, and those of exporters and importers, have had little effect on reducing assistance levels. Such a conclusion overlooks a number of important points, including:

-- In the absence of such representations, present assistance levels may have been higher;

-- The majority of IAC reports have been accepted, or substantially accepted, by the government;

-- Tariff assistance to manufacturing industry has declined; and

-- The representations may have assisted in changing the tenor of the structural adjustment debate from "if" it should occur to "where, when, and at what rate" it should occur.

III. FRANCE, SWITZERLAND

The French Government now officially recognises some twenty organisations as representing the consumer at the national level. Broadly speaking, they fall into three categories:

- -- Organisations whose sole concern is consumer affairs, even though their activities at times overlap into allied but separate domains, such as the environment;

- -- Family organisations, for which consumer affairs are but one aspect -- albeit an increasingly important one -- of their concerns and activities;

- -- Trade union organisations.

The various specific concerns contained in the latter two categories are embodied in correspondingly separate organisations, accounting for the high number of officially recognised groups.

Completing the picture is the co-operative movement (also officially recognised), which has a hand in production and trade as well as consumer problems, and a number of other organisations formed to represent the interests of consumers exclusively in specific areas (i.e., housing, telephones, urban transport, etc.).

To be sure, all of these organisations are concerned with the quality-price relation. Several, however, take into account equally such considerations as product safety, the environment and employment. Thus, government authorities and economic agencies are confronted not with one absolute "Point of View of the Consumer" but many, which are not always in harmony.

The National Consumer Institute was formed in 1967; the make-up of its board of directors at that time was such that one had consumer organisations, business and industry representatives and government authorities around the same table. But it was only in 1973, when organisations were officially granted the right to intiate civil lawsuits in the courts, that their influence really increased. Their acquisition of a legal weapon carrying financial consequences proved a strong incentive for business and industry to enter into negotiation.

As for the government, although it had played a major role in the emergence of consumer movements since the 1950s, only in 1976 was there formed a Secretariat of State for Consumer Affairs, the creation of which symbolised real recognition of these organisations as institutional partners. Nevertheless, results remained modest until 1981, when new emphasis was given to the reinforcement of consultation procedures. On the one hand, government aid to the organisations increased considerably; on the other, the unity between organisations strengthened.

Since 1981, these organisations have been invited to participate on departmental price committees, the national product safety commission, and the advisory councils for agro-alimentation, professional technical centres, national firms, the French Standardisation Bureau, etc. The National Council on Consumer Affairs, which joined together consumer organisations, business and industry in the latter half of 1983, was recognised as having the role of government adviser for consumer legislation, but also on issues such as the degree of importance that should be accorded comparative advertising, changes in food products or the regular inspection of automobiles. Admittedly, questions of trade policy have only been touched on by the Council even though it enjoys considerable breadth of agenda, as those questions are still accorded a secondary importance by the consumer organisations themselves.

Consumer influence in Switzerland has also increased in the last few years, as was demonstrated by the success of the recent government initiative on price surveillance. The Swiss Constitution and federal laws leave much to the discretion of the government regarding trade policy measures (customs laws, rules regarding country of origin, quantitative restrictions, etc.); however, before taking any important measures, federal authorities carefully consult with all parties concerned, including consumer representatives. This consultation usually takes the form of standing committees: the Federal Commission for Customs Tariffs, the Agricultural Law Enforcement Advisory Committee, etc. In the balance struck between the parties concerned in these different committees, consumer representatives are in the minority and do not always win the support of importers and producers. Thus when authorities expect especially vociferous reaction to a particular measure, they complement the normal consultation procedures with talks held with consumer organisations or the Federal Consumer Committee, where consumers are in the majority.

IV. THE EUROPEAN ECONOMIC COMMUNITY

From the earliest years of the European Economic Community, the need for consumer consultation was recognised. As early as 1962, five years after the founding of the Community, the EEC Commission set up a Consumer Contact Committee. For want of funds and research facilities, it fell into disuse. The 1972 Summit meeting in Paris of heads of state and government gave a new impetus to consumer affairs at Community level by calling on the Commission to intensify and co-ordinate actions for the protection of the consumer. This led to the establishment of the Consumers' Consultative Committee (CCC), which exists to this day by successive three-year mandates.

The Committee was given the task of "representing consumer interests to the Commission and advising the Commission on the formulation and implementation of policies and actions regarding consumer protection and information, either when requested to do so by the Commission or on its own initiative". The members of the CCC are appointed by the Commission for a period of three years. Originally, the Committee was made up of 25 members; since the last amendment of its rules of procedure in 1980 it has 33 members. The four European associations recognised by the Commission as far back as 1972 as European consumer organisations -- BEUC (European Office of Consumer Unions), COFACE (Committee of Family Organisations in the European Community), EUROCOOP (European Community of Consumer Co-operatives) and ETUC (European Confederation of Trade Unions) -- each have six members on the Committee; nine seats are reserved for persons with special knowledge of consumer questions (experts). The nomination procedure takes account of the idea that as far as possible all the member states of the Community should be represented on the Committee. The nine-member Steering Committee of the CCC is made up of the chairman, the deputy chairmen, an expert and one member of each of the four above-mentioned consumer organisations.

From the time of its founding until the end of 1983, the Committee adopted a total of 75 opinions and 33 declarations, decisions or reports, which deal in particular with the following fields: the common agricultural policy; the harmonization of laws; foodstuff legislation; prices, price policy, competition; product safety.

Since the autumn of 1981, the Committee's opinions have been disseminated as follows. They are not published -- which would present insoluble problems if only because of the many languages involved -- but are sent by the Commission to the European Parliament, the Economic and Social Committee and those government officials in the member states who are responsible for consumer questions. They are likewise forwarded to the European consumer organisations, which are at liberty to pass them on to their national member associations as they see fit. Requests for these opinions from other quarters (suppliers, the media, universities) are generally complied with. To avoid confusion, the title page of each opinion bears a statement to the effect that it is an opinion of the CCC (as opposed to an official Commission opinion).

The Committee makes practically no public appearances. The four European consumer organisations, but not the CCC as such, are regularly invited to hearings of the European Parliament or to take part in events or meetings. However, there are meetings between the Committee, its Steering Committee and commercial and agricultural organisations. The CCC restricts itself to advising the Commission and its departments, while the European and national consumer organisations represent the consumer's interests in the public sphere vis-à-vis the European Parliament, the Council of Ministers, the governments of the member states, etc. The CCC also has power to nominate representatives to various other advisory committees existing within the EC institutional framework, including those for foodstuffs, for customs matters and for veterinary questions. Similarly, the various sectoral advisory committees dealing with agricultural products include consumer representatives who are nominated by the CCC.

In addition, because of the importance to consumers of ensuring that European standards meet the appropriate standards of safety for consumer products, the Commission has negotiated an observer status for one representative, nominated by the CCC, on each of the technical committees of the Comité Européen de Normalisation (CEN) and the equivalent body for electrical standards (CENELEC) which deals with consumer product standardization.

Finally, there are other channels apart from the CCC through which consumer opinion can influence the deliberations of the Community institutions:

-- The European Parliament's Committee on the Environment, Public Health and Consumer Protection, which passed many resolutions favourable to the realisation of the Community programmes of 1975 and 1981, and also exerts influence through parliamentary questions; and

-- The Community's Economic and Social Committee, comprising representatives of various categories of social and economic activity from each member state -- including representatives of national consumer organisations -- appointed by the Council, which has the task of assisting the Council and Commission in an advisory capacity.

V. THE UNITED STATES

In operating its Trade Agreements Program, the U.S. Government relies on the input of the private sector for guidance on trade policy issues. Different avenues exist for receiving this input. Specific trade statutes provide uniformity and fairness to the trade policy process and ensure that interested parties are involved in pending trade policy developments.

With regard to specific statutes, in certain situations consumers and consumer organisations are allowed the opportunity to submit their opinions to the official body reviewing individual cases. For example, the administration of anti-dumping and countervailing duty laws is a transparent process, with abundant opportunities for oral and written comments, for explanations to and from the Department of Commerce and the International Trade Commission and for the receipt of relevant information to determine whether products are being traded unfairly and injuriously. When deciding whether to provide a remedy for an unfair practice, the Commission must consider among other things the effect the remedy would have on consumers. Further, in determining whether to provide import relief under the escape clause provisions of the 1974 Trade Act dealing with fair but injurious imports from all sources, the President is directed by section 202(c)4 to take into account "the effect of import relief on consumers (including the price and availability of the imported article and the like or directly competitive article produced in the United States) and on competition in the domestic markets for such articles".

The Trade Act of 1974, which gave the President authority to negotiate reductions in non-tariff trade barriers, provided for the establishment of a system of private sector advisory committees to ensure the existence of a formal mechanism to maintain a continuous dialogue between government, the private sector and consumer groups regarding trade negotiations, called the Private Sector Advisory Committee System. This system is managed by the Office of the U.S. Trade Representative (which is charged with the responsibility for setting and administering overall U.S. trade policy) in co-operation with the Departments of Commerce, Agriculture, Labor and Defense.

The committees fall into three categories. At the top level of the system is the Advisory Committee for Trade Negotiations (ACTN). This is a committee of 45 members, appointed by the President, representing various elements of the United States economy with international trade interests. While the U.S. Trade Representative convenes the meetings of the ACTN, the sessions are chaired by a private sector member who is elected by the Committee. The mandate of the ACTN is to provide overall policy guidance on international trade issues to the President, the Congress and the U.S. Trade Representative. The second level of committees in the structure is composed of policy advisory committees in the specific areas of industry, agriculture, labour, defence, services, investments, steel, wholesale, retailing and commodities. Their responsibility is to advise the U.S. Government on how trade issues affect the economies in their respective sectors. Finally, there are technical and sectoral advisory committees, which are composed of experts from the respective fields. The ATACs (Agricultural Technical Advisory Committees), ISACs (Industry Sector Advisory Committees) and Labor Sector Advisory Subcommittees provide specific and technical information on problems within the private sector (in such areas as automobiles, steel, wheat, aircraft or poultry) which are affected by trade policy. New sectoral committees whose interests were not represented during the Multilateral Trade Negotiations (MTN) have been formed in the areas of energy and small and minority business and services. In addition, functional committees have been established to monitor certain of the Codes of Conduct which were negotiated during the Tokyo Round.

From 1975 to 1979, during the Tokyo Round of the MTN, the committees communicated to the U.S. negotiators their concern and advice on overall U.S. negotiating objectives and bargaining positions. At the conclusion of the negotiations, the committees submitted a comprehensive report [U.S. Senate, Subcommittee on International Trade (1979) Private Sector Committee Reports on the Tokyo Round of the Multilateral Trade Negotiations, Washington, D.C.: U.S. Government Printing Office]. The reports submitted to Congress contained detailed analyses on the non-tariff codes that had been negotiated, including agricultural agreements, aircraft, counterfeiting, customs valuation, government procurement, import licensing safeguards, standards and subsidies and countervailing duties. The reports also discussed the balance of concessions obtained during the negotiations.

Throughout the Tokyo Round, the advisory committee members, who number approximately 1 000, were kept fully informed of the issues as they evolved during the five-year negotiating period. During this time span, a combined total of 650 meetings of the 45 committees took place. The committees supplied detailed information, advice and recommendations on every industrial, agricultural and labour sector issue that was affected by the negotiations. This information and advice was then integrated into the government's interagency trade policy development process, from which ultimately the U.S. negotiating position was formulated. For the most part, government negotiators followed the advice of the advisory committees, although it was not always possible to obtain from other countries all the concessions recommended by the committees.

The overwhelming success of the Private Sector Advisory Committee System during the Tokyo Round was reflected in the Trade Agreements Act of 1979, in which Congress continued the committee structure established in the 1974 Trade Act with a broadened mandate to include advice on the implementation of trade agreements and overall trade policy issues. Also, new advisory committees have been established, reflecting the increasing importance of trade to the domestic and international economy.

VI. CONCLUSION

The discussion and critical assessment of the various mechanisms showed that an effective impact of consumer policy considerations depends on several factors:

a) At which stage of the decision-making process can consumer interests be effectively brought to the attention of policy-makers? What time constraints are involved?

b) What is the general legal framework for trade policy decisions? Do consumer representatives have a statutory right to participate? Are they in a position to request judicial review?

c) Are the issues at stake clearly identified? When considering a trade measure, are governments sufficiently aware of the likely effects of these measures on consumer welfare?

d) Are decision-makers clearly identified? Are decisions transparent or are they taken through informal channels?

e) How well are consumers and consumer representatives informed on pending trade policy decisions, relevant procedures and criteria? Are they aware of the impact of such decisions on their interests? Do they have sufficient means and resources to put forward their views in a convincing manner?

Regardless of the specific institutional mechanism adopted, it became evident that at least the following prerequisites have to be met:

a) Consumers have to be sufficiently informed of the interests at stake, i.e., the economic cost of the different categories of trade restrictions and their effects on consumer welfare, including income distribution effects. Such information should be available to individual consumers and to consumer organisations, and include procedures (and criteria for trade decisions), the results of relevant studies and explanations of the reasons for trade policy decisions;

b) Sufficient resources -- that is, public money -- should be available to enable consumer views to have a bearing in the decision-making process. Funding for research and analysis of trade restrictions could be provided either to consumer organisations or directly to independent research institutes;

c) Groups or industries claiming protection should be required to substantiate their case and produce evidence not only of the economic benefits of the suggested measure but also of the overall economic consequences;

d) Consumer organisations should make the general public more aware of the effects of trade policy decisions (and here the important role of the media was stressed), thus strengthening the position of consumers as partners in the decision-making process;

e) Consumer organisations need to co-operate, both among themselves and with other groups likely to be affected by trade measures;

f) Consumer representatives should have access to real decision-makers.

Finally, there was widespread support for the recommendations contained in the OECD Committee on Consumer Policy Report (see Mr. Koopman's Introductory Statement). Many participants felt that these recommendations should be addressed to governments as well as to consumer organisations, and that measures should be taken for their implementation. It was suggested that a review mechanism be established within the Committee by which governments, in consultation with consumer organisations, would submit reports at regular intervals on their action in accordance with the recommendations, and an evaluation of the results. Further, it could be useful for the country or countries involved to focus on specific sectors or measures of particular importance to consumers.

RESULTS OF THE 1984 OECD SYMPOSIUM AND PROGRAMME OF ACTION (1)

by

the OECD Committee on Consumer Policy

I. THE SYMPOSIUM

From 27th to 29th November 1984, more than 150 representatives from governments, international organisations, business and industry, trade unions, universities and consumer organisations gathered in Paris to attend an OECD Symposium on Consumer Policy and International Trade. They met under the auspices of the OECD Committee on Consumer Policy to discuss and debate the relationship between trade policy and the consumer interest. The sessions centred on a report on this topic prepared by the Committee, as well as on an impressive series of written contributions provided by speakers at the Symposium. The Symposium brought together officials responsible for trade and consumer policies and representatives from various groups concerned with trade and consumer policy decisions in order to consider consumer interests in current trade policies and ways in which these interests could be better reflected in the international trade policy process.

In organising the Symposium the Committee had the following objectives:

-- To test and to deepen the analysis of trade and consumer policy issues contained in the Committee's earlier report [CCP(84)6] and to assist the Committee in developing its future activities on these issues;

-- To identify as completely as possible the consumer interest in international trade, notably by showing how the impact of trade policy measures on consumers can best be assessed;

-- To consider how the consumer interest can be given proper weight in the assessment of trade policy measures at the national and international levels;

-- To contribute to an increase in the general awareness of the link between consumer policy considerations and international trade.

The Symposium was opened by Mr. Paye, Secretary-General of the OECD. Opening statements were presented by Mrs. Lalumière, Secretary of State for

Consumer Affairs (France); Mrs. Knauer, Special Adviser to the President of the United States on Consumer Affairs; Mr. Koopman, Chairman of the Committee on Consumer Policy; and Mr. Löwbeer, Chairman of the Committee of Experts on Restrictive Business Practices. The discussions, which were introduced by a number of written contributions, focussed on the following themes:

-- The effect of trade policy on consumer interests;

-- The impact of consumer protection on international trade;

-- The consideration of consumer interests in the formulation of trade policy.

In-depth discussions on some of the issues raised in these themes took place in three simultaneously held workshops dealing, respectively, with the impact of trade measures in selected sectors, transparency and consumer information on trade matters and the representation of consumer views in trade policy formation. Summaries were presented in the final session of the Symposium by the chairmen of the three themes and the workshops. The Symposium concluded with remarks by the Chairman of the Committee on Consumer Policy.

The Committee believes that the Symposium achieved its objectives. It instituted a constructive dialogue between those primarily concerned with trade policy decisions, i.e., government officials representing trade and consumer policy authorities, business, labour and consumer representatives. It succeeded in raising problem awareness of the interaction between consumer, trade and other economic and industrial policies. While differences appeared in the views expressed, the Symposium established the very real and costly impact that trade restrictions have on consumer interests, and the need to consider those interests when trade policy decisions are taken. There was general support for the recommendations contained in the Committee's report on Consumer Policy and International Trade, which served as a reference document for the discussions. A number of comments and suggestions were made which usefully complemented those recommendations.

The Committee appreciates the valuable contributions made by participants, whether in writing or orally, in the course of the discussions. It welcomes the dialogue that was established at the Symposium between those interested in international trade and consumer policy issues, and hopes that the dialogue will continue both at the national and international levels.

In the following sections of this report, the main issues to emerge from the Symposium are summarised, the challenges ahead are highlighted and a number of practical steps to meet these challenges are proposed. The Committee wishes to emphasize in particular one of the main steps forward which it proposed earlier and which was generally supported at the Symposium, the use of a broad-ranging checklist for the systematic scrutiny of proposed and existing trade measures. The Committee, in co-operation with the Committee of Experts on Restrictive Business Practices and after consultation with the Trade Committee, has elaborated the attached checklist (Annex) (2) which is proposed to the Council for endorsement in a separate report.

II. MAIN ISSUES TO EMERGE FROM THE SYMPOSIUM

A. Consumer interests in trade policy

Individuals can and do play several roles, whether as voters, taxpayers, employees, investors or consumers. As consumers they use or dispose of their incomes in buying goods and services. They need comprehensive and varied market access and reliable information to exercise informed choices, so as to translate their spending and buying activities into improved standards of living and higher economic welfare, as well as to be able to transmit correct market signals to producers.

The development of international trade serves consumers globally, whether the consumer is seen as a purchaser of goods or services or as a citizen or a member of a community with more general interests. For the purchaser, the development of trade means that he will have access to a more extensive and attractive choice of products. Depending on market structures, the resulting competition on the market between domestic and foreign firms will result in economic efficiencies. This competition will have beneficial effects on quality, choice and supply. As a citizen it is in his interest to belong to a dynamic, economically efficient community, and experience shows that participation in an open trading system is a powerful force contributing to dynamic and efficient economic structures.

Efforts through the GATT or other arrangements to lower tariffs and open markets benefit consumers. The increasing resort in recent years to protectionist measures and to circumvention of the international discipline of an open multilateral trading system has without doubt had an unfavourable impact on consumers in many ways.

There is considerable scope for common cause between consumers and other groups affected by trade policy decisions. Restrictive trade measures are not only harmful to consumers; they also adversely affect importers and retailers, since other businesses are often users or consumers of imported supplies, equipment, services and other goods. Domestic exporters can suffer from import restrictions either directly or as a result of retaliation, or as reduced exchange earnings abroad inhibit access to those markets. In many cases it is even doubtful whether trade restrictions are beneficial to the industries protected, as they lessen the competitive pressures for these industries to innovate and to adjust. As consumers are not alone in reaping benefits from an open and expanding trading system, they should not stand alone in opposing distortions or restrictions to that system.

It has to be recognised that in a period when unemployment is high, conflicts between different societal interests can become very sharp. Consumer representatives do not deny this. Employees threatened by unemployment and the industries affected by rapid structural change are numerous in claiming protection through restrictive trade measures. Public policy must seek judicious compromises among conflicting demands, but under present arrangements there is no guarantee of sufficient transparency, or that all relevant considerations will be given their proper weight.

In resisting protectionist pressures, consumers may often find it difficult to attract sufficient attention vis-à-vis well-organised groups defending sectoral interests. Consumer concerns in the trade policy area are often not well focussed or expressed, and this fact also weakens their impact. Governments can help to redress the balance by giving proper weight to consumer policy considerations.

B. The impact of specific types of trade measures on consumer interests

Restrictive trade measures vary significantly in their impact on consumers. Non-tariff barriers may be particularly harmful as they often reduce or limit the range of available goods, especially low-cost products, and often operate as a regressive tax on low-income consumers. They also lack transparency and the form which some of these measures take (e.g. voluntary export restraints, technical and administrative obstacles) make it difficult for consumers to understand and to react to them.

Too little is being done to subject the effects of trade policy measures to systematic analysis and monitoring, and the questions being asked in this regard are too limited. Support was expressed for a more systematic use of cost-benefit analysis. In addition, it would be especially important at the present juncture, when many trade measures escape scrutiny in the framework of internationally recognised rules and procedures, if Member countries were to reach agreement on a comprehensive approach towards the scrutiny of proposed as well as already existing trade measures. It was stressed that existing measures should not be excluded. The use of the attached checklist would be of help to decision-makers in making rational choices on a broad range of options and in identifying the least costly (i.e., economically least harmful) trade policy measures.

However, in some instances governments may be led to adopt restrictive trade measures despite the costs to consumers and overall economic costs. Measures taken in these cases should observe the following principles:

-- Preference should be given to measures which have the least harmful effect on the functioning of markets, which, as far as possible, are limited in time and which are phased out according to fixed schedules;

-- Those supporting protectionist measures should have the burden of showing the likely benefits of such measures;

-- Criteria should be established to determine those circumstances under which trade restrictions may be introduced;

-- All interested parties should, to the extent possible, have the opportunity to comment or offer their views before action is taken;

-- Restrictions imposed should be overt and transparent;

-- After measures are adopted, they should be monitored to determine whether they are effective or whether they could be terminated at an earlier stage than originally foreseen.

C. Impact of consumer protection on trade

It is one of the primary interests of consumers that products are reasonably safe and reliable and that adequate warranties and after-sales services are provided. In order to avoid such measures creating barriers to trade, it is important that health and safety regulations as well as other product-related requirements, e.g. packaging and labelling provisions, are applied on an equal basis to both domestically produced and imported goods and services.

International harmonization of product standards deserves thorough consideration. Such harmonization is, however, often difficult to achieve. Where product standards differ between Member countries, importing countries should consider whether the standards of the exporting country, while different, provide an equivalent degree of protection to meet the basic concerns of the regulations in the importing country. In such cases, other co-operative efforts between governments should be considered to prevent national standards from creating barriers to international trade, and to avoid in particular the misuse of consumer protection requirements as protectionist devices.

Product safety is a special concern of consumers. They wish to see not only proper, internationally accepted product standards but also a rapid exchange of information on standards and other measures taken in Member countries. At the level of the OECD, priority should be given to the evaluation and effective application of the informal notification system on product safety measures operated by the Committee on Consumer Policy, the consideration of possible improvements to that system and exchanges of views on follow-up measures taken after notifications. A continued exchange of information, as well as the development of common principles as to basic methods and policies in the product safety field, will in the long run contribute to more harmonized approaches to product safety in Member countries for the benefit of consumers and international trade.

D. The consideration of consumer interests in trade policy formulation

Consumers and consumer representatives are often at a disadvantage in terms of influencing trade policy decisions. Consumer interests are generally more diffuse geographically and in terms of product coverage than those of domestic producers of a particular commodity. Further, having focussed to date their efforts on the implementation of consumer protection laws, for lack of resources or other reasons, consumer representatives may not always have been aware of the consumer impact of trade policy measures and thus may not have taken full advantage of existing possibilities to exert influence on trade policy decisions. Indeed, they may not always have been aware of the consumer impact of trade policy measures. An important obstacle in this respect is the inherent lack of transparency and the complexity of many restrictive trade measures, in particular those most frequently associated with the rise of the new forms of protectionism (i.e., voluntary export restraints, administrative and technical barriers). There is a need to address these problems in a pragmatic manner so as to establish the necessary conditions for consumer policy considerations to be given greater weight in trade policy decisions.

Better information as to pending trade measures will enable consumers to make a greater input into trade policy decisions. Consumers themselves should take an initiative to raise the awareness of the importance of trade policies for their interests. The media have an important role to play in this process. Consciousness about trade policy matters at the grass-roots level would strengthen the position of consumers in the decision-making process. Increased efforts should be made to develop, obtain and disseminate objective information about the quality of domestic and imported products in order to promote trade, improve consumer purchasing decisions and counteract "Buy-National" campaigns.

Attention needs to be given to consumer interests at all levels of trade policy decision-making, having due regard to the time constraints under which some of these decisions are taken, i.e.:

-- Trade policy formulation;

-- Preparation of bilateral and multilateral trade negotiations;

-- Implementation of trade policy decisions and, to the extent possible, application of laws relating to unfair trade practices;

-- Assessment and monitoring of restrictive trade measures.

A number of institutional options to give greater weight to consumer interests in trade policy formulation have been identified. These options have to be seen in the legal and political context of each country. Some of these approaches are not necessarily alternatives, but rather could reinforce or complement each other:

-- Action by independent bodies set up for the review of trade policy measures.

Such reviews can highlight the importance of objective criteria in trade policy formulation and strengthen the hands of governments to resist protectionist measures. They are, however, no substitutes for the consideration of consumer interests in the political decision-making process.

-- Consumer advocacy role of government bodies such as competition and consumer authorities.

Through their expertise with the functioning of markets and the enforcement of competition and/or consumer protection laws, such bodies are in a position to contribute to governmental discussions and trade law proceedings affecting competition and consumer interests. Consumer representatives agree that they could gain by receiving more support from competition authorities.

-- Consultative procedures established in the policy-making process, either of a formal or informal nature, where interest groups such as producers, employees and consumers can participate.

Such broad procedures have the advantages of raising problem awareness of participants, facilitating a dialogue between those directly concerned and identifying means for balancing conflicting interests. They can be applied both at national level and within international organisations having responsibility in trade policy matters.

III. THE CHALLENGE

On a theoretical level, there is general agreement on the harmfulness of most if not all restrictive trade measures, not only for international welfare and the harmony of trading relations but also for the country taking these measures. As a major OECD study ["Costs and Benefits of Protection" (3)] has demonstrated, the costs of protection fall heavily on the protecting country. A shift from present protectionist instruments towards a policy approach more supportive of adjustment is therefore first and foremost in the interest of the countries now imposing import controls. Participants declared they knew of no in-depth study of trade protection that had shown that consumers were not expected to bear directly or indirectly the major element of the costs.

Yet in recent years protectionist measures have been taken with increasing frequency. Despite obvious differences between countries, there is a general trend towards greater vulnerability of trade policy formation to the pressure of sectoral interest groups. Therefore options need to be identified and analysed for better management of this process, widening its base and increasing its transparency. As the Symposium has demonstrated, raising awareness of consumer interests can make an important contribution to this process.

In order to achieve progress, continuing efforts are needed:

-- To gather convincing data to describe the costs and benefits of specific trade measures which will enable decision-makers to give greater weight to consumer interests in trade policy formulation;

-- To promote consumer information and education and to enable consumers and/or consumer representatives to articulate clearly and substantiate their viewpoints;

-- To develop practical suggestions to assist governments in obtaining informed consumer comment;

-- To encourage consumers to take a greater interest in trade policy issues and to co-operate among themselves and with other interested groups in order to be in a position to make an effective representation of their interests.

It is recognised that there is not one common solution for improving the decision-making process which would be applicable to all OECD countries. It would be for each Member country to consider which of the various possibilities would be most suitable to the political, legal and institutional arrangements applying in that country. There are, however, a number of steps that can be taken to create the necessary conditions and methods under which consumer policy considerations can have an actual impact on trade policy decisions. The following suggestions for action, developed from the Committee's earlier recommendations and reinforced by the results of the

Symposium and the study on costs and benefits of protection, are addressed to these points.

IV. SUGGESTIONS FOR ACTION

Trade policy and consumer policy share a common objective, at least in the long run, which is to enhance economic welfare by eliminating distortions in competition and international trade. The Committee therefore wishes to express its strong support for efforts under way within the GATT and the OECD to maintain and promote an open international trading system, to extend international discipline to national trade measures and to progressively reduce existing trade restrictions. The Committee also welcomes the proposals set forth in the report by the Committee of Experts on Restrictive Business Practices, "Competition and Trade Policies: Their Interaction" (4), which are designed to maintain and, where threatened, to restore effective competition in international trade. On the basis of the considerations set forth in this report, the Committee makes the following suggestions which it believes would enhance the influence of consumer policy considerations on trade policy decisions, both at the national level and within the OECD.

A. Action at the national level

a) Improving information for decision-making

1. Increasing transparency

Efforts should be made to ensure that consumers have adequate information on trade policy measures likely to have a significant impact on their interests. Decision-makers and decision-making channels should be clearly identified. Trade policy measures should be made more transparent, for example through public disclosure of the action taken or envisaged and, where possible, of the criteria being applied and of the reasons for a particular decision.

2. Raising problem awareness

Consumers and consumer organisations and other groups affected by restrictive trade measures in Member countries are encouraged to take a continuing interest in trade policy issues of significant impact on consumer interests, and organisations involved should keep members informed on such issues.

3. Assessment and evaluation

Efforts should be encouraged to develop, in co-operation with government authorities, research institutes, consumer representatives and other interested groups, studies to evaluate the economic effects of specific trade policy measures, including their impact on consumer interests. The Committee is therefore of the view that policy-makers should, when considering a prospective trade measure, undertake as systematic and comprehensive an evaluation as possible of the likely effects of the measure along the lines of the attached checklist (Annex). This checklist would serve as a guide to decision-makers, it being understood that government policy considerations would determine the weight to be given to the various factors. Governments should periodically review the effectiveness of any trade measure taken and assess whether the measure has or has not achieved its stated policy objectives, whether the actual gains and losses correspond to those expected, and whether, in the light of experience, there is a need to maintain the measure. Among the methods to ensure that consumer interests are adequately taken into account when introducing trade policy proposals or decisions, the inclusion of consumer impact statements, the provision of sunset clauses, and review or programme evaluation mechanisms should be considered.

b) Improving the institutional framework

Given the diversity of government structures in Member countries, it is neither possible nor desirable to propose a single institutional model to ensure that proper consideration is given to consumer policy considerations in the decision-making process on trade issues. While it appears that the absence of any procedural arrangement in this respect would constitute a major impediment to the representation of consumer interests in the field of trade policy, the existence of a formalised procedure is in itself no guarantee that these interests can exercise any significant influence on the outcome of the decision-making process. Effective representation of consumer interests can also take place without formalised procedures. In general, trade policy authorities should be encouraged to adopt more open decision-making procedures or processes so as to allow better representation of consumer interests.

In considering an appropriate framework for reflecting the interrelationship between trade and consumer policies, stress should be laid not on rigid institutional structures but rather on creating the necessary conditions and methods under which consumer policy considerations can have an actual impact on trade policy decisions. To achieve this, the following aspects appear to be of particular importance for the consideration of governments, where appropriate:

i) Trade officials should take into account the consumer policy implications and in general seek the advice of consumer policy officials before taking decisions likely to have a significant impact on consumer interests. There are various options for organising such participation, e.g. informal but regular contacts, establishment of standing interdepartmental committees or task forces, and arrangements providing the possibility for authorities responsible for consumer and competition policies to make written or oral presentations in public hearings;

ii) Consumer and competition policy authorities should be provided relevant information in a timely manner on the nature and the motivation of proposed trade policy decisions, and should have adequate resources to be able to exert an influence on such decisions. Through their experience with the functioning of markets, such authorities are in a position to contribute to governmental decisions and trade law proceedings affecting competition and consumer interests;

iii) With respect to consumer protection measures such as product safety, packaging and labelling requirements, governments should exercise care that such measures are not used as barriers to trade; where product-related requirements differ between Member countries, importing countries should consider whether the standards of the exporting country, while different, provide an equivalent degree of protection to meet the basic concerns in the importing country;

iv) Consumers and/or consumer representatives should be given an opportunity, through appropriate means such as public hearings or more informal proceedings, to express their views on their country's trade policy measures likely to have a significant consumer impact, it being recognised that such proceedings may impose a heavy burden on the resources of those involved; when, due to time constraints, this cannot be done prior to taking a trade decision, opportunities to comment should be provided as soon as possible and in the course of monitoring the measure;

v) Member countries should encourage independent analysis of their trade policy measures. Where independent bodies for the review of such measures exist, consumers and/or consumer representatives should be given an opportunity to express their views in the proceedings of these bodies;

vi) Interested groups claiming trade protection should be required to substantiate their claims. Care should be exercised that proceedings under laws dealing with unfair trade practices (in particular anti-dumping and countervailing actions) are not misused for protectionist or anti-competitive purposes. Injury and its causal relationship to unfair trade practices should continue to be assessed on the basis of objective criteria in accordance with the GATT rules and following procedures in which all interested parties can make their views known.

B. Action at the level of the OECD

The Committee on Consumer Policy should continue to give high priority to the questions arising from the interrelationship between consumer policy and international trade through regular exchanges of views on issues of current concern, including the following:

i) Consideration of specific trade policy areas of significant interest to consumers;

ii) Consumer interests and the enforcement of laws dealing with unfair trade practices (i.e., anti-dumping and countervailing); economic and legal aspects;

iii) Impact on international trade of safety, labelling and other product-related requirements, including origin-marking;

iv) Ways and means of improving information available to consumers on relevant trade policies;

v) The interrelationships between consumer behaviour and specific trade measures.

The Committee will, in accordance with its mandate, consult with BIAC and TUAC and obtain the views of international consumer organisations. In addition, the Committee may find it useful to exchange views with other international organisations, such as those concerned with product standards.

The Committee on Consumer Policy, the Trade Committee and other bodies of the Organisation dealing with trade-related questions should closely co-operate when dealing with issues involving consumer interests. The Committee on Consumer Policy will therefore continue to provide its advice to these bodies on issues likely to have a bearing on consumer interests.

In its Annual Reports on developments in the field of consumer policy in Member countries, the Committee on Consumer Policy will give special attention to recent developments in international trade relevant to consumers.

The Committee will review the implementation of the above recommendations. For this purpose, Member governments will be invited to report on their action in accordance with the recommendations and the experience acquired in this respect. In this context the Committee, in co-operation with the country or countries concerned, may focus on specific sectors or measures of particular interest to consumers.

INDICATIVE CHECKLIST FOR THE ASSESSMENT OF TRADE POLICY MEASURES (5)

a) Is the measure in conformity with the country's international obligations and commitments?

b) What is the expected effect of the measure on the domestic prices of the goods or services concerned and on the general price level?

c) What are the expected direct economic gains to the domestic sector, industry or firms in question (technically, the increase in producers' surplus)?

d) What types of jobs are expected to be affected by the measure? What are the net employment effects of the measure in the short and long term?

e) What are the expected (direct) gains to government revenues (e.g. from tariffs, import licences, tax receipts) and/or increased government costs (e.g. export promotion, government subsidies, lost tax revenues)?

f) What are the direct costs of the measure to consumers due to the resulting higher prices they must pay for the product in question and the reduction in the level of consumption of the product (technically, the reduction in consumers' surplus)? Are there specific groups of consumers which are particularly affected by the measure?

g) What is the likely impact of the measure on the availability, choice, quality and safety of goods and services?

h) What is the likely impact of the measure on the structure of the relevant markets and the competitive process within those markets?

i) In the medium and longer term perspective, will the measure, on balance, encourage or permit structural adaptation of domestic industry leading over time to increased productivity and international competitiveness, or will it further weaken and delay pressures for such adaptation? Is the measure of a temporary nature? Is it contingent on, or linked to, other policy measures designed to bring about the desired structural adjustment?

j) What will be the expected effect on investment by domestic firms in the affected sector, by potential new entrants and by foreign investors?

k) What could be the expected economic effects of the measure on other sectors of the economy, in particular, on firms purchasing products from, and selling products to, the industry in question?

l) What are the likely effects of the measure on other countries? How can prejudice to trading partners be minimised?

m) How are other governments and foreign firms likely to react to the measure and what would be the expected effect on the economy of such actions? Is the measure a response to unfair practices in other countries?

NOTES AND REFERENCES

1. The OECD Council has agreed to the suggestion for action set out in section IV of this report at its meeting on 30th April 1985.

2. The indicative checklist for the assessment of trade policy measures has been approved by the OECD Council at its meeting on 30th April 1985, it being understood that government policy considerations would determine the weight to be given to the various factors therein. Moreover, the Council called upon Member governments to undertake, on the basis of the checklist, as systematic and comprehensive an evaluation as possible of proposed trade and trade-related measures as well as of existing measures when the latter are subject to review.

3. OECD, Paris, 1985.

4. OECD, Paris, 1984.

5. This checklist applies to all trade policy measures other than laws relating to unfair trade practices.

OECD SALES AGENTS
DÉPOSITAIRES DES PUBLICATIONS DE L'OCDE

ARGENTINA - ARGENTINE
Carlos Hirsch S.R.L.,
Florida 165, 4º Piso,
(Galeria Guemes) 1333 Buenos Aires
Tel. 33.1787.2391 y 30.7122

AUSTRALIA-AUSTRALIE
D.A. Book (Aust.) Pty. Ltd.
11-13 Station Street (P.O. Box 163)
Mitcham, Vic. 3132 Tel. (03) 873 4411

AUSTRIA - AUTRICHE
OECD Publications and Information Centre,
4 Simrockstrasse,
5300 Bonn (Germany) Tel. (0228) 21.60.45
Local Agent:
Gerold & Co., Graben 31, Wien 1 Tel. 52.22.35

BELGIUM - BELGIQUE
Jean de Lannoy, Service Publications OCDE,
avenue du Roi 202
B-1060 Bruxelles Tel. 02/538.51.69

CANADA
Renouf Publishing Company Limited/
Éditions Renouf Limitée Head Office/
Siège social – Store/Magasin :
61, rue Sparks Street,
Ottawa, Ontario KIP 5A6
Tel. (613)238-8985. 1-800-267-4164
Store/Magasin : 211, rue Yonge Street,
Toronto, Ontario M5B 1M4.
Tel. (416)363-3171
Regional Sales Office/
Bureau des Ventes régional :
7575 Trans-Canada Hwy., Suite 305,
Saint-Laurent, Quebec H4T 1V6
Tel. (514)335-9274

DENMARK - DANEMARK
Munksgaard Export and Subscription Service
35, Nørre Søgade, DK-1370 København K
Tel. +45.1.12.85.70

FINLAND - FINLANDE
Akateeminen Kirjakauppa,
Keskuskatu 1, 00100 Helsinki 10 Tel. 0.12141

FRANCE
OCDE/OECD
Mail Orders/Commandes par correspondance :
2, rue André-Pascal,
75775 Paris Cedex 16
Tel. (1) 45.24.82.00
Bookshop/Librairie : 33, rue Octave-Feuillet
75016 Paris
Tel. (1) 45.24.81.67 ou/ou (1) 45.24.81.81
Principal correspondant :
Librairie de l'Université,
13602 Aix-en-Provence Tel. 42.26.18.08

GERMANY - ALLEMAGNE
OECD Publications and Information Centre,
4 Simrockstrasse,
5300 Bonn Tel. (0228) 21.60.45

GREECE - GRÈCE
Librairie Kauffmann,
28 rue du Stade, Athens 132 Tel. 322.21.60

HONG KONG
Government Information Services,
Publications (Sales) Office,
Beaconsfield House, 4/F.,
Queen's Road Central

ICELAND - ISLANDE
Snæbjörn Jónsson & Co., h.f.,
Hafnarstræti 4 & 9,
P.O.B. 1131 – Reykjavik
Tel. 13133/14281/11936

INDIA - INDE
Oxford Book and Stationery Co.,
Scindia House, New Delhi 1 Tel. 45896
17 Park St., Calcutta 700016 Tel. 240832

INDONESIA - INDONESIE
Pdin Lipi, P.O. Box 3065/JKT.Jakarta
Tel. 583467

IRELAND - IRLANDE
TDC Publishers – Library Suppliers
12 North Frederick Street, Dublin 1
Tel. 744835-749677

ITALY - ITALIE
Libreria Commissionaria Sansoni,
Via Lamarmora 45, 50121 Firenze
Tel. 579751/584468
Via Bartolini 29, 20155 Milano Tel. 365083
Sub-depositari :
Ugo Tassi, Via A. Farnese 28,
00192 Roma Tel. 310590
Editrice e Libreria Herder,
Piazza Montecitorio 120, 00186 Roma
Tel. 6794628
Agenzia Libraria Pegaso,
Via de Romita 5, 70121 Bari
Tel. 540.105/540.195
Agenzia Libraria Pegaso, Via S.Anna dei
Lombardi 16, 80134 Napoli. Tel. 314180
Libreria Hœpli,
Via Hœpli 5, 20121 Milano Tel. 865446
Libreria Scientifica
Dott. Lucio de Biasio "Aeiou"
Via Meravigli 16, 20123 Milano Tel. 807679
Libreria Zanichelli, Piazza Galvani 1/A,
40124 Bologna Tel. 237389
Libreria Lattes,
Via Garibaldi 3, 10122 Torino Tel. 519274
La diffusione delle edizioni OCSE è inoltre
assicurata dalle migliori librerie nelle città più
importanti.

JAPAN - JAPON
OECD Publications and Information Centre,
Landic Akasaka Bldg., 2-3-4 Akasaka,
Minato-ku, Tokyo 107 Tel. 586.2016

KOREA - CORÉE
Pan Korea Book Corporation
P.O.Box No. 101 Kwangwhamun, Seoul
Tel. 72.7369

LEBANON - LIBAN
Documenta Scientifica/Redico,
Edison Building, Bliss St.,
P.O.B. 5641, Beirut Tel. 354429-344425

MALAYSIA - MALAISIE
University of Malaya Co-operative Bookshop
Ltd.,
P.O.Box 1127, Jalan Pantai Baru,
Kuala Lumpur Tel. 577701/577072

NETHERLANDS - PAYS-BAS
Staatsuitgeverij Verzendboekhandel
Chr. Plantijnstraat, 1 Postbus 20014
2500 EA S-Gravenhage Tel. 070-789911
Voor bestellingen: Tel. 070-789208

NEW ZEALAND - NOUVELLE-ZÉLANDE
Government Printing Office Bookshops:
Auckland: Retail Bookshop, 25 Rutland Street,
Mail Orders, 85 Beach Road
Private Bag C.P.O.
Hamilton: Retail: Ward Street,
Mail Orders, P.O. Box 857
Wellington: Retail, Mulgrave Street, (Head
Office)
Cubacade World Trade Centre,
Mail Orders, Private Bag
Christchurch: Retail, 159 Hereford Street,
Mail Orders, Private Bag
Dunedin: Retail, Princes Street,
Mail Orders, P.O. Box 1104

NORWAY - NORVÈGE
Tanum-Karl Johan a.s
P.O. Box 1177 Sentrum, 0107 Oslo 1
Tel. (02) 801260

PAKISTAN
Mirza Book Agency
65 Shahrah Quaid-E-Azam, Lahore 3 Tel. 66839

PORTUGAL
Livraria Portugal,
Rua do Carmo 70-74, 1117 Lisboa Codex.
Tel. 360582/3

SINGAPORE - SINGAPOUR
Information Publications Pte Ltd
Pei-Fu Industrial Building,
24 New Industrial Road No. 02-06
Singapore 1953 Tel. 2831786, 2831798

SPAIN - ESPAGNE
Mundi-Prensa Libros, S.A.,
Castelló 37, Apartado 1223, Madrid-28001
Tel. 431.33.99
Libreria Bosch, Ronda Universidad 11,
Barcelona 7 Tel. 317.53.08/317.53.58

SWEDEN - SUÈDE
AB CE Fritzes Kungl. Hovbokhandel,
Box 16356, S 103 27 STH,
Regeringsgatan 12,
DS Stockholm Tel. (08) 23.89.00
Subscription Agency/Abonnements:
Wennergren-Williams AB,
Box 30004, S104 25 Stockholm. Tel. 08/54.12.00

SWITZERLAND - SUISSE
OECD Publications and Information Centre,
4 Simrockstrasse,
5300 Bonn (Germany) Tel. (0228) 21.60.45
Local Agent:
Librairie Payot,
6 rue Grenus, 1211 Genève 11
Tel. (022) 31.89.50

TAIWAN - FORMOSE
Good Faith Worldwide Int'l Co., Ltd.
9th floor, No. 118, Sec.2
Chung Hsiao E. Road
Taipei Tel. 391.7396/391.7397

THAILAND - THAILANDE
Suksit Siam Co., Ltd.,
1715 Rama IV Rd.,
Samyam Bangkok 5 Tel. 2511630

TURKEY - TURQUIE
Kültur Yayinlari Is-Türk Ltd. Sti.
Atatürk Bulvari No: 191/Kat. 21
Kavaklidere/Ankara Tel. 17.02.66
Dolmabahce Cad. No: 29
Besiktas/Istanbul Tel. 60.71.88

UNITED KINGDOM - ROYAUME UNI
H.M. Stationery Office,
Postal orders only:
P.O.B. 276, London SW8 5DT
Telephone orders: (01) 622.3316, or
Personal callers:
49 High Holborn, London WC1V 6HB
Branches at: Belfast, Birmingham,
Bristol, Edinburgh, Manchester

UNITED STATES - ÉTATS-UNIS
OECD Publications and Information Centre,
Suite 1207, 1750 Pennsylvania Ave., N.W.,
Washington, D.C. 20006 - 4582
Tel. (202) 724.1857

VENEZUELA
Libreria del Este,
Avda F. Miranda 52, Aptdo. 60337,
Edificio Galipan, Caracas 106
Tel. 32.23.01/33.26.04/31.58.38

YUGOSLAVIA - YOUGOSLAVIE
Jugoslovenska Knjiga, Knez Mihajlova 2,
P.O.B. 36, Beograd Tel. 621.992

Orders and inquiries from countries where Sales
Agents have not yet been appointed should be sent
to:
OECD, Publications Service, Sales and
Distribution Division, 2, rue André-Pascal, 75775
PARIS CEDEX 16.

Les commandes provenant de pays où l'OCDE n'a
pas encore désigné de dépositaire peuvent être
adressées à :
OCDE, Service des Publications. Division des
Ventes et Distribution. 2. rue André-Pascal. 75775
PARIS CEDEX 16.

69482-03-1986

OECD PUBLICATIONS, 2, rue André-Pascal, 75775 PARIS CEDEX 16 - No. 43469 1986
PRINTED IN FRANCE
(24 86 01 1) ISBN 92-64-12813-1